COMPETITION LAW AND
INDUSTRIAL POLICY IN THE EU

Competition Law and Industrial Policy in the EU

DR WOLF SAUTER

CLARENDON PRESS · OXFORD
1997

Oxford University Press, Walton Street, Oxford OX2 6DP
Oxford New York
Athens Auckland Bangkok Bogota Bombay
Buenos Aires Calcutta Cape Town Dar es Salaam
Delhi Florence Hong Kong Istanbul Karachi
Kuala Lumpur Madras Madrid Melbourne
Mexico City Nairobi Paris Singapore
Taipei Tokyo Toronto
and associated companies in
Berlin Ibadan

Oxford is a trade mark of Oxford University Press

Published in the United States by
Oxford University Press Inc., New York

British Library Cataloguing in Publication Data
Data available

Library of Congress Cataloging in Publication Data
Sauter, Wolf.
Competition law and industrial policy in the EU / Wolf Sauter.
p. cm.
Includes bibliographical references and index.
ISBN 0–19–826493–3
1. Competition—European Union countries. 2. Antitrust law—
European Union countries. 3. Telecommunication—Law and
legislation—European Union countries. I. Title.
KJE6456.S28 1997
341.7′53—dc21 97–12927

1 3 5 7 9 10 8 6 4 2

Typeset by Graphicraft Typesetters Ltd., Hong Kong
Printed in Great Britain by
Biddles Ltd., Guildford and King's Lynn

To Z.A.P.

Foreword

FRANCIS SNYDER*

The end of the twentieth century is a time of constitutional debate. Especially in the European Union, but also as distant from Europe as China, different models of society, polity, and economy are competing for public attention. But in Europe this time, the second in the history of European integration, citizens are not merely attentive, satisfied to wait and listen. Instead, as recent elections in the EU Member States have shown, they are participating in the political process, trying to influence the outcome of the debate. They realise how profoundly their lives, and those of their children, are and will be influenced by the relationship between state and market. The competition between different models has therefore become a competition, not simply for public attention, but also for economic support and political legitimacy.

Macro-economic processes on the world stage have provoked a debate on the future of the European social model. As a result of globalisation, world competition, and perhaps the end of inflation, at least in the West, we in the European Union are now, to paraphrase the late Deng Xiaoping, in search of 'capitalism with European characteristics'. What, if anything, can lawyers and legal scholars contribute to this inquiry? Legal scholars, at least those toiling in the field of European Union law, do not usually address such grand questions.

This book by Dr Wolf Sauter is a singular, though I hope not unique, exception. It offers us both a broad and a detailed examination of the European Union's 'economic constitution', set against the background of a systematic conception of its political constitution. Focusing on the European Community, the author rejects the view of the German Ordoliberals regarding the Rome Treaty. He argues that the Community's founding treaties, and their amendments, condone a mixed economy within the limits set by Community law. He treats this economic constitution as a subset of the Community's (and now Union's) political constitution. Economic and monetary union (EMU) may, as the author admits, pose a challenge to this conception. However, since this book was written, the political and at least the quasi-legal framework of EMU have evolved in a direction consistent with the principal arguments set forth in this book.

The main focus of this careful study is the relationship between EC industrial policy and EC competition law. The author helps us to understand this

---

* Professor of European Community Law, European University Institute; Professor of Law, College of Europe, Bruges; Honorary Visiting Professor of Law, University College London.

relationship by combining two methods. First, he examines each policy area separately but with an eye on the other. Secondly, using the technique of a case study, he dissects Community policy and law regarding telecommunications. This case study is ideal for the purpose. As Dr Sauter shows, telecommunications embodies multiple facets of the relationship between industrial policy and competition policy in the European Union.

More generally, few sectors are more central than telecommunications to the broader processes to which this book draws the reader's attention, and with regard to which the book calls for the reader's participation. I refer to the process of globalisation of the world political economy, on the one hand, and to the process of constitutionalisation in the European Union, on the other. The continuing discussions within the World Trade Organisation testify to the former. With regard to the latter, we have only to consider the crucial role played by telecommunications in the creation or denial of social solidarity, the maintenance or erosion of boundaries, or the creation or frustration of a European Union legal and constitutional culture. These broad processes are of course interrelated, though often in extremely complex ways which are only now beginning to be understood.

This book began as the author's PhD thesis at the European University Institute in Florence. It has been nurtured and brought to fruition mainly in Florence and Brussels. As these few remarks make clear, however, its message extends far beyond its specific subject and these particular cities. I hope that readers will agree with me that Dr Sauter is to be congratulated for this thorough, informative and thought-provoking book.

Acknowledgements

The basic research for this publication was conducted at the law department of the European University Institute, Florence (1991–1995), and at the EC Commission in Brussels (Spring 1994). Additional work was completed inter alia under a research fellowship at the European University Institute (Spring 1996), and at the Brussels offices of Weil, Gotshal & Manges LLP (1996–1997). Research funding was generously provided by the Dutch Ministry of Education, the European University Institute, and by the EC Commission. Various assistantships to Professor Francis Snyder have provided me with inspiration and a sound basis for existence. Among the numerous people who have contributed their guidance and assistance in various forms, I would like to thank in particular Giuliano Amato, Richard Cawley, David Chijner, Marcel Haag, Nicole Haag, Christian Joerges, Emir Lawless, Giandomenico Majone, Phedon Nicolaides, Harm Schepel, Volker Schneider, Francis Snyder, and Ellen Vos. Among the institutions which have shaped my views is, foremost, the European Law Journal. My editors at OUP have been both supportive and constructive. Without the support of my family this book would not have been written.

W.S.

Table of Contents

Table of Documents

[Note: not included are Community legislation in force, Council resolutions and conclusions, and speeches.]

Analysis ltd, *Performance of the Telecommunications Sector up to 2010 under Different Regulatory and Market Options: Final Report to the Commission of the European Communities* (Executive report; Cambridge, 1992).

'Broad Economic Policy Guidelines and Convergence Report', (1995) *European Economy* 55.

COM(95) 379, Proposal for a European Parliament and Council Directive on Interconnection in Telecommunications: Ensuring Universal Service and Interoperability through Application of the Principles of Open Network Provision.

COM(95) 158, Consultation on the Green Paper on the Liberalisation of Telecommunications Infrastructure and Cable Television Networks.

COM(94) 682, Green Paper on the liberalisation of telecommunications infrastructure and cable television networks. Part Two: A common approach to the provision of infrastructure for telecommunications in the European Union.

COM(94) 513, Present Status and Future Approach for Open Access to Telecommunications Networks and Services (Open Network Provision).

COM(94) 492, Communication on the Consultation on the Green Paper on Mobile and Personal Communications.

COM(94) 440, Green Paper on the liberalisation of telecommunications infrastructure and cable television networks. Part One: Principles and Timetable.

COM(94) 347, Europe's Way to the Information Society: An Action Plan.

COM(94) 319, An Industrial Competitiveness Policy for the European Union.

COM(94) 217, Commission's Recommendations for the Broad Guidelines of the Economic Policies of the Member States and the Community drawn up in conformity with Article 103(2) of the Treaty on European Union.

COM(94) 161, *23rd Competition Report from the Commission: 1993.*

COM(94) 145, Towards the Personal Communications Environment: Green Paper on a Common Approach in the Field of Mobile and Personal Communications in the European Union.

COM(83) 573, Communication on lines of action in the field of telecommunications.

COM(83) 547, Discussion paper for the special Council meeting of 20–21 September on the question of improving the international competitive position of European firms.

COM(83) 371, Communication on prospects for the development of new policies.

COM(83) 329, Communication concerning telecommunications in the Community.

COM(79) 650, European Society Faced with the Challenge of New Information Technology: A Community Response.

COM(70) 100, La Politique Industrielle de la Communauté.

Comité intergouvernemental creé par la Conférence de Messine, Rapport des Chefs de délégation aux Ministres des Affaires étrangères (Brussels, 1956).

Commission communication on the implementation of the Community measures of the growth initiative ((1993) OJ C60/2).

Commission communication on the application of Articles 92 and 93 of the EEC Treaty and of Article 5 of the Commission Directive 80/723 EEC to public undertakings in the manufacturing sector ((1991) OJ C273/2).

'Commission Declaration: Notes on Council Regulation (EEC) No 4064/89', in Community Merger Control Law, *EC Bull* Supplement 2/90.

Commission of the EC, *26th General Report on the Activities of the EC: 1993* (Brussels, 1994).

Commission of the EEC, *21st Report on Competition Policy: 1991* (Brussels, 1992).

Commission of the EEC, *20th General Report on the Activities of the European Community: 1990* (Brussels, 1991).

Commission of the EC, *20th Report on Competition Policy* (Brussels-Luxembourg, 1990).

Commission of the EEC, *Improving Competitiveness and Industrial Structures in the European Community* (Brussels, 1987).

Commission of the EEC, *15th Report on Competition Policy: 1985* (Brussels, 1986).

Commission of the EEC, *13th Report on Competition Policy: 1983* (Brussels, 1984).

Commission of the EEC, *The Competitiveness of European Community Industry* (Brussels, 1982).

'Intergovernmental Conferences: Contributions by the Commission', *Bull EC* Supplement 2/91.

Monopolkommission, *Hauptgutachten 1990/1991: Wettbewerbspolitik oder Industriepolitik* (Baden-Baden, 1992).

Monopolkommission, *Hauptgutachten 1988/1989: Wettbewerbspolitik vor neuen Herausforderungen* (Baden-Baden, 1990).

Monopolkommission, *Sondergutachten 17—Konzeption einer europäischen Fusionskontrolle* (Baden-Baden, 1989).

'Objectives and Instruments of a Common Policy for Scientific Research and Technological Development', *Bull EC* Supplement 6/72.

OECD, *Economies in Transition: Structural Adjustment in OECD Countries* (Paris, 1989).

OECD, *Structural Adjustment and Economic Performance* (Paris, 1987).

OECD, *Positive Adjustment Policies: Managing Structural Change* (Paris, 1983).

ONP Analysis report on intelligent network functions; network management; local loop; and broadband communications ((1994) OJ C215/18).

Proposal for a European Parliament and Council Directive on the application of open network provision (ONP) to voice telephony (COM(92) 247 (Council Directive)/ COM(94) 689 (Council and European Parliament Directive) ((1995) OJ C122/4).

Proposal for a Council Decision on a series of guidelines for the development of ISDN as trans-European network (93/C 259/05; (1993) OJ C259/5).

Proposal for a Council Decision adopting a multi-annual Community action concerning the development of ISDN as a trans-European network (TEN-ISDN) (93/C 259/06; (1993) OJ C259/7).

SEC(95) 545, Communication on the Status and Implementation of Directive 90/388/EEC on Competition in the Markets for Telecommunications Services.

SEC(95) 308, Draft Commission Directive amending Commission Directive 90/388/EEC regarding the abolition of the restrictions on the use of cable television networks for the provision of telecommunications services.

SEC(94) 645, Draft Inter-Institutional Agreement on Comitology.

SEC(92) 1986, Industrial Competitiveness and protection of the Environment.

SEC(92) 1050, Towards Cost Orientation and the Adjustment in Pricing Structures—Telecommunications Tariffs in the Community.

SEC(92) 1049, The European Telecommunications Equipment Industry: The State of Play, Issues at Stake and proposals for Action.

SEC (92) 1048, 1992 Review of the Situation in the Telecommunications Services Sector.

SEC(91) 629, Promoting the Competitive Environment for the Industrial Activities Based on Biotechnology.

SEC(91) 565, The European Electronic and Information Technology Industry: State of Play, Issues at Stake and Proposals for Action.

SEC(73) 3824, Action Programme in the Field of Industrial and Technology Policy.

'The Community's Industrial Policy: Commission Memorandum to the Council', *Bull EC* Supplement 4/70.

'The Programme of the Commission in 1993–94', Address by Commission President Jacques Delors to the European Parliament, Straßbourg, 10 February 1993, *Bull EC* Supplement 1/93.

R. Toulemon, *Report No. 1: Stage Reached in Work on Industrial Policy in the Community*, Conference 'Industry and Society in the European Community' (Commission of the EEC, Venice, 1972).

'Towards the establishment of a European Industrial Base', *Bull EC* Supplement 7/73.

Wissenschaftliches Institut für Kommunikationsdienst GmbH (WIK), 'Network Interconnection in the Domain of ONP', (Study for DG XIII, 1994).

Table of Cases

EUROPEAN COURT OF JUSTICE AND COURT OF FIRST INSTANCE

(Numerical)

EUROPEAN COMMUNITY DECISIONS

OTHER JURISDICTIONS

GERMANY

USA

Table of European Community Legislation and Treaties

DECISIONS

DIRECTIVES

NOTICES

RECOMMENDATIONS

REGULATIONS

[1] Shown as OJ L53/5 on p. 125.   [2] Shown as OJ L359/46 on p. 125.

[3] Shown as OJ L393/1 on pp. 125, 133.

RESOLUTIONS

RULES OF PROCEDURE OF THE COUNCIL

Table of International Agreements and Conventions

Table of Abbreviations

AG	Advocated General
AJCL	American Journal of Comparative Law
Bull EC	EC Bulletin
BVerfGE	Bundesverfassungsgericht
CAP	Common Agricultural Policy
CDE	Cahiers de Droit Européen
CEN	European Committee for Standardization
CENELEC	European Committee for Electrotechnical Standardization
CEPT	European Conference of Postal and Telecommunications Administrators
CMLR	Common Market Law Review
CMLRep	Common Market Law Reports
COREPER	Committee of Permanent Representatives
DG	Directorate General
EBLR	European Business Law Review
EC	European Community
ECB	European Central Bank
ESCB	European System of Central Banks
ECSC	European Coal and Steel Community
EEC	European Economic Community
ECLR	European Competition Law Review
ECR	European Court Reports
ECU	European Currency Unit
EEA	European Economic Area
ELR	European Law Review
EMS	European Monetary System
EMU	Economic and Monetary Union
ETSI	European Telecommunications Standardization Institute
EU	European Union
EuR	Europarecht
Euratom	European Atomic Energy Community
GATT	General Agreement on Tariffs and Trade
ICLQ	International and Comparative Law Quartely
ISDN	Integrated Services Digital Network
IT	Information Technology
ITU	International Telecommunications Union
JCMS	Journal of common Market Studies
LIEI	Legal Issues of European Integration

MLR	Modern Law Review
NRA	National Regulatory Authority
OECD	Organization for Economic Cooperation and Development
OJ	Official Journal
ONP	Open Network Provision
RdMC	Revue du Marché Commun
R&D	Research and Development
RTDE	Revue Trimestrielle de Droit Européen
SEA	Single European Act
SEW	Sociaal-Economisch Weekblad
TEN	trans-European network
TEU	Treaty on European Union
TO	Telecommunications Operator
ULR	Utilities Law Review
YEL	Yearbook of European Law
WTO	World Trade Organization

1

Introduction

Worldwide, economic competition is in ascendance. In the European Community, as elsewhere, this is accompanied by retreat of the state from direct intervention in the economy. After decades of acting as participants in the economic process, the Member States are now divesting state holdings, and in many areas are proceeding to market regulation at arm's length. National competition policies are increasing their independence from the political process, in tandem with strict enforcement by the Community of the state aid and competition rules of the EC Treaty against the Member States themselves.

Yet at the same time, new theories on how competitiveness of nations may be actively promoted by public authorities have gained ground. Such theoretical prescriptions have affected practice at Community level: in the last few years, the European Community has adopted a common concept of industrial policy, aimed at the promotion of structural adjustment, and has received a formal competence on 'industry' under the Treaty on European Union. Simultaneously therefore, the Member States are reducing their commitment to economic intervention, in part as a result of pressure exerted by the European Community, and the Community itself is increasing its involvement in industrial policy.

These developments seem to be contradictory. It appears that the Member States collectively have recovered at the European level a degree of control over the economy which they had previously lost at the national level. It further appears that within the single framework of Community law the Member States are now collectively pursuing those policies at the Community level which the same law bars them from pursuing individually at the national level.

This apparent contradiction is reinforced by the fact that the ideal types of competition policy and industrial policy are usually presented as diametrically opposed forms of government-industry relations. In this binary conceptual scheme, competition policy is seen as the 'rule of economic law', characterised by strict procedures which aim to balance individual interests, but are founded on the application of general rules which aim to protect the intrinsic value of the *process* of economic competition. According to this view, Competition policy is based on rules, procedure and precedent, the institutional independence of competition authorities, as well as on the transparency of procedures involved.

Industrial policy on the contrary is seen as focused on the *structure* of the economy and its international competitiveness. It aims to achieve diverse social and political values such as growth, regional cohesion and employment. Consequently, in their pursuit of industrial policy, public authorities widely identify and promote 'strategic' economic sectors as well as economies of scale, and often perceive economic competition as wasteful and leading to unfair business practices. Opportunist and discretionary rather than principled and rule-based in its approach, industrial policy primarily derives its logic from the political process. As a result, industrial policy is characterised by ad hoc decisions which do not assign an intrinsic value to procedure or precedent.[1]

The contrast between industrial and competition policy is often perceived as being mirrored by the national traditions of the Member States. These national traditions differ with regard to the relative importance assigned to industrial and competition policy, with France playing the archetype of state interventionism facing Member States such as Germany (and to a lesser extent Britain) as the self-styled advocates of market based competition. These distinct policy preferences of the Member States may also be read in the clashes between them, and between individual Member States and the Community.

The most famous example is the public outcry which resulted the first time that the Commission decided to block a merger under the new Merger Regulation.[2] On this occasion, the French Minister of Industry and Telecommunications of the day (Mr Gérard Longuet, who ended his political career under investigation on corruption charges) demanded that the Commissioner for competition policy (Sir Leon Brittan, a British national, and now the Commissioner responsible for international trade) step down, and that the merger regulation be modified to give greater importance to national industrial policy considerations. In recent years, the Commission's strict application of the competition and state aid rules has led to repeated and well-publicised confrontations with protection-minded Member States before the European Court of Justice.[3]

Yet resistance against Community incursions on national economic policies cuts across ideologies in the Member States. Rather than springing from particular political preferences, such conflicts may be the result of competing claims of competence in a multi-level system of government. Below the surface of the debate on industrial and competition policy in the Community lies the issue of the horizontal and vertical division of powers. Related issues are the remaining scope for national economic policy (or economic sovereignty) in the context of European integration; and that of the orientation of the economic order of the Community itself. These problems have existed since the earliest

---

[1] H. Dumez and A. Jeunemaître, 'L'État et le Marché en Europe. Vers un État de droit économique?', (1992) 42 *Revue Française de Science Politique* 263; H. Dumez and A. Jeunemaître, *La concurrence en Europe: De nouvelles règles du jeu pour les entreprises* (Paris, 1991).

[2] Council Regulation 4064/89 ((1989) OJ L395/1; corrected version (1990) OJ L257/14); Commission Decision IV/M.053, *Aerospatiale/Alenia/de Havilland* ((1991) OJ L334/42).

[3] Cf. Case C-310/87, *France v Commission* [1990] ECR I-307 ('Boussac'); Joined Cases 188–190/80, *France et al v Commission* [1982] ECR 2545 ('Transparency Directive'); Joined Cases C-271/90, C-281/90 and C-289/90, *Spain, Belgium and Italy v Commission* [1992] ECR I-5833 ('Services Directive'); Case C-202/88 *France v Commission* [1991] ECR I-1223 ('Terminal Directive'); Case C-325/91, *France v Commission* [1993] ECR I-3283; Case C-327/91, *France v Commission* [1994] ECRI-3641 ('EC-US Competition Policy Agreement').

days of the Community. However, they have been brought to the fore by the Treaty on European Union of 1993, which included the Title on industrial policy, and has highlighted the ambiguity of the integration process.

Under the original EEC Treaty of 1957, negative integration, or completion of the internal market through application of the four freedoms and competition policy, was the overriding priority of the European Community. The Single European Act of 1987 introduced new methods of market integration (as well as some new shared competences), but on the whole appeared to leave the original priorities intact. Nevertheless, among its unintended consequences were, on the one side, much more intensive liberalisation than most Member States had bargained for, and on the other, an increased demand for co-operation in order to manage the effects of this liberalisation. With the Treaty on European Union, which was concluded in preparation of Economic and Monetary Union, new principles and objectives, as well as a number of new joint competences were added to the Treaty. The scope of the Community now clearly extends beyond market integration, toward increasingly close co-ordination of economic and monetary policies.

The paradox is therefore that although political consensus for extending the expansionist logic of the earlier concept of the internal market based on negative integration may have been eroded, and the Member States have become increasingly concerned with protecting their competences, the progress of convergence of the actual policies of the Member States has continued. Consequently, the debate on the allocation of competences and the relations between the different levels of government has been reopened. The main dilemma in this debate is how to achieve, simultaneously, a balance of power between the two levels of government in the Community system, and an acceptable balance between state and market.[4] Although the allocation of power between the two levels of government, and between the public and private spheres, is contentious in a large number of fields, industrial policy is an area where it is currently debated most urgently.

As set out earlier, it is usually claimed that industrial policy, representing a commitment to state planning and public intervention in the economy, and competition policy, charged with removing private (and public) distortions of the market process, are incompatible. Further, in defense of economic sovereignty the Member States have long resisted a Community policy in this area. The EC Commission claims not merely that the two are compatible at Community level, but also that Community competition policy itself forms an important

---

[4] F. Snyder, 'EMU—Metaphor for European Union? Institutions, Rules and Types of Regulation', in R. Dehousse (ed.), *Europe After Maastricht: An Ever Closer Union* (München, 1994), p. 81. On the balance between state and market cf. Ch. Joerges, 'Markt ohne Staat? Die Wirtschaftsverfassung der Gemeinschaft und die Renaissance der regulativen Politik' in R. Wildenmann (ed.), *Staatswerdung Europas? Optionen für eine politische Union* (Baden-Baden, 1991).

instrument of industrial policy.[5] The Commission has further asserted that, under the Treaty on European Union, the Community has acquired a coherent legal basis to promote the competitiveness of European industry including Titles XII to XV (covering trans-European networks (TENs), industry, economic and social cohesion, and R&D) and VIII (social policy and industrial change) TEU.[6]

The Community still does not have a truly common policy for industry, in the sense that it has a common agricultural policy, and possibly it never will. However, the introduction of industrial policy into the Treaty suggests that an important step has been taken in the further co-ordination of economic policies. The study below examines the reasons for the development of a Community industrial policy and the question whether the industrial and competition policies of the Community are compatible or in conflict. The results should cast light on the current state of relations between the two levels of government and the market.

On a closer view, three debates on industrial policy in the Community can be distinguished. These debates are only partially informed of each other.

1. First, there is a political debate, with pragmatic arguments in favour of Community industrial policy on the one hand, and principled arguments focusing on democratic legitimacy and national sovereignty on the other. At issue is the balance between the Community institutions and the Member States. The allocation of industrial policy competence and the modalities for policy co-ordination are crucial (and contested) since they affect the economic sovereignty of the Member States, the competitiveness of European industry, and ultimately general welfare. The general context of this debate is the potential redefinition of the shape and scope of the European Union in the 1996 Intergovernmental Conference, which was intended to set out the future course of economic and political integration.

2. Second, there is an economic debate that demonstrates the difficulty of squaring theoretically optimal solutions (free trade) with the political reality of regional trading blocs. Proponents of free trade and unhampered competition argue against economic planning and strategic trade. Proponents of industrial policy argue that the promotion of structural adjustment is required by the new international division of labour which is developing as the result of global economic integration. Both sides agree that internationalisation is the result of economic, technical, and cultural developments within an emerging regulatory framework which aims to maximise trade as a source of welfare. The economic polices which are proposed in reaction to this phenomenon range from state co-ordination of structural adjustment

---

[5] COM(90) 556, Industrial Policy in an Open and Competitive Environment: Guidelines for a Community Approach.

[6] COM(94) 319, An Industrial Competitiveness Policy for the Community.

(industrial policy) and strategic trade policy on the one hand, to leaving adjustment to be settled by free trade in a market regulated by competition policy on the other.

3. Third, the legal debate has so far focused on formal arguments regarding the legality of various types of positive and negative integration at the progressive stages of European integration. For a long time, industrial policy, regarded as interventionist positive integration by definition has been regarded as contrary to the economic constitution of the Community. Now the Community has obtained a concurrent competence on industrial policy under the Treaty on European Union, the legal issues have changed. Article 130 EC, which aims to promote the competitiveness of European industry within the framework of market competition and European integration, has brought the conflict over how to allocate power in the Community system, and achieve an acceptable balance between state and market, to the heart of European law. The main legal problems concerning industrial and competition policy consist now of defining the division of competence in this area, and determining the limits to the powers of the Member States and the Community.

This study will focus on the perceived contradiction between the competition policy and the industrial policy of the Community. Its objective is to examine the relationship between these Community policies, both in their own right, and as they reflect changes in the economic order, or 'economic constitution', of the Community. The main questions addressed are whether industrial and competition policy are compatible; whether the Community assigns a clear priority between the two; how they affect the policies of the Member States, the division of power and the methods of co-ordination of policy in the Community framework; and, in particular, how the emergence of the industrial policy competence of the Community fits into the process of European integration.

Hence, Industry Title XIII must be placed in the context of the system of Community law, and the relationship between the provisions concerning industrial and competition policy must be established. The legal questions which arise concern: the balance between Community competition rules and the industrial policies of the Member States (Articles 3f, 5(2) and 85 EC; and Articles 90 to 94 EC); the balance between the industrial and competition policies of the Community itself (Article 130 EC); the problem of the limits of Community competence, in particular in view of the principle of proportionality and subsidiarity (now in Article 3b EC); and the new forms of policy co-ordination which have been established.

These issues will be examined with the help of three hypotheses:

1. The first hypothesis is that industrial and competition policy can be compatible at the Community level. This position is taken by the Commission, as a self-fulfilling prophecy imposed by its role as the guarantor of the

unity of Community law. Although counter-intuitive from a traditional view, this appears to be a more appropriate basis for an analysis centred on the Community than the theory of conflict usually proposed in economic and state-centred discussions of the subject.

2. The second hypothesis is that the new industrial policy title must be seen in the context of the progressive development of European integration toward multi-level policy-co-ordination. For a long time, the process of European integration has been interpreted as jointly determined by attempts to achieve the internal market by means of negative integration (or liberalisation), and by attempts to create a positive integration (or common policies). The failure of positive integration in the early years of the Community has been followed by a period of concentration on negative integration. Specifically as a result of the widespread application of negative integration, policy-co-ordination is now widely employed in order to manage its effects.

3. The third hypothesis is that the new industrial policy title forms an expression of a new balance between state and market, which is the result of a new degree of European integration. The joint increase of importance attributed to the promotion of competition and industrial competitiveness suggests that a new level of integration has been reached which requires co-ordination of policies in these fields, irrespective of wider political preferences. This may provide an answer to the question why the Member States, in spite of apparent disagreement on the direction of integration, and their fundamental reluctance to cede competence to the Community, have nevertheless adopted the Industry Title.

These three general hypotheses will be addressed in a three step process, in which the relationship between industrial and competition policy will be studied at different levels: at the highest systemic level of Community law, that of the Treaty as a whole; at the intermediate level of industrial and competition policy; and at the level of sectoral policy, in a case study of telecommunications. Horizontal and vertical analysis will thus be combined.

The general theoretical framework will be provided by the 'economic constitution' of the European Community. The discussion of the economic constitution is intended to address three related questions. First, whether the Treaty functions as an economic constitution in the sense that it establishes a comprehensive and enforceable body of economic law which determines the limits on state and Community intervention in the market. Second, whether the Treaty was at any stage of its development intended to prescribe a particular economic order, at the national or at the Community level. Third, whether the process of economic integration favours certain forms of economic organisation over others in practice. The Rome Treaty before and after the Single European Act, and the Treaty on European Union will be compared, to determine whether the economic constitution of the Treaty has changed over time, and whether such a change can be linked to the three general hypotheses.

Although the concept of the Treaty as an economic constitution is useful to analyse the general economic orientation of the Community, the economic constitution by itself does not suffice to explain the relationship between industrial and competition policy. First, industrial policy will be defined, and the definition of industrial policy adopted by the Community will be placed in the context of economic theory on free trade and regional integration. Here it should become clear whether there is theoretical support for the hypothesis that industrial and competition policy may be compatible. Next, it should be seen whether the Industry Title has, in fact, changed the economic orientation of the Community, or merely formed a codification of earlier practice. For this purpose, the questions how and why the Community obtained its competence on industrial policy must be answered. In order to assess whether it is linked to a change in balance between state and market, and to the increase of policy co-ordination, as hypothesised, the emergence of industrial policy at the Community level will be related to the general process of European integration. Further, the individual provisions of the Industry Title should be analysed to determine their direct significance for the distribution of decision making power on economic policy in the Community.

After the discussion of the economic orientation of the Community and the nature of its industrial policy competence, the role of competition policy under the economic constitution will be examined, in order to establish how industrial and competition policy are linked. First, the principles and objectives of the competition policy of the Community will be identified. Second, the claim that competition policy can function as an instrument of industrial policy, which may promote the competitiveness of European industry, will be verified. On this basis, it should become clear whether it is industrial policy or competition policy which has priority under Community law, and whether the two are compatible, or whether, (given their difference in focus as the process of competition, and the structure of industry), an underlying tension remains. Third, the question whether the limits competition policy imposes on the industrial policies of the Member States have affected the balance between state and market (and the new willingness to proceed beyond negative integration) must be answered.

This theoretical and comparative exercise will subsequently be completed with a case study of telecommunications. This in-depth sectoral study will add a vertical dimension to the analysis, and will illustrate how industrial and competition policy interact in practice. In the 1990s, telecommunications has surpassed information technology as the most widely identified strategic economic sector, and it is undoubtedly at the centre of the current industrial policy initiatives of the EC. In the last few years, industrial and competition policy in this sector have clearly converged, with rapid liberalisation as the result. Moreover, the regulatory framework within which this industry operates has been transformed by Community policy. Telecommunications should therefore be regarded as the critical case for an analysis of Community industrial and competition policy in this decade. Finally, telecommunications liberalisation gives rise to a number of regulatory issues of wider relevance, which allow the telecommunications sector to be used to examine new forms of regulation and policy co-ordination.

The discussion is organised as follows. The second chapter deals with the 'economic constitution'. The third chapter describes the emergence of the industrial policy of the European Community. The fourth chapter examines the competition policy of the Community in the light of the industrial policy. The case study on telecommunications forms the fifth chapter. In chapter six the conclusion will recapitulate the findings in reverse sequential order, and expand on the theoretical conclusions based on the analysis of the relationship between industrial and competition policy.

2

The Political and the Economic Constitution
of the European Union

I. INTRODUCTION

Since the founding of the EC, the nature of the relations between market, Member States and Community has been contested. This is all the more true because the Community is a divided power system, in which the question of the need for intervention and the level at which this intervention should be decided and conducted are intimately connected. This debate has largely been conducted in legal terms.[1] It has focused on the question whether the Rome Treaty itself prescribed or favoured a specific economic paradigm for the Member States, or whether a plurality of economic systems at the national level might be compatible with the economic law of the Community.

In the first place, this raises the issue of the remaining scope for national economic policy, which has been a recurrent theme in the case law of the European Court of Justice. This in turn leads to more fundamental questions of how far European integration should proceed, and how decision making power should be allocated between the different levels of government. At issue therefore, is the relationship between the level of decision making, and the orientation of the economic order.

In the second place, the further question arises whether the Community itself may pursue a variety of economic policies, or whether it should always give priority to market principles and free competition. The question whether an industrial policy at the European level would be compatible with the system of undistorted competition in the common market has been at the heart of the debate on these matters. This question gained greater relevance with the ratification of the Treaty on European Union. The latter inaugurated a further phase of integration by establishing a timetable for economic and monetary union, and by elaborating for the first time the procedures for the co-ordination of the

---

[1] The EC has been described as a legal phenomenon in three respects: as a creature and source of law as well as a legal order in its own right. Ch. Joerges, 'Markt ohne Staat? Die Wirtschaftsverfassung der Gemeinschaft und die Renaissance der regulativen Politik', in R. Wildenmann (ed.), *Staatswerdung Europas? Optionen für eine politische Union* (Baden-Baden, 1991), citing W. Hallstein, *Die Europäische Gemeinschaft* (5th edn., Düsseldorf, 1974). It is with the last dimension that this chapter is essentially concerned.

economic and monetary policies of the Member States. The Treaty on European Union also introduced other new competences for the Community, and gave the Union (which it created) responsibilities regarding common foreign and security policy, and co-operation on justice and home affairs. Thus European integration is scheduled to progress well beyond establishing the internal market. However, the Treaty on European Union has become a lightning rod for dissent on European integration, bringing out an undercurrent of resistance of unexpected strength. At its most articulate, this dissent has focused on the horizontal and vertical division of power in the Community system, and is motivated in particular by concern over the democratic legitimacy of the decision making process.

Although its popular image in the ratification debates has usually been that of unbridled liberalism, the economic orientation of the Treaty on European Union is a complex one. On the one hand, it has introduced the principle of free competition in open markets, supplementing and extending the prior provision Article 3(f) EEC (Article 3(g) EC).[2] This principle, which has been included in Articles 3a, 102 and 105(1) EC, is linked to the new objectives of the Community, notably economic and monetary union. The Treaty on European Union sets out in detail the manner in which these objectives are to be achieved, and spells out for the first time the modalities of economic and monetary policy co-ordination alongside the long standing provisions establishing the internal market.

On the other hand, the Treaty on European Union also introduced a Community competence on measures to improve the competitiveness of European industry. This is remarkable, as industrial and competition policy are commonly perceived as logical opposites. Moreover, the text of the Treaty does not suggest a clear hierarchy between the two. Article 3(1) EC introduces the strengthening of the competitiveness of the European industry as one of the activities of the Community required for the pursuit of the objectives set out in Article 2 EC, alongside Article 3(g) EC on ensuring a system of undistorted competition. In the body of the Treaty, the promotion of the competitiveness of European industry is then developed in Part III EC on Community policies, alongside those policies (free movement of goods, persons, services and capital, transport, and agriculture) which were formerly ranked in Part II EEC as foundations of the Community. Hence, industrial and competition policy appear to be of equal importance, adding insult to injury for the opponents of industrial policy. The introduction of industrial policy into the Treaty has given rise to

---

[2] Article 3(g) EC appears to codify the case law. Cf. Case 202/88 *France v Commission* [1991] ECR I-1223 para. 41 p. 1229: 'as the Court has consistently held, Articles 2 and 3 of the Treaty set out to establish a market characterized by the free movement of goods where the terms of competition are not distorted'. The Court made reference to its judgement in Case 229/83 *Leclerc v Au Blé Vert* [1985] ECR 1, para. 9 p. 30 where it stated: 'Articles 2 and 3 of the Treaty set out to establish a market characterized by the free movement of goods where the terms of competition are not distorted'.

vociferous dissent, in particular from economic liberals, to whom Industry Title XIII EC has become emblematic for all that is contestable in the structure of the European Union.

This chapter will examine this apparently contradictory development of the economic orientation of the Treaty. For this purpose two theoretical perspectives are used, which regard the Treaty as the political constitution and the economic constitution of the European Union respectively.

The view that the Treaty represents the political constitution of the Community is fairly well established. At the same time however, the Treaty is widely considered to be unsatisfactory as a political constitution, both in terms of logic and coherence, and in terms of legitimacy.

The debate on the economic constitution of the European Community can be summarised as revolving around three related issues. The first of these is the question whether the Treaty functions as an economic constitution in a *functional* sense, by establishing an orderly set of principles as the basis of a comprehensive and enforceable body of economic law, which allows conflicts over the limits on state and Community intervention in the market to be resolved. The second question is whether the Treaty was intended to create or prescribe a particular economic regime in the range of possibilities between the two extremes of centralised economic planning and laissez-faire capitalism. This regards the *normative* role of the economic constitution.

The third question is whether the process of European integration favours certain forms of economic organisation and policy over others *in practice*.[3] This question goes beyond the problem of the economic constitution by asking whether the Community itself is adequately equipped to deal with such matters as now escape the administrative scope of its Member States individually, given the practical and legal constraints on the economic policies pursued by the Community. This issue is known as that of the 'regulatory deficit' of the Community.

Below, the views of the Treaty as a political and economic constitution will be discussed and compared. Next, it will be seen whether the Treaty defines the economic order of the Member States and the Community, and whether it limits their freedom of action.

---

[3] This is the pragmatic approach of P. VerLoren van Themaat in 'Die Aufgabenverteilung zwischen dem Gesetzgeber und dem Europäischen Gerichtshof bei der Gestaltung der Wirtschaftsverfassung der Europäischen Gemeinschaften', in E.-J. Mestmäcker, H. Möller and P. Schwartz (eds.), *Eine Ordnungspolitik für Europa: Festschrift für Hans von der Groeben zu seinem 80. Geburtstag* (Baden-Baden, 1987). Cf. P. VerLoren van Themaat, 'Einige Bemerkungen zu dem Verhältnis zwischen den Begriffen Gemeinsamer Markt, Wirtschaftsunion, Währungsunion, Politische Union und Souveränität', in J. Baur, P.-Ch. Müller-Graf and M. Zuleeg (eds.), *Europarecht, Energierecht, Wirtschaftsrecht: Festschrift für Bodo Börner zum 70. Geburtstag* (Cologne, 1992); U. Everling, 'Die Koordinierung der Wirtschaftspolitik in der Europäischen Wirtschaftsgemeinschaft als Rechtsproblem', (1964) No. 296/297 *Recht und Staat* 14, reprinted in U. Everling, *Das europäische Wirtschaftsrecht im Spannungsfeld von Politik und Wirtschaft: Ausgewählte Aufsätze 1964–1984* (Baden-Baden, 1985).

II. THE POLITICAL CONSTITUTION OF THE EUROPEAN UNION

A. The Process of Constitutionalisation of the Treaties

There is a rich vein of legal writing which analyses the constitutionalisation of European law as the result of its teleological interpretation by the European Court of Justice.[4] The constitutional approach has, in fact, become one of the main general legal theoretical approaches to European law.[5] This approach has three important characteristics. First, in order to establish the constitutional nature of the Treaty it does not hold it to the standard of the constitution of a modern nation state, notably regarding its democratic legitimacy. Second, rather than focusing on the text of the Treaty as a 'formal constitution' this approach concentrates on the Treaty as interpreted by the Court of Justice, the 'material constitution'.[6] Obviously, these devices facilitate finding that the Community has a constitution. Third, however, even the material constitution is not seen as complete. Instead, a process of constitutionalisation of the Treaty is observed, which is explained as a consequence of attempts to progressively bridge the gap between the formal and the material constitution of the Community.

The most elaborate account of the constitutionalisation of the Treaty distinguishes three separate phases of this process.[7] The first phase is that of constitutionalisation by the Court by its development of the doctrines of its direct effect, supremacy, implied powers, and human rights. During this phase of legal integration, political integration regressed. The Member States responded to this tightening of the framework of European law by taking control of the Community's decision making process. During the second phase, legal and political

---

[4] Cf. S. Cassese 'La Costituzione Europea', (1991) 11 *Quaderni Costituzionali* 187; L.-M. Diez-Picazo, 'Reflexiones sobre la Idea de Constitucion Europea', (1993) 20 *Revista de Instituciones Europeas* 533; A. Easson, 'Legal Approaches to European Legislation: The Role of the Court and Legislator in the Completion of the European Common Market', (1989) 12 *Revue d'Integration Européen* 101; T. C. Hartley, 'Federalism, Courts and Legal Systems: The Emerging Constitution of the European Community', (1986) 34 *American Journal of Comparative Law* 229; F. G. Jacobs, 'Is the Court of Justice of the European Communities a Constitutional Court?', in D. Curtin and D. O'Keeffe (eds.), *Constitutional Adjudication in European Community and National Law* (London, 1992); K. Lenaerts, 'Constitutionalism and the many Faces of Federalism', (1990) 38 *American Journal of Comparative Law* 205; G. F. Mancini, 'The Making of a Constitution for Europe', (1989) 26 CMLR 295; T. Sandalow and E. Stein, *Courts and Free markets: Perspectives from the United States and Europe* (Oxford, 1982); J. J. H. Weiler, 'The Transformation of Europe' (1991) 100 *The Yale Law Journal* 2403; D. O'Keeffe and M. Twomey (eds.), *Legal Issues of the Maastricht Treaty* (London, 1994), Part 2: 'Subsidiarity'.

[5] For a comparison of different approaches cf. Ch. Joerges, 'European Economic Law, the Nation State and the Maastricht Treaty', in R. Dehousse (ed.), *Europe After Maastricht: An Ever Closer Union* (München, 1994); Ch. Joerges, 'Die Europäisierung des Rechts und die rechtliche Kontrolle von Risiken', (1991) 74 *Kritische Vierteljahresschrift für Gesetzgebung und Rechtswissenschaft* 416; E. U. Petersmann, 'Grundprobleme der Wirtschaftsverfassung der EG', (1993) 48 *Aussenwirtschaft* 389.

[6] Cf. E. U. Petersmann, 'Constitutionalism, Constitutional Law and European Integration', (1991) 46 *Aussenwirtschaft* 15, p. 28.

[7] Cf. Weiler, above, n. 4; and id., 'Community, Member States and European Integration: Is the Law Relevant?', (1983) 21 JCMS 42.

integration progressed in tandem, and the competences of the Community were transformed. This occurred as the principle of enumerated powers was relaxed, primarily by an extensive use of Article 235 EEC. The resulting expansion of the powers of the Community was possible since the Member States continued to hold veto power. In the third phase, political power started gravitating to the Community level. This phase is identified with the Single European Act, and with the majority voting that was re-introduced in order to complete the internal market. With this change in decision making procedures, limiting the competences of the Community has become of the utmost importance to the Member States.[8] Therefore, although further pooling of sovereignty is taking place, the Member States have taken care to include explicit safeguards of their competences in the Treaty on European Union. For the same reason more recently, the role of the Court and the Commission themselves have become the object of particular scrutiny and at times open resistance.

The basic principles of the 'material constitution' are derived from the Court's early case law on direct effect, supremacy, implied powers, and human rights.[9] The doctrines of direct effect and supremacy allow individuals to rely on Community law before national courts, even against the Member States and the Community itself. In this way the Treaty offers individuals enforceable constitutional guarantees even against decisions which are legitimised by democratic means (as Community law cannot be overruled by national law). Further, the Treaty establishes the institutions of the Community, their decision making procedures, and the rules by which the Treaty itself can be amended.

Hence, if the core characteristics of a constitution are held to be limited government under the rule of law, expressed through the embodiment of fundamental norms, of separation of powers, and of guarantees enforceable by minorities and individuals against majoritarian decisions, a credible claim can be made that the Treaty, as interpreted by the European Court of Justice, meets the minimum standards of a constitutional charter.

The Court of Justice itself has gone beyond its implicit constitutionalisation of the Treaties to explicitly claiming constitutional status for the EEC Treaty. In the landmark cases setting out the fundamental principles of direct effect and supremacy, it has already suggested that the Treaty amounts to a constitution for the Community.[10] More recently, the Court has consistently referred to the Treaties as the basic constitutional charter of a Community based on law.[11]

---

[8] J. J. H. Weiler, 'Journey to an Unknown Destination: A Retrospective and Prospective of the European Court of Justice in the Arena of Political Integration', (1993) 31 JCMS 417.

[9] It has been observed that '. . . the essential consequence of the constitutionalization of Community law is that it is in the national courts that Community law is applied'. Easson, above, n. 4, p. 109.

[10] Case 26/62 *Van Gend en Loos* [1963] ECR 1; Opinion of Advocate General Lagrange on Case 6/64 *Costa v ENEL* [1965] ECR 585, p. 605.

[11] Case 294/83 *Parti écologiste 'Les Verts' v European Parliament* [1986] ECR 1339, para. 23 p. 1365. Repeated in Case C-2/88 *Zwartveld et al* [1990] ECR I-3365, para. 16 p. 3372.

The Court has tied together the various elements of the constitutionalisation thesis most explicitly in its Opinion 1/91 on the draft treaty establishing the European Economic Area. When contrasting that agreement with the EC Treaty, the Court stated:

(T)he EEC Treaty, albeit concluded in the form of an international agreement, none the less constitutes the constitutional charter of a Community based on the rule of law. As the Court of Justice has consistently held the Community treaties established a new legal order for the benefit of which the States have limited their sovereign rights, in ever wider fields, and the subjects of which comprise not only the Member States but also their nationals . . . The essential characteristics of the Community legal order which has thus been established are in particular its primacy over the law of the Member States and the direct effect of a whole series of provisions which are applicable to their nationals and to the Member States themselves.[12]

Two further steps in the constitutionalisation of the Treaty can be traced back to this Opinion. Starting with this Opinion, the Court appears to have begun to move towards establishing a hierarchy both of the principles developed in its case law and of the norms explicitly laid down in the Treaty.[13] Finally, the Court has furthered the 'fundamental democratic principle' by promoting both the locus standi of the European Parliament, and by imposing the involvement of the Parliament in the adoption of legislation as well as in external relations as a fundamental requirement for the validity of Community acts.[14]

During the second phase of integration, the competences of the Community were extended on an ad hoc basis. The Single European Act codified these changes, and modified the political constitution by increasing the role of the European Parliament, re-introducing majority voting procedures in the Council, and streamlining the delegation procedure from the Council to the Commission.[15] Since then, political consolidation of constitutional developments has

[12] Opinion 1/91 [1991] ECR I-6079, para. 21 p. 6102, with reference to Case 26/62 *Van Gend en Loos*, above n. 10. Cf. D. O'Keeffe, 'The Agreement on the European Economic Area', (1992) 8 LIEI 1.

[13] This further major step in the constitutionalisation of the Treaties was seen by some in the reference by the Court to a conflict 'with Article 164 of the EEC Treaty and the very foundations of the Community'. Opinion 1/91, above, n. 11, para. 46 p. 6107. These foundations would include the uniform application of Community law, the principle of non-discrimination, legal certainty, the unity of the market and the identity of the Community in its external relations. Cf. O'Keeffe, above, n. 12. Contrast, M. Heintzen, 'Hierarchierungsprozesse innerhalb des Primärrechts der Europäischen Gemeinschaft', (1994) 29 EuR 35.

[14] Cf. Case 22/70 *Commission v Council* [1971] ECR 263 ('ERTA'); Case 138/79 *Roquette Frères v Council* [1980] ECR 3333 and Case 139/79 *Maizena v Council* [1980] ECR 3393 ('Isoglucose Cases'); Case 13/83 *Parliament v Council* [1985] ECR 1513; Case 294/83 *Les Verts,* above, n. 11; Case 302/87 *Parliament v Council* [1988] ECR 5615 ('Comitology'); Case C-70/88 *Parliament v Council* [1990] ECR I-241 ('Chernobyl'). For an overview see G. F. Mancini and D. T. Keeling, 'Democracy and the European Court of Justice', (1994) 57 MLR 175.

[15] Arguably the most important changes concerning the latter were not included in the SEA as such, but in the amendment to Article 5 of the Council's rules of procedure which facilitated resorting to the majority vote ((1987) OJ L291/27); and the Council Decision of 13 July 1987 laying down procedures for the exercise of implementing powers conferred on the Commission ((1987) OJ L197/33), which standardised the comitology procedures.

taken place in the Treaty on European Union, where numerous provisions have codified the constitutional case law of the Court of Justice. The codification of the respect of fundamental rights as general principles of Community law in Article F(2) TEU is a prime example of this codification, which has narrowed the gap between the 'material constitution' developed in the case law of the Court, and the 'formal constitution' of the Treaty.

Further, the Treaty on European Union has extended the scope of the Community's constitution on at least three important points.[16] First, a concept of citizenship of the Union was introduced in part II of the EC Treaty. Under the EEC Treaty, the individual had been ignored completely. Under the EEC Treaty as interpreted by the Court, the position of the individual as the subject of economic law was improved (mainly by improving the means of the enforcement of its economic rules), but the political dimension of citizenship was left undeveloped. Although under the EC Treaty the new citizenship of the Union remains very limited in its practical meaning, taken together with the recognition of the principles of human rights and democracy noted earlier, it forms a significant advance over the way the individual was previously conceived under European law, and thereby adds to the development of a full political constitution.[17]

Second, the institutional reform introduced by the Treaty on European Union has extended the constitution. The direct democratic legitimation of the Community has been strengthened by an increased role for the European Parliament, and by the introduction of a Committee of the Regions. Moreover, an explicit commitment to democracy was first expressed in the preamble to the Treaty on European Union.[18]

Third, the emphasis which the Treaty on European Union has placed on the co-ordination of economic and monetary policies has further modified the constitution of the Community. In particular, it has reduced the margins of national sovereignty, while introducing new procedures for the co-ordination of economic policy.

---

[16] Cf. U. Everling, 'Reflections on the Structure of the European Union', (1992) 29 CMLR 1053; V. Constantinesco, 'la structure du traité instituant l'Union européenne—Les dispositions communes et finales—Les nouvelles compétences', (1993) 29 CDE 251; T. C. Hartley, 'Constitutional and Institutional Aspects of the Maastricht Agreement', (1993) 43 ICLQ 213; O'Keeffe and Twomey (eds.), above, n. 4, 'Part 1: Treaty Framework and Constitutional Change'. Critical: D. Curtin, 'The Constitutional Structure of the Union: A Europe of Bits and Pieces', (1993) 30 CMLR 17.

[17] Cf. O'Keeffe and Twomey (eds.), above, n. 4, 'Part 3: Citizenship and Fundamental Rights'; 'Special Issue on Sovereignty, Citizenship and the European Constitution', (1995) 1 *European Law Journal*; and the discussion of the European Parliament's Resolution on the Constitution of the European Union (EP Doc A3-0064/94), 'A Constitution for Europe?', EUI Working Paper RSC 95/9 (Florence, 1995). This dimension is now also developed in EC Commission, *Conférence intergouvernementale 1996: Rapport de la Commission pour le Groupe de réflexion* (Brussels, 1995).

[18] Where the contracting parties confirm 'their attachment to the principles of liberty, democracy and respect for human rights and fundamental freedoms and of the rule of law'. This respect for the democratic principle is repeated in Article F(1) of the common provisions, and for the common foreign and security policy in Article J1 TEU. Also, the fifth consideration of the preamble of the Treaty on European Union states the desire of the contracting parties to 'enhance further the democratic and efficient functioning of the institutions'.

In spite of these changes, which point to its development beyond the minimalist definition of 'limited government under the rule of law', the constitution of the Community is still subject to criticism. Arguments that sources of legitimacy are to be found in the constitution of the Community itself, such as the normative legitimacy of the Treaty and Community law, functional legitimacy in relation to the goals codified as the objectives of the Community, and political legitimacy derived from the horizontal and vertical division of powers laid down in the Treaty, are ultimately based on the rule of law.[19] Yet the rule of law is widely perceived as inadequate: regardless of its new found general commitment to democracy, the legitimacy of the Community is suffering as the result of the widely perceived 'democratic deficit'. Since the Community does not constitute a polity, full direct democratic legitimation of its actions would be difficult to achieve even if the powers of the European Parliament were enhanced further.[20] For the foreseeable future, the legitimacy of the Community will be derived, indirectly, from the Member States' national parliaments. This lack of direct democratic legitimacy, and the problem of finding an adequate substitute for the national polity, remain a major weakness of the Community as a modern constitutional system.

Other weak points of the constitution are the convoluted institutional structure of the Union (exacerbated by the three pillar structure), the ambiguous division of competences between the Member States and the Community, and the lack of a clear hierarchy of Community acts.[21] These problems have been complicated rather than resolved by the Treaty on European Union. Some commentators have argued that none of these problems, including the democratic deficit, could be resolved by means of 'constitutionalization through the back door' by the Court of Justice, or by intergovernmental conferences of the Member States. They believe that what is needed at this stage to bootstrap

[19] H. Von der Groeben, 'Probleme einer Europäischen Wirtschaftsordnung', in Baur, Müller-Graf and Zuleeg (eds.), *Europarecht, Energierecht, Wirtschaftsrecht: Festschrift für Bodo Börner zum 70. Geburtstag* (Cologne, 1992), pp. 113–14; Cf. H. Von der Groeben, *Legitimationsprobleme der Europäischen Gemeinschaft* (Baden-Baden, 1987). Cf. J. Habermas, 'Wie ist Legitimität durch Legalität möglich?', (1987) 20 *Kritische Justiz* 1; J. Raz, 'The Rule of Law and its Virtue', (1977) 93 *The Law Quarterly Review* 195. Critical of the concept of legitimation as such: A. Hyde, 'The Concept of Legitimation in the Sociology of Law', (1983) 54 *Wisconsin Law Review* 379.

[20] Under these circumstances, decision making by consensus by the Council is the most important source of (indirect) political legitimation. Cf. J. J. H. Weiler, 'Problems of Legitimacy in Post 1992 Europe', (1991) 46 *Aussenwirtschaft* 411, p. 421. For a view focused on individual rights and direct democratic legitimacy see E.-J. Mestmäcker, 'On the Legitimacy of European Law', (1994) 58 *Rabelszeitschrift* 615. The absence of independent democratic legitimation formed the crux of one branch of the BVerfG Maastricht judgment. The German Constitutional Court argued that in the absence of a united European polity ('*Volk*'), ultimate political control should remain with the national parliaments for the foreseeable future. It asserted that, as an association of states, within the Community sovereignty remained with the Member States, and the powers of legitimation with the national parliaments. See below, n. 24.

[21] Cf. K. Lenaerts, 'Some Reflections on the Separation of Powers in the European Community', (1991) 28 CMLR 11; E. U. Petersmann, 'Constitutionalism, Constitutional Law and European Integration', (1991) 46 *Aussenwirtschaft* 15, p. 28.

a democratic European polity is nothing less than a 'constitutional moment': the emphatic affirmation of a common democratic identity by a constitutional convention.[22]

Such proposals ignore the fact that, notwithstanding the explicit statements by the Court of Justice on the constitutional nature of the Treaties, and the narrowing of the gap between the formal and the material constitution, the constitutionalisation thesis as such is still contested. In the controversy over the Maastricht Agreement the persistence of the view of the Treaty as no more than an international agreement between sovereign states has again been demonstrated.[23] This point was driven home in a particularly painful manner by the 'Maastricht Judgment' of the German Constitutional Court. Ostensibly concerned with refuting a constitutional challenge to Germany joining the Economic and Monetary Union, the *Bundesverfassungsgericht* in passing denied any claims to supranationalism in the Treaty. Its analysis remained strictly within the framework of public international law, asserting the sovereignty of the Member States, and explicitly considering them the sovereign masters of the Treaty (*Herren der Verträge*). As a result, the judgment undermined fundamental tenets of Community constitutional law by denying the primacy of European law and of its interpretation by the Court of Justice, and reasserting the right of the Member States to withdraw from the Community.[24]

A full-fledged revolt by the national judiciary would be fatal to the constitutionalisation of the Treaty, since the denial of constitutional status by the highest courts of the Member States could become a self-fulfilling prophecy.[25] Much as the European Court of Justice has played a central role in developing the constitution of the Community, it has always depended on the co-operation and receptiveness of the national courts and the broader legal community for

[22] Cf. Curtin, above, n. 16. Cf. B. A. Ackerman, *The Future of Liberal Revolution* (New Haven, 1992); R. Bellamy, V. Bufacchi and D. Castiglione (eds.), *Democracy and Constitutional Culture in the Union of Europe* (London, 1995), on the distinction between the democratic deficit, the federal deficit, and the constitutional deficit of the European Community.

[23] Although the usefulness of the concept of sovereignty in legal discourse has of course been questioned, this does not make the threat to the integration project posed by its reassertion any less real. Cf. N. MacCormick, 'Beyond the Sovereign State', (1993) 56 MLR 1; and '*The Maastricht Urteil*: Sovereignty Now', (1995) 1 *European Law Journal* 255, developing the critique on the concept of sovereignty by H. L. A. Hart in *The Concept of Law* (Oxford, 1961), pp. 215ff.

[24] BVerfG, Urt v 12.10.1993—2BvR 2134/92 und 2BvR 2159/92, *Manfred Brunner et al v The European Union Treaty* [1994] 1 CMLR 57. Cf. M. Herdegen, 'Maastricht and the German Constitutional Court: Constitutional Restraints for an "Ever Closer Union"', (1994) 31 CMLR 235; D. Hanf, 'Le jugement de la Cour constitutionelle fédérale allemande sur la constitutionalité du Traité de Maastricht: Un nouveau chapitre des relations entre le droit communautaire et le droit national', (1994) 30 RTDE 391. On the competing perspectives of the Community system as a *Rechtsgemeinschaft* (Community under the rule of law) or *Staatenverbund* (confederation of states) that are at play here, Ch. Joerges, 'Das Recht im Prozeß der europäischen Integration: Plädoyer für die Beachtung des Rechts durch die Politikwissenschaft', in M. Jachtenfuchs and B. Kohler-Koch (eds.), *Europäische Integration* (Opladen, 1995).

[25] D. R. Phelan, 'Revolt or Revolution: The Constitutional Boundaries of the European Community', Ph.D. thesis (Florence, 1995).

the success of its approach. The problems for the unity of European law that would arise if institutionalised resistance were to be encountered from within the judicial system were already spelled out by Advocate General Tesauro in the Opinion on the very Case in which the supremacy of European law was first confirmed: 'It is apparent that a conflict between the Court of Justice and the highest national courts could be of such a nature as seriously to prejudice the system of judicial review instituted by the Treaty, which rests upon a necessary, and frequently even organic co-operation between the two jurisdictions.'[26]

Throughout the 1996–97 intergovernmental conference required by Article N. TEU, alternative visions of Europe will abound. Yet at least formally, the constitution of the European Union as established by the Court of Justice will not be under threat. At the intergovernmental conference, the results of the constitutionalisation of the Treaties so far will be protected as *acquis communautaire* under Articles B and C TEU.

B. The Structure and Objectives of the European Constitution

As the 'constitutional charter' of the Community, the Treaty provides both the structure of the constitution, and its objectives. Yet although it sets out under separate headings principles, foundations, policies, and institutional provisions, the Treaty does not clearly distinguish goals, principles, and instruments at various levels in an explicit hierarchy of norms and legal acts, such as would normally be the case in a written constitution. This is the result of the fact that it was written as an international agreement intended to bind the contracting governments, and not as a constitution intended to set out and legitimise a coherent and independent political structure before a critical polity. The debate on the ratification of the Treaty on European Union has made clear that subsequent revisions should take account of a wider audience both in tone and in content. However, the TEU has made some improvements in the structure of the EC Treaty,[27] and redrawn the balance between its provisions on the internal market and the co-ordination on economic policy.

In its opening articles, the EEC Treaty established the objectives of the Community, the instruments to realise these objectives, and the general principles which guide the use of the instruments.[28] These objectives may be distinguished

---

[26] Case 6/64 *Costa v ENEL* [1965] ECR 585 at p. 601.

[27] The three pillar structure of the Treaty on European Union indicates more clearly the division of competences between supranational and intergovernmental forms of co-operation within the framework of general rules of Articles A to F TEU, and L to S TEU. Thus an incomplete but hierarchical structure of legal rules is becoming discernable, which covers differentiated rules for supranational and intergovernmental areas, and mixed forms of co-operation. However, as is demonstrated by Article L TEU, it is debatable to what extent at least the provisions of the intergovernmental pillars could be seen as part of the constitutional charter of a Community based on the rule of law.

[28] As elaborated by L.-J. Constantinesco, 'La constitution économique de la C.E.E.', (1977) 13 RTDE 244. It is also found in P. J. G. Kapteyn and P. VerLoren van Themaat, *Introduction to the Law of the European Communities* (2nd ed., Deventer, 1990), L. W. Gormley (ed.).

between intermediate and sectoral goals on the one hand, and general objectives on the other. The general objectives, listed in Article 2 of the Rome Treaty, were the harmonious development of economic activities throughout the Community, a continuous and balanced expansion, an increase in stability, an accelerated raising of the standard of living, and closer relations between the Member States. The intermediate and sectoral goals can be further divided into two categories, according to the instruments by which they are to be realised, as linked either to the establishment of the common market or to the approximation of the economic policy of the Member States.

The two most immediate goals of the Community were establishing the two instruments: the common market and the approximation of economic policy. Consequently, the establishment of the common market and, to a lesser extent, the co-ordination of the economic policies of the Member States have so far played a decisive role in shaping the Community. Neither of the two has been fully realised, and until the adoption of the Treaty on European Union the focus has been on establishing the common market. This priority was largely determined by the different nature of the relations between the Community and the Member States in these two spheres.[29]

The common market was characterised by vertical relations aimed at economic integration, and based on the principle of Community 'solidarity' enshrined in Article 5 EC.[30] The field of approximation of economic policies was dominated by horizontal relations aimed at achieving co-operation, based on the principle of 'sovereignty' of the Member States. The legal instruments used were distributed accordingly, with the application of directives and regulations for the common market, and of recommendations for the approximation of economic policy. This reflected the fact that there was a qualitative difference in the nature of the (positive) consensus between the Member States which is required to establish the co-ordination of economic policy, as opposed to the negative consensus required to create a free trade area and a common market.

It is on this point that the Treaty on European Union has made the most significant advances. In the first place Article 2 EC has been modified by the introduction of new general objectives (such as a high degree of convergence of economic performance, and a high level of employment and social protection), and the elaboration of existing objectives (such as sustainable and non-inflationary growth respecting the environment, instead of a continuous and

---

[29] L.-J. Constantinesco, ibid., p. 259.

[30] Article 8a to 8c EC were introduced by the Single European Act to revitalise the common market objective by introducing both a timetable and changes in decision making procedures to attain the objective of the 'internal market'. Defined by Article 8a(2) EEC as 'an area without internal frontiers in which the free movement of goods, persons, services and capital is ensured in accordance with the provisions of this Treaty'. Cf. P. VerLoren van Themaat, 'Some Preliminary Observations on the Intergovernmental Conferences: The Relations between the Concepts of a Common Market, a Monetary Union, an Economic Union, a Political Union and Sovereignty', (1991) 28 CMLR 291, pp. 293ff.

balanced expansion; or economic and social cohesion and solidarity among the Member States, rather than 'closer relations' between them). In the second place, and more importantly, the second instrument of the EEC Treaty (that of the progressive approximation of the economic policies of the Member States) has now been replaced by the establishment of economic and monetary union, and supplemented by 'implementing the common policies or activities referred to in Articles 3 and 3a'. As a result, the objectives of the Community under the Treaty on European Union are not only much broader than they were under the original Treaty, but also cover a much wider range of policies for their realisation (as is reflected in the expansion of the policies covered by Article 3 EC).

This elaboration of the objectives of the Community gives rise to three observations. First, the changes to Article 2 reflect the fact that the EC Treaty now provides detailed rules for the (intergovernmental) co-ordination of economic policy and the definition and conduct of a single monetary and exchange-rate policy (which is progressively upgraded to a supranational policy).[31] Second, by establishing an institutional structure (including the European Central Bank as an institution of the Communities) and a detailed three stage system of 'phased obligations', the Treaty on European Union redresses the imbalance between the internal market objective and the co-ordination of economic policies that had characterised the original Rome Treaty.[32] Third, the juxtaposition of the common market, economic and monetary union, and the policies and activities set out in Articles 3 (and 3a) EC makes it clear that there is no hierarchical relationship between the latter and the two main intermediate objectives.

This is worth noting in the context of an assessment of the economic orientation of the Treaty, since Article 3 EC includes among the policies and activities of the Community a system whereby competition in the internal market is not distorted (under 3(g) EC), and the competitiveness of Community industry is strengthened (under 3(l) EC). Further, the 'open market economy with free competition' is introduced as a principle in the first and second paragraphs of Article 3a EC, and repeated in the new Title VI EC on economic and monetary policy where the implementation of Article 3a EC is developed. Similarly, Article 130(1) of Industry Title XIII (which aims at implementing Article 3(l) EC on the promotion of competitiveness) states that the action of the Community and the Member States shall be 'in accordance with a system of open and competitive markets'. Further, Article 130(3) EC repeats that 'this Title shall not provide a basis for the introduction by the Community of any measure

---

[31] Cf. F. Snyder, 'EMU—Metaphor for European Union? Institutions, Rules and Types of Regulation', in Dehousse (ed.), *Europe After Maastricht: An Ever Closer Union* (München, 1994); J. Pipkorn, 'Legal Arrangements in the Treaty of Maastricht for the Effectiveness of the Economic and Monetary Union', (1994) 31 CMLR 263; P. J. Slot, 'The Institutional Dimension of the EMU', in D. Curtin and T. Heukels (eds.), *Institutional Dynamics of European Integration: Essays in Honour of Henry G. Schermers* (Dordrecht, 1994).

[32] Snyder, ibid.

which could lead to a distortion of competition'. This raises the question whether priorities can be assigned between the various policies with the help of constitutional principles; and the further question whether the open market economy with free competition has itself the status of a constitutional principle under Community law.

C. The Constitutional Principles of the European Union

There is no generally accepted exclusive catalogue or hierachy of constitutional principles for the European Union. The classification of the constitutional principles of the European Union which is developed here is based on a distinction between: (i) legal priciples versus political principles; (ii) general principles of law versus constitutional principles; and (iii) principles binding the Member States versus principles binding the Community.

The first distinction made here is that between political and legal principles. There can be no doubt that the constitution of the European Union includes both types of principles, and political principles have become more numerous with the Treaty on European Union.[33] For example, the principles which guide the co-ordination of the economic policies of the Community, or the common monetary and exchange rate policy, are of a political nature since they are primarily to be guaranteed by political means. They represent an attempt to bind economic policy to the pursuit of certain economic objectives, which are further circumscribed by the convergence criteria for Monetary Union.[34] As such, the principle of free competition in open markets of Article 3a EC, which is linked explicitly to the provisions on Economic and Monetary Union, should be considered a political principle.

This does not necessarily mean that such political principles have no legal relevance. The political principles included in the Treaty are cast in legal form, and are justiciable to various degrees. However, even political principles which in theory may be perfectly well justiciable may involve value judgements which the courts are reluctant to subject to anything other than limited judicial review for manifest illegality. These political principles are to be pursued and guaranteed foremost by political means. They appear to play a further role in particular where co-ordination of polices of the Member States is involved.

[33] This includes the principles of liberty, democracy, respect for human rights and fundamental freedoms and the rule of law listed in the preamble. In Article F(1) the principle of democracy (as the foundation of the systems of government of the Member States, to be respected by the Union) is repeated. In Article 3a(1) the principle of an open market economy with free competition (repeated in Article 102a and 105(1) EC) is mentioned, as are the guiding principles of stable prices, sound public finances and monetary conditions and a sustainable balance of payments.

[34] Beyond the principle of an open market economy with free competition, Article 3a identifies as a 'primary objective' of both economic and monetary policy to maintain price stability and, without prejudice to this objective, to support the general economic policies in the Community, as well as the 'guiding principles' of 'stable prices, sound public finances and monetary conditions, and a sustainable balance of payments'.

The second distinction is that between the general principles of law and the principles of Community law (although the two categories partially overlap). The Court of Justice has established the general principles of law as an independent source of Community law, alongside the Treaty, secondary legislation, and agreements with third countries.[35] As such the general principles of law have been described as 'Community common law'.[36] The Court has repeatedly read general principles of law into provisions of the Treaty, many of which have subsequently been applied as representing general principles of Community law in their own right. An example is Article 7 EC, which forms the basis for the extensive Community law doctrine of equality, or the principle of non-discrimination. The Court's method has been called 'inductive-deductive'.[37] Hereby, the general principles of law are in fact derived from the legal traditions of the Member States, or international law.[38]

The general principles of law are used to interpret the constitutional rules of the Community. They are used by the Court of Justice both where constitutional rules are lacking, and where conflicts among such rules are to be resolved. As these general principles of law are applied and developed by the Court itself, they are established as general principles of Community law. This process is completed unequivocally when general principles of law are codified as principles of Community law in the Treaty. Yet it should be noted that not all general principles of Community law can also be considered to form general principles of law. The most obvious examples of this are the fundamental Community law principles of direct effect and supremacy, which are evidently not to be found in the legal traditions of the Member States. Other important principles of Community law, which are derived directly from the Treaty, and not from the general principles of law, are the free movement of goods and persons.[39]

If general principles of law as a category are nevertheless regarded as constitutional principles, they should be considered part of the material constitution

---

[35] The application of general principles of law has been based on Articles 164, 173, and 215(2) EC. For a study of the application of these general principles by the Court see A. Arnull, *The General Principles of EEC Law and the Individual* (Leicester, 1990).

[36] T. C. Hartley, 'Federalism, Courts and Legal Systems: The Emerging Constitution of the European Community', (1986) 34 *American Journal of Comparative Law* 229, p. 242.

[37] T. C. Hartley, *The Foundations of European Community Law* (3rd ed., Oxford, 1994), ch. 5 'General Principles of Law'.

[38] For a principle to be respected by the Community, it will suffice that it is recognised as such in the constitution of only one of the Member States. The argument is that the Member State in question cannot be assumed to have signed away the protection of the constitutional right concerned by acceding to the Community, and the respect of this right by the Community is therefore implicit. ibid., p. 136, with reference to the Opinion of Advocate General Warner in Case 7/76 *IRCA* [1976] ECR 1213, p. 1237.

[39] H. G. Schermers and D. Waelbroeck, *Judicial Protection in the European Communities* (5th ed., Deventer, 1992), para. 45 p. 28. These authors distinguish between 'compelling legal principles', 'regulatory rules common to the laws of the Member States', and 'general rules, native to the Community legal order'.

(that is the Treaty as interpreted by the Court of Justice) rather than as part of the formal constitution of the Community (or the Treaty itself). The general principles of law are not derived directly from the Treaty and there is no established list of the general principles of law applied by the Court of Justice.[40] Given their nature as the product of creative judicial activity, there could not be an exhaustive enumeration of the general principles of law, although it may be possible to identify the most important of these principles. As part of the process of constitutionalisation, some general principles of law have been explicitly codified in the Treaty as principles of Community law (such as fundamental human rights and the principle of proportionality in Article 3b TEU).[41] However, there is a qualitative difference between such general constitutional principles which have found their basis in a fundamental political consensus, and the general principles of law found by the Court in order to resolve what may not amount to more than a single case.

The principles of Community law can be classified by their objectives. The first category is that of principles concerned with limited government under the rule of law. This includes the fundamental human rights mentioned in Article F TEU, 'due process' and procedural rules of administrative law such as are protected by Article 173 EC. The second category is that of principles concerned with liberalisation and the freedom of the market process, such as non-discrimination, the unity of the market, and equality, which are exemplified by Articles 6, 7 and 7a EC. The third category is that of the principles concerned with common policies and redistribution, of which the principles of solidarity (or good faith), included in Article 5 EC, and Community preference, of Article 44(2) EC are examples.[42]

---

[40] Although authoritative sources are available, even their classifications show considerable variation. Compare for example L.-J. Constantinesco, 'La Constitution de la C.E.E.', (1977) 13 RTDE 244; VerLoren and Kapteyn, *Introduction to the Law of the European Communities* (2nd ed., Deventer, 1990), L. W. Gormley (ed.); Hartley, above, n. 37; J. Mertens de Wilmars, 'The Case-Law of the Court of Justice in Relation to the Review of the Legality of Economic Policy in Mixed Economy Systems', (1983) 10 LIEI 1; J. Mertens de Wilmars, 'Réflexions sur l'ordre juridico-économique de la Communauté européenne' in J. Dutheil de la Rochère and J. Vandamme (eds.) *Interventions Publiques et Droit Communautaire* (Brussels, 1988); P. Pescatore, 'Les objectifs de la Communauté européenne comme principes d'interprétation dans la jurisprudence de la Cour de Justice', in *Miscellanea Ganshof van der Meersch*, Vol. 2 (Brussels, 1972); Schermers and Waelbroeck, above, n. 39; J. Temple Lang, 'Article 5 of the EEC Treaty: The Emergence of Constitutional Principles in the Case Law of the Court of Justice', (1987) 10 *Fordham International Law Journal* 503.

[41] The legal basis for respect of human rights has now been laid down explicitly in Article F(2) TEU, which states: 'The Union shall respect fundamental rights, as guaranteed by the European Convention for the Protection of Human Rights and Fundamental Freedoms signed in Rome on 4 November 1950 and as they result from the constitutional traditions common to the Member States, as general principles of Community law'.

[42] Under this classification some principles are found in more than one category. For example, the principles of non-discrimination and solidarity are general principles of Community law, but they are also present in numerous individual Treaty provisions. Further, as was noted on the evidence of Article 3b TEU, there seems to be a tendency towards the constitutionalisation of the general principles of law as general principles of Community law and political constitutional principles.

Within the first category of general principles of Community law a further threefold classification is possible, which identifies principles as:

(i) relating to the rule of law as such;

(ii) as relating to the institutional structure (such as the autonomy of the institutions and their loyal co-operation) and the horizontal division of power between the institutions; and

(iii) as relating to the vertical division of powers between the Community and the Member States (including supremacy and direct effect).[43]

These three categories can be seen as defining the rule of law, by providing the basic criteria, the structure, and the process involved. This subdivision is attractive since the rule of law and the horizontal and vertical division of powers presently form the core of the constitution of the European Union. As such, the principles on the horizontal and vertical division of powers deserve some further attention.

The basic rules on the horizontal division of power are well established. For example, the composition and particular duties of Community institutions and the various auxiliary bodies as well as their instruments and detailed decision making rules are set out in Part Five of the Treaty.[44] The objective of the horizontal division of powers is to achieve a balance between the institutions which provides mutual checks on the exercise of power. The institutional balance between the institutions of the Community is largely the result of the allocation of powers in the specific area, the relevant decision making rules, as well as (more generally) of the rules on judicial review by the Court of Justice. Beside the Treaty, other sources of constitutional rules regarding the institutional balance include, for example, inter-institutional agreements. The principle of institutional balance itself, however, is a general principle of Community law, which is regularly invoked by the Court to settle inter-institutional disputes.[45] Other sources of political rules are formed by the rules of procedure of the various institutions and auxiliary bodies, and other functional rules based on specific and general authorisations by the Treaty.[46]

---

[43] N. A. Neuwahl, 'Principles of Justice: Human Rights and Constitutional Principles Within the European Union—A Framework for Analysis', COST A7 Project, *The Evolution of Rules for a Single European Market* (1995).

[44] Cf. K. Lenaerts, 'Some Reflections on the Separation of Powers in the European Community', (1991) 28 CMLR 11, who explains how the legislative, executive and judiciary functions are exercised by the four institutions according to a 'functional division of powers', which only remotely reflects purer forms of the *trias politica*. Especially the executive and legislative functions are confused, with the Council retaining partly executive functions, whereas the European Parliament has still not attained the status of full co-legislator. Of course this unusual arrangement reflects the fact that the Member States, in the Council, in fact provide both the real locus of power and the main source of (indirect) democratic legitimation.

[45] Notably in Case 294/83 *Les Verts*, [1986] ECR 1339; Case C70/88 *Chernobyl*, [1990] ECR I-241. Cf. G. Guillermin, 'Le principe de l'équilibre institutionnel dans la jurisprudence de la Cour de justice des Communautés européennes', (1992) 119 *Journal du droit international* 319.

[46] Neuwahl, above, n. 43.

The vertical division of powers, which is the subject of Article 3b EC, has recently become more problematic. Here, the principles of limited powers and proportionality, which had previously been developed in the case law of the Court, and the principle of subsidiarity (hitherto found in Article 130r EEC), are brought together. The objective of these principles is to limit the powers of the Community and safeguard those of the Member States, while ensuring that decisions are taken as close as possible to the citizens of the Union. Beyond the general statement of subsidiarity, Articles 126f, 128, 129 and 129a EC explicitly limit the expansion of Community activity at the expense of the Member States in the relevant policy areas.

Of the three principles codified in Article 3b, subsidiarity is the most contested.[47] Three observations may be made. First, whereas proportionality applies whether or not the action concerned is within the exclusive competence of the Community, the principle of subsidiarity only applies where there are concurrent powers under the EC Treaty. Second, even where the application of subsidiarity excludes Community action, the Member States are still bound by the Community solidarity clause of Article 5 EC. Third, although 'the interpretation of this principle, as well as review of compliance with it by the Community institutions are subject to control by the Court of Justice',[48] its application is primarily a political matter.[49]

The third and last general distinction is that between the constitutional principles which are applied primarily to the Member States, and those which bind the Community. In some cases, the Treaty refers exclusively to the Member States, as is the case in Article 5(2) EC, which forms the basis for the principle of solidarity. Article 3a TEU on the other hand imposes compliance with

---

[47] Expressions of subsidiarity are also found in the 11th consideration of the preamble of the Treaty, and Articles A, B(2), F(1), and K3 TEU. Cf. H. Bribosia, 'Subsidiarité et répartition des compétences entre la Communauté et ses États membres', (1992) 4 *Revue du Marché Unique Européen* 165; V. Constantinesco, 'La subsidiarité comme principe constitutionel de l'Integration Européenne', (1991) 46 *Aussenwirtschaft* 439; R. Dehousse, 'Does Subsidiarity Really Matter?', EUI Working Paper LAW 92/32 (Florence, 1993); N. Emiliou, 'Subsidiarity: An Effective Barrier Against the Enterprises of Ambition?', (1992) 17 ELR 383; European Institute of Public Administration, *Subsidiarity: The Challenge of Change. Proceedings of the Jacques Delors Colloquium, Maastricht 21–22 March 1991* (Maastricht, 1991); L. A. Geelhoed, 'Het subsidiariteitsbeginsel: Een communautair principe?', (1991) 39 SEW 422; K. Lenaerts and P. Van Ypersele, 'Le principe de subsidiarité et son contexte: étude de l'article 3B du Traité CE', (1994) 30 CDE 3; D. O'Keeffe and M. Twomey (eds.), *Legal Issues of the Maastricht Treaty* (London, 1994), Part 2: Subsidiarity; A. Toth, 'The Principle of Subsidiarity in the Maastricht Treaty', (1992) 29 CMLR 1079; M. Wilke and H. Wallace 'Subsidiarity: Approaches to power-sharing in the European Community' *RIIA Discussion Paper* No. 27 (London, 1990). Cf. SEC(92) 1990, *The Principle of Subsidiarity*, Communication from the Commission to the Council and the European Parliament of 27 October 1992; *Conclusions of the Presidency*, Edinburgh European Council, 11–12 December 1992.

[48] Conclusions of the Presidency, ibid.

[49] The Court of Justice will be reluctant to go beyond a marginal test where the judgement required is essentially one of efficiency. Indeed, even the legitimacy of judicial review of such political decisions on the relative efficiency of various paths of action may be doubted. Dehousse, above, n. 47, p. 18.

the principles of free competition in open markets, stable prices, sound public finances and monetary conditions, and a sustainable balance of payments, on both the Member States and the Community. Here it is a straightforward matter to decide whether the principles concerned apply, regardless of whether they are political or legal in nature. In other cases determining the addressee is more difficult.

Ostensibly the requirements of the four freedoms and the system of competition are aimed at the Member States, and the fundamental freedoms and principles of administrative law bind the Community (whereas the Member States are bound to these directly both by their national law, as well as by Community law). Attempts have been made to demonstrate that the Community is bound by the four freedoms and competition as well.[50] This position presupposes that competition and the other market freedoms are regarded as constitutional principles in their own right.[51] The most radical position is that competition is the guiding principle of the (economic) constitution of the Community.[52] Finally, competition may be seen as a specific expression of the principles of non-discrimination and unity of the common market.[53] Alternatively, when competition, solidarity, and equity are held to be compatible, the economic neutrality of the Treaty itself may be proposed as a principle. In the choice between these various positions, both the remaining margins for national economic policies and the economic orientation of the Community are at stake.

III. THE ECONOMIC CONSTITUTION OF THE EUROPEAN UNION

A. The Concept of the Economic Constitution

In the early twentieth century, German economists first used the concept of *Wirtschaftsverfassung*, or 'economic constitution', interchangeably with 'economic order' to describe the principles and relations which characterised a

---

[50] For example, Möschel holds that the *effet utile* case law on Articles 5 and 85 EEC can be applied to the Community. W. Möschel 'Hoheitliche Maßnahmen und die Wettbewerbsvorschriften des Gemeinschaftsrechts' in *Weiterentwicklung der Europäischen Gemeinschaften und der Marktwirtschaft. Referate des XXV. FIW-Symposions* (Cologne, 1992) p. 102. Cf. A. Bach *Wettbewerbsrechtliche Schranken für staatliche Maßnahmen nach europäischem Gemeinschaftsrecht* (Tübingen, 1992); E.-J. Mestmäcker, 'Zur Anwendung der Wettbewerbsregeln auf die Mitgliedstaaten und auf die Europäischen Gemeinschaft', in Baur, Müller-Graf and Zuleeg (eds.), above, n. 3; Monopolkommission, *Hauptgutachten 1988/1989: Wettbewerbspolitik vor neuen Herausforderungen* (Baden-Baden, 1990), pp. 386ff; B. Van der Esch, 'Die Artikel 5, 3f, 85/86 und 90 EWGV als Grundlage der wettbewerbsrechtlichen Verpflichtungen der Mitgliedstaaten', (1991) 155 ZHR 274.

[51] E. U. Petersmann, 'Constitutionalism, Constitutional Law and European Integration', (1991) 46 *Aussenwirtschaft* 15, pp. 256ff.

[52] Mestmäcker, above, n. 50.

[53] L.-J. Constantinesco, 'La Constitution de la C.E.E.', (1977) 13 RTDE 244, at p. 273.

national economy.[54] Between the First and the Second World Wars, it was developed and transposed into the central concept of a theory of economic law which was developed by the Freiburg School of law and economics.[55] The economic constitution formed the subject of extensive debate in the founding years of the German Federal Republic, and even today 'Ordoliberalism' (the form of neo-liberalism from which this concept originated) remains the dominant school of thought on the economic order in Germany.

Classic liberalism had sought to ban the state from the economy, and saw only a minimal role for a 'watchman' state. The main conceptual innovation on classic liberalism introduced by the Ordoliberals of the Freiburg School was that they considered a coherent legal framework to be essential to guarantee individual freedoms and the economic process.[56] Taking this view, the economic constitution indicated not merely the factual coexistence of the component elements of an economy, but the legal structure which determines the kind of economic system (or economic order) a state is committed to pursue, and sets out a system of principles which bind economic policy accordingly.[57] Hence, the state serves as the guarantor of the economic order by enforcing the economic constitution.

This theory has been mainly developed for the neo-liberal market economy, and after the Second World War for the social market economy (*soziale Marktwirtschaft*), which seeks to combine open markets with social justice and individual freedom.[58] When the economic constitutions of other economic systems

---

[54] English language references on this topic are still limited. Cf. D. J. Gerber, 'Constitutionalizing the Economy: German Neo-liberalism, Competition Law and the "New" Europe', (1994) 42 *American Journal of Comparative Law* 25; Ch. Joerges, 'Die Europäisierung des Rechts und die rechtliche Kontrolle von Risiken', (1991) 74 *Kritische Vierteljahresschrift für Gesetzgebung und Rechtswissenschaft* 416. M. E. Streit and W. Mussler, 'The Economic Constitution of the European Community: From "Rome" to "Maastricht"', (1995) 1 *European Law Journal* 5. Further references in Gerber, ibid., at n. 2, Joerges, ibid., at n. 25.

[55] The most important representatives of the Freiburg School were the economist Walter Eucken and the lawyer Franz Böhm. The latter first introduced the preoccupation with freedom of competition into the discussion. Cf. L.-J. Constantinesco, above, n. 53. Recently, the contribution of Friedrich Hayek has been emphasised. Hayek forms the bridge between the Freiburg School and the neo-liberal economics of the Austrian and Chicago schools. See M. E. Streit, 'Economic Order, Private Law and Public Policy: The Freiburg School of Law and Economics in Perspective', (1992) 148 JITE 675.

[56] The term *Ordoliberal* is linked to the concept of distinguishable economic, legal and political 'orders', which was fundamental to this German school of neo-liberalism. Their main forum has been the *ORDO* journal of law and economics. On the various strands of the Freiburg School cf. Gerber, above, n. 54.

[57] Used in a descriptive manner, the term simply refers to 'all economic rules which constrain the conduct of economic agents, i.e. that are particularly relevant to the economy as a societal subsystem'. Used in a functional manner, the economic constitution refers to 'those legal rules which, according to experience and research, are constitutive for, or conducive to a specific type of economic system'. Streit and Mussler above, n. 54, pp. 5–6. In this sense, it has been used as a benchmark for the legality of economic policy. The economic constitution could also be seen as an element of the Community constitution, which would then comprise both a political and an economic constitution.

[58] Cf. A. Müller-Armack, *Wirtschaftsordnung und Wirtschaftspolitik* (Freiburg, 1964).

have been analysed, this has mainly served to underline the contrast between the market economy and 'central planning' or 'the command economy'.[59] The theory of the economic constitution contains a strong normative element in favour of a free market economy. As such, its demands are rarely satisfied by political practice. Nevertheless, both the German Federal Republic and the European Community have at various times been identified as political systems based on an (Ordo-) liberal economic constitution.

The economic constitution approach builds on the idea of the state based on the rule of law (*Rechtsstaat*). The assertion that a state is based on the rule of law is generally held to mean that not only political power, but also economic power, are bound by legal rules which are enforceable by individuals, and that conflicts between the political and economic spheres can be resolved through legal procedures. The economic constitution goes a step further than the general view of the rule of law as constituted by procedural guarantees, by claiming to provide the basis of a legal framework which fulfills qualitative objectives by enabling an optimal functioning of the economy. This legal framework defines the relation between the economic and the political processes, by means of ensuring their strict functional separation. The guarantees of the economic constitution are formed by its inclusion of justiciable criteria, which amount to self-constraint imposed on the state. These constraints can take various forms, such as clear constitutional objectives for the economic policy of a state, limits on state competence, limits on the instruments of state action, and, in particular, directly enforceable individual economic rights.[60]

The economic order to be protected by a liberal economic constitution is essentially that of a private law society (based on the freedom of contract) supplemented by minimal public intervention. Within this framework, economic competition and competition policy play a central role. Competition is seen as a 'discovery procedure' which can resolve the problem of partial information of market participants. Competition policy in turn serves both to protect the evolutionary process of competition as such, and to prevent the concentration of private power to the detriment of both the competitive and the political processes. Consequently, competition is considered as a value in its own right, which goes beyond considerations of efficiency. In this view, the economic constitution serves, first, to guarantee the basic equality of individuals as economic subjects, second, to back up the private law society by public authority, and third, to protect civil liberties.[61]

The Ordoliberal approach to the economic constitution presupposes that a meaningful separation between political and economic decisions is possible. A

---

[59] For a critique of such rhetorical devices cf. D. Rahmsdorf, 'Eine zweite Euro-Ordo-Debatte', (1980) 3 *Integration* 156.

[60] Cf. P. Behrens, 'Die Wirtschaftsverfassung der Europäischen Gemeinschaft', in G. Brüggemeier (ed.), *Verfassungen für ein ziviles Europa* (Baden-Baden, 1994).

[61] Streit, above, n. 55.

deep suspicion of the vulnerability of the democratic state to 'rent-seeking' by interest groups leads many of its adherents to deny that democracy can hope to pursue the general interest in a meaningful way, beyond enshrining fundamental freedoms in constitutional form. From this perspective, the role of the legislature is that of defining the economic constitution, and then stepping back.

The economic constitution is to guarantee that politically defined 'group interests' can but rarely override individual economic interests. Paradoxically, it is these individual economic interests which are seen as an expression of the 'general interest', which are equated with the foundations of the market economy, and 'liberty'. Consequently, under the Ordoliberal economic constitution, economic rights and freedoms are given equal status with the traditional political freedoms defined by means of majoritarian decision making. The practical effect of these liberal economic rights is, therefore, that limits are imposed on the scope of public intervention in the economy. Limiting public intervention is considered to be the most effective way of guaranteeing the economic constitution, and one that is close to the liberal ideal of the private law society.

Ordoliberalism takes the widely identified tension between the constitutional guarantees of individual (economic) rights and the democratic principle to an extreme:[62] under an Ordoliberal economic constitution, the activities of all three branches of government would be severely limited. Ideally, the clarity and market logic of the rules laid down in the economic constitution would make them fully self-evident and usually self-enforcing, removing almost all need for judicial interpretation. Administrative and legislative action would then be wholly circumscribed by the original charter. One of the main dynamic elements of government that would remain would be the active application of a body of competition rules. Yet even in the case of the application of the competition rules, the objective would be to minimise administrative discretion.

Extreme as they may appear to be on first reading, Ordoliberal theories have a relevance which goes well beyond academic debate. The Ordoliberals, who had generally resisted the widespread belief in economic planning under National Socialism, played a prominent role in the politics of German reconstruction after the Second World War, and their theoretical advances were applied to the drafting of the new German constitution of 1949.[63] The thesis that this new constitution prescribed a specific form of the market economy, *soziale Marktwirtschaft* or *Ordoliberalismus*, was hotly debated by economic

---

[62] Today, most Ordoliberals acknowledge the general legitimacy of intervention in the economic system when justified by the democratic political process, even where this might lead to results that would be sub-optimal from an economic point of view. However, even in this case market-conform solutions would be required where possible, based on a strict reading of the proportionality principle.

[63] For an extensive (and idealised) account of the role of the Freiburg School in the resistance against nazism, during the formation of the Federal Republic, and in establishing the European Community, see Gerber, above, n. 54.

lawyers in the German Federal Republic of the 1950s.[64] This debate helped to secure the *Kartellgesetz*, the German competition law originally imposed by the United States in order to break up the industrial cartels which were considered to have formed the backbone of the German war effort. The *Kartellgesetz* became the basis for the development of an active competition policy in Germany, a type of policy which was relatively new to Europe, but which was subsequently (at German request[65]) also introduced at the Community level. As a consequence of this, many of the issues regarding competition and public policy which would be discussed in the context of the Community were derived directly from the German debate.

The German constitutional court has resolved the German debate on the economic constitution by denying economic liberalism constitutional status for the Federal Republic. A contrary decision would have saddled the courts with the unenviable task of deciding on the constitutionality of economic policy measures on the basis of a (disputed) theory of political economy.[66] The constitutional court did, however, rule that there were strict limits to administrative discretion in the exercise of economic policy (hereby presaging the position later adopted by the Court of Justice of the Community). However, the Ordoliberals have argued that transgressions of the market rules, which may be legitimised democratically in the Member States, are by definition out of bounds for the Community, which lacks such democratic legitimation. The economic constitution of the Community would therefore require an even purer form of the market economy than the *soziale Marktwirtschaft* at the national level.

The concept of the 'economic constitution', and the claims that it prescribed 'as much competition as possible and as little planning as unavoidable', were subsequently introduced at the Community level by prominent Ordoliberal lawyers.[67] Nevertheless, only a few lawyers outside Germany have systematically used the concept. Undeterred by their conceptual isolation, Ordoliberals

---

[64] See G. Gutman *et al* (eds.), *Die Wirtschaftsverfassung der Bundesrepublik Deutschland* (Stuttgart, 1976).

[65] Cf. H. Von der Groeben, *Die Europäische Gemeinschaft und die Herausforderungen unserer Zeit: Aufsätze und Reden 1967–1987* (Baden-Baden, 1987), P. R. Weilemann (ed.).

[66] The Constitutional Court held that the constitution guaranteed neither economic neutrality nor the limitation of economic policy to market instruments ('weder die wirtschaftspolitische Neutralität der Regierungs- und Gesetzgebungsgewalt noch eine nur mit marktkonformen Mitteln zu steuerende soziale Marktwirtschaft'). Hence the state was free to pursue any economic policy it thought appripriate, within the limits set by the constitution ('sofern er dabei das Grundgesetz beachtet'). BVerfGE 4, 7, 17f ('Investitionshilfeurteil'). This was confirmed in BVerfGE 30, 292, 315 ('Erdölbevorratung'); and BVerfGE 50, 290, 338 ('Mitbestimmung'), cited in Behrens, above, n. 60. Herewith, the main question became determining the limits on state policy. See U. Everling, *Das europäische Wirtschaftsrecht im Spannungsfeld von Politik und Wirtschaft: Ausgewählte Aufsätze 1964–1984* (Baden-Baden, 1985), p. 211. 'Aus der Debatte ist ... festzuhalten, das es jedenfalls Grenzen gibt, die zu überschreiten den staatlichen Organen verwehrt ist. Hier liegt auch die Lösung des Problems in der Gemeinschaft. Es kommt darauf an, die Grenzen des hoheitlichen Eingriffs in der Gemeinschaft festzustellen'.

[67] Such as Von der Groeben, Müller-Armack, Ophüls and Mestmäcker.

have continued to use the economic constitution approach to criticise not only the legitimacy of individual Community policies and acts, but even the legitimacy of the Single European Act and the Treaty on European Union. From the Ordoliberal perspective, the Rome Treaty is often idealised as the original free market constitution of the Community, a covenant which has been broken by its subsequent modifications.[68]

B. The Rome Treaty as an Economic Constitution

In the debate on the hypothetical choice between *planification* and *Ordnungspolitik* as economic models for the Community, the concept of the 'economic constitution' was introduced by German liberals to support their position that the signatories of the Treaty had already (even if possibly unintentionally[69]) opted for the latter.[70] Among the founding Member States, the debate on the economic order of the Community saw Germany, where the Ordoliberal view predominated, opposing France (and, less markedly, Italy), where state ownership and planning were applied in a market framework. In this debate, the Benelux countries held the middle ground. Some lawyers have attempted to defuse this conflict at a theoretical level by making the case for the economic neutrality of the Treaty.[71] They claimed the Treaty sanctioned a 'mixed economy', within certain limits on the discretion of both the Member States and the Community.[72] Below, the normative Ordoliberal approach will be covered.

---

[68] Cf. Behrens, above, n. 60; E.-J. Mestmäcker, 'Widersprüchlich, verwirrend und gefährlich', 10 October 1992 FAZ 10; M. Seidel, 'Die Weisheit einer höheren Instanz', 14 March 1992 FAZ 15; E. Steindorff, 'Quo vadis Europa? Freiheiten, Regulierung und soziale Grundrechte nach den erweiterten Zielen der EG-Verfassung', in *Referate des XXV. FIW-Symposions*, above, n. 50; Streit and Mussler, 'The Economic Constitution of the European Community: From "Rome" to "Maastricht"', (1995) 1 *European Law Journal* 5.

[69] This has been described as a 'ruse of reason' in the Hegelian sense. Ch. Joerges, 'Markt ohne Staat? Die Wirtschaftsverfassung der Gemeinschaft und die Renaissance der regulativen Politik', in R. Wildenmann (ed.), *Staatswerdung Europas? Optionen für eine politische Union* (Baden-Baden, 1991).

[70] Cf. Rahmsdorf, above, n. 59, and id., *Ordnungspolitischer Dissens und europäischer Integration* (Kehl am Rhein, 1982).

[71] L.-J. Constantinesco, 'La constitution économique de la C.E.E.', (1977) 13 RTDE 244, at p. 278, cites three positions: (1) the French, pro-planification; (2) German, 'soziale Marktwirtschaft'; and (3) 'others' of the opinion it should be defined in a negative manner, as 'une Constitution économique ouverte, de telle sorte que son orientation concrète pourrait être fixée par une décision politique, toutefois limitée par certaines barrières'. The latter group was formed by writers such as Pescatore, Mertens de Wilmars, VerLoren van Themaat, and Constantinesco himself, who have used the concept to construct a dynamic interpretation of the limitations on Community powers while insisting on the economic neutrality of the Treaty.

[72] Cf. Mertens de Wilmars, 'Reflections sur l'ordre juridico-économique de la Communauté européenne' in J. Dutheil de la Rochère and J. Vandamme (eds.), *Interventions Publiques et Droit Communautaire* (Brussels, 1988), p. 26, on the 'ambivalence économique des instruments juridiques communautaires'; Everling, on public versus private property and the economic order of the Community: 'Neutralität der Gemeinschaft gegenüber den Eigentumsordnung, aber Befugnis zur Eigentumsbindung'. 'Eigentumsordnung und Wirtschaftsordnung in der Europäischen Gemeinschaft',

In many ways, the Ordoliberals considered that the Rome Treaty, which seemed to concern exclusively economic rights, formed an improvement over the national constitutions of the Member States, with their emphasis on political rights. It is central to the Ordoliberal reading of the Rome Treaty as an economic constitution that strict priorities are awarded to the goals and principles it establishes. The price mechanism is regarded as the dominant organisational principle of the economy. This claim is based on the fact that the establishment of the internal market and the co-ordination of the economic policies of the Member States are, according to Article 2 EEC, to form the instruments for attaining the objectives of the Community. Hereby, the market mechanism is identified as the primary mechanism of integration in a decentralised market system.[73] Further, the autonomy of private economic subjects, which lies at the basis of the market system, is thought to be guaranteed by the four freedoms listed in Article 3 EEC.

The competition rules of Articles 85 and 86 EEC protect the realisation of these 'individual liberties' from private restraints on competition. Public restrictions are to be removed first of all by the realisation of the four freedoms, which form the legal basis for limits on state intervention. The material basis for these limits is found in the general anti-discrimination principle of Article 7 EEC. It should be emphasised that in this perspective the four freedoms, although enforceable by individuals, serve to defend the general interest. This squares with the Ordoliberal conviction that the law should serve to protect both diffuse general interests against politically involved 'special interests', and individual liberties against majoritarian decisions.[74]

Beyond the constraints imposed by the general anti-discrimination principle and the four freedoms, further limits of state intervention are specified in the Treaty. These include the requirement of the removal of the distortions of competition due to state aids, in Articles 92 to 94 EEC, and of distortions due to state regulations, which are dealt with in Articles 101 to 104 EEC, as well as those resulting from the existence of undertakings granted special and exclusive rights, covered by Article 90 EEC.

In the Ordoliberal view those elements of the Treaty which go beyond (or are at odds with) its perception of the process of integration as primarily (or

---

in U. Everling, *Das europäische Wirtschaftsrecht im Spannungsfeld von Politik und Wirtschaft: Ausgewählte Aufsätze 1964–1984* (Baden-Baden, 1985), p. 306. Cf. VerLoren, 'Einige Bemerkungen zu dem Verhältnis zwischen den Begriffen Gemeinsamer Markt, Wirtschaftsunion, Währungsunion, Politische Union und Souveränität', in J. Baur, P.-Ch. Müller-Graf and M. Zuleeg (eds.), *Europarecht, Energierecht, Wirtschaftsrecht: Festschrift für Bodo Börner zum 70. Geburtstag* (Cologne, 1992), p. 439.

[73] Cf. Behrens, above, n. 60.

[74] The paradox of this position is that majoritarian decisions are identified with rent seeking special interests, and individual liberties with the general interest, whereas the laws that protect the general interest are ultimately decided by democratic means. For this reason a central position is assigned to the constitution (which requires an extraordinary majority, presumably reducing the impact of special interests).

exclusively) based on market integration by means of a wide interpretation of the principles of the free market, free competition and anti-discrimination, form flaws to the liberal economic constitution. Sectoral policies, such as those on coal and steel in the ECSC Treaty and the common agricultural policy (CAP), are seen by definition as prone to capture by rent-seeking interest groups, at the expense of the more diffuse general interests of consumers and taxpayers.[75] These 'functional deficiencies' of the Treaty system are held to cause a vicious cycle, or 'spill over' of distortions and protectionism, for example into the common commercial policy.[76]

Another Ordoliberal objection is that the Rome Treaty does not explicitly require the Community in the exercise of its own powers to respect the four freedoms and the system of undistorted competition. Since the relevant provisions of the Treaty are specifically addressed to the Member States and undertakings, their application cannot easily be generalised to include the Community. Nevertheless, attempts have been made to construe strict limits on Community action by reading Treaty provisions for Community intervention as mere exceptions to the rule of liberal market integration. It is held that the characterisation by the Court of Justice of the Treaty as 'the fundamental charter of a Community based on the rule of law', proves the existence of constitutional legal restraints which have regard to not only the division of competences between the Member States and the Community, but also to Community and state intervention in the economy.

It is generally accepted that limits on the Community competences follow, first, from the principle of the limited attribution of powers, and, second, from the limits on the exercise of these powers (such as more recently imposed on concurrent powers by the subsidiarity principle). In the Ordoliberal interpretation, the four freedoms and the principle of free competition limit the Community in the exercise of its powers, as general principles of Community law, guaranteed by the Court of Justice.[77]

In this reading, market integration is seen as the guiding light of the division of competences between the Community and the Member States, and the attribution of supranational powers to the Community is seen as primarily directed at (and limited to) the realisation of the common market.[78] This is

---

[75] See Streit and Mussler, above, n. 68, pp. 16ff. This observation is based on the work of M. Olson, *The Rise and Decline of Nations* (New Haven, 1982).

[76] For a critique of the common commercial policy based on an analysis of the economic constitution cf. E. U. Petersmann, 'Constitutionalism, Constitutional Law and European Integration', (1991) 46 *Aussenwirtschaft* 15, p. 28; E. U. Petersmann, 'Constitutional Principles Governing the EEC's Commercial Policy', in M. Maresceau (ed.), *The European Community's Commercial Policy after 1992; The Legal Dimension* (Dordrecht, 1993).

[77] Cf. the references in n. 50, above; especially Monopolkommission, ibid., p. 409.

[78] This has sometimes been construed as imposing an additional obligation on Community legislation to respect the unity of the market, to be enforced as a minimum requirement by the Court under the application of the proportionality test. This would mean that the Community is barred from taking or maintaining in force measures which threaten the unity of the internal market, that

supported by the argument that intergovernmental co-operation is dominant in the area of economic policy co-ordination. As a consequence, the proportionality principle is held to require an evaluation aimed at restricting public intervention at the Community level to a minimum. As a general rule therefore, the methods of mutual recognition and competition among rules are to be given preference over harmonisation. Community intervention in such areas as agriculture, transport and commercial policy is to remain an exception.

The fact that the constraints which Community law has imposed on economic intervention by the Member States have not generally been compensated for by a corresponding increase in competences at the European level is cited as evidence that the constraints on Community action mirror those imposed on the Member States.[79] The result, based on competition between economic systems, and competition among rules, is described as integration from below (as opposed to integration from above, associated with harmonisation). The net effects of European integration would therefore be deregulation, and strengthening of the market principle. The observation that the process of European integration involves liberalisation and deregulation, whereas the scope of Community powers and 're-regulation' remain comparatively limited is not unique to Ordoliberalism. But political factors are rarely as ignored in favour of a deterministic reading of the founding charter as they are by the Ordoliberals. This restrictive interpretation of the Rome Treaty has been contradicted by the subsequent modifications of the latter by the Single European Act and in particular by the Treaty on European Union, which together have confirmed the advance of policy co-ordination to facilitate and supplement market driven economic integration.

C. The Treaty on European Union as an Economic Constitution

The successive changes to the Rome Treaty, which was (in spite of its weaknesses) considered a model market-oriented economic constitution, have been sharply criticised from the Ordoliberal point of view. These objections can be seen as motivated by a general desire to limit the Community to negative integration. The Single European Act of 1987 was already considered to have sharpened the contrast between 'integration by regulation and integration

is supporting state measures which are contrary to the Treaty, or to erecting new barriers between the Member States. Cf. Mestmäcker, above, n. 50, pp. 283–284, citing Joined Cases 80 and 81/77 *Ramel* [1978] ECR 827; and Case 18/83 *Denkavit* [1984] ECR 2171. Others have denied that the unity of the 'common market' as such imposes any constraints on Community legislation beyond those imposed by the general principles of Community law. Instead a prohibition of 'the geographical partitioning of the common market' as the sole constraint on the Community may be derived from the case law of the Court regarding the equality principle (with the aid of the proportionality rule). R. Barents, 'The Community and the Unity of the Common Market', (1990) 33 *German Yearbook of International Law* 9.

[79] Generally cited in this context is Case 120/78 *Rewe Zentral AG v Bundesmonopolverwaltung für Branntwein* [1979] ECR 649 ('Cassis de Dijon').

by competition'.[80] Although aimed at establishing the internal market, the new approach to harmonisation was thought to contain contradictory methods. Whereas Article 100b EEC introduced the method of mutual recognition, which is favoured by Ordoliberals as it opens the way to 'competition among rules', Article 100a(3) EEC established a minimum level of protection for consumers, and of health, safety, and the environment.[81] In terms of liberalisation, minimum level harmonisation under Article 100a EEC was clearly seen as a second best solution compared with mutual recognition and competition among rules. Article 100a EEC was further considered to be at odds with the principle of enumerated powers, as this Article does not limit the scope of the areas which may be harmonised for internal market purposes.[82] Finally, the Ordoliberals claimed that the meaning of the minimum level of protection ensured by Article 100a(3) EC could be stretched to cover protectionist abuses to the detriment of free trade both within the Community and with third countries.

Title VI EEC (Articles 130f to 130q), which introduced a Community competence on the co-ordination of Research and Development (R&D), was held to be even more objectionable. Targeted funding of R&D was seen as an ill-boded attempt to 'pick winners' at Community level. In the Ordoliberal view only the market can supply accurate information, and state involvement in R&D will inevitably introduce self-defeating distortions. The new R&D Title was therefore considered nothing more than a thinly disguised excuse for a Community industrial policy of funding uncompetitive undertakings at the expense of both successful industries and taxpayers at large. A final affront to the logic of the market was seen in the new responsibility for economic and social cohesion in Title V EEC (Articles 130a to 130e). The funds for social and economic cohesion were seen as the results of political blackmail (the price paid to the peripheral Member States in return for the support on the internal market programme and the Single Act), which moreover lacked the democratic legitimacy of similar transfers at the national level.[83] In sum, the Single Act was considered to have strengthened both the non-market elements of the original Treaty and discretionary policy making.[84]

The Ordoliberals viewed the 1993 Treaty on European Union as a further step in the wrong direction. This may seem surprising at first, in particular

---

[80] Streit and Mussler, above, n. 68, p. 20.

[81] Cf. COM (85) 310, *Completing the Internal Market*, on the application of 'mutual recognition', building on the Court's ruling in Case 120/78 *Cassis de Dijon*, above, n. 79.

[82] *Gutachten des Wissenschaftlichen Beirats beim Bundesministerium für Wirtschaft: Ordnungspolitische Orientierung für die Europäische Union* (Tübingen, 1994), p. 6. Further, the use of directives (which is favoured by Article 100a EEC as an instrument of market integration) was held to form a threat to the uniform application of Community law.

[83] In the Ordoliberal interpretation, regional disparities represent mere differences in comparative advantage (such as low labour costs in peripheral and depressed regions) and require liberalisation to unleash the wealth producing mechanisms of the market, rather than the introduction of subsidies for the periphery which protect labour market rigidities elsewhere. ibid., pp. 53ff.

[84] Streit and Mussler, above, n. 68, p. 22.

given the introduction of the principle of free competition in open markets in Article 3a EC and elsewhere in the Treaty, which appears to confirm the Ordoliberal claims of constitutional status for competition.[85]

For example, there are repeated references to the principle of competition in the new Treaty. First, Article 3(g) EC includes among the activities of the Community, for the purposes set out in Article 2 EC, 'a system ensuring that competition in the internal market is not distorted'. Second, the 'open market economy with free competition' is introduced as a principle in the first two paragraphs of Article 3a EC.[86] Third, the principle of an open market economy with free competition is repeated in the body of the Treaty in the new Title VI EC on economic and monetary policy. There, it is found both in Article 102a EC (at the beginning of Chapter 1 on economic policy) and in Article 105 EC (at the opening of Chapter 2 on monetary policy). Here it is required that the Member States, the Community, and the European System of Central Banks respectively, shall act 'in accordance with the principle of an open market economy with free competition, favouring an efficient allocation of resources'. The overriding objective of Article 105 EC in particular is formulated as price stability, in compliance with the other economic principles set out in Article 3a(3) EC.

However, in the EC Treaty the principle of free competition in open markets is strictly linked to the co-ordination of economic policy, and the common monetary and exchange rate policy of the Community. Since economic and monetary union as such is not of central importance to the Ordoliberal agenda, it has not gained much by progress on this front. It is more important that economic policy co-ordination, aimed at achieving economic and monetary union, has come alongside changes which negate the absolute priority of open markets and free competition. Therefore, the Treaty on European Union, which not only involved a significant expansion of the 'cohesion funds', but moreover introduced industrial policy as such, was seen as a dramatic break with the original economic constitution.

---

[85] The argument for the constitutional nature of freedom of competition as one of the general principles of Community law alongside the free movement of goods was previously based on the judgments of the Court in Case 139/79 *Maizena v Council* [1980] ECR 3393; and Case 240/83 *Procureur de la République v Association de défense des brûleurs d'huiles usagées (ADBHU)* [1985] ECR 531 ('Used Oils'). Cf. B. Van der Esch, 'Dérégulation, autorégulation et le régime de concurrence nonfaussée dans la CEE', (1990) 26 CDE 499, p. 520.

[86] Article 3a(1) EC specifies that 'the adoption of an economic policy, which is based on the close cooperation of Member States' economic policies, on the internal market and on the definition of common objectives', and to be conducted in accordance with this principle. Article 3a(2) EC makes a similar provision for the single monetary and exchange-rate policy, 'the primary objective of both of which shall be to maintain price stability and, without prejudice to this objective, to support the general economic policies in the Community, in accordance with the principle of an open market economy with free competition'. Further, Article 3a(3) EC stipulates that these activities shall be in compliance with the guiding principles of 'stable prices, sound public finances and monetary conditions, and a sustainable balance of payments'.

The Ordoliberal objections against the Treaty on European Union focus on six main points. The most fundamental objections have been raised against Article 2 EC.

1. This article adds the establishment of an economic and monetary union to that of the common market as an instrument to attain the objectives of integration set out in that same Article.
2. Apart from rephrasing the economic objective to include the more modern perspective of 'sustainable and non-inflationary growth respectful of the environment', Article 2 EC adds 'a high degree of convergence', 'economic and social cohesion', and 'solidarity among Member States' as objectives of the Community. These objectives evidently extend beyond negative integration and the common market and appear to require further redistribution. It is this expansion of the objectives of the Community, rather than the widely criticised provisions regarding industrial policy, which some commentators regard as the major break with the economic order established by the Rome Treaty.[87]
3. Article 3 EC lists the new policy responsibilities for the Community linked to the expanded objectives of Article 2 EC. The Community will assume some of the responsibilities that the Ordoliberals would have preferred to see removed from the realm of public policy as such, since they are thought to harbour possibilities for protectionist abuse. Beyond the expansion of the provisions on R&D and economic cohesion with general authorisations for the Community to take the necessary measures, new Community competences were introduced on education, vocational training and youth, culture, public health, consumer protection, and trans-European networks.
4. Further, the blurring of the division of competences between the Community and the Member States has been criticised. At first it would appear that the Treaty on European Union has addressed precisely this problem as never before under Community law. The principle of the attribution of specific powers has been codified in the first paragraph of Article 3b(1) EC, which states that 'The Community shall act within the limits of the powers conferred upon it by this Treaty and of the objectives assigned to it therein'.[88] In addition, the Treaty on European Union has explicitly excluded the harmonisation of legislation in the new policy areas of education, vocational training, culture and public health.[89]

---

[87] Cf. Steindorff, above, n. 68, p. 9.

[88] Formerly based on Article 4(1) EEC and the case law on limited powers and implied powers of the Court of Justice. Joined Cases 7/56 and 3–7/57 *Algera v Common Assembly* [1957–1958] ECR 39; Case 8/55 *Fédération Charbonière de Belgique v High Authority* [1954–1956] ECR 245; Case 20/59 *Italy v High Authority* [1960] ECR 133; and Case 25/59 *Netherlands v High Authority* [1960] ECR 355.

[89] Articles 126(4), 127(4), 128(5) and 129(4) EC.

Yet, in spite of these new safeguards against the expansion of the competence of the Community, it has been suggested that the Maastricht Treaty seems to allow the Community both to create new instruments, and to use existing instruments for purposes for which they were not originally designed (following the use made of Articles 100a and 235 under the EEC Treaty). Such claims have been based in the first place on Article F(3) TEU, which states (in contrast to Article 3b EC) that 'The Union shall provide itself with the means necessary to attain its objectives and carry through its policies'. Further, the obligation of the Community to take account of the objectives of cultural policy, industrial policy, economic and social cohesion, and environmental policy in the pursuit of its other policies and activities under the provisions of the Treaty is seen as a threat to the primacy of the market principle.[90]

5. The provisions of Article 130 EC play a central role in these objections: Article 130 EC can be seen as the linchpin of a system designed to pursue interventionist policies of structural adjustment, flanked by the provisions of Title XII and XV on trans-European networks and R&D, or even including Titles VIII, XIV and XV on social policy, regional development and economic and social cohesion.[91] With Article 130 EC as the basis for an alternative economic order, the Commission could now use its competition policy powers to pursue industrial policy goals (in particular under the block exemptions of Article 85(1) EC and the derogation of Article 85(3) EC, as well as the Merger Regulation) to pursue an interventionist industrial policy.

6. The principle of subsidiarity is regarded as a final threat to the original economic constitution. With many other critics, the Ordoliberals point out that whereas subsidiarity is barely justiciable, it may potentially undermine the current division of competences of the Community (in particular regarding the internal market). Consequently, it is feared that subsidiarity may come to threaten the unity of the internal market, and the uniform application of Community law. This negative reading of Article 3b EC is surprising, since this article primarily codifies the constraints on Community action (limited attribution of powers, subsidiarity and proportionality) which had earlier been found implicit in the economic constitution. The rejection of subsidiarity may be explained by the mainly political nature of this principle, and the fact that, when it comes to respecting the economic constitution, the Ordoliberals regard the Member States with even greater suspicion than the Community itself.

---

[90] Articles 128(4), 130(3), 130b(1) and 130r(2) EC.
[91] Streit and Mussler, 'The Economic Constitution of the European Community: From "Rome" to "Maastricht"', (1995) 1 *European Law Journal* 5, p. 26.

Hence, from an Ordoliberal point of view, the Treaty on European Union no longer contains a liberal economic constitution, and thus distorts the original economic constitution of the Community to a degree that can only be remedied by formal Treaty amendment.[92] The politicisation of a process which the Ordoliberals had so eagerly construed as the retreat of national politics before the advent of the rule of European economic law has led to charges that the future Union will deteriorate to a 'rent seeking Community'.[93]

The changes made by the Treaty on European Union have undeniably increased the scope and objectives for policy making at the Community level. Yet rather than as the perversion of a liberal economic constitution, this could be seen as the logical result of the beginning of a next phase of European integration (notably that towards economic and monetary union), legitimised, moreover, by the increased role played by the European Parliament. This change could be described, most concisely, as a shift in emphasis toward positive integration: whereas negative integration can largely be achieved by the enforcement of legal rules, positive integration, which involves redistributive choices, is more dependent on political decisions, policy co-ordination and administrative discretion.[94] This raises the further question whether the Rome Treaty itself ever formed a liberal economic constitution, or whether it was, in fact, always the constitution of a mixed economy.

IV. COMPARING THE POLITICAL AND ECONOMIC
CONSTITUTION APPROACHES

A. Neutrality Regarding the Economic Policies of the Member States

The Rome Treaty undeniably formed a move away from the *dirigiste* approach of the ECSC Treaty, both in its scope and purposes. Since the EEC largely relied on intergovernmental decision making, the competence of the Commission was more restrictively defined than that of the High Authority. Further, the four freedoms and the competition rules appeared to match the requirements of directly enforceable individual economic rights, and the guarantee of competition as an economic value, which would be expected to form part of a liberal economic constitution.

[92] This inspired proposals for the removal of Article 130 EC and the reflection of an unequivocal commitment to economic liberalism in the text of the Treaty for the 1996 Intergovernmental Conference which will be called under the terms of Article n. TEU. *Gutachten des Wissenschaftlichen Beirats*, above, n. 82.

[93] Streit and Mussler, above, n. 91, pp. 25ff.

[94] W. Molle, *The Economics of European Integration: Theory, Practice, Policy* (Aldershot, 1990), pp. 11ff, 27ff.

At the same time however, it is relatively simple to establish that the Rome Treaty never comprised a liberal economic constitution in a formal sense. There is no evidence that the market oriented elements of the Treaty ever had a higher formal legal status than the clauses which justify intervention. Moreover, it was the European Court of Justice which constitutionalised the Treaty over time, rather than the contracting Member States at its conclusion. The Court of Justice did this in particular by developing the doctrines of direct effect and supremacy, implied powers and pre-emption, by interpreting widely the four freedoms (notably Article 30 EEC) and by stressing the *effet utile* of the competition rules. Hence, the Rome Treaty could not reasonably be seen as the formal economic constitution of a liberal market economy. The more interesting question which remains is whether the material economic constitution of the Community prescribes a particular economic system at the national or the Community level, or whether it perhaps favours certain forms of economic organisation and policy over others.

Advocates of the position that the economic constitution of the Community sanctions a mixed economy have based their argument on the juxtaposition of other principles, such as equality and solidarity, with competition: there is no hierarchy between these principles.[95] The most direct reference in the Rome Treaty on which the argument for the existence of the mixed economy in the Community can be based is Article 222 EEC, which provides that the Treaty 'shall in no way prejudice the rules in the Member States governing the system of property ownership'.[96] Article 222 EEC has at various times been used to justify state monopolies and other methods of Member State intervention in the economy. Further provisions of the Treaty which have often been cited in support of this position are Article 90 EEC (which deals with the application of the Treaty rules to the public sector), and Article 37 EEC (on the respect of the anti-discrimination rules by state monopolies of a commercial character).[97]

The Ordoliberals have side-stepped this absense of hierarchy by arguing that no other principles could exist at Community level other than the four freedoms and competition. Their main argument is that its lack of independent democratic legitimation precludes the Community from assuming responsibility beyond the functioning of the internal market. On this view, only the individual Member

---

[95] The 'mixed economy' here should be taken to mean a system which includes public as well as private ownership of the means of production, and allows state intervention for reasons other than enhancing economic efficiency and the functioning of the market mechanism (primarily for purposes of spatial and interpersonal redistribution) in the economic process. In particular, this includes both intervention and direct involvement of the state in the economy, the latter through such means as nationalisation, state participation in corporate ownership, and public companies. Cf. Rahmsdorf, 'Eine zweite Euro-Ordo-Debatte', (1980) 3 *Integration* 156, pp. 53–55.

[96] An early example is the successful justification of the nationalisation of the Italian electricity sector in Case 6/64 *Costa v ENEL* [1965] ECR 585.

[97] An early suggestion that the EEC Treaty, although suggesting a liberal economic constitution, remained a mixed one, was found in Opinion 1/78 *International Agreement on Natural Rubber* [1979] ECR 2871, para. 44 p. 2913. Cf. Petersmann, above, n. 76, p. 26.

States as democratic entities may legitimately base their actions on the principles of equality or solidarity rather than free competition (albeit within certain constraints).[98] It should be noted that both sides in this argument agree on the existence of constraints on administrative discretion of the Member States. The disagreement is on the remaining margins for national public policy.[99] To settle this problem, it is useful to refer to the case law of the European Court.

Central to the Ordoliberal view of the economic constitution is the argument that very strict constraints on state intervention in the economy follow from the competition rules and the four freedoms. The so-called *effet utile* case law of the Court was held to indicate that European law posed restrictive limits on the remit of national public policy with anti-competitive effects, since Article 5(2) EEC (which requires that the Member States abstain from any measure which could jeopardise the attainment of the objectives of the Treaty) demanded an active policy of the Commission to ensure equal respect of the competition rules by Member States and private undertakings.[100]

The main question involved was whether, beyond public measures encouraging, reinforcing or requiring collusive behaviour, or delegating public authority to a cartel, legislation which rendered collusion superfluous would also fall under the *effet utile* rules. An expansive interpretation would cover many measures of economic or monetary policy, such as legislation setting minimum prices. Likewise, the expanding scope of Articles 30 and 59 EEC was held to roll back state regulation.[101] Against this interpretation of Community law, it has been pointed out that the text of the Treaty clearly distinguishes between private and

---

[98] This is how Mestmäcker can accept the neutrality of the German constitution while insisting on the market-oriented vision underlying the Community, 'Auf dem Wege zu einer Ordnungspolitik für Europa', in Mestmäcker *et al* (eds.), *Eine Ordnungspolitik für Europa: Festschrift für Hans von der Groeben zu seinem 80. Geburtstag* (Baden-Baden, 1987), pp. 16ff. Cf. Joerges, 'Markt ohne Staat? Die Wirtschaftsverfassung der Gemeinschaft und die Renaissance der regulativen Politik', in R. Wildenmann (ed.), *Staatswerdung Europas? Optionen für eine politische Union* (Baden-Baden, 1991).

[99] For a summary of the debate cf. P. Pescatore, 'Public and Private Aspects of European Community Competition Law', (1987) 10 *Fordham International Law Journal* 373; and G. Marenco, 'Competition between National Economies and Competition between Businesses—A Response to Judge Pescatore', (1987) 10 *Fordham International Law Journal* 420.

[100] Articles 85 and 86 concern the conduct of undertakings and not the law or regulations of the Member States. Yet by virtue of Articles 3(g) EEC (3(f) TEU) and 5(2) EEC, the latter are barred from adopting or maintaining in force any measures which deprive the competition rules of their effectiveness. Cf. Case 13/77, *GB-INNO-BM v ATAB* [1977] ECR 2115, where the Court held that 'The Treaty requires the Member States not to take or maintain in force measures which could destroy the effectiveness of Article 86', para. 31 p. 2144. The case law of the Court of Justice on the *effet utile* of the competition rules has been well developed in recent years. Cf. Case 229/83 *Leclerc v Au Blé Vert* [1985] ECR 1; Case 231/83, *Cullet v Leclerc* [1985] ECR 305; Cases 209–213/84, *Asjes* [1986] ECR 1425; Case 311/85, *Vereniging van Vlaamse Reisbureaus* [1987] ECR 3801; Case 267/86, *Van Eycke* [1988] ECR 4769.

[101] Following the celebrated judgments in Case 8/74 *Dassonville* [1974] ECR 837; and Case 120/78 *Cassis de Dijon* above, n. 79. Concerning Article 59 EC cf. Case C-288/89 *Stichting Collectieve Antenne Voorziening Gouda* [1991] ECR I-4007; and Case C-353/89 *Commission v The Netherlands* [1991] ECR I-4069.

public standards of behaviour, especially where wider public responsibilities are at stake.[102]

In what has been called the 'November Revolution' of 1993, the Court set out a more restrictive approach to the *effet utile* rule,[103] and likewise took the road of judicial restraint on Article 30 EEC.[104] The balance between the competition rules of the Treaty and the remaining margins for national economic policy seems to have been found in a compromise which both permits restrictive state measures which respect the principle of non-discrimination concerning Article 30 EEC, and requires evidence of collusion between undertakings for the application of Articles 3(g) EEC (now 3(f) EC), 5(2) and 85 EEC.

These developments indicate that the Court of Justice is unwilling to go into an evaluation of the merits of the economic policies of the Member States where the Community interest is not at stake, and that the latter is defined more restrictively than was widely presumed in the heyday of the expansive application of Article 30 EC. This is the case in particular where these policies or the rules established by them are non-discriminatory, or are aimed to advance non-economic public interest objectives, in so far as these do not significantly affect trade between the Member States. This attitude of judicial restraint on the legitimacy of economic policy is much like that reached by the German Constitutional Court in the 1950s. In this manner, within certain constraints, decisions on the pursuit of a mixed economic system would remain at the national level.

Hence, the Ordoliberal claims that the Treaty imposes strict limits on the public policy of the Member States must be rejected. At the national level, liberal market economies, social market economies, and mixed economies are all compatible with the Treaty. The Rome Treaty can be seen as an economic constitution that is neutral regarding the economic policies pursued at the national level, within certain constraints that are directly linked to the objective of economic integration.

---

[102] This has been described in terms of a constitutional conflict, especially where the economic and monetary policies of the Member States would thereby be circumscribed by the competition rules of the Treaty, whereas under Articles 102a to 108 EEC the former are the subject of progressive harmonisation. This argument would hold *a fortiori* regarding the new provisions on economic and monetary policy in Title VI EC, introduced by the Maastricht Treaty. L. Gyselen, 'State Action and the Effectiveness of the EEC Treaty's Competition Provisions', (1989) 26 CMLR 33.

[103] Case C-185/91, *Reiff* [1993] ECR I-5801, Case C-2/91, *Meng* [1993] ECR I-5751, and Case C-245/91, *Ohra* [1993] ECR I-5851. Cf. N. Reich, 'The "November Revolution" of the European Court of Justice: *Keck*, *Meng* and *Audi* Revisited', (1994) 31 CMLR 459, p. 479ff, who reads an implicit rejection of a liberal economic constitution for the Community in the November cases, and in particular in the Opinion of Advocate General Tesauro in Case C-292/92, *Hünermund* [1993] ECR I-6787.

[104] Joined Cases C-267 and 268/91 *Keck* [1993] ECR I-6097 and Case C-292/92 *Hünermund* [1993] ECR, above, n. 103, noted by Roth (1994) 31 CMLR 845. Article 30 does not apply to state measures where these do not discriminate in law or in fact against imports. Cf. Reich, above, n. 103. This new line of judicial restraint could be interpreted as the return to minimalism predicted in T. Koopmans, 'The Role of Law in the Next Stage of European Integration', (1986) 35 ICLQ 925.

B. Constitutional Limits to Community Action

As the controversy on economic sovereignty at the national level and the principle of the free market economy allegedly enshrined in the Rome Treaty died down, it was replaced by the debate on the perceived conflict between industrial and competition policy of the EC.[105] This concerns the question whether, in spite of the apparent economic neutrality of the Treaty, there are constitutional limits which restrict the Community to the pursuit of liberal market policies, and therefore, whether at Community level the economic order preordained by the Treaty is a liberal one.

The theory of the constitutional limits to Community action is based on the doctrine of attribution of powers. Hereby, with few exceptions, the Community only enjoys those powers delegated to it by the Member States as expressed in the Treaty.[106] Apart from the limited attribution of powers, legal limits to Community action have been derived from the general principles of Community law. In the Treaty on European Union, specific limits were set on the expansion of Community competence in the provisions on education, culture and public health, and an attempt was made to introduce a general constraint on Community competence in Article 3b EC. The Member States' determination to impose tighter limits on Community action can only have been reinforced by the debate around the ratification of the Treaty on European Union.[107] The question addressed here is whether the Ordoliberal thesis which holds that

---

[105] 'Der Gegensatz von Wettbewerbspolitik und mittelfristigen Wirtschaftspolitik hat sich als Scheinproblem erwiesen. Der konzeptionelle und praktische Gegensatz von Industriepolitik und Wettbewerbspolitik ist dagegen höchst real. Bei der Industriepolitik handelt es sich um einen Gegenentwurf zum System unverfälschten Wettbewerbs'. Mestmäcker, above n. 98, p. 27.

[106] The most important exceptions are based on the Article 235 EC, which provides the Community may by Council unanimity take appropriate action where necessary to realise the objectives of the Treaty, in the absence of explicit provisions. Further, in particular in the area of external relations, the Court has developed the doctrine of 'implied powers' to justify Community action. Case 22/70 *Commission v Council* [1971] ECR 263; Joined Cases 3, 4 & 6/76 *Kramer et al* [1976] ECR 1279; Opinion 1/76 [1977] ECR 741. Recently however, the Court has exercised considerable restraint in this area: cf. Cases C-181 and C-248/91 *Parliament v Council and Commission* [1993] ECR I-3685 ('Bangladesh Development Aid'); Case C-327/91, *France v Commission* [1994] ECR I-3641 ('EC-US Competition Agreement'); Opinion 1/94 [1994] ECR I-5267.

[107] It may be noted that the German Constitutional Court is strongly opposed to any incremental softening of the limited attribution of powers, in the belief that explicit Treaty amendments are required: 'Whereas a dynamic extension of the existing treaties has so far been supported on the basis of an open-handed treatment of Article 235 of the EEC Treaty as a competence to 'round-off the Treaty' as a whole, and on the basis of considerations relating to the 'implied powers' of the Communities, and of Treaty interpretation as allowing maximum exploitation of Community powers ('*effet utile*'), in future it will have to be noted as regards interpretation of enabling provisions by Community institutions and agencies that the Union Treaty as a matter of principle distinguishes between the exercise of a sovereign power conferred for limited purposes and the amending of the Treaty, so that its interpretation may not have effects that are equivalent to an extension of the Treaty. Such an interpretation of enabling rules would not produce any binding effects in Germany'. BVerfGE, Cases 2BvR 2134/92 and 2159/92, *Manfred Brunner et al v The European Union Treaty* [1994] 1 CMLR 57, para. 99 p. 105.

fundamental rights and competition impose strict constitutional constraints on Community policy is correct.[108]

Property rights and the right to trade had been established as fundamental rights in some Member States, notably in Germany.[109] Consequently, much of the early case law of the Court of Justice on fundamental rights was triggered by actions where private parties charged that their property rights had been infringed by Community law, and claimed constitutional protection before national courts. Thus, in Case 4/73 *Nold v Commission*, a property right and the right to the free pursuit of business activity, as protected by the German basic law, was at stake.[110] In this case, the Court phrased the well-known formula that was codified in the Treaty of European Union:

As the Court has already stated, fundamental rights form an integral part of the general principles of law, the observance of which it ensures.

In safeguarding these rights, the Court is bound to draw inspiration from constitutional traditions common to the Member States, and it cannot therefore uphold measures which are incompatible with fundamental rights recognized and protected by the Constitutions of those States.

Similarly, international treaties for the protection of human rights on which the Member States have collaborated or of which they are signatories, can supply guidelines which should be followed within the framework of Community law.[111]

Yet the Court, after having stated the requirement of respect of fundamental rights by Community legislation, proceeded to limit the scope of the fundamental right of property:

If rights of ownership are protected by the constitutional laws of all the Member States and if similar guarantees are given in respect of their right freely to choose and practice

---

[108] The idea that the competition rules form a coherent system was first expressed in Case 32/65, *Italy v Council and Commission* [1966] ECR 389, p. 405, and developed in Case 6/72, *Euroemballage & Continental Can Co Inc v Commission* [1973] ECR 215, paras. 23–24 p. 244. Pescatore draws the conclusion from this case law that 'the fundamental economic aim of the Community is to ensure the free exchange of goods and services under conditions of fair competition'. Above, n. 99, p. 379.

[109] Articles 12 and 14 of the German Basic Law.

[110] [1974] ECR 491. This dictum was intended to ensure that the *Bundesverfassungsgericht* would not break the ranks of the judiciary by limiting the direct effect and supremacy of European law by itself not merely examining the compatibility of measures of Community institutions with Articles 14 and 12 of the *Grundgesetz*, but declaring them unconstitutional. The German Constitutional Court had, after the judgements of the European Court of Justice in Case 29/69 *Stauder v Ulm* [1969] ECR 419, and Case 11/70 *Internationale Handelsgesellschaft v Einführ und Vorratsstelle Getreide* [1970] ECR 1125, taken the position that, in the absence of a codification of human rights under Community law, it was impossible to decide whether these were equivalent to those guaranteed under the German constitution. Although it did examine the Community act concerned, it never found any such acts to be unconstitutional during the period this approach was taken. *Solange I* BVerfGE 37, 271; [1974] 2 CMLR 540. This position was only reversed by *Solange II* BVerfGE 73, 339; [1987] 3 CMLR 225. See Hanf, 'Le jugement de la Cour constitutionelle fédérale allemande sur la constitutionalité du Traité de Maastricht: Un nouveau chapitre des relations entre le droit communautaire et le droit national', (1994) 30 RTDE 391, pp. 406ff; Hartley, *The Foundations of European Community Law* (3rd ed., Oxford, 1994), pp. 242ff.

[111] Case 4/73 *Nold*, ibid., para. 13 p. 507.

their trade or profession, the rights thereby guaranteed, far from constituting unfettered prerogatives, must be viewed in the light of the social function of property and the activities protected thereunder.

For this reason, rights of this nature are protected by laws subject always to limitations laid down in accordance with the public interest.

Within the Community legal order it likewise seems legitimate that these rights should, if necessary, be subject to certain limits justified by the overall objectives pursued by the Community, on condition that the substance of these rights is left untouched.[112]

This case law was confirmed and developed in Case 44/79 *Hauer v Rheinland-Pfalz*, concerning viticulture.[113] Here, the Court recalled that right to property guaranteed by the first Protocol to the European Convention for the Protection of Human Rights was (by virtue of that protocol), nevertheless, subject to restrictions where these could be justified as necessary for the protection of the general interest.[114] Considering the constitutional rules and practices in the Member States, the Court found that in all cases the legislature was entitled to restrict the use of private property in accordance with the general interest. Further, the Court found that in the wine-producing countries of the Community, restrictions on the cultivation of this particular agricultural product existed concerning the practices affected by the contested Community legislation.

More importantly, the Court went beyond this comparative exercise, and the doctrine that the public interest may justify the limitation of individual rights, in order to state that:

Even if it is not possible to dispute in principle the Community's right to restrict the exercise of the right to property in the context of a common organization of the market and for the purposes of a structural policy, it is still necessary to examine whether the restrictions introduced by the provisions in dispute in fact correspond to the objectives of general interest pursued by the Community or whether, with regard to the aim pursued, they constitute a disproportionate and intolerable interference with the right of the owner, impinging upon the very substance of the right of property.[115]

The result of this case law is that in the final analysis the general principles of administrative law, such as proportionality and non-discrimination, form the ultimate test of the legality of measures of Community law. Subsequent cases where the right to property and the right to carry on an established business were in issue were answered on the basis of the positions described above.[116]

---

[112] ibid., para. 14 p. 508.   [113] [1979] ECR 3727.
[114] ibid., para. 17–19 pp. 3746ff.   [115] [1979] ECR 3727, para. 23 p. 3747.
[116] The Court refined its argument on the right to carry on economic activities to the effect that undertakings cannot claim vested rights to the maintenance of advantages obtained from the common organization of the market. In such cases a reduction in this advantage cannot be regarded as constituting an infringement of a fundamental right. Case 230/78 *Eridiana v Minister of Agriculture and Forestry* [1979] ECR 2749, para. 20ff p. 2768; and Case 59/83 *Biovilac v EEC* [1984] ECR 4057, para. 23 p. 4080. T. Frazer, 'Competition Policy After 1992: The Next Step', (1990) 53 MLR 609, uses these cases to argue by analogy that 'competition policy in the EEC is not a constitutional norm, nor is it itself limited by constitutional norms. There are therefore no constitutional obstacles to prevent it evolving to meet new demands'. ibid., p. 615.

Thus, although the right to property can be seen as a principle of Community law, other general principles of Community law must be applied to determine the scope of this principle. The principle of proportionality is especially important in this regard.[117] Parallels can be found in the case law on free competition as a principle of Community law.

Beside the limits on discretionary action which are enforced under the limited judicial review exercised by the Court of Justice on the basis of the general principles of law, it has sometimes been claimed that the system of undistorted competition imposes directly effective constraints not only on the Member States and undertakings, but on the Community as well. As will be recalled, the Ordoliberals considered free competition to form a fundamental principle of the economic constitution of the Community.

The relative importance of the system of undistorted competition compared to other objectives of the Treaty was established in Joined Cases 41–44/70 _NV International Fruit Company v Commission_.[118] Here, Commission decisions regarding protective measures established by Council regulations dealing with the organisation of the fruit market were contested on a number of grounds (although the principle of competition was not mentioned as such). The Court stated: 'In accordance with the general objectives of the Treaty the protective measures permitted by Regulations Nos 2513/69 and 2514/69 can only be adopted in so far as they are strictly necessary for the attainment of the objectives specified in Article 39 of the Treaty, and impair as little as possible the functioning of the common market'.[119]

Hence, the Commission was bound to ensure that competition in the common market was not distorted, in accordance with Article 3(f) EEC. However, the Court pointed out that Article 3 EEC placed the common agricultural policy on the same level as the system of undistorted competition. Further, Article 42 EEC provided explicitly that the provisions relating to competition should apply to the production and trade in agricultural products only to the extent determined by the Council, in view of the objectives of the common agricultural policy as stated in Article 39 EEC.[120] Finally, since they were based on objective criteria which made it possible to avoid discrimination, the measures in question were found to meet the demands of anti-discrimination and proportionality.

Consequently, in Case 139/79 _Maizena v Council_, when examining the possible 'breach of the principles of the right of competition' which had been submitted in an action for annulment of a Council regulation fixing production quota, the Court stated (upon citing Article 42 EEC): 'That [Article 42] explicitly recognizes the precedence the agricultural policy has over the aims

---

[117] The principle of proportionality can be found in Articles 3b, 36, 90(2), 223(1b), and 226(3) EC. It was first accepted as a general principle of Community law in Case 11/70 _Internationale Handelsgesellschaft_, above, n. 110, and developed (for example), in Case 114/76 _Bela-Mühle Josef Bergman KG v Grows-Farm GmbH_ [1977] ECR 1211 ('Skimmed-Milk Powder').

[118] [1971] ECR 411.   [119] ibid., para. 64 p. 427.   [120] [1971] ECR 411, paras. 68–70.

of the Treaty in relation to competition and the power of the Council to decide how far the rules of competition should apply to the agricultural sector. The Council has a wide discretion in the exercise of that power as it has in the implementation of the whole agricultural policy'.[121] The Court then went on to examine the contested regulation on the more traditional grounds of a possible breach of the general principles of proportionality and non-discrimination, factual error, and infringement of essential procedural requirements.[122]

The most explicit statement on the constitutional status of the system of undistorted competition and the limits on Community action is found outside the area of the common agricultural policy in Case 240/83 *Used Oils*.[123] In response to a preliminary reference concerning the question whether a directive dealing with the disposal of waste oils (which introduced, inter alia, a system of permits and exclusive collection rights) was compatible with the principles of free trade, free movement of goods, and freedom of competition, the Court stated: '. . . it should be borne in mind that the principles of free movement of goods and freedom of competition, together with freedom of trade as fundamental rights, are general principles of Community law of which the Court ensures observance'.[124] This was a clear statement of the constitutional status of the principle of free competition. However, the Court continued: '. . . it should be observed that the principle of freedom of trade is not to be viewed in absolute terms but is subject to certain limits justified by the objectives of general interest pursued by the Community provided that the rights in question are not substantively impaired'.[125]

The Court found that, since the contested directive should be seen in the light of environmental protection ('one of the Community's essential objectives') and care had been taken to ensure that the principles of proportionality and non-discrimination would be observed, the limits of intervention justified by the public policy objective concerned had not been exceeded. Concerning the free movement of goods the Court found that the directive did not create barriers to intra-Community trade, and concluded:

It follows from the foregoing that the measures prescribed by the directive do not prescribe barriers to intra-Community trade, and that in so far as such measures . . . have a restrictive effect on the freedom of trade and of competition, they must nevertheless neither be discriminatory nor go beyond the inevitable restrictions which are justified by the pursuit of the objective of environmental protection, which is in the general interest. That being so, Articles 5 and 6 cannot be regarded as incompatible with the fundamental principle of Community law mentioned above.[126]

---

[121] Above, n. 14, para. 25 p. 3421.
[122] As is well known, the Court declared the contested regulation void since the European Parliament had not been adequately consulted. ibid.
[123] Above, n. 85.   [124] ibid., para. 9 p. 548.   [125] ibid., para. 12 p. 549.
[126] ibid., para. 15 p. 549–550.

Consequently, it is clear that the Court has declared the principle of competition, the four freedoms, and the principle of free trade, to be general principles of Community law. As such, they form principles of the economic constitution of the Community (or inversely, their existence could be taken as evidence that the Community has an economic constitution). However, the case law also shows that the economic constitution is not exclusively defined by these market principles. The four freedoms, free competition, and free trade may be limited in the pursuit of other legitimate objectives pursued by the Community.[127] Given the pursuit of legitimate objectives, the yardstick for the constitutionality of Community actions is formed by those principles of Community law that are concerned with the rule of law, such as proportionality and non-discrimination. The observation that the economic constitution of the Community allows the Member States to pursue (within certain constraints) mixed economic policies holds true for the policies pursued at the Community level as well.

However, the economic constitution of the EC is not 'neutral' regarding the Community itself, to the extent that it is predominantly oriented towards establishing the internal market. This is accompanied by the common policies, and more recently, notably by the establishment of the economic and monetary union. For the latter, the objective of the 'open market economy with free competition' is explicitly established.

The Court of Justice could cite the principle of freedom of competition as the basis for a strict proportionality test, such as has been applied to national policy measures under Article 36 EC: that the measures concerned must not restrict trade between the Member States any more than is strictly necessary, and that no alternative, less restrictive ways of attaining the legitimate objectives are possible.[128] But the criterion of the least possible intervention would then be applied on the basis of a comparison of various possible tools according to the degree to which they would restrict competition. So far, the Court of Justice has been reluctant to substitute its own views for those of the

---

[127] Similarly, for example, the public policy exception of Article 36 EC has allowed the Member States exceptions from the free movement of goods, among others, in the pursuit of consumer protection, environmental protection, the protection of public health and culture. The list of Community objectives as provided by Articles 2 and 3 EC provides such exceptions for the Community.

[128] For the Member States, the Court usually employs a strict proportionality test which requires that the 'least restrictive means' of attaining legitimate objectives is employed, for example under Article 36. Cf. Case 261/81 *Walter Rau Lebensmittelwerke v De Smedt PvbA* [1982] ECR 3961. However, in highly contentious cases involving the Member States, the Court has sought to avoid application of the proportionality test altogether. Case 238/82 *Duphar v Netherlands* [1984] ECR 523; Case 72/83 *Campus Oil v Minister for Industry and Energy* [1984] ECR 2727; Case C-159/90 *SPUC v Grogan* [1991] ECR 4685; Case C-169/91 *Council of the City of Stoke-on-Trent v B&Q plc* [1992] ECR I-6635. The Court employs a loose definition of proportionality in assessing the legality of the Community acts, in particular where discretionary powers are involved ('manifestly unsuitable'). Cf. Case C331/88 *R v Minster for Agriculture, Fisheries and Food, ex parte Fedesa* [1990] ECR I-4023. G. De Búrca, 'Proportionality in EC Law', (1993) 13 YEL 105.

Community institutions in the application of the proportionality test to discretionary policy making. Rather, the trend seems to be that of judicial restraint even regarding policy making at the national level.

C. The Political versus the Economic Constitution

As has been seen, the idea of the constitution of the European Union has multiple sources. Most importantly, it has been developed in the case law of the Court of Justice, which progressed from the interpretation of the Treaty as the functional equivalent of a constitution, to explicit statements on the Community based on the rule of law, and finally to a declaration that the Treaty constitutes the constitutional charter of the Community.

Another source of the idea of a European constitution was the Ordoliberal reading of the Treaty as a liberal economic constitution. By conceptualising the constraints that follow from the four freedoms and competition as individual economic rights, the Ordoliberals have made a major contribution to the constitutional theory of the European Union. However, under Community law, these economic rights are not boundless. They go no further than is necessary to establish the internal market, are subject to public interest exceptions, and therefore do not impose the strict constitutional constraints of a liberal economic order on the Member States.

The rigorous theoretical perspective of Ordoliberalism has always seemed at odds with a number of provisions of the original Rome Treaty, as well as established Community policies (such as the CAP), and has misread the case law of the Court of Justice on human rights and the freedom of competition. The limitations of the Ordoliberal reading of the Treaty have become evident in particular with the Treaty on European Union, which not only expanded the policies pursued at the Community level, but strengthened the role of the European Parliament, added the concept of citizenship and respect for democracy and human rights, and spelled out principles for the allocation of power between the various levels of government.

The Treaty is gaining credibility as a political constitution, and the balance between political and economic rights has become an issue in the horizontal and vertical distribution of powers in the Community. This balance is addressed not only in terms of subsidiarity, but also in the attempts by the Court of Justice to draw a new line between public policy considerations and the demands of the integration objective. Hence, the Ordoliberal view ignores a large part of the economic as well as the political constitution. This becomes readily apparent when the component elements of the neo-liberal economic constitution and the Treaty of European Union constitution of the Community are compared, as set out in the table below.

	Ordoliberal Economic Constitution	**Political Constitution of the European Union**
objectives of constitution	internal market; individual economic freedom	Article B ,TEU: economic and social goals; common foreign and security policy; ever closer Union. Article 2 EC: economic and social goals; internal market; economic and monetary union; implementing common policies and activities of Articles 3 and 3a EC
constitutional principles	economic freedoms; competition	general principles of Community law (including human rights); political principles
integration process	market process	economic and political integration; increase of democratic legitimacy
method of integration	competition among rules	harmonisation; policy co-ordination; mutual recognition
role of constitution	guarantee individual economic freedom; limit role of the state and democratic principle; limit private economic power	guarantee limited government under the rule of law; horizontal and vertical division of powers; political legitimacy
nature of constitution	static (Rome Treaty)	dynamic (emerging)
concept of individual	economic actor	citizen (both economic and political actor)

Table 1: A Comparison Between the Ordoliberal view of the Economic Constitution and the Political Constitution of the European Union.

The economic constitution of the Community imposes constraints on the economic policies of the Member States and the Community. When the legitimacy of the objective of the national measures and the minimal effect on trade between the Member States are established, judicial review will be restricted to a marginal test based on the general principles of Community law concerned with protecting the rule of law (such as non-discrimination). Constraints on Community action follow from the limited attribution of powers, the principle of subsidiarity, and from the general principles of Community law. Exceptions to market freedoms and competition are acceptable in the pursuit of the other policy objectives of the Community, subject to judicial control based on the principles of Community law concerned with protecting the rule of law. Thus, the principle of open markets with free competition is a principle of the economic constitution of the Community, but does not exclude the pursuit of other public policy objectives.

The flaws of the Ordoliberal approach result from its tendency to underestimate the importance of the political dimension and the dynamism of the European integration. Given the emphasis on establishing the common market in the Rome Treaty, it was thought that market led integration would roll back the state and establish a liberal economic order. Until the negotiation of the Treaty on European Union, the co-ordination of economic policies was neglected, and as given the practical limits on positive integration, the case law of the Court likewise focused on negative integration. The Ordoliberals overinterpreted these characteristics (which were read by others as the (temporary) ascendance of normative (legal) supranationalism and the stagnation of decisional (political) supranationalism) as conditioned by an immutable liberal economic constitution.

The question remains whether, in practice, the process of integration has reduced the margins for public policy. The limits imposed by the four freedoms and the guarantees of free competition have narrowed with progress towards a common market. This is largely the result of the growth of trade between the Member States, which has led to expansion of the anti-discrimination rationale. This development has in turn been interpreted as favouring economic liberalism, private capital, and the market mechanism over planning, public capital, and state intervention.[129] It could therefore be claimed that the practical limitations on Member States' potential to conduct effective economic policy which were imposed by the economic effects of the common market have resulted in a liberal 'practice' of an economic constitution, which was in principle neutral regarding the economic policies pursued at the national level.[130]

This result occurred especially where the Community institutions themselves were not authorised to fill the gap created by the limits imposed on national

---

[129] Joerges, above, n. 98.

[130] Widely cited in this context is the failure of national anti-cyclical economic policy attempted by the newly elected French socialist government in 1981 and 1982. Mertens de Wilmars, 'Reflections sur l'ordre juridico-publique de la Communauté européenne', in J. Dutheil de la Rochère and J. Vandamme (eds.), *Interventions Publiques et Droit Communautaire* (Brussels, 1988), [1988], p. 36; cf. VerLoren, 'Some Preliminary Observations on the Intergovernmental Conferences: The Relations between the Concepts of a Common Market, a Monetary Union, an Economic Union, a Political Union and Sovereignty', (1991) 28 CMLR 291, pp. 293ff, p. 302.

economic policy by Community law.[131] This was the result of the institutional and political constraints on the decision making procedures of the Community, most notoriously that of unanimity decision making in the shadow of the de facto veto introduced by the Luxembourg Accord.[132] Therefore, it has been observed that 'the policy-making capacities of the Union have not been strengthened nearly as much as capabilities at the level of the member states have declined'.[133] This phenomenon has been described as the 'regulatory deficit' of the Community.[134]

However, economic deregulation by Community law, the demise of public policy making at the level of the Member States and the indefinite persistence of the constraints on positive action at the Community level should not be deemed foregone conclusions. First, Community involvement has usually gone beyond mere liberalisation, even where fully fledged common policies were not developed to compensate for the retreat of the Member States. This tendency has been strengthened with the institutional reforms of the Single Act and the Maastricht Treaty, where decision making procedures were streamlined and upgraded, and the powers of the European Parliament were extended. This made it possible to proceed beyond decision making by default, including in principle pro-active redistributive policies at the Community level.

In this context, the trend toward an extensive use of Article 100a EC to promote joint liberalisation and re-regulation has been widely noted. Such economic re-regulation has taken a number of forms, which range from new techniques of harmonisation, with the pervasive introduction of comitology procedures, to the introduction of European agencies. In this manner complex methods of decentralised policy making are developing, based on networks of experts and

---

[131] Cf. Everling regarding Community competences in this regard: 'Marktintervention und Planifikation stoßen also weniger deshalb auf Schwierigkeiten und Grenzen, weil sie einer—angeblichen—Ordnungspolitischen Entscheidung des Vertrages nicht entsprechen, als vielmehr weil die Hoheitsgewalt fehlt, die sie beschließen und durchsetzen könnte'. *Das europäische Wirtschaftsrecht im Spannungsfeld von Politik und Wirtschaft: Ausgewählte Aufsätze 1964–1984* (Baden-Baden, 1985), p. 214. This conclusion may also be drawn from Mestmäcker, 'Zur Anwendung der Wettbewerbsregeln auf die Mitgliedstaaten und auf die Europäischen Gemeinschaften', in Baur, Müller-Graf and Zuleeg (eds.), *Europarecht, Energierecht, Wirtschaftsrecht: Festschrift für Bodo Börner zum 70. Geburtstag* (Cologne, 1992), and Möschel, 'Hoheitliche Maßnahmen und die Wettbewerbsvorschriften des Gemeinschaftsrechts' in *Weiterentwicklung der Europäischen Gemeinschaften und der Marktwirtschaft. Referate des XXV. FIW-Symposions* (Cologne, 1992).

[132] Cf. J. J. H. Weiler, 'The Community System: The Dual Character of Supranationalism', (1982) 1 YEL 267; F. W. Scharpf, 'The Joint-Decision Trap: Lessons From German Federalism and European Integration', (1988) 66 *Public Administration* 239.

[133] F. W. Scharpf, 'Community and Autonomy: Multi-Level Policy-Making in the European Union', (1994) 1 *Journal of European Public Policy* 219, p. 220.

[134] R. Dehousse, C. Joerges, G. Majone and F. Snyder (with M. Everson), *Europe After 1992: New Regulatory Strategies* Working Paper Law 92/31 (Florence, 1992), p. 6. The constraints on regulatory policy at the Community level have included *de facto* unanimity requirement for decision making in the Council, the marginal legitimising role the European Parliament was able to fulfil, and the material constraints on the Commission. Combined, the formal requirements of institutional balance and the practical ones of political expediency have come at a clear cost to effectiveness, and, paradoxically, (democratic) legitimacy.

occasionally independent national regulators.[135] Although complicating the horizontal and vertical division of powers (and therefore open to criticism that they lack democratic legitimacy, or threaten the institutional balance), such structures clearly go a long way toward closing the regulatory deficit. The comitology structures form a way of reconciling the autonomy of national policy making with the need for policy co-ordination.

The reaction of the Member States against seepage of their autonomous decision making powers, both due to the expansive interpretation of the market freedoms by the Court, and the expansion of harmonisation under the new decision making rules, has led to rethinking of the level at which authority should be exercised. Further withdrawal of the Member States should not be taken for granted, as is indicated both in the Treaty on European Union itself, with the introduction of the principle of subsidiarity, and in the recent case law of the Court of Justice. Consequently, there appears to be a clear tendency to seal off part of the policy making powers of the Member States from the expansionist logic of the internal market.

With the Treaty on European Union, the economic neutrality of the economic constitution *vis-á-vis* the economic order of the Member States may nevertheless be under threat. Henceforth, the real constraints on the economic policies of the Member States will not be so much those of the market freedoms as those of economic and monetary union. The constraints involved range from the general objective of stability and the principles of stable prices, sound public finances and a sustainable balance of payments set out in Articles 3a, 102a and 105(1) EC, to the convergence criteria which impose enforceable standards of conformity with these principles.[136] These constraints are reminiscent of the directive, in that they are binding as to the result to be achieved, but leave the choice of form and method to the Member States. Nevertheless, the discipline of the capital markets will condition the methods used. Further, to guarantee the commitment of the Member States to economic and monetary union, in the area of economic and monetary policy itself, a politically neutral, but norm-based system (with price stability as its central objective) has been established: a technocratic system which is one step removed from democratic politics.

---

[135] Cf. Joerges, above, n. 5.

[136] That is: (1) reduction of public deficits; (2) stable monetary policies; (3) anti-inflationary policies; and arguably (although not formally included) an open economy in the context of GATT and EEA. More precisely, the convergence (including excessive deficit) criteria set under Article 104c(2) and Article 109j EC are: price stability (a maximum inflation rate of the average of the three Member States with the lowest rate, plus 1.5 per cent); balanced long terms interest rates (at a maximum of the average of the three Member States with the lowest rate, plus 2 per cent); a budget deficit lower than 3 per cent of GDP and a public debt ratio lower than 60 per cent of GDP; currency remaining within the normal band of the EMS for at least 2 years (maximum fluctuation of 2.25 per cent on either side of target rate). Treaty on European Union: Protocols Nos 5 ('on the excessive deficit procedure') and 6 ('on the convergence criteria referred to in Article 109j of the Treaty establishing the European Community').

The complex institutional system developing toward full economic and monetary union goes beyond the simple dichotomy between intergovernmental and supranational decision making. It could not, however, be seen as a withdrawal of public policy. Its rationale is that of reasserting public control over economic and monetary policy, albeit pooled at the Community level, and within strict constraints. The importance of public policy is thus reaffirmed both at the national and the Community level.

This is in line with the suggestion by integration theorists and historians of the European Community that the Union is not primarily an expression of the demise of the nation state but an attempt to lift the management of the market to a higher systemic level, which it is hoped may be more effective, while at the same time securing the existence of the component units.[137] Through participation in such transnational structures, national states attempt to increase their ability to address problems which escape the effective political control of even the largest individual states. At the same time, the pooling of sovereignty is restricted to the necessary minimum, in order to limit the pressures toward fragmentation of the state.[138] As is demonstrated by the debate on subsidiarity, the problem becomes that of the co-ordination of regulatory action at the various levels of public intervention.

Yet in the context of the European integration, the need to compensate for the reduced capacity of the individual Member States to act effectively, while remaining within the institutional constraints on the Community, is problematic. Where a basic consensus exists on methods and objectives, there may be a tendency to delegate specific policy decisions to independent professional bodies. An important example is provided by the role played by the European Central Bank, and the network of other specialised bodies that surround it. The 'comitology' structures involved in the implementation of Community law, which provide an interface between the Commission, national authorities, and communities of experts, play a similarly important role on a much wider scale. The emergence of dual, or multi-level policy making remains to be studied in greater detail. One question is what the role of such structures is, particularly where they clearly complicate further the horizontal and vertical division of powers given by the constitution of the European Union. Another question is whether there is a tendency to formalise such networks in a move toward establishing independent agencies?

---

[137] For example the neo-institutionalist view expressed by A. Moravcsik, 'Preferences and Power in the European Community: A Liberal Intergovernmentalist Approach', (1993) 31 JCMS 473. See also the historical view pioneered by A. S. Milward, *The European Community: The Salvation of the Nation State* (London, 1994).

[138] S. Cassese, 'Oltre lo Stato: i limiti dei governi nazionali nel controllo dell'economia', in F. Galgano, S. Cassese, G. Tremonti and T. Treu, *Nazioni senza ricchezza, ricchezze senza nazione* (Bologna, 1993).

V. CONCLUSION

The three main questions posed at the beginning of this chapter can now be answered. First, the Rome Treaty was not intended to create or prescribe a particular economic regime for the Member States, and the Ordoliberal concept of the 'ruse of reason' must be rejected. The Rome Treaty does not require particular economic policies at the national level, and as such condones the mixed economy within certain limits set by Community law. Nevertheless, the Treaty can be approached as the basis of the formal economic constitution of the European Community, which has functioned in spite of disagreement regarding its precise content. This was possible since on the one hand the Member States retained a large measure of freedom to pursue their national policies, while on the other hand the Court of Justice formulated limits to the discretion of the Member States. Filling the gap left by political disagreement, the Court found and applied a set of principles which allowed it to settle such conflicts between the various levels of public policy and individual economic rights (creating the material economic constitution).

This economic constitution can be seen as a subset of the emerging political constitution of the Community which, although incomplete, is maturing. In the process, the debate is shifting to the methods and legitimacy of positive integration. Consequently, the democratic quality of decision making and the constitution of a pan-European polity play an important part in the discussion which accompanies this development. However, the modalities chosen for proceeding toward economic and monetary union appear to minimise the role of democratic institutions, and instead seek to isolate this important policy area from political interference. The question is whether this represents a model which can be more widely applied to the new areas of Community competence.

Concerning the second question, it can be concluded that the economic order at the Community level is that of a market system which guarantees individual economic rights within certain limits imposed by the public interest, subject to limited judicial review. Under the Treaty on European Union, this economic order is based on co-ordination of the Member States' economic policies, on the internal market and on the definition of common objectives, and conducted in accordance with the principle of an open market economy with free competition, as required by Article 3a EC. However, this order is not absolute to the extent that legitimate public policy goals may justify exceptions from market policies also at the Community level. Here, political decisions are decisive, although they are submitted to a restrained form of judicial control. As such, there is no hierarchical order between the various intermediate objectives of the Treaty set out in Article 3 EC.

This leaves the third question posed at the outset of this chapter, which asked whether the process of economic integration as such favours certain forms of economic organisation and policy over others, in particular those associated with economic liberalism over those associated with state ownership, planning, and intervention. This question can be answered in the affirmative. Under the Treaty on European Union, economic and monetary union is linked to the principle of free competition in open markets. With the overriding objective of price stability and the stringent criteria aimed at achieving economic convergence, monetary union imposes new constraints on the economic policies of the Member States. Although legally the Member States retain a certain freedom, and are not bound to particular methods to reach the economic objectives set by the Treaty, in practice there is a bias toward liberal market policies.

However, this will not inevitably result in a complete and permanent retreat of the state, as had been hoped by the Ordoliberals. New and more effective ways of pursuing public interest goals may be found, which are compatible with the demands of European law and the new economic constraints alike. These will involve regulation at arm's length rather than the various forms of direct intervention and state ownership which were typical of the mixed economy.

In summary, the economic constitution can be seen as part of a European constitution in the making. This constitution guarantees the rule of law, provides principles guiding the horizontal and vertical division of power, the legal basis for Community actions and common policies, an institutional structure, and the basic elements of the economic order, but lacks a clear hierarchy, and a matching political structure. The question whether industrial or competition policy has priority cannot be answered on the basis of a general examination of the constitution. Although free competition forms a principle of Community law, the objective of promoting competitiveness can legitimise exceptions.

At this point the Ordoliberal argument that industrial policy in the EC would be illegal as such, since it would be at odds with the principles of the Treaty, has lost its relevance. It has been seen that the economic order of the Community has always been a mixed one, or at least allowed the pursuit of public policy objectives beyond liberalisation. In the absence of a strict hierarchy in the economic constitution it does not appear that including a title on industrial policy amounts to a qualitative change of the economic order of the Community. This supports the hypothesis that industrial and competition policy need not be considered to be incompatible or mutually exclusive. Instead it should be seen how the two are reconciled. A closer examination of the nature of Community industrial policy is required.

3

The Emergence of the Industrial Policy of the European Union

I. INTRODUCTION

Paradoxically, the globalisation of production and the growth of international commerce due to trade liberalisation have led to a renewed interest in industrial policy. First, seeking to explain the predominance of trade between advanced countries with a similar industrial structure, recent developments in economic theory have modified standard assumptions about the general benefits of free trade. The new trade theory suggests that states can effectively change comparative advantage in their favour by adopting strategic behaviour. Second, a certain degree of consensus seems to have formed among economists that industrial policies aiming to remedy market failures may be both beneficial and successful. Third, the economic success of Japan and the East Asian New Industrial Countries has given rise to further debate on the role of the state in promoting industrial competitiveness in the United States and Western Europe.[1] Finally, this debate has been fuelled by analyses stressing the importance of technological change as a factor conditioning economic growth, and the way in which the appropriate institutional structures may maximise such benefits.

However, no generally accepted definition of industrial policy has yet been established, and the new theories remain contested. Further, in countering the new trade theory, public choice and rent-seeking theories have drawn attention to the danger that state intervention and protection will be captured by economic interest groups, to the detriment of general welfare: in practice, this risk may outweigh the advantages that industrial policy could render in theory. However, beside economic arguments, there are also political reasons for pursuing industrial policy. In the final analysis, the merits of public policy based on democratic decisions cannot be judged on efficiency arguments alone.

Industrial policy is usually discussed in the context of efforts to change the terms of economic competition between states. The general arguments regarding the need to address market failures and the possible gains from strategic

---

[1] For a critical review of this debate cf. P. R. Krugman, 'Competitiveness: A Dangerous Obsession', (1994) 73 *Foreign Affairs* 28; and the responses by C. V. Prestowitz, L. C. Thurow, R. Scharping, S. C. Cohen and B. Steil in 'The Fight over Competitiveness: A Zero-Sum Debate?', (1994) 73 *Foreign Affairs* 186. Cf. P. R. Krugman, 'Economic Integration in Europe: Some Conceptual Issues', in T. Padoa Schioppa *et al* (eds.), *Efficiency, Stability and Equity: A Strategy for the Evolution of the Economic System of the European Community* (Oxford, 1987).

behaviour in principle apply to the European Community as well. In addition however, there is a specific argument regarding the need for co-ordination of the national industrial policies of the Member States, which may otherwise form a threat to the internal market. For this reason an industrial policy at the Community level could serve to resolve possible conflicts between industrial policies at the level of the Member States. This need for co-ordination of industrial policy has increased with the co-ordination of economic policy required in the run-up to economic and monetary union.

Until recently, such considerations were purely academic. Active and explicit industrial policy has long remained within the competence of the Member States, which individually pursued more or less interventionist national policies. The Community, and especially the Commission, (which has sought such powers since its creation), was excluded from pursuing active industrial policy. Instead, it was restricted to passive measures of industrial policy (or the removal of the internal barriers to the four freedoms). In the original EEC Treaty, the focus was on the establishment of the common market through 'negative integration', and the co-ordination of economic policies was not well developed. As a consequence, the Treaty has been interpreted as a liberal economic constitution. However, the economic constitution of the Community has been extended and modified. In 1990 the Commission presented a 'coherent industrial policy concept' which was accepted by the Council, and in 1993 Title XIII of the Treaty on European Union gave the Community a concurrent competence on industrial policy.

This chapter examines the process of constitutionalisation of the industrial policy of the European Community. The basic question is how and why the Community obtained its competence on industrial policy in spite of apparent disagreement on whether this was desirable. Did the Industry Title or the 'new industrial policy concept of the Community' form a decisive break with earlier practice? The wider issue to be addressed on this basis considers the significance of the emergence of a Community industrial policy for the distribution of decision making power on economic policy in the Community, and whether this is related to a redefinition of the role of the state in the economy.

The three hypotheses formulated in the general introduction will be addressed:

   (i) that industrial and competition policy should not a priori be considered incompatible, and indeed that in the EC, under the principle of the unity of Community law, the two should be aligned;

  (ii) that the new industrial policy title must be seen in the context of Economic and Monetary Union, in particular the co-ordination of economic policy;

 (iii) that the new industrial policy competence of the Community could be seen not only as the result of a next phase of European integration, but also as an expression of a new balance between state and market.

Below, alternative definitions of industrial policy will be compared, followed by an overview of the arguments for strategic industrial policy. Next, the progressive constitutionalisation of industrial policy in the EC is discussed chronologically, concluded by an evaluation of the new Industry Title and a sketch of recent developments.

II. REASONS FOR INDUSTRIAL POLICY

A. Defining Industrial Policy

There is no general consensus on the meaning of the concept of industrial policy. First, the concept is not clearly defined, neither in law, nor in politics or economics. Second, apart from a wide range of definitions being available at any given time, their focus has shifted over time. Third, there is no agreement even on the use of the term industrial policy as such. Alternative concepts in English include 'competitiveness policy',[2] 'enterprise policy', 'innovation policy',[3] 'government industry relations',[4] 'structural policy', and even such convoluted constructions as 'continuous forward-looking structural adjustment'. Across languages, the problems obviously increase, especially when conscious attempts are made to avoid using the label 'industrial policy' for its interventionist connotations. For example, whereas the term *Industriepolitik* is anathema to most German observers, *Standortwettbewerb* (competitiveness policy) is not, although the distinction is not obvious and does not easily lend itself to translation.[5]

Perhaps the widest definition available is that 'industrial policy embraces all acts and policies of the state in relation to industry'.[6] This definition covers both positive or active (state intervention) and negative or passive (minimising state intervention) industrial policy, and would certainly include competition policy. According to a less sweeping view, '(I)ndustrial policy is taken to refer to a set of measures used by governments to influence the investment decisions of individual enterprises—public and private—so as to promote such objectives as lower employment, a healthier balance of payments and a generally more

[2] Cf. the references in Krugman, above, n. 1.

[3] S. Ostry, *Governments and Corporations in a Shrinking World: Trade and Innovation Policies in the United States, Europe, and Japan* (New York, 1990).

[4] This term has been favoured by British social scientists. Cf. S. Wilks, 'Government-Industry Relations: A Review Article', (1986) 14 *Policy and Politics* 491; S. Wilks, 'Government-Industry Relations: Progress and Findings of the ESCR Research Initiative', (1989) 67 *Public Administration* 329; M. Wright, 'Policy community, policy network and comparative industrial policies', (1988) 36 *Political Studies* 593.

[5] Cf. H. Siebert, 'Standortwettbewerb—nicht Industriepolitik', (1992) *Die Weltwirtschaft* 409.

[6] B. T. Bayliss and A. M. El-Agraa, 'Competition and Industrial Policies with an Emphasis on Competition Policy', in A. M. El-Agraa (ed.), *The Economics of the European Community* (3rd ed., New York, 1990), p. 137.

efficient industrial economy'.[7] An emphasis on objectives rather than instruments is found in the following definition:

'Industrial policy' is the label that has come to be used to describe a wide-ranging, ill-assorted collection of micro-based supply side initiatives primarily directed at firms, which are designed to improve market performance in a variety of occasionally mutually inconsistent ways. The performance criteria usually include productive and allocative efficiency, equity of market outcomes, progressivity of firms, and flexibility of production structures, and action is typically demanded in cases of egregious 'market failure' involving public goods or externalities, or where major changes need to be effected quickly.[8]

From these otherwise disparate definitions, the following two conclusions can be drawn: first, industrial policy concerns various forms of state involvement in the economy in the pursuit of a variable mix of social and economic goals; and second, it is focused on industrial undertakings and improving the framework in which they function.

Again, this understanding of industrial policy would include competition policy. An additional specification can be derived by comparing some further definitions. Industrial policy has been defined as: 'the set of measures applied by governments to deal with the process of structural adjustment associated with changes in comparative advantage. It includes measures aimed at declining sectors as well as policies oriented toward the future';[9] and as 'any state measure designed primarily to affect the allocation of resources between industrial activities, in other words, to impose a new direction on market structures'.[10] This focus on the dynamic nature of industrial policy, as concerned with steering the economy toward specific economic activities (or structural adjustment) is found most explicitly in the seminal work by Johnson: '. . . industrial policy means the initiation and co-ordination of governmental activities to leverage upward the productivity and competitiveness of the whole economy and of particular industries in it. Above all, positive industrial policy means the infusion of goal oriented, strategic thinking into public economic policy. (. . .) In more abstract terms, industrial policy is the logical outgrowth of the changing concept of comparative advantage'.[11] A more recent and succinct expression of the same idea is that: 'industrial policy is an attempt by a government to shift the allocation of resources to promote economic growth'.[12]

    [7] W. Grant, *The Political Economy of Industrial Policy* (London, 1982), p. 2.

    [8] P. A. Geroski, 'European Industrial Policy and Industrial Policy in Europe', (1989) 5 *Oxford Review of Economic Policy* 20, p. 21.

    [9] P. Buigues and A. Sapir, 'Community Industrial Policies', in Ph. Nicolaides (ed.), *Industrial Policy in the European Community: A Necessary Response to Economic Integration?* (Maastricht, 1993), p. 21.

    [10] V. Curzon-Price, 'Competition and industrial policies with an emphasis on industrial policy', in El-Agraa (ed.), above, n. 6, p. 157.

    [11] C. Johnson, Introduction: 'The Idea of Industrial Policy' in C. Johnson (ed.), *The Industrial Policy Debate* (San Francisco, 1984), p. 8.

    [12] P. Krugman and M. Obstfeld, *International Economics: Theory and Policy* (2nd ed., New York, 1991), ch. 11: 'Industrial Policy in Advanced Countries', p. 281.

The third conclusion that can be drawn is that the present focus of industrial policy is on facilitating industrial change, or structural adjustment of the economy. The promotion of structural adjustment can take two forms. General policies which affect the internal structure of industry include both the reduction of barriers to trade (forcing the rationalisation of industrial structures) and competition policy. Hereby, competition policy may again be considered to form a subset of industrial policy. By contrast, sectoral policies aim at affecting the allocation of resources between sectors, or toward specific sectors. Many observers would limit their definition of industrial policy to such cases, excluding competition policy.

The distinction between general and sectoral measures should be retained. It has been observed that there is no agreement among economists as to how industrial policy should be pursued, or indeed if it is worth pursuing at all. Disagreement on whether governments should pursue industrial policy is obviously linked with the definition of industrial policy used. Yet while it remains true that there is no common definition of industrial policy, a certain measure of consensus seems to have emerged on which types of industrial policy measures would be appropriate in a market economy. To proceed beyond the problem of definition and identify the area of consensus, industrial policy measures can further be divided into passive (efficiency enhancing) versus active (shaping industrial structure according to preconceived standards) measures.

This four-fold division allows a classification of state measures aimed at enhancing the competitiveness of industry which illustrates that the disagreement on the desirability of industrial policy is one of degrees.[13] Passive general (as well as sectoral) measures of liberalisation are generally held desirable. Active general measures, aimed at correcting market failures, are also generally accepted, although some economic liberals already warn of rent-seeking in this area. The focal point of disagreement is active sectoral measures, which involve the identification and active promotion of strategic industries. Like the more general division between 'negative' and 'positive' integration, which to some degree it overlaps, this classification of industrial policy measures is ambiguous.[14] Most actual policies combine measures across categories, and some types of measures

[13] This distinction is borrowed from Ph. Nicolaides, 'Industrial Policy: The Problem of Reconciling Definitions, Intentions and Effects', in Ph. Nicolaides (ed.), *Industrial Policy in the European Community: A Necessary Response to Economic Integration?* (Maastricht, 1993), pp. 5–6. Cf. D. B. Audretsch, 'Industrial Policy and International Competitiveness', in Nicolaides Ph. (ed.) ibid.; Curzon-Price, above, n. 10, pp. 156ff. Bayliss and El-Agraa use a less revealing distinction between 'negative' and 'positive' industrial policy in El-Agraa (ed.), above, n. 6, ch. 7: 'Competition and Industrial Policies with an Emphasis on Competition Law'.

[14] The distinction between negative and positive integration was first made by J. Tinbergen, *International Economic Integration* (Amsterdam, 1954). It was further developed for the Community by J. Pinder, 'Positive and Negative Integration: Some Problems of Economic Union in the EEC', (1968) 24 *The World Today* 88, reprinted as 'Problems of European Integration', in G. R. Denton (ed.), *Economic Integration in Europe* (London, 1969). Tinbergen's definition of positive and negative integration is based on the distinction whether (national) policy instruments are eliminated or new (common) policies formed, whereas Pinder distinguishes between the purpose of removing discrimination, or maximising welfare in other ways. Pinder, ibid. p. 145, n. 1.

which surely have an impact on competitiveness (such as those which shape national education systems) are not adequately captured. Consequently, there is little point in attempting to providing an exact classification of all measures of public policy on this basis. Nevertheless, these criteria are useful to identify broad shifts in policy making.

B. Reasons for an Active Industrial Policy

Policies focused on adjustment directed toward specific industrial sectors are once again in vogue. This is the result of recent work on the comparative and competitive advantage of nations, done by political economists building on theoretical developments in international economics.[15] New or 'strategic' trade theory was developed in the 1980s to explain why 'intra-industry' trade between developed countries (rather than inter-industry trade between countries at different levels of development) represents the bulk of global trade, something that is not readily accounted for by traditional notions of comparative advantage.

The core idea derived from the new trade theory is that governments can sometimes be successful at directing their economies toward high growth and value added activities. In other words, it is thought that comparative advantage is not merely the product of different natural endowments, but can be created.[16] Often, the term 'competitive advantage' is used to express this voluntarist notion. Given the strategic behaviour of states and firms, some authors emphasise the advantages of public actors over private ones in influencing structural adjustment, and argue for industrial policy on this basis.[17] In this view, the

[15] Cf. E. Helpman and P. Krugman, *Trade Policy and Market Structure* (Cambridge, 1986); P. R. Krugman (ed.), *Strategic Trade policy and the New International Economics* (Cambridge, 1986).

[16] Cf. S. S. Cohen and J. Zysman, *Manufacturing matters: The Myth of the Post-Industrial Economy* (New York, 1987); L. D'Andrea Tyson, *Who's Bashing Whom: Trade Conflict in High-Technology Industries* (Washington, 1992); I. C. Magaziner and R. B. Reich, *Minding America's Business: the Decline and Rise of the American Economy* (New York, 1983); M. J. Piore and C. F. Sabel, *The Second Industrial Divide: Possibilities for Prosperity* (New York, 1984); M. E. Porter, *The Competitive Advantage of Nations* (London, 1990); R. Reich, *The Work of Nations: Capitalism in the 21st Century* (New York, 1991).

[17] An approach to industrial policy which falls outside mainstream economics (but is related to the new trade theory) looks at institutional failure, rather than market failure. The argument of institutional failure was developed to explain the differences in performance between nations with similar industrial structures. It identifies differences in the systemic properties of states (in particular in their approach to innovation, their financial system, management methods, education, and training) as determinants for success in structural adjustment. Where institutional failure is identified as the cause of market failure, this is to be remedied by institutional reform. Cf. M. Sharp and K. Pavitt, 'Technology Policy in the 1990s: Old Trends and New Realities', (1993) 31 JCMS 129, pp. 141–143; U. Hilpert (ed.), *State Policies and Techno-Industrial Innovation* (London, 1991). Many studies on this subject have focused on comparisons with Japan. Cf. R. Dore, *Flexible Rigidities: Industrial Policy and Structural Adjustment in Japan 1970–80* (London, 1986); C. Freeman, *Technology Policy and Economic Performance—Lessons from Japan* (New York, 1987); C. Johnson, *MITI and the Japanese Miracle* (Stanford, 1982); S. Ostry, above, n. 3; S. Wilks and M. Wright (eds.), *The Promotion and regulation of Industry in Japan* (London, 1991); S. Wilks and M. Wright (eds.), *Comparative Government-Industry Relations: Western Europe, the United States and Japan* (Oxford, 1987).

strengths of public authorities would be their almost infinite legal and financial resources, their inherent inertia, and potential recourse to force as well as other means of ensuring co-operation, all of which lend credibility to their strategies (and thereby create a stable environment for the decisions taken by private enterprise). At the same time it is usually emphasised that strategic public policies should be pursued with restraint, and within the overall framework of the market economy.

Although strategic trade arguments have lately been fashionable, the reasons in favour of active industrial policy are often intermeshed with older and more general notions. In the debate, four broad categories can be distinguished: (i) general (popular) arguments; and more specific arguments based on (ii) the notion of 'defensive' industrial policy; (iii) or 'market failure'; (iv) or on strategic trade theory.

The first category is that of the 'popular' arguments which are commonly used by governments to defend the promotion of 'national champions' by a variety of means, ranging from subsidies, credit and public procurement policies, as well as import protection, to nationalisation. Many of these arguments do not hold up to modern economic analysis. For example, the idea that industries which provide a high added value per worker, 'linkage industries' producing intermediate goods that are used in various sectors, or industries with future growth potential should be especially encouraged is rejected by standard economic theory.[18] In the past these claims were usually formulated as 'infant industry' arguments. The aim of correcting 'market failures' is regarded more favourably. However, usually arguments in favour of targeting strategic sectors are not based on evidence of such market failure. Further, governments can rarely hope to increase the market allocation of resources to targeted sectors without negative consequences for growth and employment elsewhere. Hence, in general the given allocation of resources between economic sectors (although it may not be concentrated in 'strategic' sectors) should be considered to be an optimal distribution.

The second set of arguments focuses on protecting sectors first targeted in other countries: this is defensive industrial policy. Economists have given a mixed reaction to such arguments. On the one hand, the point is made that defensive policies are misconceived, since they would merely reproduce flawed and counterproductive constraints devised elsewhere.[19] On the other hand, it has been argued that the primary value of industrial policy is precisely a defensive one. Although international free trade remains the optimal solution, in order to reach this stage it may be necessary even for liberal market oriented states to devise strategic trade and industrial policy measures in order to improve their

---

[18] Krugman and Obstfeld, above, n. 12, pp. 263ff. Cf. Monopolkommission, *Wettbewerbspolitik oder Industriepolitik: Hauptgutachten 1990/1991* (Baden-Baden, 1992), ch. 7: 'Wettbewerb und strategische Handelspolitik'.

[19] Krugman and Obstfeld, above, n. 12, p. 266.

bargaining position.[20] This can be related to the general case for international negotiations and trade policy. In the absence of effective global competition and trade rules, unilateral adoption of free trade would neither be productive nor politically feasible (given the interest in protection of highly organised pressure groups). Mutual tariff reductions and linkages across sectors in multilateral trade negotiations facilitate the adoption of free trade policies and increase their immediate benefits.[21] In the context of such negotiations, industrial and trade policy instruments are bargained away to the benefit of all parties involved.

A third group of arguments in favour of industrial policy, based on the theory of market failure (in combination with more recent insights in strategic trade theory), is more sophisticated. Market failure occurs where, in the absence of public intervention, the supply of certain (public) goods by the market would be sub-optimal from the perspective of society as a whole. An important example of market failure is anti-competitive behaviour and monopolisation of markets by firms, which is countered by competition policy. This is one type of public intervention in the market which is usually advocated by economic liberals. Another case of market failure that is of particular importance is that of investment in high technology industries (such as information technology, aerospace and biotechnology). Such investment is often sub-optimal from the perspective of the important beneficial effects for the economy as a whole (externalities) that may be involved. This problem is related to that of the limited appropriability (through effective protection of intellectual property) of the results of research and development (R&D) in these areas. For example, government support of non-appropriable R&D through subsidies, or improved protection of intellectual property may help to counter this market failure.

Although the argument of market failure is widely accepted, the remaining problem is that it is impossible to measure the externalities involved accurately, and hence equally impossible to establish the appropriate level of the subsidies required. Further, state intervention leads to the problem of rent-seeking, as it stimulates entrepreneurs to compete for profits generated in the political arena rather than the economic market. Through lobbying, entrepreneurs seek to establish and guarantee economic advantage over their competitors, be it in the form of subsidies, tariff, or non-tariff protection, or domestic regulation. It has therefore been suggested that decisions on state intervention in the economy should take into account the rents that might be generated, the private resources devoted to obtaining them, and the incentive provided to waste further resources in attempts to obtain similar benefits (rather than invest them for more widely beneficial productive purposes).[22]

---

[20] Cf. G. Bletschacher and H. Klodt, *Strategische Handels- und Industriepolitik: Theoretische Grundlagen, Branchenanalysen und wettbewerbspolitische Implikationen*, Kieler Studien No. 244 (Tübingen, 1992). Strategic trade theory thus presents governments pursuing free trade with a prisoners' dilemma. Monopolkommission, above, n. 18, pp. 382ff.

[21] Krugman and Obstfeld, above, n. 12, ch. 9: 'The Political Economy of Trade Policy'.

[22] With these arguments, strategic trade theory has been countered by the theories of public choice and rent seeking. Cf. Curzon-Price above, n. 10, pp. 164ff.

The fourth category of arguments is based on two further insights from strategic trade theory. The first of these is that in some markets conditions of imperfect competition lead to monopoly rents (profits in excess of marginal cost), due to high barriers to entry, for example, the level of investments required, or to the advanced state of development of the technology involved. In such cases, government subsidies[23] may lend credibility to market entry, thereby stimulating international competition in the market concerned. In this way, strategic trade policy would target sectors subject to imperfect competition, aiming at the excess profits available there. In this way, if successful, profit would be shifted to the domestic firm, thereby increasing national welfare at a cost to general welfare (assuming at least that the resulting profits would exceed the cost of the subsidy required). The problem in this case is not only that of information (and of distortions in the rest of the economy) but also that of possible retaliation, which can have destructive consequences reaching far beyond the sector originally targeted.[24]

Second, strategic trade theory has also shown that it is in theory possible to devise 'optimal tariffs', which would allow the increase of the welfare of a nation at the expense of its trading partners, and therefore be preferable to free trade. In industries characterised by important economies of scale and learning effects, import tariffs will help domestic firms to gain foreign market share as a result of cost and learning advantages obtained in their protected home markets.[25] However, it has been pointed out that these arguments for strategic trade policy are valid only for countries where the size of the domestic market is large enough to exploit such economics of scale and learning effects. Although this size may be reached by the United States, Japan, and the internal market as a whole, in most industries this is not the case for the individual Member States of the Community.[26] Again, public choice and rent-seeking theories explain how tariffs tend to be taken hostage by particular national interest groups at a cost to domestic welfare as well as foreign producers. Finally, the argument about the threat of retaliation regarding subsidies applies to tariffs as well.[27]

In so far as the four categories of arguments given here have not been rejected outright, they are of limited use in guiding public policy, and often more effective policies exist. For example, where market failures involving public goods or externalities have been identified, the generally accepted argument is that these should be addressed as directly as possible, rather than through the use of strategic trade or industrial policy instruments. This can take the shape of removing domestic legal and institutional constraints, such as result for example

---

[23] R&D subsidies, production subsidies, or export promotion. Monopolkommission, above, n. 18, p. 379.

[24] De Grauwe, 'Economic Policy and Political Democracy', (1989) 3 *European Affairs* 66, p. 67.

[25] The entry into the aerospace market by the European Airbus consortium is often given as an example.

[26] De Grauwe, above, n. 24, p. 68.   [27] ibid.

in labour market rigidities and illiquid capital markets.[28] In most cases industrial policy will form a second best solution, unless it addresses the market failure directly.

This discussion has been limited to the main economic reasons for active industrial policy, based on standard arguments. However, there are not only other economic arguments for active industrial policy (such as improving the balance of payments or protecting employment), but many non-economic ones as well. Examples of non-economic reasons for industrial policy measures range from regional development, as well as national military and economic security, to income redistribution. Here again, the observation applies that from an economic point of view the most direct means of addressing such issues are assumed to be the most effective.[29] In many cases this need not involve active industrial policy measures. For political reasons however, active industrial policy measures are sometimes preferred to 'first best' solutions which may have distributional effects or a degree of visibility that makes them impracticable: sound economic theory may make bad politics. However, the result is that active industrial policies which go beyond the limited theoretical case impose (often hidden) additional costs, and therefore have adverse redistributive effects. Hence, although there is a generally accepted limited theoretical case for industrial policy, it is difficult to translate into practice.

C. Industrial Policy at the Community Level

For the Community, the general arguments given above are not exhaustive. Usually, industrial policy is advocated in terms of improving national comparative advantage, or facilitating national structural adjustment in the context of a global economic competition, not merely between companies, but between nation states. Likewise, the case for a Community industrial policy is often argued in terms of the dangers of lagging European competitiveness compared with the United States and Japan.[30] Yet although it is probably necessary to accept the case for an active national industrial policy in order to accept the case for a European one, this does not mean that the arguments overlap completely.

Regarding the EC level, there are additional legal, economic, and political reasons for industrial policy related to the process of economic integration to be considered, as well as specific problems of legitimacy and multi-level government. The legal and economic arguments are standard ones. The political reasons can be linked to the hypothesis that the constitutionalisation of industrial policy is connected to economic and monetary union.

[28] K. Stegemann, 'Wirtschaftspolitische Rivalität zwischen Industriestaaten: Neue Erkenntnisse durch Modelle strategischer Handelspolitik?', in M. E. Streit (ed.), *Wirtschaftspolitik zwischen ökonomischer und politischer Rationalität. Festschrift für Herbert Giersch* (Wiesbaden, 1988).

[29] Curzon-Price, above, n. 10, pp. 163–164.

[30] Cf. Philips spokesman W. Grünsteidl, 'An industrial policy for Europe', (1990) 4 *European Affairs* 14.

From the perspective of Community law the removal of barriers to the four freedoms forms a constitutional obligation to engage in passive general measures of industrial policy. Similarly, the principles, objectives and instruments of the economic constitution provide a framework for economic policy which over time has developed to provide a basis not only for passive industrial policy, but increasingly also for active measures. Hence, with the progressive expansion of the objectives and the instruments of the Community (to include establishing the internal market, an economic and monetary union, and implementing an increasing range of common policies or activities), the legal basis for industrial policy has expanded. In terms of industrial policy, the enforcement of the four freedoms has been supplemented by harmonisation of rules and the co-ordination of active policies, such as the promotion of R&D. By the same token, the margins for industrial policy at the national level have been reduced by the strict application of the four freedoms and the competition rules of the Treaty. This process of constitutionalisation of industrial policy at the European level in tandem with the restriction of autonomous national industrial policies has followed both economic and political logic.

Economic reasons for a Community industrial policy are provided by the general arguments in favour of establishing an internal market (efficiency benefits in terms of scale, competition, and mobility).[31] Given the objective of market integration, there are two areas where a European industrial policy may be warranted on economic grounds. The first concerns trade barriers. Where national and economic (efficient) markets do not coincide, and national barriers to trade impede the free movement of goods and services within the Community there is a case for a passive industrial policy, aimed at removing these barriers. This involves liberalisation and harmonisation. Although the primary objective will be the removal of market distortions (which have often been created by national industrial policies) the harmonisation of legislation also involves establishing common standards implicitly or explicitly expressing positive public policy goals. Harmonisation therefore bridges the categories of passive and active industrial policy. Second, the co-ordination of policies and the introduction of common policies at the European level may be required where externalities and other forms of market failure occur. The most important example is the competition policy of the EC.

For another example, active measures of industrial policy are clearly involved in Community support for R&D. Where the latter concerns general support for

---

[31] More precisely: (1) enhanced efficiency in production due to increased specialization in accordance with comparative advantage; (2) increased production levels due to better exploitation of economies of scale in an increased market; (3) an improved international bargaining position leading to better terms of trade; (4) enhanced efficiency by increased competition; (5) changes in volume and quality of factors of production due to technological changes; (6) increased factor mobility. El-Agraa, *The Economics of the European Community* (3rd ed., New York, 1990) ch. 4, 'The Theory of Economic Integration', p. 79; Cf. W. Molle, *The Economics of European Integration: Theory, Practice, Policy* (Aldershot, 1990) ch. 2, 'Fundamental Concepts'.

R&D based on the externalities argument, this means addressing a case of market failure. Based on the arguments of strategic trade, strategic industries could be identified and targeted at the Community level (leading to active sectoral industrial policy). The case for European intervention based on these arguments is a good one, since the desired scale and learning effects are more likely to be achieved in the Community as a whole than within the individual Member States.

With progress toward economic and monetary union, the emphasis of industrial policy will shift from market integration by removing trade barriers to policy co-ordination in the pursuit of wider social and economic goals. The economic reason for this is that the effectiveness of the co-ordination of macro-economic policies (crucial to economic and monetary union) can be improved by simultaneous co-ordination of structural measures. Under the EC Treaty, the constitutional context is that provided by the objectives of stable growth and employment, and the principles to which the policies concerned are subject.[32] The co-ordination involved may range from reforming the regulatory framework in order to facilitate competition and business restructuring, to market creation, infrastructural investments, and the promotion of the development and diffusion of high technology.

The political reasons for the emergence of the industrial policy of the Community are closely linked to these economic arguments. Economists remain divided on the actual benefits of economic integration, and the question whether the various stages which have been identified follow a necessary sequence.[33] Yet it is widely accepted that, although economic arguments are commonly used to promote economic integration, political motives are ultimately decisive, and that '(E)conomic integration favours integration in other areas for political motives'.[34] In the area of industrial policy the progress of negative integration appears to have led to a perceived need for positive integration.[35] Thus, as

[32] Notably the principle of an open market economy with free competition, favouring an efficient allocation of resources; and the principles of stable prices, sound public finances and monetary conditions, and a sustainable balance of payments. Articles 3a, 102a and 105 EC.

[33] The exact measure of these benefits has been contested, starting from the observation that trade diversion as well as trade creation occur, in J. Viner, *The Customs Union Issue* (New York, 1950). For an overview of the debate see El-Agraa, above, n. 31, ch. 4. Seven stages of economic integration, ranging from a free trade area to full economic union were first identified in B. Balassa, *The Theory of Economic Integration* (New York, 1961).

[34] Molle, above, n. 31, p. 29.

[35] Whereas negative integration mainly concerns the allocative function (aimed at the efficient use of resources), positive integration involves decisions on the stabilisation and redistributive functions of government. The latter are aimed respectively at such objectives as high growth rates, price stability and full employment, to be achieved primarily using macro-economic and monetary policy instruments, and at income redistribution where the market mechanism fails to achieve an equitable outcome. Achieving a balance between the three functions requires political decisions as well. This now standard distinction between the three functions of government was pioneered in R. A. Musgrave and P. Musgrave, *Public Finance in Theory and Practice* (Auckland, 1985). It has been applied to the Community in Padoa Schioppa *et al*, *Efficiency, Stability and Equity: A Strategy for the Evolution of the Economic System of the European Community* (Oxford, 1987). In this report priority was given to evaluating the efficiency and stabilisation functions, and their interplay, in the context of the 1992 programme and the EMS.

European integration evolved from a customs union to a common market and economic and monetary union, general measures of passive industrial policy have generated a perceived need for active general measures, and sometimes for active sectoral measures as well. In turn, this has resulted in the progressive constitutionalisation of the measures involved.

There are two ways of explaining this process.[36] First, it could be that in order to consolidate negative integration, positive integration had to follow as active measures of industrial policy were necessary to make the earlier passive measures fully effective. Second, positive integration may have followed in order to compensate for the reduction of national economic policy instruments by negative integration. Under the second explanation, introducing active industrial policy at the Community level was an attempt to reassert a measure of political control in the wider context of a progressive transfer of decision making powers on economic policy to the Community. Evidently these two explanations do not necessarily contradict each other, although they remain to be tested on the basis of the historical evidence. Thus, the first hypothesis, which stated that the new industrial policy title of the EC Treaty must be seen in the context of the move toward economic and monetary union, can be based more firmly on general considerations which arise from the theory of economic integration.

Although they cannot be developed in detail here, it should be noted that apart from providing additional reasons for industrial policy, the context of European integration also raises problems related to multi-level policy making.[37] The first of these problems is that of identifying the appropriate level of intervention. This level should be determined according to the effectiveness criterion of the principle of subsidiarity. Accordingly, the co-ordination of local and national industrial policies may be the most important task to be exercised at the Community level.[38] Second, there is the problem of joint decision making, which poses additional constraints on the types of problems that can hope to be resolved.[39] Under these circumstances, the principle of subsidiarity can become a barrier to policy formulation. The third problem is that of the

---

[36] These explanations are based on the predictions offered by Pinder, above, n. 14, (writing in 1968) with regard to positive and negative integration. For a more general discussion of the consequences of the mismatch between economic factors and the administrative control of the nation state, and the results of attempts to reassert control through international co-operation and supranational institutions see S. Cassese, 'Oltre lo Stato: i limiti dei governi nazionali nel controllo dell'economia', in F. Galgano, S. Cassese, G. Tremonti and T. Treu, *Nazioni senza Ricchezza, Ricchezze senza Nazioni* (Bologna, 1993).

[37] Cf. recently F. W. Scharpf, 'Community and Autonomy: Multi-Level Policy-Making in the European Union', (1994) 1 *Journal of European Public Policy* 219.

[38] Thus: 'as one moves up the policy hierarchy from local to national policy and then to supranational policy, the appropriate policy stance must shift from policy design to policy coordination to reflect the comparative advantages of policy makers at each level'. Geroski, 'European Industrial Policy and Industrial Policy in Europe', (1989) 5 *Oxford Review of Economic Policy* 20, p. 29.

[39] Cf. J. J. H. Weiler, 'The Community System: The Dual Character of Supranationalism', (1982) 1 YEL 267; F. W. Scharpf, 'The Joint-Decision Trap: Lessons From German Federalism and European Integration', (1988) 66 *Public Administration* 239.

legitimacy of public policy at the Community level.[40] Here the dilemma is that, while the Treaty obligations on negative integration progressively limit the scope of national industrial policy, the Community may lack the necessary democratic legitimacy for similar redistributive measures. Given the specific reasons for an industrial policy at the Community level, and the problems of multi-level policy making, such a Community policy will not replicate prior national industrial policies. It is likely to be more limited in its ambitions, and to use different instruments, in particular regulation, programmatic proposals, and co-ordination of initiatives by other (public and private) actors.

III. THE SEARCH FOR CONSENSUS ON INDUSTRIAL POLICY: 1957–1990

A. Industrial Policy under the EEC Treaty before the Single European Act

In contrast to the ECSC and Euratom Treaties, the original EEC Treaty did not provide the instruments for active sectoral industrial policies.[41] The reason why a common industrial policy was not included in the Rome Treaty has not been clearly established.[42] It has been suggested that the state aid rules of Articles 92–94 EEC were considered adequate to deal with the distortions which resulted from the industrial policies of the Member States.[43] According to the Ordoliberal

---

[40] Cf. J. J. H. Weiler, 'Problems of Legitimacy in Post 1992 Europe', (1991) 46 *Aussenwirtschaft* 411, p. 421; E.-J. Mestmäcker, 'On the Legitimacy of European Law', (1994) 58 *Rabelszeitschrift* 615; H. Von der Groeben, *Legitimationsprobleme der Europäischen Gemeinschaft* (Baden-Baden, 1987).

[41] Thus, the ECSC Treaty provides for guided investment to promote production and modernisation (Articles 3d and 9); supported by the obligation to notify the High Authority of investment plans (Articles 46, 54), its participation in joint planning of investments (Article 46), or financial participation (Articles 54, 56). Further, the High Authority may intervene by means of production quota (Article 58), maximum and minimum prices (Article 61), and import quota (Article 74). The Euratom Treaty provided for the promotion of investment (Article 2c), facilitation of co-operation among undertakings (Article 40), and for the founding of common undertakings (Articles 45–51). Cf. R. Hellman, 'Industriepolitik', in H. Von der Groeben, J. Thiesing and C.-D. Ehlermann (eds.), *Kommentar zum EWG-Vertrag*, Vol. 4 (4th ed., Baden-Baden, 1991), p. 6274. For an exhaustive overview of the scope and organisation of industrial policy under the EEC Treaty prior to the SEA see D. Vaughan (ed.), *Law of the European Communities*, Vol. 1 (4th ed., London, 1986), paras. 6.01–6.85.

[42] The European Community was set up first of all as a common market protected by common external tariffs. The harmonisation of laws, the control of state aids and the competition rules were to guarantee free competition in an open market. This does not mean that the Community was limited to negative integration. Common agricultural, transport, social, fiscal and commercial policies were provided for in the EC Treaty, to provide for a common approach in sectors where state intervention made it necessary to resolve the resulting distortions of trade at the Community level. Yet, in spite of the fact that interventionist sectoral industrial policies prevailed in the Member States, no common industrial policy was provided for.

[43] Curzon-Price, 'Competition and industrial policies with an emphasis on industrial policy', in El-Agraa (ed.), *The Economics of the European Community* (3rd, ed., New York, 1990), pp. 167–168.

interpretation, industrial policy was omitted since it was incompatible with the liberal economic constitution. Alternatively, it has been suggested that at the time the EEC Treaty was negotiated the contracting parties simply did not anticipate the issues of industrial policy which might arise beyond their intermediate goal of establishing a Customs Union.[44]

In fact, discussion of industrial policy at the Community level was not documented before the mid-1960s. During this period the degree of interpenetration of the economies of the Member States was still relatively low, economic growth was high and consistent, and state interventionism was rarely questioned. The Member States pursued active national industrial policies, involving subsidies, protectionist public procurement policies and a variety of other non-tariff trade barriers. Against the background of reconstruction and persistent growth, national industrial policies may not have been considered problematic, nor an active industrial policy at the Community level necessary. This remains to be explored by economic historians. Meanwhile, the general observation that the Member States have only surrendered competence where necessary to support domestic policy choices suggests that diffuse reasons rather than a principled decision may explain why a formal competence on (active) industrial policy was originally withheld from the Community.[45]

Although from at least 1970 onward the Commission of the EC has tried to obtain such powers, a considerable lapse of time occurred before the first firm foothold for active industrial policy was introduced in the Rome Treaty by the Single European Act of 1987. Four phases can be identified in the Community approach to industrial policy between the conclusion of the EEC Treaty and the Single Act.[46] These are, first, a period between 1958 and the mid-1960s, when the belief prevailed that competition in the newly integrated market would be adequate to foster industrial restructuring; a second period, between the mid-1960s and mid-1970s, when the creation of industrial structures of European dimensions, and a Community-wide home market were (ineffectively) promoted; a third period, until the early 1980s, when the Community approach was defensive (aimed at restructuring in crisis sectors); and a fourth phase, leading up to the Single Act, when the promotion of high technology industries became a priority. Although this periodisation does indicate general trends, the actual picture is more complex, especially if the distinction between active and passive measures of industrial policy is kept in mind.

During the first ten year period following the conclusion of the EEC Treaty, the focus of integration was on establishing the customs union. Hence, the industrial policy of the EC was limited solely to passive measures. By the late

---

[44] Hellman, above, n. 41.

[45] Cf. A. S. Milward, *The European Rescue of the Nation-State* (2nd ed., London, 1994).

[46] V. Lauber, 'The Political Economy of Industrial Policy in Western Europe', in S. A. Shull and J. E. Cohen (eds.), *Economics and Politics of Industrial Policy: The United States and Western Europe* (Boulder, 1986), pp. 28ff.

1960s however, it had become clear that the customs union and free trade area would not form a true home market for European industry. Moreover, worries about the lagging competitiveness of European firms, in particular in relation to United States multinationals spurred interest in a more active approach to industrial policy at the Community level.[47]

During the second stage of the emergence of a European industrial policy, these concerns slowly translated into concrete proposals for Community action, which remained, however, largely unimplemented. Initially, most of the Commission's activity concerning industry was limited to requesting, collecting and processing sector-specific data, and making suggestions directly to industrial organisations. On that basis, The Committee for Medium-term Economic Policy identified a need for co-ordinated action to allow industry to attain the maximum benefits from the expanding market.[48] This concerned especially the restructuring of enterprises in terms of size (aimed at realising economies of scale) and the promotion of technological development.[49] In this context Community efforts were to promote both the creation of European firms large enough to compete with the largest United States companies, and of a home market of comparable size necessary to sustain them.[50]

In anticipation of a more active stance, with the merger of the Commission for the EEC and Euratom with the High Authority in 1967, a Commissioner was charged with responsibility for a new industrial policy DG III, and a Commission working group on the subject was created.[51] In 1969 the Commission

---

[47] The beginnings of a push for a coherent industrial policy for the European Communities may be dated back even further, to the work begun on medium-term economic policy planning in 1963 under Article 104 EEC. From the outset, the Commission attempted to use the ideas formulated in the medium-term economic policy programmes 'to work out more explicit guidelines concerning the development of and changes in industrial sectors'. Commission of the EEC, *Third General Report on the Activities of the Communities 1969* (Brussels, 1970), p. 190.

[48] Council Decision of 15 April 1964 setting up a Medium-term Economic Policy Committee ((1964) OJ L64/1031). The Committee did not begin operations until 1966. H. Von der Groeben, *The European Community: The Formative Years. The Struggle to Establish the Common Market and the Political Union (1958–66)* European Perspectives Series (Brussels-Luxembourg, 1985), pp. 121–213.

[49] R. Toulemon, *Report No. 1: Stage Reached in Work on Industrial Policy in the Community*, Conference 'Industry and Society in the European Community' (EEC Commission, Venice, 1972). The recommendations of the Committee reflected the national industrial policies of the time, which 'sought to exploit the link between size and competitiveness which was widely believed to exist'. These national policies mainly promoted horizontal mergers at the national level, but were still believed inadequate to capture the perceived economies of scale.

[50] Cf. P. A. Geroski and A. Jacquemin, 'Industrial Change, Barriers to Mobility and European Industrial Policy', in A. Jacquemin and A. Sapir (eds.), *The European Internal Market: Trade and Competition—Selected Readings* (Oxford, 1989); E. De Ghellinck, 'European industrial policy against the background of the Single European Act', in P. Coffey (ed.), *Main Economic Areas of the EEC—Towards 1992* (Deventer, 1988).

[51] Questions were raised regarding the legal basis for the authority with which the Commission had invested itself, and were answered (then, as at present), that the former did not sanction more than a loose form of co-ordination of pre-existing powers. Cf. U. Everling, 'Rechtsfragen einer Industriepolitik im gemeinsamen Markt', (1968) 3 EuR 175.

decided to prepare a structural analysis of Community industry for the Council, at the initiative of Italian Commissioner Colonna di Palliano and in response to demands from the European Parliament. The ensuing Memorandum (*Colonna Report*) on industrial policy was presented to the Council in March 1970.[52] The *Colonna Report* contained basic guidelines and qualitative socioeconomic goals for European industrial policy, as well as an extensive analysis of the situation of European industry, and formed a programmatic statement for the newly created DG III. It was accompanied by studies commissioned by the French, German and Italian governments.

In the *Colonna Report*, the main factors determining industrial development in the EC were held to be not industrial policy, but general economic policy: regulating supply and demand, co-ordinating economic policies and establishing monetary union. Nevertheless, a Community industrial policy was held indispensable to achieve three central objectives: the establishment of firm foundations for the economic and political unity of Europe, the maintenance of economic growth, and a reasonable degree of technological independence from the United States.[53] Instead of providing a definition of industrial policy, the *Colonna Report* proposed that the latter should be understood in terms of these three objectives. The industrial policy approach of the Community was to be forward looking, and support market-led structural adjustment both by means of an active commercial and competition policy, and by promoting new technologies and infrastructure.

The basic guidelines of the *Colonna Report* emphasised liberalisation and measures to facilitate the creation of European multinationals. The Commission stressed first, that the main aim was completing the customs and economic union; second, that many problems would remain under national or regional responsibility (and that it did not aim to redistribute economic growth); and third, that growth industries and industries in difficulties in particular, should be targeted.[54]

---

[52] COM(70) 100, La Politique Industrielle de la Communauté: Memorandum de la Commission au Conseil. The first part of this document ('principles') was reprinted as 'The Community's Industrial Policy: Commission Memorandum to the Council', *Bull EC* Supplement 4/70.

[53] ibid., p. 4.

[54] The five qualitative objectives were the following: (1) improvements in the conditions and dignity of labour; (2) increased worker participation; (3) harmonisation of education (and mutual recognition of diplomas); (4) increased environmental protection; and (5) a more equitable global distribution of wealth. 'The Community's Industrial Policy: Commission Memorandum to the Council', *Bull EC* Supplement, pp. 7ff. These socio-economic goals required more positive measures of integration than provided by the five basic guidelines. Little progress has been made on the former, whereas the latter were essentially covered by further market liberalisation and the 1992 program.

The five basic guidelines: (1) completion of the single market (the removal of technical barriers to trade and liberalisation of public procurement); (2) unification of the legal, fiscal and financial framework (adoption of a European Company Statute; proposal of a European economic interest grouping; reducing barriers to multinational mergers and further harmonisation of VAT, excise and direct taxes; the creation of a common capital market); (3) restructuring of firms (promotion of transnational mergers to attain economies of scale in high technology); (4) measures to organise change or adaptation related to industrial restructuring; and (5) extension of Community solidarity in economic relations with third countries. ibid., pp. 12ff.

With this, the basic agenda for a Community industrial policy for the 1970s had been set.[55]

The Council's reaction to the *Colonna Report* (which was described by one well-placed observer as the 'equivalent of the Mansholt Plan for agriculture')[56] was largely a positive one. The Council listed its own priorities accordingly, and assigned them for further study to a working group composed of senior civil servants reporting to the Coreper.[57] To provide a forum for wider discussion, the new Industry Commissioner Spinelli organised a Conference, with tripartite and expert representation on the theme of Industry and Society in the EC, in Venice in 1972. Finally, at the October 1972 Paris Summit (otherwise devoted to the first enlargement of the EEC) the European Council recognised the need 'to try and provide a uniform basis for industry throughout the Community',[58] and suggested that the necessary measures could be based on Article 235 EEC.

In response, the Commission presented a new Memorandum on the technological and industrial policy programme in 1973.[59] This Memorandum set five priorities, calling for:

  (i) the removal of barriers to trade;
 (ii) the progressive and effective opening-up of public and semi-public contracts;
(iii) promoting competition between companies at the European level;
 (iv) special measures regarding both high technology and industries facing crisis conditions;
  (v) the co-ordination of the industrial policy with the other objectives of the Community.

[55] The qualitative socio-economic objectives have aged less gracefully: 'To reconcile industry and society means first liberating the industrial worker from the evil spells still binding him; not only material squalor, which is still with us, but the moral poverty bred by monotonous jobs, the ever-faster rhythm, conveyor-belt work, the inconveniences of transport, the harmful effects of city life and above all the lack of standing. This means providing work for men near their birthplace and where their forefathers lived. Europe must not turn into a Far West of rootless people nor a melting pot drowning national and regional characteristics'. 'The Community's Industrial Policy' *Bull EC* Supplement, p. 31.

[56] Commission president Hallstein: 'ein Gegenstück zum Mansholt-Plan für die Landwirtschaft'. W. Hallstein, *Die Europäische Gemeinschaft* (4th ed., Düsseldorf, 1973), p. 192.

[57] These priorities were: (1) the realisation of the common market in certain sectors of advanced technology and capital goods; (2) the promotion of industrial progress and technological development; (3) measures facilitating trans-national industrial regrouping; (4) technological co-operation with third countries; (5) finding a common approach to foreign direct investment; (6) facilitating collaboration between undertakings; (7) the territorial aspects of industrial policy; (8) co-ordination and rationalisation of Community funds for economic development; (9) the role of public enterprises in the industrial policy of the EC. Toulemon, above, n. 49, pp. 3–4. Cf. *Law of the European Communities*, above, n. 41, para. 6.01.

[58] *Bull EC* 5-1973, para. 1101. At the time developing a Community industrial policy was seen as an enticement for British entry into the Community.

[59] SEC(73) 3824, Action Programme in the Field of Industrial and Technology Policy; (sometimes identified as the '*Spinelli Report*') published as 'Towards the establishment of a European Industrial Base', *Bull EC* Supplement 7/73.

On the basis of declaration by the 1972 Paris European Council and the new Commission Memorandum, the Council finally adopted a resolution on an action plan on industrial policy in December 1973. This action plan formed a combination of liberalisation, harmonisation and export support measures.[60]

The industrial policy proposals of this period can be divided into two parts. The first part concerns measures of negative integration (passive industrial policy), aimed at completing the internal market. Many of these were to reappear in the 1992 programme. The separation of national markets was to be countered not only by liberalisation measures, including the opening of public procurement (for which even the use of Commission directives under Article 90 EEC was proposed), but by creating an appropriate fiscal and legal framework stimulating co-operation between undertakings across borders (including the adoption of a merger regulation). The second part of the industrial policy proposals was formed by flanking measures of positive integration (active industrial policy), in particular in the areas of social, regional, environmental and R&D policy.[61] Apart from general measures, this involved specific proposals concerning the high-technology and crisis sectors which were to form the concentration points of positive action: aeronautics, data-processing, heavy mechanical and electrical plants, uranium enrichment, shipbuilding, textiles and paper.[62] Again, many of these policies were taken up by the 1992 programme and the Single Act.

It should thus be noted that even at this stage, Community industrial policy should not be equated with interventionism. Rather, the proposals aimed at completing the internal market and promoting industry were conceived as a whole, or, perhaps more accurately, they were packaged jointly in a programmatic manner in an attempt to focus and accelerate the process of European integration. Thus, the widespread perception that the performance of European firms was flagging in relation to their United States competitors was used by the Commission to persuade the Member States of the potential benefits of common action, with an emphasis on liberalisation. The problems of European industry were to be resolved primarily by completing, and moving beyond, the common market, in a manner not dissimilar to the 1992 programme.

---

[60] Council Resolution of 17 December 1973 on industrial policy ((1973) OJ C117/1). Listed as priorities for Community action were: (1) the abolition of technical barriers to trade in foodstuffs and industrial products; (2) the gradual and effective liberalisation of public contracts; (3) the abolition of fiscal barriers to closer relations between undertakings; and (4) of legal barriers to closer relations between undertakings; (5) European promotion of competitive advanced technology undertakings (aeronautics and data processing); (6) the conversion and modernisation of certain sectors of industry (shipyards and the paper sector); (7) the preparation of measures to guarantee that concentrations affecting undertakings established in the Community are in keeping with Community economic and social objectives, and the maintenance of fair competition both in the Common Market and on outside markets in accordance with the provisions of the treaties (control of concentrations); (8) measures concerning exports (in particular credit insurance); and concerning (9) supplies of raw materials, in particular of non-ferrous metals.

[61] Cf. Supplements 1/73 to 8/73, *Bull EC*.   [62] *Bull EC* 5-1973, para. 1105.

Three points, which still surface in the discussion of industrial policy today, should be stressed in particular. First, already in the 1970s integration toward economic and monetary union was sketched as the general context of the industrial policy proposals: 'La création d'une assise industrielle européenne constitue l'un des aspects essentiels de la réalisation de l'Union économique et monétaire'.[63] The internal market was to be the basis of the industrial policy of the Community: 'Cette assise industrielle européenne est fondée sur l'existence d'un marché unique fonctionnant comme un marché intérieur dans lequel les personnes, les biens, les services, les capitaux et les sociétés circulent sans entraves'.[64] Second, even at this early stage the complementarity of the competition and industrial policies of the EEC was stressed:

La politique industrielle et la politique de la concurrence poursuivies par la Commission sont étroitement complémentaires. En effet, le renforcement de la lutte contre les cartels et les efforts entrepris pour réprimer les abus de position sont le complément indispensable des encouragements que la Communauté doit donner au rapprochement des entreprises à travers les frontières. Les deux visent à augmenter l'éfficacité de l'industrie communautaire par l'amélioration de ses structures et le maintien d'une situation de concurrence.[65]

Third, the active or sectoral dimension of industrial policy at the Community level was not conceived as an exercise in central planning:

. . . la politique industrielle de la Communauté ne peut et ne doit pas être conçue comme une politique unitaire gerée par les institutions communautaires. Elle est et continuera à être en large partie fondée sur la libre initiative des entreprises, sur des accords librement conclus entre organismes syndicaux et professionels, sur les programmes poursuivis par les autorités publiques, régionales et nationales.[66]

It is evident that the Community industrial policy of the 1970s struck a tone which was decidedly more liberal than the practice of the Member States at that time. The Commission's proposals formed a package which emphasised the elements that were to re-emerge at the core of the internal market programme. Also, these proposals were not drafted in obscurity: they clearly formed an exercise in agenda setting, and an attempt to unite the Member States behind a common project designed to promote further integration as such. Thus, by 1973 a relatively liberal industrial policy seemed to have moved to the centre of the Community agenda. Instead however, it fell victim to controversy over the division of tasks and powers between the Community and the Member States, and no significant follow-up measures were taken. The industrial policy committee which had been under discussion since 1970 was not created, and many of the concrete steps that had been planned (such as a merger regulation) were not

[63] *Bull EC*, Supplement 7/73, para. 1.　　[64] ibid., para. 2.
[65] *Bull EC*, Supplement 7/73, para. 29.　　[66] ibid., para. 8.

implemented.[67] As a result, the industrial policy of the Community moved into its third, defensive phase. During this period, progress was made in co-ordinating national restructuring efforts in certain industrial sectors, as Community industrial policy now concentrated 'on the task of simultaneously encouraging the restructuring of traditional manufacturing sectors and cushioning the impact of that process'.[68] But it would take almost two decades before a new consensus on industrial policy concerns was arrived at.

How can the failure to establish a lasting consensus as a basis for action in the 1970s be explained? There are two sets of explanations. The first centres on the general reasons for the stagnation of integration. Although the two are related, the second is more specific to industrial policy.

Given that the bulk of the industrial policy proposals actually concerned completing the internal market, at a general level the reasons for failure were identical to those responsible for the widely documented 'Eurosclerosis' which affected the Community roughly between the first oil-shock and the Commission's 1985 White Paper.[69] As the economic crises of the 1970s eroded the consensus, industrial interests turned to national governments for support. In response, interventionist national industrial policies intensified, and the Member States resorted to a variety of measures, including controls on wages, prices, credit, and imports as well as the 'wholesale direct subsidization of loss-making industries'.[70] The re-introduction of (non-tariff) barriers threatened the common market, but compliance with the Community rules on competition and state aids was not monitored effectively, and at least initially the actions of the Member States were hardly questioned by the Commission.

Moreover, when national interests diverged, European integration hit the doldrums, and the constraints on the decision making process of the Community (notably the unanimity requirement imposed by the Luxembourg Accord) rendered the latter unworkable. The failure of the traditional harmonisation process under Article 100 EEC (aiming at Community-wide uniform legislation) to remove such barriers under conditions of unanimity voting, has been widely documented as a result of the institutional shortcomings of the Community.[71] Enlargement and the budgetary conflict complicated these institutional problems. It is clear that the industrial policy programme of the Community (which

[67] An exception was formed by the liberalisation of public procurement: Council Directive 71/305/EEC concerning the coordination of procedures for the award of public works contracts ((1971) OJ L185/5); and Council Directive 77/62/EEC coordinating procedures for the award of public supply contracts ((1977) OJ L13/1).

[68] F. McGowan, 'EC Industrial Policy', in A. M. El-Agraa (ed.), *The Economics of the European Community* (4th ed., London, 1994), p. 197.

[69] Cf. A. Schout, *The Institutional Framework for Industrial Development: New Directions for a European Industrial Policy* (Maastricht, 1990).

[70] Curzon-Price, above, n. 43, p. 169.

[71] Cf. Scharpf, 'Community and Autonomy: Multi-Level Policy-Making in the European Union', (1994) 1 *Journal of European Public Policy* 219; 'The Joint-Decision Trap: Lessons From German Federalism and European Integration', (1988) 66 *Public Administration* 239.

was entirely based on Articles 100 and 235 EEC) was doomed to fare poorly under these circumstances.

More specific explanations point to constitutional problems, conflicting interests and ideologies between the Member States, the fear of supra-nationality (especially among the larger Member States), and insufficient resources.[72] The constitutional problem was that of the absence of a firm legal basis in the Treaty. Conflicts of interest occurred since the national structures of the Member States varied widely in relation to firm size, capital intensity, and profitability between sectors. Conflicting ideologies found their extremes in Germany (and later the United Kingdom) which took a pro-market stance on European integration, versus France which promoted state intervention.[73] The problem of supranationalism occurred where the Member States were reluctant to cede authority to the Community given the lack of a clearly identifiable 'Community interest' commensurate with the national interest. Finally, the limited resources of the Community did not allow active policies based on financial transfers, whereas the principle of *juste retour* obstructed policies that would have had redistributive effects.

Taking these factors together, the failure of Community industrial policy in the 1970s can be explained by the negative interaction between divergent national interests and unfavourable institutional conditions. At a time of economic crisis, national solutions were considered more effective or preferable to a common approach, and as a result, both positive and negative integration suffered. The lack of a joint long-term perspective effectively foreclosed co-operative solutions, and therefore the political and constitutional hurdles were not tackled.[74]

B. R&D Co-operation and Industrial Policy under the Single European Act

The fourth period of industrial policy prior to the Single European Act saw a change of focus to the promotion of high technology. Technology policy is

---

[72] Lauber, above, n. 46, pp. 41ff. A. Dumont, 'Technology, Competitiveness and Cooperation in Europe', in M. S. Steinberg (ed.), *The Technical Challenges and Opportunities of a United Europe* (London, 1990); A. Jacquemin, 'European Industrial Policies and Competition', in P. Coffey (ed.), *Economic Policies of the Common Market* (London, 1979), pp. 37ff.

[73] A related but less credible explanation is that suspicions of structural policy aspirations inspired by 'dirigisme' kept the Member States from allowing the development of a common industrial policy. The industrial policies proposed by the Commission in the 1970s were not more interventionist than those which were habitually practised by the Member States. Further, through unanimous decision making in the Council and comitology structures, the Member States kept tight control over political decision making and implementing rules alike. Quite to the contrary Commission's proposals seem to have been resisted primarily since they required further liberalisation.

[74] An exception was provided by the Commission's management of the European steel crisis, but with the ECSC Treaty steel (where the European dimension of the industry was recognised immediately after the Second World War) had from the outset been the major exception regarding industrial policy. Cf. Y. Mény, V. Wright and M. Rhodes (eds.), *The Politics of Steel: Western Europe and the Steel Industry in the Crisis Years (1974–1984)* (Berlin, 1987).

generally considered to form a central element of an active industrial policy.[75] The general argument for government involvement in R&D is that of market failure, as the result of the limited appropriability of research results.[76] The arguments for Community involvement in R&D go beyond the externalities which apply also at the national level. By improving the co-ordination of national programmes, the Community can help to avoid the waste associated with the duplication of research. A Community-wide basis can provide additional economies of scale and learning. Further, the joint development of core technologies may lead to spill-over effects, and can benefit European producers by the development of common standards, which may be exported. Finally, it has been observed that a European industrial policy will make it easier to identify 'European' firms than it previously was to identify 'national' ones. The Community R&D policy could therefore in theory hope to appropriate results more successfully.

As with active industrial policy in general, the EEC Treaty (in contrast to the ECSC and Euratom Treaties) did not provide for Community action on R&D, and the early efforts of the Commission to develop a common approach remained fruitless.[77] The present technology policy of the EC has its roots in the late 1970s and early 1980s, when large European companies turned away from national technology strategies to support market opening and Community R&D efforts. By the mid-1980s the Member States agreed to shift significant resources from national to Community projects, and with the Single European Act of 1987 the EEC received a formal competence for research and technological development. R&D policy currently forms the most developed element of active Community industrial policy.

From the early 1950s onward, worries over a technological gap between Europe and the United States led to repeated proposals for a 'European Technological Community', and the EC made several false starts in this direction. In 1965 the Community's Medium Term Economic Policy Committee set up a committee to study scientific and technical research policy, which was charged with proposing measures for a co-ordinated Community policy on R&D. As had happened with Industry DG III, after the merger of the ECSC, Euratom and

---

[75] Hence, it has been observed that industrial policy in the Treaty on European Union was an innovation only in so far as it exceeded the R&D competences introduced by the SEA. Cf. W. Möschel, 'Hoheitliche Maßnahmen und die Wettbewerbsvorschriften des Gemeinschaftsrechts', in *Weiterentwicklung der Europäischen Gemeinschaften und der Marktwirtschaft. Referate des XXV. FIW-Symposions* (Cologne, 1992), p. 89.

[76] Market failure justifies a range of policies towards technology, including public subsidies for basic research, the promotion of common technical standards, the dissemination of information to small firms, competition and regulatory policies, and promoting the (international) protection of intellectual property rights. Cf. Sharp and Pavitt, 'Technology Policy in the 1990s: Old Trends and New Realities', (1993) 31 JCMS 129, pp. 131–132.

[77] The Euratom Treaty includes wide-ranging provisions on R&D, while the ECSC Treaty provides a firm basis in Article 55. The EEC Treaty only dealt with research related to agriculture in its Article 41, in a cursory manner.

EEC in 1967, the Commission installed a directorate general for science and research and development (DG XII) to explore closer co-operation in core technologies. A first meeting of the Council of science ministers took place that year.

The early R&D initiatives of the Community formed an integrated part of the industrial policy proposals discussed above, as is made clear by the 1973 Council Resolution on the Commission's action plan on industrial and technological policy.[78] The results of these R&D initiatives were meagre.[79] Most productive has been the relatively low-profile COST programme (Coopération européenne dans le domaine de la Recherche Scientifique et Technique), which was established in 1971. COST provided financing on a national basis, and involved all European OECD members, but did not pursue projects in core technologies. The first enlargement of the EC provided a certain stimulus for Community R&D as well, and after the creation of the Comité de la Recherche Scientifique et Technologique (CREST)[80] in 1974 a general R&D policy seemed to be developing on the basis of Article 235 EEC. However, with the exception of the nuclear research co-ordinated under the Euratom Treaty (which also can at best be characterised as a qualified success), most large scale technological co-operation between the Member States took place outside the Community framework. This included projects such as Concorde, Airbus, and the European Space Agency.[81] Thus, the first twenty years of the EC showed little progress on R&D co-operation.

This changed when, by the early 1980s, the focus of leading industrialists shifted from a national orientation to one aimed at the European Community. Within a few years a series of new initiatives (ESPRIT, the Framework programmes and EUREKA) were launched, and an R&D Title was included by the Single Act. The information technology (IT) or microelectronics industry provides a good example to illustrate these developments. Concerns about the technology gap between the United States and Western Europe intensified in the 1960s, fuelled especially by the advances of the American computer industry.[82] In the 1960s and 1970s, most European governments embarked upon costly efforts to create national champions in semiconductors and computers. Apart from research subsidies and the protectionist public procurement policies of national PTTs, the Member States used standard setting to favour domestic

---

[78] Council Resolution of 17 December 1973, above, n. 60.

[79] 'Objectives and Instruments of a Common Policy for Scientific Research and Technological Development', *Bull EC* Supplement 6/72.

[80] Council Resolution of 14 January 1974 ((1974) OJ C 7/2).

[81] M. Sharp, 'The Single Market and European Technology Policies', in C. Freeman, M. Sharp and W. Walker (eds.), *Technology and the Future of Europe: Global Competition and the Environment in the 1990s* (London, 1991).

[82] C. Servan-Schreiber, *Le Défi Americain* (Paris, 1967); C. Layton, *European Advanced Technology: A Programme for Integration* (London, 1969); S. Nora and A. Minc, *l'Informatisation de la Société* (Paris, 1978). The latter triggered the French *Plan télématique* and inspired COM(79) 650, European Society Faced with the Challenge of New Information Technology: A Community Response.

producers, and stimulated mergers among national electronics companies to create the desired economies of scale.[83]

European efforts in this area were not taken up seriously, and the national governments preferred to act autonomously to maximise their freedom of action: in fact the national champion strategies were mutually exclusive. Also, since United States undertakings were more advanced in information technology, they were often found more attractive partners for collaboration than European ones.[84] For example Unidata, an attempt to organise a collaborative venture in computer production analogous to the Airbus project, collapsed three years after its founding in 1972, when the French government decided to pursue a national strategy based on a trans-Atlantic alliance between national champion CIT and Honeywell-Bull instead (Groupe Bull).[85]

Although during the 1970s the level of public support of industry in Europe was at least as high as in the United States, and in most cases significantly higher than in Japan, by the end of the decade the technology gap between European firms and their American and Japanese counterparts was largely perceived to have widened. There are several reasons why public expenditure on national champions in Europe was unproductive. Most Member States chose to focus on the same industries, thereby reducing their chance of success, while overlapping national research efforts wasted R&D resources. Different standards and other non tariff barriers foreclosed the realisation of a common market, which in turn made it impossible for European firms to attain the economies of scale to which they aspired. Protectionist public procurement policies further reduced firms' competitiveness while perpetuating market segmentation.[86] Finally, the nurturing of national champions in captive markets occurred at the expense of smaller firms, reducing competition, productivity and innovation.

---

[83] It is estimated that France spent FFR 640 million on its first *plan calcul*, launched in 1966, FFR 1400 million on its third *plan calcul*, which ended in 1980, and over FFR 1000 million on two microelectronics support programmes aimed at the semiconductor industry. The three electronic data processing programmes of the German Federal Republic, spent DM 387 million, DM 2.41 billion and DM 1.58 billion respectively, between 1967 and 1979. The German semiconductor industry is thought to have absorbed DM 800 million between 1974 and 1983. Britain pursued similar programmes, but on comparatively meagre budgets. W. Sandholtz, 'ESPRIT and the politics of international collective action', (1992) 30 JCMS 1, pp. 6–7.

[84] By the early 1980s the fact that only a quarter of the agreements between high-tech industries took place between EC-based partners gave rise to concern among European policy makers. Cf. L. K. Mytelka and M. Delapierre, 'The Alliance Strategies of European Firms in the Information Technology Industry and the Role of ESPRIT', (1987) 24 JCMS 231. For a discussion of the logic of the firms' behaviour cf. R. Van Tulder and G. Junne, *European Multinationals in Core Technologies* (Chichester, 1988); A. F. P. Wassenberg, 'Games within Games: On the Politics of Association and Dissociation in European Industrial Policy-Making', in B. Marin (ed.), *Governance and Generalized Exchange: Self-Organizing Policy Networks in Action* (Boulder, 1990).

[85] Unidata was a collaborative venture between Siemens, Philips and CIT, independent of the EC.

[86] Van Tulder and Junne, above, n. 84, p. 211. They cite three counterproductive effects of close relationships between national governments and domestic producers: (1) denying economies of scale; (2) decreasing the incentive to develop a competitive design; and (3) delaying product innovation due to long time lapses before development costs are recovered in small markets.

By 1980, when the potential for co-operation at the national level had largely
been exhausted, yet the international competitiveness of European firms remained
in doubt, the ground had been prepared for a European approach.[87]

This was the context for the efforts of Industry Commissioner Davignon
and the 'roundtable' of leading industrialists that he brought together in 1979.
After initially having directed his efforts towards the co-ordination of restructuring in traditional industries such as steel and shipbuilding, Davignon set
out to create a framework for discussions with leaders of European industry
on improving competitiveness in growth sectors, especially information technology. In particular, a core of European IT firms which already maintained close
contacts was encouraged to meet and co-ordinate R&D plans. The resulting
'Big 12 Round Table', which was formed in 1981–1982, developed the principles for the ESPRIT programme, and promoted its adoption by the Member
States:[88] '(T)hus, the Commission helped engineer an industrial consensus for
new collaborative schemes, was supported by industry in urging the transfer
of authority over technology policy to the EC level, and was ultimately able
to convince governments to launch the Esprit programme in 1983'.[89] The roundtable, which bypassed both established European interest groups and other communication channels, became a driving force behind (and prime beneficiary of)
not only the Community's R&D programme, but also its 1992 programme as
a whole.[90]

[87] R. Van Tulder and G. Junne, n. 84 above, p. 212. 'It was not until 1980 that the Community
was able to take a strategic view of science and technology'. K.-H. Narjes, 'Europe's Technological
Challenge: A View From the European Commission', (1988) 15 *Science and Public Policy* 395,
p. 396.

[88] This group consisted of Bull, CIT-Alcatel (CGE) and Thomson from France, AEG, Nixdorf
and Siemens form Germany, GEC, ICL and Plessey from the United Kingdom, Olivetti and STET
(IRI) from Italy, and Philips from the Netherlands.

[89] J. Peterson, 'Technology Policy in Europe: Explaining the Framework Programme and Eureka
in Theory and Practice', (1991) 29 JCMS 269, p. 276. The influence of the large information technology firms (through membership of the 'IT task force', which took primary responsibility for
distributional decision-making within ESPRIT) on shaping ESPRIT and their subsequent locking
in of the benefits from the programme, was striking. More than 80 per cent of all ESPRIT contracts in its first pilot phase of 1983 was awarded to firms represented on the round table and the
IT task force. ibid., p. 277; Cf. Mytelka and Delapierre, above, n. 84, p. 245.

[90] The Big 12 Round Table was followed by the creation of the G17 Round Table of European
Industrialists (with an overlapping membership), which lobbied the governments of the Member
States in favour of the 1992 programme. These round tables are at the centre of networks of indus-
trialists on which the Community has since drawn regularly in order to devise industrial strategies.
Cf. M. Green, 'The Politics of Big Business in the Single Market Program', Paper presented to the
European Community Studies Association Third Biennial Conference, May 27, 1993, Washington
DC. The 'trigger events' that led to involvement of big business have been identified as: (1) 'anti-
MNC legislation' at the EC level as proposed by industry Commissioner Altiero Spinelli, and the
Vredeling proposal (the 5th Company directive on work councils); and (2) the economic recession
that struck in the 1970s. Sharp has identified the 1983 deregulation of AT&T and the growing
intensity of competition from Japanese firms (notably the setting up of production facilities for semi-
conductors within the EC) as the crucial events for information technology. M. Sharp, 'Changing
Industrial Structures in Western Europe', in D. Dyker (ed.), *The European Economy* (London,
1992), p. 250.

ESPRIT established general principles of pre-competitive collaborative research for the Community. This was to involve industrial partners from separate Member States, obliged to match Community funding, with research projects proposed by the applicants within broad areas and priorities established by the Commission, and subject to management and close monitoring by it.[91] This formed the model for a series of initiatives.[92] A pilot phase in 1983–1984 was followed by ESPRIT I (1984–1988),[93] which was subsumed under the First Framework Programme for Community R&D policy (including similar programmes for a range of industries such as telecommunications and biotechnology), running from 1987 to 1991 and followed by a series of similar five year programmes.[94] In 1985, the EUREKA programme was launched on a proposal from the French President Mitterand to counter the American Strategic Defense Initiative (which, it was feared, threatened to lure away leading European scientists).[95] Finally, by 1987, technology policy was included as Title VI (Articles 130a–130q EEC) in the Rome Treaty by the Single European Act.[96] This formed the legal basis for the subsequent Framework Programmes.

The introduction of Title VI EEC (XV EC) by the Single Act is often seen as the first introduction of a common industrial policy in the Treaty.[97] This is confirmed by Article 130f(1) EEC, which stated that 'The Community's aim shall be to strengthen the scientific and technological bases of Community industry and *to encourage it to become more competitive at international level*'.[98] In the first place the Community aimed to encourage the co-operation between undertakings (including SMEs, research centres and universities) in their R&D activities, notably by completing the internal market in regard to the liberalisation of public procurement, standardisation, and the removal

[91] Sharp, above, n. 81, p. 69.
[92] Cf. COM(85) 84, Strengthening the Technological Base to Restore the Community's Competitiveness; and COM(85) 530, Towards a European Technology Community.
[93] ((1984) OJ L67/64).
[94] Council Decision 87/516 ((1987) OJ L302/1), as amended by Council Decision 88/193 ((1988) OJ L89/35).
[95] In 1983, the French President proposed a 'European Technological Community'. At the national level, France had launched a series of plans aimed at developing the *filière électronique* as the core of its industrial strategy. For a discussion linking the French and European R&D strategies cf. M. Richonnier, 'Europe's Decline is not Irreversible', (1984) 22 JCMS 227. EUREKA, which is open to all European countries, operates under much looser rules than the Framework programmes, and is funded by the participating states on a project by project basis. In general, EUREKA projects are closer to the market than those of the EC framework programmes.
[96] Cf. J. Elizalde, 'Legal Aspects of Community Policy on Research and Technological Development', (1992) 29 CMLR 309.
[97] Hellmann, 'Industriepolitik', in H. von der Groeben, J. Thiesing and C.-D. Ehlermann (eds.), *Kommentar zum EWG-Vertrag*, Vol. 4 (4th ed., Baden-Baden, 1991). p. 6270.
[98] Cf. Narjes, above, n. 87 (emphasis added). The Treaty on European Union widened the objectives of Community R&D policy beyond industrial policy. Article 130f (1) EC now also requires the promotion of all the research activities deemed necessary by virtue of other chapters of the Treaty. Also, in the second Delors Commission from 1989 onward, R&D policy was (for the first time) administered separately from industrial policy.

of legal and fiscal barriers to co-operation. Article 130f(3) EEC emphasised: '. . . the connection between the common research and technological development effort, the establishment of the internal market and the implementation of common policies, particularly as regards competition and trade'.[99] Hereby, the R&D policy of the Community was firmly grounded in the internal market programme.

Further, Articles 130g and 130h EEC made clear that the activities of the Community were to be complementary to those carried out by the Member States, and to be co-ordinated jointly. Thus, the activities of the Community are subsidiary to those of both private industry and the Member States. This is the main constitutional dimension of the approach to R&D policy taken in the Single Act.[100] Articles 130i to 130q EEC set out rules for the operation of Community activities under multi-annual framework programmes. These framework programmes define scientific and technological objectives, broad guidelines for the R&D activities of the Community, and fix the rules for the financial participation of the latter for a period of four years. Under Article 130i *juncto* Article 130q(1) EEC, the framework programmes were to be adopted in council by unanimity after consultation of the European Parliament and the Economic and Social Committee. Specific programmes to implement the framework programme (and supplementary programmes involving only certain Member States under Article 130l EEC were subject to decision making by qualified majority vote under a co-operation procedure set out in Article 130q(2) EEC.[101] Actual projects were selected by the Commission, assisted by specialised advisory committees.[102] Projects operated on the basis of matching EEC funding, and had to involve partners from at least two Member States.

It is worth noting that the emergence of the Community R&D policy has been used to explain the 1992 project as a whole, triggering a new debate between the neo-functionalist and neo-realist schools of integration theory.[103]

[99] Replaced by the Treaty on European Union.

[100] Elizalde, above, n. 96, p. 314. This complementarity is demonstrated by the fact that 97 per cent of R&D in the Community is financed directly by the Member States, merely 3 per cent from the Community budget. ibid.

[101] Article 130q was repealed by the Treaty on European Union, which generally revised the R&D Title. Now, Article 130i EC provides for the use of the procedure of Article 189b EC (co-decision), with the specification that the Council shall act unanimously throughout this procedure (instead of by qualified majority vote as is normally the case). Interinstitutional conflict had arisen between Council and European Parliament, in particular regarding the budgetary provisions of Articles 130i, 130k and 130p EEC. Elizalde, above, n. 96, pp. 317ff. Article 130o EC now provides for a consultation procedure for decisions regarding the setting up of joint undertakings under Article 130n EC, and the use of the co-operation procedure regarding implementing rules and supplementary programmes. For a theoretical exposition on the problems around the R&D budget see H. Ward and G. Edwards, 'Chicken and Technology: The Politics of the European Community's Budget for Research and Development', (1990) 16 *Review of International Studies* 111.

[102] Elizalde, above, n. 96, pp. 324ff.

[103] Cf. the overview in J. Caporaso and J. Keeler, 'The EC and Regional Integration Theory', Plenary address at the Third Biennial International Conference of the European Community Studies Association 1993, pp. 26ff.

Neo-functionalists have suggested that the 1992 process was triggered by changes in the international economic structure, but that policy entrepreneurship by '(t)he Commission of the EC, aided by business, was able to mobilize a coalition of government elites that favoured the overall objective of market unification'.[104] In this view, the leadership of European multinational corporations forms a new and influential set of elite actors which shapes and promotes European integration. This applies in particular to the roundtable of European industrialists, which lobbied national governments and gave essential support to the Commission's initiatives: 'In short, the 1992 process is repeating the pattern established by ESPRIT; major businesses have allied with the Commission to persuade governments, which were already seeking to adapt to the changed international structure'.[105]

This view of the Single Act as an élite bargain has been criticised by the intergovernmentalist (realist) approach to European integration, which emphasises the role of domestic politics, lowest common denominator bargaining and strict limits on the transfer of sovereignty.[106] In response to this criticism, attempts have been made to account in greater detail for the role of business groups and multinationals in setting the agenda of the Community, and in shaping the interests of the Member States.[107] A third view has pointed to the importance of the development of policy networks spanning the public and private sectors, and the various levels of government.[108]

Although the thesis that business interests made a decisive contribution is contested regarding the Single Act as a whole, it is widely accepted that collaboration in R&D prior to the single market programme led to the R&D Title in the SEA and strengthened political momentum for the single market. It is important to note that the Single Act did not merely codify procedures which had already been established in practice, in close collaboration with participating

[104] W. Sandholtz and J. Zysman, '1992: Recasting the European Bargain', (1990) 42 *World Politics* 95, p. 96.

[105] ibid., pp. 117–118.

[106] Cf. A. Moravcsik, 'Negotiating the Single Act: National Interests and Conventional Statecraft in the European Community', (1991) 45 *International Organization* 19; and 'Preferences and Power in the European Community: A Liberal Intergovernmentalist Approach', (1993) 31 JCMS 473; M. A. Pollack, 'Creeping Competence: The Expanding Agenda of the European Community', (1994) 14 *Journal of Public Policy* 95.

[107] Green, above, n. 90, W. Sandholtz, 'Institutions and Collective Action: The New Telecommunications in Western Europe', (1993) 45 *World Politics* 242; W. Sandholtz, 'Choosing Union: Monetary Politics and Maastricht', (1993) 47 *International Organization* 1.

[108] Cf. P. Kenis and V. Schneider, 'Policy Networks and Policy Analysis. Scrutinizing a New Analytical Toolbox', in B. Marin and R. Mayntz (eds.), *Policy Networks: Empirical Evidence and Theoretical Considerations* (Frankfurt, 1991); Peterson, above, n. 89; V. Schneider, 'The Structure of Policy Networks: A Comparison of "Chemicals Control" and "Telecommunications Policy" in Germany', (1992) 21 *European Journal of Political Research* 109. A synthesis of the various approaches (the EC as a network; spill-over and supranationality; and the EC as based on intergovernmental bargains) is found in R. O. Keohane and S. Hoffmann, 'Institutional Change in Europe in the 1980s', in R. O. Keohane and S. Hoffmann (eds.), *The New European Community: Decision-Making and Institutional Change* (Boulder, 1991).

undertakings. It also provided a legal framework which facilitated establishing critical evaluation of the projects involved, and consequently reduced the influence of the largest firms which dominated the early initiatives.

The strategic and mission oriented approach of a select group of élite actors was thus followed by the slow grind of bureaucratic procedure, aimed at a much wider clientele. Although it has made the decision making processes involved longer and more burdensome, the proceduralisation of R&D policy has occurred to the benefit both of smaller undertakings and the Commission itself, which had gained a new policy competence while reducing its dependence on the big information technology firms.[109] Finally, the procedure for the selection of projects (which is a fraction of proposed projects) combines qualitative and political criteria: it has been claimed that instead of as traditional subsidies on demand the EC funds are distributed as premiums for excellence.[110] Consequently, although EC expenditure on R&D is minor in comparison to that by the Member States, the Community R&D policy has established collaborative networks of firms across national borders, and introduced new standards of public policy in this area.

C. Guidelines for Industrial Policy in an Open and Competitive Environment

The performance of the European economies in the 1970s was marked by slow economic growth, increasing unemployment and high inflation. Moreover, European industry seemed to be falling behind the United States and, increasingly, Japan.[111] This suggested that in Europe the process of structural adjustment to the economic and technological changes which were accelerating in a globalising economy was faltering. In response to the economic crisis, the Member States had relied initially on various traditional macroeconomic measures (such as exchange rate policies, credit and interest rate policy, and demand management by regulating public expenditure) without much success.[112] As a result, the Member States increasingly resorted to micro-economic measures instead, including various subsidies, encouragement of concentrations and R&D, and preferential public procurement. These measures were usually aimed at crisis sectors, and often contradictory. In fact, the economic distortions which resulted from these policies slowed rather than facilitated the adjustment process, as productive and private firms were burdened further in order to protect loss-making and public enterprises, and market barriers were erected.

---

[109] Peterson, above, n. 89. Cf. Elizalde, above, n. 96.   [110] Elizalde, above, n. 96, p. 333.

[111] Economic and Social Committee, 'Opinion on Industrial Change and Employment—A Review of the Community's industrial policy and Future Prospects' ((1977) OJ C292/16); Commission of the EEC, *The Competitiveness of European Community Industry* (Brussels, 1982).

[112] Cf. Commission of the EEC, *Report of the Study Group on Industrial Policies in the Community: State Intervention and Structural Adjustment* (Brussels, 1981), and the other studies cited there.

During this period the Commission was first of all involved in restructuring efforts in crisis sectors, such as steel. In addition, it collected information comparing approaches to structural adjustment in the Member States, and sought to formulate a role for the Community in this process. Commission studies done in the early 1980s found the role of the Community in facilitating structural adjustment to be that of reinforcing the single market, ensuring respect for the rules of the Treaty, providing a stable environment (in the context of the EMS), and promoting positive adjustment through R&D co-operation.[113] These priorities were ultimately addressed in the internal market programme, accompanied by stricter monitoring of the rules on competition and state aids.[114]

The R&D Title was accompanied by other Community legislation favourable to technological collaboration: the Commission adopted block exemptions for licensing agreements, franchising and R&D collaboration,[115] and in the same year the European Economic Interest Grouping was created. Regarding the industrial policy dimension of the 1992 programme in general, the most important point is that it covered the proposals which had originally formed part of the 1973 industrial policy guidelines in the areas of public procurement, standardisation, and fiscal harmonisation. The success of an internal market programme has been largely attributed to the consensus on its limited focus (Article 8a EEC), and the consequent agreement on important changes in decision making rules, as they are principally reflected in Articles 100a and 100b EEC, introduced by the Single Act.[116] Consequently, the 1992 programme and the Single Act achieved a large part of the proposals which were grouped as 'industrial policy' in the 1970s. With its combination of market opening measures and technology policy the Single Act established what has been called the 'twin track approach' of Community industrial policy, which balanced intervention and the promotion of competition.[117]

In this new co-operative setting, the Council requested the Commission to prepare proposals for a concerted approach to growth and employment, to

---

[113] Cf. COM(85) 84 and COM(85) 530, above, n. 92.

[114] Cf. COM(85) 310, *Completing the Internal Market*, White Paper.

[115] Commission Regulation 2349/84 on patent licensing agreements ((1984) OJ L219/15; corrigendum (1985) OJ l280/32; amended by Regulation 151/93, (1993) OJ Ll21/8); Commission Regulation 418/85 on R&D agreements ((1985) OJ L53/1); Commission Regulation 4087/88 on franchising ((1988) OJ L369/46); and Commission Regulation 556/89 on know-how licensing ((1989) OJ L61/1). Cf. Commission of the EEC, *Fifteenth Report on Competition Policy: 1985* (Brussels, 1986), pp. 11–12, and pp. 225–226; Monopolkommission, *Wettbewerbspolitik vor neuen Herausforderungen: Hauptgutachten 1988/89* (Baden-Baden, 1990) ch. VII: 'Kooperation in Forschung und Entwicklung'.

[116] Cf. G. A. Bermann, 'The Single European Act: A New Constitution for the Community?', (1989) 27 *Columbia Journal of Transnational Law* 528; R. Dehousse, '1992 and Beyond: The Institutional Dimension of the Internal Market Programme', (1989) 16 LIEI 109; C.-D. Ehlermann, 'The Internal Market Following the Single European Act', (1987) 24 CMLR 361; J. J. H. Weiler, 'The Transformation of Europe', 100 *Yale Law Journal* 2403.

[117] Sharp, above, n. 90, p. 251; Sharp, above, n. 91, p. 75.

complement the internal market programme.[118] In the closing days of 1989 the Commission produced an analysis on the state of Community industry and the consequent requirements for 'a Community approach' to industrial policy.[119] The aim of these Industrial Policy Guidelines was to make EC policies affecting the competitiveness of European industry more systematic and to provide the 'appropriate conceptual framework' which the debate on industrial policy in the Community had so far lacked. The central assumption underlying the Industrial Policy Guidelines was that, after years of debate on the necessity and form of industrial policy, consensus had been reached.[120] The theoretical basis of this consensus was that market allocation of resources could be corrected by state intervention, in particular in order to accelerate structural adjustment, improve industrial competitiveness, and establish a long-term technological framework:

The main question is not whether an industrial policy is opportune, as governments are increasingly recognized to have, in advanced economies, an important influence on industrial development and performance. On the contrary, the main issue is which conditions need to be present in order to strengthen the optimal allocation of resources by market forces, towards accelerating structural adjustment and towards improving industrial competitiveness and the industrial and particularly technological long term framework.[121]

The definition of industrial policy used was based on the concept of structural adjustment.[122] 'Behind the Community's approach, therefore, to industrial policy lies the will to promote the most efficient functioning of markets. A dynamic industrial policy concerns the effective and coherent implementation of all those policies which impinge on the structural adjustment of industry'.[123]

By this definition, the Community's approach covered both active and passive, general and sectoral policies, including competition policy. Structural adjustment in turn was understood as 'the process by which industry adapts on a permanent basis to signals provided by the market', which 'comprises the steady shifting of resources in reply to these signals to the most productive

---

[118] COM(85) 570, Annual Economic Report 1985–1986. Cf. Commission of the EEC, *Improving Competitiveness and Industrial Structures in the European Community* (Brussels, 1987).

[119] COM(90) 556, Industrial Policy in an Open and Competitive Environment: Guidelines for a Community Approach (hereafter 'Industrial Policy Guidelines'), with an Annex on 'European Industry in the 1990s' providing a comparison with industrial performance in the United States and Japan.

[120] On consensus as a necessary condition for an effective industrial policy see D. G. Mayes, 'European Industrial Policy', in M. Macmillen, D. G. Mayes and P. van Veen (eds.), *European Integration and Industry* (Tilburg, 1987).

[121] Industrial Policy Guidelines, above, n. 119, p. 1.

[122] Structural adjustment was placed on the economic policy agenda by the OECD in its comparative analyses of post-war economic developments. Cf. OECD, *Positive Adjustment Policies: Managing Structural Change* (Paris, 1983); OECD, *Structural Adjustment and Economic Performance* (Paris, 1987); OECD, *Economies in Transition: Structural Adjustment in OECD Countries* (Paris, 1989).

[123] Industrial Policy Guidelines, above, n. 119, pp. 5–6.

outlets'. Hence, '(T)hrough providing a home market of the requisite size and quality, the program to complete the internal market can be considered as industrial policy par excellence'.[124] The main responsibility for structural adjustment was to lie with the economic operators themselves. This pointed to a new and more restricted role for the state in the economy: 'The role of public authorities is above all as a catalyst and pathbreaker for innovation. The main responsibility for industrial competitiveness must lie with firms themselves, but they should be able to expect from public authorities clear and predictable conditions for their activities'.[125]

The new role for public authorities was based on a negative assessment of the experience of national industrial policy: '. . . the experience of the 1970s and 1980s has shown that sectoral policies of an interventionist type are not an effective instrument to promote structural adaptation. They have failed to make industry competitive by delaying the requirement to implement necessary adjustments, led to grave misallocation of resources and exacerbated problems of budgetary imbalances'.[126] These policy failures provided arguments both for the new market oriented approach presented by the Commission, and for the co-ordination of industrial policy. Apart from being more limited, state intervention in the economy was to be co-ordinated between the Member States, while respecting the principle of subsidiarity.[127]

The Industrial Policy Guidelines credited economic recovery after the crises of the 1970s to factors for which the Community had provided the framework: macroeconomic stabilisation, completion of the internal market, and substantial measures aimed at strengthening the economic and technological base. In line with this evaluation, the Community R&D effort was given as an example of the type of policy co-ordination between the public and the private sector, and between the various levels of government, which would be required to achieve a coherent and effective approach. The Community approach to industrial policy was to be primarily horizontal, to rely on the co-ordination of existing instruments and policies, and on market funding. Sectoral policies should henceforth aim to facilitate rather than delay adjustment. The three principal objectives of public policy were to maintain a favourable business environment; to implement a positive approach to adjustment; and an open approach to markets.[128]

Given these principles, the proposed concept of industrial policy was based on three key elements:

---

[124] ibid., p. 11.   [125] Industrial Policy Guidelines, above, n. 119, p. 1.
[126] ibid., p. 19.
[127] Earlier, the Commission had taken a more circumspect attitude in particular in regard to public undertakings, while however insisting that 'Where they are operating in competitive sectors, the authorities should not grant them special privileges that result in distorting competition'. COM(70) 100, above, n. 52, p. 11. Cf. Toulemon, *Report No. 1: Stage Reached in Work on Industrial Policy in the Community*, Conference 'Industry and Society in the European Community' (EEC Commission, Venice, 1972), p. 18.
[128] Industrial Policy Guidelines, above 119, p. 5.

   (i) stable long term conditions, including a competitive environment (vigil-
      ance on concentrations and close scrutiny of state aids), high standards of
      education and social cohesion, and a stable macro-economic environment;
  (ii) catalysts for structural adjustment, primarily the completion of the internal
      market (including the establishment of technical standards and the cre-
      ation of trans-European networks in education, energy, telecommunica-
      tions and transport), and an active trade policy;
 (iii) the development of the instruments to accelerate structural adjustment
      and enhance competitiveness, focused on the development of the tech-
      nological capacity of the Community and policy towards SMEs.

These policies were ordered systematically in a diagram, reproduced below.

STRUCTURAL ADJUSTMENT		
Prerequisites	**Catalysts**	**Accelerators**
Competition	Internal Market	R&D, Technology, Innovation
Economic Context		Training
Educational Attainment		Small and Medium Size Enterprises
Economic and Social Cohesion	Commercial Policy	Business Services
Environmental Protection		

*Table 2: The Variables affecting Structural Adjustment in the European
Community (Source: COM(90) 556, Industrial Policy in an Open and
Competitive Environment, 16.11.1990)*

    In its conclusions, the Commission summarised the Industrial Policy
Guidelines as follows: '. . . the concept that Community industrial policy should
promote is permanent change in an open and competitive market. It is based
on the principle of free trade and on the competitive functioning of markets
around long term industrial and technological perspectives'.[129] The emphasis
was thus on a horizontal approach, the creation of a general market environment which is in line with the principle of free competition in open markets
of Article 3a EC. The role of the state was to change from an active particip-
ant engaged in 'micro-management' to that of a 'catalyst', providing positive

---

[129] ibid., p. 21.

incentives for change within a stable environment. Finally, it should be stressed that this new 'dynamic' industrial policy required an active competition policy, as a precondition for structural adjustment.[130]

The Commission's analysis of the state of Community industry and its place in the global economy, and in particular its adoption of a market oriented approach based on linking existing powers and policies, earned wholehearted Council approval.[131] Accordingly, the Council requested further proposals while stressing the priority of the consistency and co-ordination of existing policies.[132] The reactions of the European Parliament and Economic and Social Committee were likewise positive, although they would have preferred a more active policy, with greater attention to regional disparities, and a reformulation of competition policy to include wider social and economic goals.[133] The European Parliament considered that '. . . the common industrial policy should be one of the main areas of European integration alongside Economic and Monetary Union'.[134] It concurred with the Economic and Social Council that industrial policy should be included in the Treaty on European Union (which was then under negotiation), and stated that this policy should be subjected to democratic control at the Community level.

Most commentators interpreted the Industrial Policy Guidelines as an apparent conversion of the Community to market oriented industrial policy.[135] Two qualifications of this apparent market orientation have been generally noted. First, the Industrial Policy Guidelines contain several subtexts, which have been seen

[130] Cf. 'Does Europe Need an Industrial Policy?', Speech by the Commissioner for Competition, Sir Leon Brittan, to the College of Europe, Bruges, 29 January 1991. For the Commission's exegesis of the Industrial Policy Guidelines cf. M. Bangemann, *Meeting the Global Challenge: Establishing a Successful European Industrial Policy* (London, 1992); M. Bangemann, 'Pour une politique industrielle européenne', (1992) 35 RdMC 367; A. Jacquemin and J.-F. Marchipont, 'De nouveaux enjeux pour la politique industrielle de la Communauté', (1992) 102 *Revue de l'Économie Politique* 69; J.-F. Marchipont, P. Ramadier and P. Vigier, 'Politique industrielle: Intérêt communautaire', (1992) 17 *L'Événement Européen* 19.

[131] *Bull EC* 11-1990, para. 1.3.110.

[132] ibid. The first examples of sector specific proposals (concerning electronics and information technology; industrial activities based on biotechnology) are found in 'European Industrial Policy for the 1990s', *Bull EC* Supplement 3/91.

[133] Economic and Social Committee, Opinion 92/C 40/15 on the Commission communication on industrial policy in an open and competitive environment ((1992) OJ C40/31); European Parliament Resolution of 11 July 1991 on the Commission comunication to the Council and European Parliament on industrial policy in an open and competitive environment—guidelines for a Community approach (COM(90) 556 final), A 3-0177/91 ((1991) OJ C240/213, 16.9.91). Cf. *Bull EC* 7/8-1991, para. 1.2.82.

[134] EP Resolution on COM(90) 556, ibid., para. 12.

[135] Cf. G. Bletschacher and H. Klodt, 'Braucht Europa eine neue Industriepolitik?', *Kiel Discussion Paper* No. 177 (Kiel, 1991); Ch.-P. Frees, 'Das neue industriepolitische Konzept der Europäischen Gemeinschaft, (1991) 26 EuR 281; C. Goybet, 'La CEE a-t-elle une politique industrielle?', (1991) 34 RdMC 753; M. Neumann, 'Industrial Policy and Competition Policy', (1990) 34 *European Economic Review* 562; Ph. Nicolaides, 'Industrial policy in the European Community: An assessment of the Bangemann Report', in CEPS, *The Annual Review of European Community Affairs* (Oxford, 1992); Ph. Nicolaides, 'EC industrial policy', (1992) 28 *European Trends* (Economist Intelligence Unit) 53.

both as reflecting the bargaining within the Commission, and as deliberate ambivalence aiming to appease liberal critics of sectoral industrial policy, while nevertheless creating a basis for Commission intervention in strategic sectors.[136] Second, it has been pointed out that although the Industrial Policy Guidelines confirm the predominance of general and passive policy, where the report deals with the Community as a global trading partner the double-edged nature of the internal market emerges. Criticism has focused on the protectionist tone struck in those parts of the document dealing with trade policy (stressing the need for reciprocity in trade relations with third countries), and analysing the perform-ance of Community industry relative to the United States and Japan.[137]

In fact, the new industrial policy seems less of a break with a past inter-ventionist attitude than is often assumed. Like the *Colonna Report* of 1970, the new industrial policy concept covers both active and passive, general and sectoral policies. As has been seen, the earlier industrial policy proposals were fairly liberal, and likewise gave priority to general passive measures, notably the completion of the internal market. Further, with the new industrial policy sectoral intervention has been sanctioned, albeit within the framework of an open market with free competition, much as had been proposed earlier. The main changes lie elsewhere. First, the new industrial policy is more coherent; second, the Member States (rather than the Commission) have changed their position on Community action in this field, apparently as the results of changes wrought by the internal market programme.

Some problems with the new approach are evident. First, the active co-operation of the Member States is required to make a subsidiarity-oriented approach workable, but it is not clear whether such co-operation will be forth-coming. Second, the new industrial policy concept does not make clear in which cases the Community is to be involved. The Community interest is not easily defined, and the static description provided in the Industrial Policy Guidelines is unsatisfactory.[138] Hence, the issue is avoided by assuming an identity of European interests as opposed to competitors in global markets.[139] However, a

---

[136] Cf. G. Ross, 'Sidling into Industrial Policy: Inside the European Commission', (1993) 11 *French Politics and Society* 20, p. 24. Cf. G. Ross, 'Inside the Delors Cabinet', (1994) 32 JCMS 499; G. Ross, *Jacques Delors and European Integration* (Cambridge, 1995).

[137] Nicolaides, above, n. 135, pp. 7ff. Hints of strategic targeting had been added: 'It is important (. . .) to avoid falling into the trap of considering certain industries as condemned to technological obsolescence and ripe for transfer overseas to lower cost sources of supply. However the generaliza-tion of technology as a source of competitive advantage implies that the control of key technologies such as advanced materials and electronics, information systems, integrated manufacturing sys-tems, life-science applications, which are important to a large number of industries, has become of crucial significance. This requires that excellence in core technologies be maintained'. Industrial Policy Guidelines, above, n. 119, Annex, p. 31.

[138] ' . . . only a competitive industry will allow the Community *to maintain its position in the world economy*, which *constitutes the essence of the Community interest*'. *Industrial Policy Guidelines*, above, n. 119, p. 2. (emphasis added).

[139] Or 'an active partnership between all interested parties (firms, social partners, scientific bodies, local, regional, national and Community authorities)'. ibid.

bias toward established industrial interests is unmistakable.[140] Much as this bias may be unavoidable, it raises doubts about the way the involvement of interested parties in Community policy making will be structured.

Third, where the Commission can in principle act independently, the question arises how it will establish priorities. Thus, the suggestion that competition could serve as an instrument of industrial policy is not without problems. The Industrial Policy Guidelines reflect a continuing preoccupation with scale, where they state the intention of the Commission to promote cross-border mergers, in the face of rising entry barriers at all levels (such as R&D costs and the size of minimum efficient operations), while eliminating national champions. They further propose the modification of the concept of the relevant geographical market to include the world market where necessary. The problem for competition policy will therefore be to establish a balance between the requirements of internal and external competition.

IV. INDUSTRIAL POLICY IN THE TREATY ON EUROPEAN UNION

A. Title XIII EC: Industry

With Title XIII (Article 130 EC) and Article 3(1) EC the Treaty on European Union introduced a formal Community competence on industrial policy into the EC. Title XIII can be seen as a codification of the 1990 Industrial Policy Guidelines which reasserted the open texture of the Treaty regarding economic policy.[141] Although the negotiation history of the industry title remains to be written, the basic elements are known.[142]

Neither the 1990 Rome European Council, which launched the two intergovernmental conferences, nor the draft treaty submitted by the Commission referred to industrial policy.[143] However, at the opening of the Intergovernmental Conference on political union in 1991, the Belgian delegation introduced a strongly interventionist proposal calling for the establishment of an industrial strategy linked to the common commercial policy. It aimed to promote the development of high-tech industry by guiding investments and temporary tariff measures. Although this project was defeated in substance, it placed industrial policy on the agenda, and the Luxembourg Presidency subsequently drafted a more restrained title on industry based on a French proposal.[144] Unlike

---

[140] For example, the Industrial Policy Guidelines state that 'it is particularly important that the representatives of industry be *fully consulted at the earliest possible stage*', while 'employees representatives must be given *sufficient opportunities to make comments*' (emphasis added). ibid., 19.

[141] Cf. C.-D. Ehlermann, 'The Contribution of EC Competition Policy to the Single Market', (1992) 29 CMLR 257, p. 273.

[142] Cf. Editorial, 'After the Maastricht Agreements—What Industrial Policy?', *Agence Europe* (four parts) Nos 5640–5643, 6–10 January 1992.

[143] 'Intergovernmental Conferences: Contributions by the Commission', *Bull EC* Supplement 2/91.

[144] *Europe Documents* No. 1722/23, 5 July 1991.

the Belgian proposal, this draft title stressed horizontal measures, rather than sectoral intervention, but it retained the possibility of the Council adopting specific measures by a qualified majority in co-operation with the European Parliament.[145] The text which was ultimately adopted was based on the Luxembourg draft. However, Industry Title XIII EC provides for decision making on specific measures by unanimity, with consultation of the European Parliament. Further, beyond affirming that measures aimed at enhancing the competitiveness for European industry would be 'in accordance with a system of open and competitive markets' a final caveat against anti-competitive measures was included in Article 130(3) EC.

Linked to the Industry Title is Article 3(l) EC, whereby the Treaty on European Union introduced the strengthening of the competitiveness of the European industry as one of the activities of the Community required for the pursuit of the objectives set out by Article 2 EC.[146] This placed the new Community responsibility on par with Article 3(g) EC on ensuring a system of undistorted competition. In the body of the Treaty, competitiveness policy was developed in Part III EC on Community policies, alongside those policies (free movement of goods, persons, services and capital, transport and agriculture) which were formerly ranked in Part II EEC as foundations of the Community. Aside from Title XIII, other new titles of relevance to industrial policy were VIII (Social Policy, Education, Vocational Training and Youth),[147] XII (Trans-European Networks), XIV (Economic and Social Cohesion) and XV (R&D). In these other titles, industrial policy objectives were of secondary importance. Here, the focus will be on Title XIII.

The central importance of Article 130 EC merits quoting it in full:

TITLE XIII: Industry—Article 130

1. The Community and the Member States shall ensure that the conditions necessary for the competitiveness of the Community's industry exist.

For that purpose, in accordance with a system of open and competitive markets, their action shall be aimed at:

---

[145] The text of this proposal is reproduced in Möschel, 'EG-Industriepolitik nach Maastricht', (1992) 43 *ORDO* 415, p. 417. The draft of the Treaty on European Union prepared by the Dutch Presidency likewise substantially followed the French text and included a co-operation procedure (Article 189c EC), although it also required the industrial policy to be 'in accordance with a system of open, competitive markets'. *Europe Documents* No. 1746/1747, 20 November 1991.

[146] Although Articles 3(l) and 130 EC mention strengthening (respectively enhancing) the competitiveness of industry, the term 'industrial policy' has been widely used in the discussion of these provisions. This general usage will be followed here.

[147] Among the aims of the European Social Fund stated in Article 123 EC is '... to render the employment of workers easier (. . .) and to *facilitate their adaptation to industrial changes and to changes in production systems* . . .'; and Article 127(2) EC states: 'Community action shall aim to:—*facilitate adaptation to industrial changes*, in particular through vocational training and retraining.' (emphasis added).

— speeding up the adjustment of industry to structural changes;
— encouraging an environment favourable to initiative and the development of undertakings throughout the Community, particularly small and medium-sized undertakings;
— encouraging an environment favourable to co-operation between undertakings;
— fostering better exploitation of the industrial potential of policies of innovation, research and technological development.

2. The Member States shall consult each other in liaison with the Commission and, where necessary, shall coordinate their action. The Commission may take any useful initiative to promote such coordination.

3. The Community shall contribute to achievement of the objectives set out in paragraph 1 through the policies and activities it pursues under other provisions of this Treaty. The Council, acting unanimously on a proposal from the Commission after consulting the European Parliament and the Economic and Social Committee, may decide on specific measures in support of action taken in the Member States to achieve the objectives set out in paragraph 1.

This Title shall not provide a basis for the introduction by the Commission of any measures which could lead to the distortion of competition.

The structure of the article is clear. Article 130(1) requires that the Community and the Member States ensure that the general conditions for the competitiveness of European industry exist, and lists four lines of action to this effect. The lines of action state the aims of promoting: (i) structural adjustment; (ii) an environment favourable to the development of undertakings, in particular SMEs; (iii) co-operation between them; and (iv) of improving the exploitation of R&D. The ways in which the general conditions for competitiveness are to be pursued are therefore of a general nature themselves. They aim at creating structural conditions for the competitiveness of industry rather than at enabling the authorisation of intervention in favour of specific regions, industries, or undertakings.[148]

Article 130(2) EC requires consultation between the Member States in their pursuit of these four lines of action, and their co-ordination where necessary. To promote such co-ordination the Commission may take initiatives, the nature of which is not limited in any way. Nor is it clear in which cases co-ordination may be deemed necessary. The Industrial Policy Guidelines suggested that this will be the case where a Community dimension (or the Community interest) is involved. Given that Article 130 EC establishes a concurrent competence, the principle of subsidiarity will come into play (as is further suggested by Article 130(3) EC).

---

[148] Although SMEs are mentioned specifically, these account for the vast majority of undertakings in the Community. Cf. N. Moussis, 'Small and Medium Enterprises in the Internal Market', (1992) 17 ELR 482.

Article 130(3) EC requires the Community itself to contribute to the industrial policy objectives set out in Article 130(1) EC, through the other activities and policies it pursues under the Treaty.[149] Under Article 130(3) EC the Council may further decide, by unanimity and upon a proposal by the Commission, measures in support of the actions taken by the Member States to achieve these objectives. The wish of the European Parliament for democratic control over industrial policy at the Community level was evidently ignored:[150] the European Parliament (and the Economic and Social Committee) need merely be consulted. There is no specification of the types of acts the Council may adopt. Therefore, it must be assumed that this provision covers the full range of legal instruments listed in Article 189 EC. The Council alone will therefore decide both on the need for Community action, and on the scope of the Community measures required. Since a concurrent competence is involved, it will have to apply the principle of subsidiarity.

The requirement in Article 130(1) EC that Community and Member States individually, or in a co-ordinated manner, act in accordance with a system of open and competitive markets, and the statement in Article 130(3) EC that the Community is barred from enacting supporting measures which lead to distorting competition, indicate that Article 130 EC seeks to reconcile two apparently contradictory objectives. One is promoting competitiveness, aimed at modifying market conditions, or industrial structures. The other seeks to guarantee respect of the system of free competition, or the market process, thereby limiting public intervention. Yet, neither the legal limits to the specific industrial policy actions of the Member States and the Community, nor the degree to which the Community can take industrial policy objectives into account in its pursuit of other policies are self-evident. Consequently, the inclusion of industrial policy in the Treaty is sometimes seen as a basic change in the economic constitution of the Community. For this reason, Article 130 EC has been the most contested individual provision of the Treaty on European Union (although not so much during the negotiations as after their conclusion), and proposals for its removal from the Treaty in the follow-up to the 1996 Intergovernmental Conference have been heard.[151]

---

[149] This obligation is repeated in the Treaty for cultural policy in Article 128(4) EC, for economic and social cohesion in Article 130b EC, and in Article 130r EC for environmental policy.

[150] EP Resolution on COM(90) 556, above, n. 133, paras. 52–54.

[151] Cf. the Scientific Advisory Council to the German Ministry of Economic Affairs in its report on the economic orientation to be pursued at the 1996 IGC, *Gutachten des Wissenschaftlichen Beirats beim Bundesministerium für Wirtschaft: Ordnungspolitische Orientierung für die Europäische Union*, Tübingen, 31 August 1994, pp. 38, 93. Strong criticism of the Industry Title appeared in newspaper articles by individual members of this body. Moreover, the *Wissenschaftliche Beirat* took the unusual step of itself publishing an open letter along similar lines in the *Neue Zürcher Zeitung* of 4 March 1992.

As its Ordoliberal critics have pointed out, Industry Title XIII EC can be interpreted in two diametrically opposed ways.[152] On the one hand it can be seen as part of a liberal trading system together with the four freedoms, the provisions regarding competition policy, state aids and public monopolies, and the system of undistorted competition. In this context, enhancing the competitiveness of European industry can be seen as merely an attempt to create the preconditions for this competitiveness, much as the completion of the internal market will enhance the competitiveness of European industry. Read in this sense, the guarantees of competition found in the first and the third paragraphs of Article 130 EC are to be interpreted restrictively, and to exclude anticompetitive measures aimed at industrial policy objectives in the pursuit of other policies under the Treaty. Control of industrial policy measures on competition grounds could be seen as guaranteed by the possibility for Member States and private parties to lodge complaints to this effect with the Commission. The unanimity requirement for Community measures can be seen as providing a further guarantee of liberal market policies.

On the other hand, the provisions of Article 130(3) EC in particular have led to the opposite interpretation. In the first place, it has been submitted that the unobjectionable supply side policies which would be pursued under the first interpretation would not require a separate title in the Treaty (or indeed be mentioned there at all). It has been noted that Article 130 EC does not explicitly exclude interventionism, and that the warnings in its first and third paragraphs do not impose strict limits on industrial policy either. In this view, the joint pursuit of industrial policy and other objectives by the Community could lead to a blurring of competences, and the abuse of instruments originally designed for the pursuit of different policy objectives. In particular, industrial policy objectives might take precedence in the implementation of Community competition policy. It is thought that this risk has increased now that the juxtaposition of Articles 3(g) and 3(l) EC appears to assign equal constitutional rank to competition and industrial policy. Finally, it has been submitted that the unanimity requirement of Article 130(3) EC need not be an insurmountable obstacle where 'package deals' can be found.[153]

The most jaundiced view of the Maastricht Treaty holds that it has established a 'rent-seeking Community', and sees Article 130 EC as 'the key to a whole network of possible interventions'.[154] Here, industrial policy is seen as

---

[152] *Gutachten des Wissenschaftlichen Beirats*, ibid., pp. 33–35; Möschel, 'Hoheitliche Maßnahmen und die Wettbewerbsvorschriften des Gemeinschaftsrechts', in *Weiterentwicklung der Europäischen Gemeinschaften und der Marktwirtschaft. Referate der XXV. FIW-Symposions* (Cologne, 1992), pp. 103–104; Möschel, above, n. 145.

[153] Möschel, above, n. 152, p. 104.

[154] M. E. Streit and W. Mussler, 'The Economic Constitution of the European Community: From "Rome" to "Maastricht"', (1995) 1 *European Law Journal* 5, pp. 22–23. Cf. the criticism by Ehlermann and Hancher in the same issue.

a 'constitutional cornerstone' of the Treaty on European Union, which forms the basis for the co-ordination of interventionist policies enabled by a much wider range of provisions, which would provide a range of financial and regulatory instruments. The network of Treaty provisions involved includes Title VII (Commercial Policy), Title VIII (Social Policy), Title XII (trans-European Networks), Titles XIV and XV (R&D and Cohesion), as well as Title V (Competition) and the merger regulation.

These Treaty provisions undeniably form the 'policy area' relevant to promoting the competitiveness of European industry. However, it is dubious whether the predictions of pervasive Community intervention based on this network of provisions around the 'linchpin' of Article 130 are realistic. Article 130 EC forms a weak co-ordinating instrument, and states only limited objectives. Moreover, Community action under Article 130 EC is limited by legal and political constraints.

The main legal constraints are imposed by the general principles of Community law, enforced by the European Court of Justice. Given the concurrent competence of the Member States and the Community spelled out in Article 130 EC, the principle of subsidiarity applies, and is in principle justiciable. Further, the principle of free competition is of particular importance. Normally, the application of this principle would take place in the context of the limited judicial review of the exercise of discretionary authority. In such cases, other policy objectives may override the principle of free competition, subject only to a loose proportionality test ('manifestly inappropriate' rather than 'least restrictive means'). It is clear from the text of Article 130(3) EC that in this case the test required will be a strict one: the scope of political discretion has been limited. Hence, the caveat of Article 130(3) EC provides an explicit basis for contesting Community measures of industrial policy on the ground that they 'could lead to a distortion of competition'. At least for this provision of the Treaty, the precedence of competition over competitiveness has been established.

The political constraints on Community action under Article 130 EC reflect the general institutional set-up of the Community, with a predominant role for the Council, agenda-setting by the Commission, and a weak position of the European Parliament. In this case, the political constraints include decision making by unanimity, the subsidiarity requirement, and the commitment to open markets with free competition (which is alluded to in Article 130(1) EC). Hence, industrial policy was cast in the mould of traditional intergovernmental decision making, controlled by the Member States.

However, especially given the changes in the legal and political framework after the Single Act and the Treaty on European Union, more complex outcomes may be expected: the institutional actors will be able to trade off between their positions of strength and weakness under the various provisions which can be used to promote industrial policy goals. Concerning harmonisation of legislation and R&D for example, the role of the European Parliament is stronger and the majority requirements in the Council are less stringent. Further, Parliament may be expected to exploit its budgetary and co-decision powers. The Commission can use leverage derived from its powers under the rules on competition and state aids to bolster its apparently weak position under the Industry Title. Although the position of the Commission under Article 130 EC itself is a weak one, it may be but a small step from surveillance of national industrial policy measures to their co-ordination. Here, Article 130(3) EC will come into play.

B. Growth, Competitiveness and Employment

So far, the Commission has attempted to formulate a co-ordinated approach to problems of structural adjustment in the form of (non-binding) communications, without explicitly resorting to Article 130 EC. These communications cover (i) general agenda setting efforts; (ii) horizontal problems;[155] and (iii) specific sectors.[156] Here, only the first category will be addressed.

The recent agenda setting proposals of the Commission show that it perceives industrial policy as central to the future of European integration, in particular in relation to employment and growth, which will be major political issues in the run-up to economic and monetary union. This first became evident in the Commission's programme for the year 1992, and the 'Delors II package' in which it set out its objectives for the five-year period following the internal market programme.[157] The general aim was to consolidate the 1992 programme, and to set the agenda for the post-Maastricht phase (soon rephrased as 'to overcome the crisis of confidence in the Community'). Market liberalisation was to be supplemented by positive measures of structural adjustment, to

[155] For example SEC(92) 1986, Industrial Competitiveness and protection of the Environment. Cf. Council Resolution 92/C331/03 concerning the Relationship between Industrial Competition and Environmental Protection ((1992) OJ C331/5); Council Resolution 92/C331/02 on Administrative Simplification for Enterprises, especially SMEs ((1992) OJ C331/3).

[156] Cf. for 1991–1993: SEC(91) 565, The European Electronic and Information Technology Industry: State of Play, Issues at Stake and Proposals for Action; SEC(91) 629, Promoting the Competitive Environment for the Industrial Activities Based on Biotechnology; COM(91) 339, Improving the Competitiveness of the Community's Textile and Clothing Industry; COM(92) 152, The Oil Market and the Refining Industry in the European Community; COM(92) 164, The European Aircraft Industry: First Assessment and Possible Community Actions; COM(92) 166, The European Motor Vehicle Industry Situation, Issues at Stake and Proposals for Action; COM(91) 476, Green Paper on the Development of the Internal Market for Postal Services; SEC(92) 1049, The European Telecommunications Equipment Industry: The State of Play, Issues at Stake and proposals for Action; COM(92) 480, Green paper: Pluralism and Media Concentration in the Internal Market. An Assessment of the Need for Community Action; COM(93) 91, Report on the State of the Shipbuilding Industry in the Community: Situation in 1991; COM(93) 159, Communication on the Consultation on the Review of the Situation in the Telecommunications Services Sector.

[157] COM(92) 2000, From the Single Act to Maastricht and Beyond: the Means to Match Our Ambitions; COM(92) 2001, The Community's Finances Between Now and 1997. Cf. *Bull EC* Supplement 1/92.

form the basis for the construction of an 'organized European space', which could sustain the European social model and reorient it toward the future.[158]

From the 'growth initiative' included in the 'Delors II package' onward, the Commission has consistently developed the themes of growth, competitiveness and employment.[159] These are to form the focus of the 'flanking measures' to economic and monetary union. In this context the objectives of competitiveness and the establishment of trans-European networks (TENs) under Title XII EC were presented as instrumental in bolstering the internal market, and competitiveness was to become 'a priority' for the Community between 1993 and 1997.[160] Apart from an investment stimulus, the TENs in transport, energy and communications will provide infrastructure to boost competitiveness and help to overcome physical market fragmentation. In order to fund the new Community actions, the Commission has proposed reform of the structure, the volume and the allocation of resources.[161]

At the 1992 Edinburgh Summit the European Council created new financial facilities (the 'Edinburgh facility' and the European Investment Fund) and agreed that the creation of TENs should be advanced in order to promote growth and employment.[162] At the subsequent Copenhagen European Council of June 1993, the idea of TENs was further developed, and the financial facilities were expanded. Commission President Delors (who in his speech to the Summit focused on 'competitiveness') made a commitment to provide a 'white paper' to set out a Community growth strategy. Immediately following the ratification of the Treaty on European Union in November 1993, the resulting White Paper on growth, competitiveness and employment was presented at the Brussels European Council.[163]

[158] Cf. Ross, above, n. 136 [1994]; Ross, above, n. 136, [1995] pp. 115ff.

[159] Commission communication on the implementation of the Community measures of the growth initiative ((1993) OJ C60/2); 'The Programme of the Commission in 1993–94', Address by Commission President Jacques Delors to the European Parliament, Straßbourg, 10 February 1993, *Bull EC* Supplement 1/93.

[160] TENs were introduced into European law by Title XII (Articles 129b–d EC), of the Treaty on European Union. Title XII provides for guidelines to identify projects of common interest eligible for Community funding, to be adopted under codecision with European Parliament and other measures (the identification of projects of common interest, and the possible Union support of financial efforts), to be adopted under co-operation procedures after consultation with the Economic and Social Committee and Committee of the Regions.

[161] The Commission proposed to create a new budget heading for 'internal policies of a horizontal nature' to improve competitiveness. This was to cover networks, transport, R&D and training. It was proposed to allocate an additional 3.5 billion ECU's for these purposes, bringing the total to 6.9 billion. The ceiling of the Community budget was to go from 1.2 per cent of GNP in 1992 to 1.37 per cent by 1997.

[162] Presidency Conclusions Edinburgh European Council, December 1992, *Bull EC* 12-1992. Annex 4 to part A, para. 1.30.

[163] COM(93) 700, Growth, Competitiveness, Employment: The Challenges and Ways forward into the 21st Century. White Paper (hereafter '1993 White Paper'); published as *Bull EC* Supplement 6/93—page references are to the latter.

In the line of the 'Delors II Package', the White Paper combined a programme to increase the financial muscle of the Community with an agenda for societal renewal.[164]

The primary objective of the 1993 White Paper is job creation: 'finding a new synthesis of the aims pursued by society (work as a factor of social integration, equality of opportunity) and the requirements of the economy (competitiveness and job creation).' At the heart of the unemployment problem is the fact that since the 1970s the potential growth rate of the European economy has been reduced from around 4 per cent to around 2.5 per cent a year. As a result, at the time the 1993 White Paper appeared, 17 million people were out of work.[165] The poor unemployment performance of the Community is explained by the constraints that unresolved distributional conflicts and insufficient structural adjustment have placed on macroeconomic policies. This has resulted in unsustainable levels of public expenditure (especially in the social field), and rising labour costs.[166]

The essential characteristic of the Community's approach to remedy this problem is that it seeks to align macroeconomic and structural policies.[167] The 1993 White Paper emphasises, first, the need to restore a stable macroeconomic framework, supporting market forces. This means that where trade-offs are made between increased growth and employment creation, economic stability is given priority over increasing employment.[168] Here the paper is consistent with the Article 103 EC Guidelines for the co-ordination of economic policy, the criteria for economic and monetary convergence, and indeed the

---

[164] 'From the Single Act to Maastricht and Beyond: the Means to Match Our Ambitions', *Bull EC* Supplement 1/92. This effort was thus also related to the Edinburgh and Copenhagen growth initiatives. At Edinburgh a new mechanism was created for EIB loans for investment in infrastructure or SMEs. The first 5 billion ECU loan was made to the *Bundespost*, end March 1993.

[165] 1993 White Paper, above, n. 163, p. 9. The sources of unemployment in Europe are cyclical, structural, and technological. Cyclical unemployment gives relatively little cause for concern. More serious is structural employment, explained by an unfavourable international division of labour (where the EU must now compete with the new industrial countries of South East Asia in the more traditional economic sectors, and lags behind the United States and Japan in high technology and advanced production techniques), the high cost of unskilled labour, and the fact that labour markets have ceased to function effectively. Added to this is the impact of technology, which under such circumstances favours replacing labour by capital investment. ibid., pp. 10–11.

[166] 1993 White Paper, above, n. 163, p. 42.   [167] ibid., pp. 48ff.

[168] Thus, the 1993 White Paper recommends aiming at high growth (at around 3 per cent) and a modest employment intensity, rather than an alternative strategy combining modest growth with high employment creation. The White Paper therefore recommends that 'the Community set itself the objective of creating at least 15 million new jobs, thereby halving the present rate of unemployment by the year 2000'. Of these 15 million jobs, 5 million must be created to avoid a further increase in unemployment rates, since labour supply will grow. *Ceteris paribus*, unemployment numbers would rise from the current 17 million to 20 million by the year 2000. The remaining 10 million jobs created would halve the current 11 per cent rate to 5 or 6 per cent (with 10 million unemployed remaining).

requirements set out in Articles 3a, 102a and 105(1) EC.[169] Second, the White Paper recommends structural actions to increase industrial competitiveness and to remove the rigidities (or domestic distortions) of the European economy. In order to underline the importance of structural adjustment, and avoid connotations of centralised interventionism, industrial policy is recast as 'competitiveness policy'.[170]

Third, the 1993 White Paper promotes the adoption of '. . . active policies and structural changes in the labour market'.[171] Yet although the White Paper calls for far-reaching changes in employment policy, it also affirms the basic soundness of the European social model.[172] Market failures are to be remedied through 'collective solidarity mechanisms', under the understanding that 'growth is not in itself the solution to unemployment'.[173] Hence, promoting the competitiveness of European industry serves the purpose of making comparatively high social costs affordable by increasing productivity.[174]

In accordance with the 1990 Industrial Policy Guidelines, the efforts to improve the competitiveness of European industry are to be compliance with competition rules, and focused on completing the internal market. Five lines of actions are proposed:

   (i) the co-ordination of laws and establishing an adequate regulatory framework to maximise the effects of the single market;

  (ii) stimulating SMEs;

 (iii) social dialogue to prepare and accompany labour market reforms;

---

[169] The 1993 broad economic policy guidelines issued under Article 103(2) EC, refer to completion of the single market including the development of TENs, the reorientation of policy in favour of industrial competitiveness towards high growth markets, and the facilitation of competitive industrial clusters and networks. Cf. (1) Council Recommendation of 22 December 1993 on the broad guidelines of the economic policies of the Member States and of the Community; (2) Commission Recommendation for the broad guidelines of the economic policies of the Member States and of the Community, drawn up in conformity with Article 103(2) of the Treaty on European Union: 'Restoring growth and employment—strengthening convergence'; and (3) Framework for the broad economic policy guidelines: 'Restoring growth and employment—strengthening convergence', in (1995) *European Economy* 55: Broad Economic Policy Guidelines and Convergence Report. Whereas the White Paper has been defined as an 'OECD-type reference document', the Broad Economic Guidelines are a binding instrument introduced by the Treaty on European Union.

[170] 'While industrial policy continues to be controversial no-one is in any doubt as to the responsibility of governments and of the Community to create as favourable an environment as possible for company competitiveness'. 1993 White Paper, above, n. 163, at 9.

[171] ibid., p. 47. Further recommendations include stimulating investment growth over consumption (with real wage rises below productivity gains), and boosting business confidence by pursuing structural adjustment, trade liberalisation, completion of the single market and the creation of TENs. The rates of national saving are to be improved through the reduction of public deficits.

[172] 1993 White Paper preamble. Cf. speech by Commission President Jacques Delors at the Conference 'Combatting Social Exclusion', Copenhagen, 4 June 1993: 'Giving a New Dimension to the Fight Against Exclusion'.

[173] 1993 White Paper, above, n. 163, pp. 15–16.

[174] Cf. COM(90) 556. Industrial Policy Guidelines, p. 10. 'With a high living-standard to preserve and improve, EC industry is condemned to technological, commercial and financial excellence in order to enable the necessary social and environmental expenses to be incurred'. ibid., p. 3.

(iv) the establishment of TENs; and

(v) preparing the 'information society' (a qualitative change in organisation and production based on complementary improvements in access and exchange of information, which is dependent on the creation of European information networks).

The primary responsibility for most of the measures regarding competitiveness required lies with the Member States. Apart from setting the common agenda, the role of the Community is focused on promoting the diffusion of high technology and the rolling out of the trans-European infrastructure networks in energy, transport and telecommunications. The Community proposals concerning the latter are based on new Treaty competences and a new understanding of the internal market, one that requires networks providing seamless physical links across national borders. To fund the TENs, the White Paper proposed a co-ordinated public works programme. Public investment was to come, first, from the Community budget (spread over the structural funds, the cohesion fund, and the R&D programmes in the telecommunications and transport areas), and second, from loans by the European Investment Bank. Third, the Commission proposed creating new financial facilities: (i) 'union bonds', issued by the Community itself; and (ii) 'convertibles', issued by companies involved in strategic TEN projects, but guaranteed by the European Investment Fund.[175]

Aimed at addressing the fundamental problems of the European economies, the 1993 White Paper may be regarded as the closing statement of the Delors Commission. The reaction of the Brussels European Council to this final agenda-setting effort was a mixed one: although the need for common action to address the problem of unemployment was recognised, the funding proposals of the Commission were regarded with scepticism. The Ecofin and General Affairs Council likewise approved the White Paper and Broad Economic Guidelines in general terms, but expressed reservations about the funding required for infrastructural investment.[176] Ultimately, the proposal for issuing 'Eurobonds' floundered, and the Council did not commit to any hard unemployment reduction targets. The conclusions of the Council emphasised the implementation of TENs and in particular information infrastructure. Further, a monitoring procedure was requested, with yearly reports by the Commission on progress toward realisation of its industrial policy proposals.[177]

---

[175] The funds needed were estimated at 150 billion ECU over 10 years for information and communication technologies alone, to be covered by private investment. Up to the year 2000 the needs for transport were estimated at 220 billion ECU, for energy at 30 billion ECU. Of the billion ECU 150 required for information and communication technologies the Community budget would contribute 5.3 billion ECU, the EIB 6.7 billion ECU in loans, and the new financial facilities 8 billion ECU through bond issues. 1993 White Paper, above, n. 163, pp. 32–34.

[176] Cf. Editorial, 'Growth, Competitiveness and Unemployment: The Challenges Facing the European Union', (1995) 31 CMLR 1.

[177] Improving the competitiveness of European industry. Conclusions of the Council of 22 April 1994, *Bull EU* 4-94, para. 2.2.1.

Progress on implementation of the 1993 White Paper has been uneven. In line with the 1994 Council conclusions, it has been most marked regarding the 'information society' project, in particular with political agreement on the liberalisation of the telecommunications sector.[178] As public financing will play only a limited role in this area, the balance will shift toward market developments. Meanwhile, a new regulatory framework taking wider Community objectives into account remains to be adopted.

The general follow-up to the White Paper has been worked out in the recent communication on an industrial competitiveness policy for the European Union, which meets the yearly reporting requirement.[179] Here, the Commission goes further than it had in the 1990 Industrial Policy Guidelines by claiming a coherent legal basis for competitiveness policy in Titles XII to XV (covering TENs, industry, economic and social cohesion, and R&D) and VIII EC (social policy and industrial change). The paper restates how the industrial policy of the Community is to further the competitiveness of European industry by liberalisation and deregulation, complemented by a tough competition policy. The four priority areas set out are: (i) the promotion of intangible investment (education); (ii) the development of industrial co-operation; (iii) ensuring fair competition; (iv) and modernisation of the role of the public authorities.[180]

Most importantly, the role of public authorities is to be redefined in the context of the liberalisation, privatisation, and regulatory reform brought about by the establishment of the internal market. The objective in this area is 'to move on from the phase of establishing a legal framework (. . .) to the phase of giving priority to co-operation', in the overall interest of promoting greater economic efficiency and more effective regulation.[181] Instead of using direct subsidies, public authorities are to mobilise private capital, notably by providing a regulatory environment conducive to private sector initiatives. In this context, it is remarkable that the Commission has cautiously begun to link the role of public authorities in promoting industrial competitiveness with

---

[178] High-Level Group on the Information Society, *Europe and the Global Information Society: Recommendation to the European Council* (Brussels, 1994); COM(94) 347, Europe's Way to the Information Society: An Action Plan; Cf. 'Growth, Competitiveness and Employment: White Paper Follow-Up', *Bull EU* Supplement 2/94.

[179] COM(94) 319, *An Industrial Competitiveness Policy for the European Union* (Published as *Bull EU* Supplement 3/94—page references here to *Bull EU*). The annexes to this document provide an analysis of the state of European industry in relation to its main competitors.

[180] Concerning the intangible investment, a human resources policy for the Community is advocated, along with more market co-operation under the Fourth Framework Programme on research and development. Industrial co-operation, the second priority area, is to see further deregulation, increased transparency, and fine-tuning of the existing instruments, along with the support of industrial roundtables. Concerning competition, strengthening the enforcement of the state aids rules, facilitating the intervention of third parties in competition procedures, and international co-ordination of competition policy are emphasised.

[181] *Bull EU* Supplement 3/94, above, n. 179, p. 35. The proposals include systematic recourse to Articles 101 and 102 EC.

privatisation.[182] Finally, although the proposals on consultation and co-operation between the Member States are mainly exhortatory in nature, they explicitly refer to their obligations in this regard under Articles 3(1) and 130 EC.

Throughout these various documents the Commission has consistently developed the approach defined in the 1990 Industrial Policy Guidelines. In its 1994 resolution on industrial policy, the Council likewise confirmed the continuity of the 1990 approach and the principles embodied there.[183] Most importantly, the 1994 Council Resolution indicated that Articles 130, 130b, 130a, 3a and 3b EC form the main framework for industrial policy. Hence, ensuring the conditions necessary for the competitiveness of industry is combined social and economic cohesion, yet 'all economic policy-measures of the Community and the Member States must also be consonant with the principle of an open market economy with free competition and the principle of subsidiarity'.[184] Hence, the consensus on the Community's new approach to industrial policy remains intact, and the concept of industrial policy as part of an 'organized European space', based on market principles but including socio-economic goals is retained. Community industrial policy has survived the backlash provoked by the Treaty on European Union and has become an integral part of the Delors legacy. Nevertheless, it remains to be seen whether the wider exercise in agenda-setting of the 1993 White Paper and its more ambitious objectives will be effectively developed by the Santer Commission.

V. Conclusion

Definitions of industrial policy and opinions on its desirability still vary widely, although there is consensus on measures aimed at promoting industrial restructuring through market reforms, as well as positive action to remedy market failures. Disagreement persists in particular with regard to the scope for public policy measures which aim to remedy market failures. Many economists agree

---

[182] 'Greater privatisation, more effective regulatory methods and the new role of public services: out of concern to achieve greater economic efficiency, most Member States have embarked on policies on the privatization of industrial activities, reduction of costs arising from the regulation and modernisation of public services. All measures which aim at improving overall economic productivity in the European Union must be encouraged, taking account of experience acquired and of national differences'. ibid., p. 13. Cf. in reference to the 1993 White Paper and the efforts required by the Member States to ensure that their economies will fully benefit form the internal market and international trade: COM(94) 217, Commission's Recommendations for the Broad Guidelines of the Economic Policies of the Member States and the Community drawn up in conformity with Article 103(2) of the Treaty on European Union, p. 5; 1993 White Paper, above, n. 163, pp. 64, 67: in the guidelines for a policy of global competitiveness: 'encouraging continuing structural adjustment by supporting privatizations'.

[183] Council Resolution of 21 November 1994 on the strengthening of the competitiveness of Community Industry ((1994) OJ C343/1). It also noted that a number of important industrial policy objectives had been achieved, including the (virtual) completion of the internal market, the GATT Uruguay Round and the adoption of the fourth framework programme.

[184] ibid.

that in practice the 'second best' strategy of pure market solutions is preferable to trying to reach a theoretical optimum through government policies. However, beside economic arguments, there are also political reasons for adopting industrial policies, which may include the pursuit of redistributive and other socially desirable goals. Contesting democratic decisions to this effect on purely economic grounds is spurious.

For the Community, the situation is more complicated. However, both given the obligations of the Member States, especially after the ratification of the Treaty on European Union with its detailed framework and timetable for economic and monetary union, and for practical reasons (avoiding overlapping and contradictory efforts), there is a case for the co-ordination of industrial policy at the Community level.

The definition of industrial policy to which the Community subscribes is that of '... the effective and coherent implementation of all those policies which impinge on the structural adjustment of industry'. This covers both active and passive, general and sectoral measures, within the framework of an open market with free competition. Competition policy is regarded both as a precondition and as a component of industrial policy. This is in line with current economic theory, yet the Community approach to industrial policy in an open and competitive environment is the outcome of a lengthy development which has been found to be essentially continuous. The Community approach presented in 1990 did not form a radical break with the past. From the outset, the industrial policy approach of the Community has aimed at the completion of the internal market. The industrial policy proposals of the Commission have, therefore, always combined both passive and active measures, or liberalisation and measured intervention aimed at facilitating the interplay of market forces. The change in emphasis of these proposals has been subtle, and has followed that of European integration. This mainly regards the increasingly forceful attitude against direct public intervention by the Member States. Further, as the Community moves from negative to positive integration, the relative importance of economic policy co-ordination and social and economic cohesion has increased.

After false starts in the 1970s, a first step toward active industrial policy was made with the take off of the technology policy of the Community and the internal market programme, codified in the Single Act. The R&D competence of the Community and the liberalisation measures facilitated by the institutional reforms of the Single Act express the 'twin tracks' of Community industrial policy, which can be identified with positive and negative integration. A second step was taken in 1990, when the Council approved the 'coherent concept of industrial policy' in an open and competitive environment. The third step was the inclusion of a title on the competitiveness of European industry in the EC Treaty by the Treaty on European Union.

The acceptance of the Community approach of the 1990 Industrial Policy Guidelines, and its subsequent codification in the EC Treaty was based on broad consensus on the failure of sectoral intervention by the Member States motivated by narrowly perceived national interests. This economic nationalism ran its course after common solutions were abandoned in the aftermath of the oil shocks of the 1970s and the resulting economic crisis. The new industrial policy proposals can thus be placed in the general context of the relaunching of European integration with the internal market programme, which realised a great part of the industrial policy proposals which had originally been submitted before 1973. Hence, whereas industrial policy is usually regarded as appropriate only where it is clear that the workings of the market have failed, Community industrial policy emerged once national industrial policies, rather than the market, had failed. This is reflected in the market orientation of the Community approach. Further, Community industrial policy has become acceptable in so far as the Member States have ceased to perform the correspondent regulatory tasks, and where a unified response is required.

Apart from the change in position by the governments of the Member States, it seems that European multinationals played an important role in this regard. Their collaboration, including 'reverse lobbying' of their national governments in support of the Commission's proposals, played an important part in establishing the R&D policy of the Community, and possibly in the adoption of the Single European act as well. However, the Single Act structured the R&D policy according to strict procedures, reducing the direct influence of important economic actors, and increasing the input of the European Parliament.

The most important innovation of the 1990 Industrial Policy Guidelines in relation to earlier proposals by the Commission was that they redefined the role of public authorities in industrial policy as one of providing a stable economic and regulatory framework for a market environment, and a 'catalytic' function of stimulating structural adjustment. This confirms the hypothesis which stated that the new industrial policy title should be seen not only as the result of a new stage of European integration, but (as such) also as an expression of the balance between state and market.

This approach was reinforced and extended by the 1993 White Paper on growth, competitiveness and employment, which cast industrial policy as a central element of the growth strategy of the Community, and as a flanking policy of the co-ordination of economic policy toward economic and monetary union. The overall strategy seeks to harness structural adjustment in the pursuit of wider social and economic goals. The first hypothesis, that the new industrial policy competence of the Community must be seen in the context of the transition from negative integration to positive integration, policy co-ordination, and in particular economic and monetary union has thus broadly been confirmed.

Industrial policy therefore appears to be more central to European integration than might have been thought. It is clear that the industrial policy proposals of the Commission have been intended to rally political will behind mission oriented efforts to promote further economic integration. It is questionable whether these proposals are as coherent in practice as their promotion for political purposes would suggest. The claim that the Community now has a basis for industrial policy initiatives under Titles VIII, XII, XIII and XV may not be inaccurate. That it is a coherent basis seems improbable.

The criticism of Title XIII of the EC Treaty as the 'linchpin' for co-ordinated Community intervention is misplaced. Article 130 EC does not provide effective means for the co-ordination of these various competences, and the various provisions of Titles VIII, XIII and XV EC merely include industrial policy objectives among a range of more specific goals. Under unanimous decision making an interventionist Community policy cannot override the principled objections of even a single Member State. In theory, the Commission could co-ordinate its own actions in this direction, and trade off advantages it has in other areas (such as competition policy). However, the Commission's approach has so far been markedly more market-oriented than that of the individual Member States.

Moreover, Article 130(3) EC itself does not leave room for industrial policy initiatives at odds with the principle of free competition. This is an explicit exception to the general rule that various public policy objectives may legitimise restrictions of the principle of free competition and the four freedoms at the Community level. Further, the limited financial resources of the Community restrict its ability to conduct industrial policy through public investment, and the consultative role of the European Parliament under Article 130 EC is ill-suited to legitimise redistributive measures. As a result of these various constraints and the new perspective on the role of public authorities, the reduction of public intervention at the national level is not replaced by Community intervention. Instead, economic regulation and co-ordination of other actors within commonly agreed rules will become more important.

This suggests that industrial and competition policy may indeed be compatible at the Community level. From a theoretical point of view it is possible to regard competition policy as part of industrial policy, and to promote structural adjustment by safeguarding open markets. The hypothesis that the industrial and competition policies of the Community are compatible is further supported by the fact that both the Commission and the Council subscribe to this view. However, competition policy per se is not concerned with the direction of structural adjustment. The opposite is true for (sectoral) industrial policy. Therefore, it is doubtful that no friction would emerge in practice.

4

The Competition Policy of the Community and the Competitiveness of European Industry

While the Community has from the outset had extensive competences in competition policy, its powers in the broader area of economic policy were limited. This is now changing. A new phase of integration is bringing about shifts in the horizontal and vertical distribution of power in the Community. First, the powers of the Member States on economic policy making are increasingly pooled, as the result of the internal market programme, and the drive toward economic and monetary union. Second, a Community competence on industrial policy has been created. Third, changes in the constitutional framework and institutional set-up of competition policy are being considered

Industrial and competition policy can be seen as being linked in two ways. First, the requirements of competition policy may impose limits on the industrial policies of the Member States. Second, as was stated above, competition policy has been described as an instrument of Community industrial policy.

Concerning the first aspect, that of the limits to industrial policy, it has been seen that although free competition forms a constitutional principle of the Community, the Treaty remains neutral in regard to the economic policies pursued at the level of the Member States. The actions of the Member States are subject only to restricted judicial review under this principle, and legitimate public policy objectives may justify exceptions to it. Nevertheless, the margin of freedom exercised by the latter has been progressively reduced by the application of the four freedoms and competition, and more recently by the requirements regarding the co-ordination of economic policy in the run-up to economic and monetary union (notably the convergence criteria). The question is what (in spite of the principle of neutrality regarding the economic order) the implications of this reduced margin of discretion are in practice.

This has a bearing on the hypothesis that the industrial policy competence of the Community emerged due to the inability of the Member States to pursue similar policies autonomously at the national level. Further, it is relevant to test the hypothesis that the industrial policy competence of the Community emerged not only in the context of the increasing co-ordination of economic policy at the European level which arose in response to European integration, but also as the result of a shifting balance between state and market, which seems to be developing in tandem with the introduction of the internal market. It should be seen to what extent this change has been influenced by competition policy.

Concerning the second aspect, the use of competition policy powers in the pursuit of industrial policy goals is considered possible given the wide margins of discretion enjoyed by the Commission in the implementation of the competition rules of the Treaty. This may have been facilitated by Article 130(3) EC, which requires the Community to contribute to the goals of industrial policy through the activities and policies it pursues under other provisions of the Treaty. However, the threshold formed by the principle of free competition was deliberately heightened for industrial policy under Article 130 EC, since in this case distortions of competition would not be covered by the normal public policy exemption.

Further, although both the competition and the industrial policy of the Community are horizontal (rather than sectoral) in nature, there are important differences between them. Competition policy has a firm constitutional basis, and takes the form of the implementation of a highly developed body of Community law, which was elaborated over the course of several decades. Although the EC has long been active in industrial policy under various guises, a policy on industry as such has only very recently been entered into the Treaty, and the new Article 130 EC does not yet have a well developed practice. Finally, whereas industrial policy is focused on industrial structures, or structural adjustment, and outcome oriented, competition policy is generally not concerned with the allocation of resources between sectors, and is process oriented.

For these reasons, even if the assertion that the industrial and competition policies of the Community are in principle compatible holds, tension between the two may be expected. Therefore, it must be seen whether the goals and instruments of competition policy are compatible with the Community concept of industrial policy. If the pursuit of industrial policy objectives under competition policy is possible, the problem may be reconsidered as a conflict internal to competition policy, rather than between the Community policies on competition and competitiveness as such. Further, it must be seen how the promotion of structural adjustment relates to recent efforts toward decentralisation of Community competition policy, and the debate on the merits of creating an independent European antitrust authority.

This chapter will discuss the purported complementarity between the industrial and competition policy of the Community, and how the latter may be used to jointly promote competition and 'competitiveness', with a brief case study of merger control. It further deals with the application of competition policy to the Member States, notably under Article 90 EC. Finally, recent proposals for changing the institutional design of competition policy are assessed.

II. PRINCIPLES AND OBJECTIVES

A. The Compatibility of EC Industrial and Competition Policy

There can be no doubt about the position of the Commission of the EC on the relationship between industrial and competition policy. In the debate on the alleged conflict with competition policy which followed the adoption of a new Community approach to industrial policy in 1990, the Commission from the outset took the position that the two were compatible.[1] Competition DG IV considers the new industrial policy of the Community, as defined in the 1990 Industrial Policy Guidelines (which embraced the system of open and competitive markets),[2] to be fully compatible with its own activities:

Industrial policy concerns the effective and coherent implementation of all those policies which impinge on the structural adjustment of industry with a view to promoting competitiveness. The provision of a horizontal framework in which industry can develop and prosper by remedying structural deficiencies and addressing areas where the market mechanism alone fails to provide the conditions necessary for success is the principal means by which the Community applies its industrial policy. Central to this approach are the three specific Community policies which promote competition within the Community: an open trade policy, completion of the internal market and an active competition policy. It would be quite incorrect, therefore, to consider that there is any conflict between the objectives or instruments of competition policy and those of industrial policy.[3]

Regardless of whether this assessment could also be interpreted as an exercise in damage control by the competition services of the Commission, it formed an intellectually tenable position.[4] As the guardian of the Treaty and the unity of Community law, the Commission is obliged to guarantee that the various goals and objectives are compatible.

The Industrial Policy Guidelines emphasised the central role of the internal market for the competitiveness of European industry, and competition policy as central to the internal market. The general horizontal measures involved, aimed at facilitating structural adjustment by removing domestic distortions and addressing market failure (for example, concerning investment in R&D), rest on widely accepted economic arguments. Seen from the perspective of competition

[1] Commission of the EEC, *20th General Report on the Activities of the European Community: 1990* (Brussels, 1991), p. 42.

[2] COM(90) 556, Industrial Policy in an Open and Competitive Environment: Guidelines for a Community Approach (hereafter 'Industrial Policy Guidelines'), published in 'European Industrial Policy for the 1990s' *EC Bull* Supplement 3/91.

[3] Commission of the EEC, *21st Report on Competition Policy: 1991* (Brussels, 1992), p. 42. This forms an elaboration of the definition of industrial policy given in the Industrial Policy Guidelines, above, n. 2, pp. 5–6.

[4] There have been suggestions that DG IV was initially less than enthusiastic. Cf. Ross, 'Sidling into Industrial Policy: Inside the European Commission', (1993) 11 *French Politics and Society* 20. Ross suggests that Competition Commissioner Sir Leon Brittan had been directly at odds with Commission President Delors on this issue.

policy, the essential element of the Industrial Policy Guidelines was that they were based on an unconditional rejection of the national policies of sectoral intervention of the 1970s.[5] The resulting approach could therefore be seen as no more than a restatement of standing Community policy.[6] The opening sentence of the Competition Policy Report for 1991 went even further, with the assertion that the Industrial Policy Guidelines confirm the growing importance of competition policy as the Community advances toward economic and monetary union and nears the completion of the single market.[7]

The issue of the compatibility of industrial and competition policy surfaced again when Industry Title XIII and Article 3(1) on promoting the competitiveness of European industry were introduced into the EC Treaty by the Treaty on European Union. The competition services of the Commission had pressed for the inclusion of a provision in Article 130(3) EC which stated that the Industry Title did not provide a basis for the introduction by the Community of any measure which might distort competition. Indeed the new Industry Title was held to demonstrate the growing importance of competition policy, to the extent that it confirmed the commitment to the system of free competition in open markets expressed in the Industrial Policy Guidelines.[8] Although the Treaty on European Union had with the Industry Title reasserted the open texture of the EC Treaty regarding economic policy, it could be concluded that 'the *Community* has the *most strongly free-market oriented constitution in the world.*'[9]

Rather than focusing narrowly on efficiency-maximising antitrust, the competition policy of the Community is broadly conceived, and is oriented towards the general goals of European integration. Competition policy has been progressively adapted to the new priorities adopted by the Community.[10] Recently, the emphasis on the general goals and priorities of the Community (and on the sectoral context of individual decisions) has become relevant, especially in relation to the innovations introduced by the Treaty on European Union, notably

[5] C.-D. Ehlermann, 'Wettbewerbspolitik im Binnenmarkt', (1993) 39 *Recht der Internationalen Wirtschaft* 793, p. 798.

[6] 'The European Community needs a policy for industry. It has such a policy in the single market programme and its many supporting actions, all backed by a vigorous application of the rules of competition', 'Does Europe Need an Industrial Policy?', Speech by Competition Commissioner Brittan to the College of Europe, Bruges, 29 January 1991. Cf. the foreword by the latter to M. Bangemann, *Meeting the Global Challenge: Establishing a Successful European Industrial Policy* (London, 1992).

[7] *21st Report on Competition Policy*, above, n. 3, Introduction.

[8] ibid.; 'Von den neuen Vorschriften des Maastrichter Vertrags droht sicherlich keine Gefahr, solange die Gemeinschaft an ihrer industriepolitischen Orientierung vom Herbst 1990 festhält'. Ehlermann, above, n. 5.

[9] C.-D. Ehlermann, 'The Contribution of EC Competition Policy to the Single Market', (1992) 29 CMLR 257, p. 273 (emphasis in the original); Cf. Ehlermann, above, n. 5.

[10] Although competition policy is based on principles enshrined in the Treaty, these 'cannot be applied mechanically without reference either to the context within which they have their impact or the main objectives and priorities of the Community'. COM(94) 161, 23rd Competition Report from the Commission: 1993, p. 2.

regarding industrial, cultural and environmental goals, and subsidiarity, as well as the grand socio-economic strategy outlined in the 1993 Delors White Paper on Growth, Competitiveness and Employment.[11]

Competition Policy has a central role to play in the Community's strategy for achieving a lasting recovery in growth and employment. The priorities which the Commission has set itself as regards competition are, therefore, largely determined by the contribution which competition policy can make to the Community's objective of growth, competitiveness and employment, as set out in the White Paper. . . .[12]

Competition encourages the efficient allocation of resources and stimulates research and development, innovation and investment. It is the mechanism by which resources and jobs are redirected towards growing sectors and away from ones with less promising futures. The importance of this traditional role of competition policy has been reinforced in recent years in two ways. Firstly, its part in making a reality of the internal market which will create jobs and stimulate growth and competitiveness is widely recognised. Secondly, it is central to the Community's industrial policy. The completion of a genuine internal market and an effective industrial policy have received first priority in the White Paper. This in itself implies the need for renewed vigour in competition policy in areas where it complements and enhances these objectives.[13]

. . . the Commission considers that, far from being the direct opposite of industrial policy, competition policy is an essential instrument, with clear complementarity between the two policies.[14]

Structural adjustment as promoted by 1993 White Paper involves the promotion of infrastructure development through the creation of trans-European networks, of technological development, and of market opening in third countries. It further includes stimulating mergers and joint ventures, preferential treatment for small and medium-sized enterprises, infrastructural investment and labour force training under the state aids regime.[15]

The compatibility or complementarity between the industrial and competition policies of the Community may be explained, first, by the specific characteristics of the competition policy of the Community. Both industrial and competition policy form part of the general economic policy of the Community.[16] Moreover,

---

[11] COM(93) 700, Growth, Competitiveness, Employment: The Challenges and Ways forward into the 21st Century. White Paper (hereafter '1993 White Paper'). Published as *Bull EC* Supplement 6/93.
[12] 23rd Competition Report, above, n. 10, p. 6.
[13] ibid., p. 7; cf. Commission of the EC, *26th General Report on the Activities of the EC: 1993* (Brussels, 1994), para. 194.
[14] 23rd Competition Report, above, n. 10, p. 79.   [15] ibid., pp. 79–81.
[16] H. Schröter, 'Die Wettbewerbsregeln der Gemeinschaft', in H. Von der Groeben, J. Thiesing and C.-D. Ehlermann (eds.), *Kommentar zum EWG Vertrag* Vol. 3 (4th ed., Baden-Baden, 1991), para. 23. Cf. H. Von der Groeben, 'Die Wettbewerbspolitik als Teil der Wirtschaftspolitik im Gemeinsamen Markt', speech to European Parliament of 16 June 1965, reproduced in H. Von der Groeben, *Europa: Plan und Wirklichkeit. Reden-Berichte-Aufsätze zur europäischen Politik* (Baden-Baden, 1967). 'Wettbewerbspolitik ist allgemeine Wirtschaftspolitik . . . und von ihr nicht zu trennen'. ibid., p. 194. From this point of view competition is a fundamental element of the economic order of the Community.

competition policy straddles positive and negative integration, since it complements the four freedoms, while making it possible to take account of the objectives of the co-ordination of social and economic policy.[17] This is especially true if
competition policy is seen alongside the competition rules on taxation and the
approximation of laws,[18] as they were originally grouped together as 'common
rules' under part III of the EEC Treaty.[19] Hence, the competition policy of the
Community can be seen as an important instrument of economic policy, and
as such take the industrial policy objectives of the Community into account.
This is all the more important since the Community has only a limited competence regarding economic policy in general, whereas it has full competence
concerning competition policy.[20] In this context, it should be emphasised that
competition is not pure law or economics, but policy.[21]

Second, this assumed complementarity can be explained by the particular
nature of the Community approach to industrial policy. The Community
approach is primarily horizontal (general) and oriented toward removing obstacles to free trade and industrial restructuring (passive). As such, it includes the
internal market, as a catalyst for structural adjustment. Under application of the
principle of subsidiarity, the active and sectoral elements of industrial policy
are largely reserved for the Member States, within the overall framework of
their obligations under Community law. According to Article 130(1) EC, similar Community measures are moreover to be 'in accordance with a system of
open and competitive markets'. Article 130(3) EC further underlines that such
measures should not give rise to distortions of competition. In the drafting of
the new industry title, care thus seems to have been taken to ensure the compatibility of the two policies at the Community level.

[17] This approach was taken in H. Von der Groeben and E.-J. Mestmäcker (eds.), *Ziele und
Methoden der Europäischen Integration* (Frankfurt, 1972). Cf. P. J. G. Kapteyn and P. VerLoren
van Themaat, in L. Gormley (ed.), *Introduction to the Law of the European Communities After the
Coming into Force of the Single European Act* (Deventer, 1990), pp. 586–587.

[18] Cf. ibid., ch. VIII: 'The Competition Policy of the Community', n. 1. This was reflected in
the portfolio of DG IV when the EC Commission was created, which amalgamated restrictive practices, state aids and harmonisation of laws and taxes, 'thus providing a good basis for a *uniform*
competition policy'. H. Von der Groeben, *The European Community: The Formative Years. The
Struggle to Establish the Common Market and the Political Union (1958–66)* European Perspectives
Series (Brussels-Luxembourg, 1985), p. 60. According to Von der Groeben this concentration of
functions was possible since at the time competition policy was generally considered to be much
less important than for example foreign trade, economic policy, agriculture and social affairs, and
some compensation was thought due to the responsible Commissioner.

[19] Schröter, above, n. 16, para. 2. Now Title V EC, 'Common rules on competition, taxation
and approximation of laws'.

[20] Cf. Ch. Joerges, 'Markt ohne Staat? Die Wirtschaftsverfassung der Gemeinschaft und die
Renaissance der regulativen Politik' in R. Wildenmann (ed.), *Staatswerdung Europas? Optionen
für eine politische Union* (Baden-Baden, 1991); M. Neumann, 'Industrial Policy and Competition
Policy', (1990) 34 *European Economic Review* 562.

[21] Cf. H. De Jong, 'Competition Policy in Europe: Stimulus, Nuisance, or Drawback?', in K.
Groeneveld and G. Maks (eds.), *Economic Policy and the Market Process* (Amsterdam, 1990).
Some detractors of course would go further, and have that it is politics, rather than policy.

This means that for the Community there is no sharp distinction between industrial policy as concerned with market structure, and competition policy as aimed at protecting the process of competition. It should therefore not come as a surprise that the complementarity of competition and industrial policy is not particular to the new approach.

Although the positions discussed above were taken in the recent debate on the compatibility of competition policy with the new approach to industrial policy, it must be stressed that although the emphasis of the Community approach to industrial policy has shifted over time, there has been no radical break in its development. From the beginning, Community proposals for industrial policy emphasised the completion of the internal market by reducing barriers to trade and competition (or passive general measures), rather than active sectoral intervention. Thus, when giving an outline of the aims and scope of Community competition policy since its inception in the *First Report on Competition Policy* of 1971, the Commission underlined that it had defined its policy on cartels and monopolies '(W)ithin the framework of the Community's medium-term economic policy and in accordance with the guidelines on the Memorandum on the Industrial Policy of the Community'.[22]

Subsequent competition policy reports consistently confirmed the role of competition policy in enhancing the economic development of European industry as well as its international competitiveness.[23] As will be recalled, the codification of the R&D competence of the Community formed a major step in the (re)-emergence of its industrial policy, which was made possible by the upgrading of their common interests by the Member States, culminating in the Single Act. Not surprisingly therefore, the link between competition policy and positive industrial policy comes out most clearly in regard to the approach taken to R&D in the early 1980s:

...the Commission's work of administering competition policy cannot be encapsulated by the sole objective of removing distortions caused by anti-competitive practices or State aids which are liable to interfere with inter-State trade. Competition policy also contributes to improving the allocation of resources and raising the competitiveness of Community industry, and thanks to this greater competitiveness, secured largely by encouragement of research and development, to enabling the Community at length to overcome the economic problems now facing it and in particular to combat structural

[22] Commission of the EEC, *First Report on Competition Policy* (Brussels, 1972), p. 23, with reference to: Council, Second Programme of Medium-term Economic Policy ((1969) OJ L129, 30 May 1969). This report also noted that the links between competition policy and structural policies (such as regional policy), and the need to enhance the effectiveness of competition by removing obstacles such as price fixing and protectionist public procurement policies, were such as had been proposed in the industrial policy guidelines the Commission issued in 1970. *First Report on Competition Policy*, pp. 12–13; Commission of the EC, *La Politique Industrielle de la Communauté, Mémorandum de la Commission au Conseil* (Brussels, 1970), ch. II: 'La coopération et la concentration des entreprises dans la Communauté'.

[23] Schröter, above, n. 16, para. 24.

unemployment. In this way competition policy can play its part, with other Community policies, in securing a lasting economic recovery.[24]

In sum, it may be noted that compatibility between the industrial and competition policies of the Community has been assumed at all important points in the development of the former, that is the 1970 guidelines, the 'technology Community' in the early 1980s, the 1990 guidelines, and finally the Industry Title of the Treaty on European Union. On this basis, some first conclusions can be drawn regarding the development of the relationship between these two policies over time.

The industrial and competition policy of the Community started out on parallel tracks. They were both envisaged as horizontal policies which formed part of the general economic policy of the Community, and as such their complementarity was in principle in-built from the outset (or at least from the time medium-term economic planning and active thinking on industrial policy commenced after the customs union was completed). However, whereas competition policy flourished under the centralised control of the Commission, the development of industrial policy at the Community level was halting and fragmented, and ultimately languished following the first oil crisis.

The industrial policy of the Community failed to take off, especially since it was for the main part dependent on unanimity in the Council. First, until relatively recently, the Commission's relatively liberal views on industrial policy clashed with those of most Member States. Second, the Member States were reluctant to compromise their economic sovereignty. Third, some Member States, notably Germany (later joined by the United Kingdom) feared that the Community might in practice resort to forms of industrial policy intervention to which they were opposed as a matter of principle (albeit honoured by frequent breach in domestic practice). Hence, industrial policy remained a national matter, and was pursued in ways which were often both counterproductive and at odds with the internal market objective.

B. The Objectives of EC Competition Policy

To allow an evaluation of the conflict and complementarity of competition and industrial policy, the objectives of the former must be examined more closely. Opinions on the value of competition per se, and therefore concerning the appropriate objectives for competition policy as well, have varied over time and between economic systems. In the Community moreover, the dimensions of multi-level government and economic integration give rise to particular considerations.

---

[24] Commission of the EEC, *13th Report on Competition Policy: 1983* (Brussels, 1984), p. 11. Cf. the remarks on the 'technology Community' in Commission of the EC, *15th Report on Competition Policy: 1985* (Brussels, 1986), pp. 13, 225.

Three categories of goals of competition policy are identified:

(i) the diffusion of economic power, to protect individual (political) freedom and individual rights and the economic freedom of market competitors;

(ii) enhancing consumer welfare by stimulating both allocative and productive efficiency; and

(iii) broader public interest goals.[25]

These goals can be identified with various schools of antitrust analysis. Competition as a value in and of itself is emphasised by those who give priority to the first category. For example Ordoliberals and followers of the neo-Austrian school of economics see competition both as linked to individual freedom and as a 'discovery procedure' central to the generation and diffusion of information in a market system.[26]

Strictly speaking, only the second category, concerned with efficiency, is based on economic arguments. The main economic reason for competition policy is the occurrence of market failures in the allocation of resources. Competition policy may correct the mis-allocation of resources which results from:

(i) static inefficiency in resource allocation, when (due to abuse of monopoly pricing power) both production and consumption remain below optimal levels;

(ii) reduced technical efficiency, since firms sheltered from competition fail to optimise their production;

(iii) dynamic inefficiency (which follows from technical inefficiency), when the innovation of production and products is stalled.

Usually, technical and dynamic inefficiency are often considered to be more serious threats to overall welfare than is static inefficiency.[27] The influential Chicago school of law and economics, however, has focused on the power of

---

[25] Cf. A. Jacquemin, 'Introduction: Competition in Market Economies', in W. S. Comanor *et al*, *Competition Policy in Europe and North America: Economic Issues and Institutions* (London, 1990), pp. 3–4; D. Hay, 'The Assessment: Competition Policy', (1993) 9 *Oxford Review of Economic Policy* 1. A further distinction can be made regarding the criteria used: market structure, behavioural aspects, or performance. Jacquemin, ibid., p. 5.

[26] Cf. D. J. Gerber, 'Constitutionalizing the Economy: German neo-liberalism, Competition Law and the "New" Europe', (1994) 42 *American Journal of Comparative Law* 25; M. E. Streit, 'Economic Order, Private Law and Public Policy: The Freiburg School of Law and Economics in Perspective', (1992) 148 JITE 675, with reference to the development of this theme by Hayek.

[27] W. Molle, *The Economics of European Integration: Theory, Practice, Policy* (Aldershot, 1990) ch. 7, 'Economic and Monetary Union', p. 146. Cf. D. G. Goyder, *EC Competition Law* (2nd ed., Oxford 1993), p. 9. For a theoretical discussion of the economic issues involved see J. A. Ordover, 'The Economic Foundations of Competition Policy', in W. S. Comanor *et al*, above, n. 25; F.M. Scherer and D. Ross, *Industrial Market Structure and Economic Performance* (3rd ed., Boston, 1990), ch. 2: 'The Welfare Economics of Competition and Monopoly'; F. Jenny, 'Competition and Efficiency', in B. Hawk (ed.), *Annual Proceedings of the Fordham Corporate Law Institute 1993: Antitrust in a Global Economy* (New York, 1994).

monopolists to raise prices (consumer welfare) and pleaded for a restrained application of the competition rules on this basis.[28]

The third category covers a wide variety of objectives, and typically includes redistributive goals such as employment promotion and regional policy. In this case the state may adopt an entrepreneurial or developmental role aimed at stimulating particular firms or industrial sectors. In general the pursuit of such goals is associated with administrative discretion (competition policy) rather than with the strict enforcement of antitrust law. Under this approach, industrial and competition policy overlap.[29]

For the Community this category of wider public policy considerations is of exceptional importance, since it includes market integration. Although there is no agreement on the importance of the other two types of goals for EC competition policy, it has generally been observed that the integration objective forms its first priority.[30] Indeed, the market integration objective forms the very reason why a system of competition rules was originally introduced in the Treaty. As was observed in the Spaak report of 1956, a Treaty which aims to achieve economic integration by abolishing the barriers between states could not be effective if it were to allow private undertakings to reconstruct such barriers by means of collusive behaviour or abuse of market power:

[28] Emblematic are R. H. Bork, *The Antitrust Paradox* (Chicago, 1978); and R. Posner, *Antitrust Law: An Economic Perspective* (Chicago, 1976). For a comparison and review of the impact of the Chicago School and the new antitrust economics in the United States and their relevance for the EC cf. B. Hawk, 'The American (Anti-trust) Revolution: Lessons for the EEC?', (1988) 9 ECLR 53; V. Korah, 'From Legal Form Toward Economic Efficiency—Article 85(1) of the EEC Treaty in Contrast to U.S. Antitrust', (1990) 35 *Antitrust Bulletin* 1009; G. Wils, 'Recente ontwikkelingen in het Amerikaanse antitrustrecht', (1991) 39 SEW 214. For the United States debate itself see, for example: D. B. Audretsch, 'Divergent Views in Antitrust Economics', (1988) 33 *The Antitrust Bulletin* 135; J. B. Baker, 'Recent Developments in Economics that Challenge Chicago School Views', (1989) 58 *Antitrust Law Journal* 645; L. Constantine, 'An Antitrust Enforcer Confronts the New Economics', (1989) 58 *Antitrust Law Journal* 661; E. M. Fox and L. A. Sullivan, 'Antitrust —Retrospective and Prospective: Where Are We Coming From? Where Are We Going?', (1987) 62 *NYU Law Review* 936; J. J. Gibbons, 'Antitrust, Law & Economics, and the Courts', (1987) 50 *Law and Contemporary Problems* 217; H. Hovenkamp, 'Antitrust Policy, Federalism, and the Theory of the Firm: A Historical Perspective', (1990) 59 *Antitrust Law Journal* 75; R. H. Lande, 'Chicago's False Foundations: Wealth Transfers (Not Just Efficiency) Should Guide Antitrust', (1989) 58 *Antitrust Law Journal* 631; R. H. Lande, 'The Rise and (Coming) Fall of Efficiency as the Ruler of Antitrust', (1988) 33 *Antitrust Bulletin* 429; J. A. Ordover, 'Conflicts of Jurisdiction: Antitrust and Industrial Policy', (1987) 50 *Law and Contemporary Problems* 165; W. H. Page, 'Ideological Conflict and the Origins of Antitrust Policy', (1991) 66 *Tulane Law Review* 1.

[29] Some observers have simply described competition policy aimed at such goals as industrial policy. M. C. Sawyer, 'Reflections on the Nature and the Role of Industrial Policy', (1992) 43 *Metroeconomica* 51.

[30] 'The preservation of the unity of the common market is and remains the basis for all new activities in the field of competition', and '(C)ompetition policy is one of the fundamental means for preserving the unity of the market'. Commission of the EC, *Sixth Report on Competition Policy: 1976* (Brussels, 1977), p. 9. Accordingly, at its outset the common competition policy had the following priorities: '(i) the opening-up of markets within the framework of a customs union and the free movement of factors of production; (ii) the removal of distortions of competition and the safeguarding of fair competition; (iii) the promotion of effective competition as an instrument for regulating the market'. Von der Groeben, above, n. 18.

Dans les conditions économiques du monde moderne, l'élargissement des marchés et de la concurrence ne suffit pas à assurer la répartition la plus rationelle des activités et le rythme le plus favorable d'expansion. Le premier fait dont il convient tenir compte, c'est la dimension atteinte par les entreprises, ou l'usage des ententes entre entreprises, et, par la suite, les pratiques de monopole, les facultés de discrimination, les possibilités de répartition du marché. Des règles de concurrence qui s'imposent aux entreprises sont donc nécessaires pour éviter que des doubles prix aient le même effet que des droits de douane, qu'un dumping mette en danger des productions économiquement saines, que la répartition des marchés se substitue à leur cloisonnement.[31]

This reasoning was confirmed and developed by the European Court of Justice, when it first applied Article 85 EEC in the *Consten-Grundig* case of 1966:

... an agreement between producer and distributor which might tend to restore the national divisions in trade between the Member States might be such as to frustrate the most fundamental objections (sic) of the Community. The Treaty, whose preamble and content aim at abolishing the barriers between States, and which in several provisions gives evidence of a stern attitude with regard to their appearance, could not allow undertakings to reconstruct such barriers. Article 85(1) is designed to pursue this aim, even in the case of agreements of undertakings placed at different levels in the economic process.[32]

The Court of Justice did not accept the argument that an increase in trade and of interbrand competition could off-set the restriction of intrabrand competition which resulted from the exclusive distribution system at issue. Hereby, the Court set the course for a competition policy emphasising the threat to the common market (directly or indirectly, in fact or potentially) rather than to competition as such.

Together with the provisions regarding state aids and the harmonisation of laws and taxation, the competition rules were intended to supplement the four freedoms in order to establish and maintain the common market, defined by the Court as 'one single market working under conditions coming as close as possible to those of an internal market'.[33] The constitutional basis for this argument was formed by Articles 2 and 3(f) EEC, which linked the institution of a system ensuring that competition in the common market was not distorted to establishing the common market as the instrument for realisation of the social and economic goals of European integration.[34]

---

[31] Comité intergouvernemental creé par la Conférence de Messine, *Rapport des Chefs de délégation aux Ministres des Affaires étrangères* (Brussels, 1956), p. 16. Cf. Goyder, above, n. 27, pp. 22–25.

[32] Joined Cases 56 and 58/64 *Consten and Grundig v Commission* [1966] ECR 299, p. 340; Cf. Case 22/78 *Hugin Kassaregister AB v Commission* [1979] ECR 1869.

[33] Case 15/81 *Gaston Schul Douane-Expediteur BV v Inspecteur der Invoerrechten en Accijnzen, Roosendaal* [1982] ECR 1409. The complementary nature of the free movement of goods, persons and services and free competition in this context has been outlined by P. Pescatore, 'Public and Private Aspects of European Competition Law', (1987) 10 *Fordham International Law Journal* 373.

[34] Indeed, competition policy has been called 'the primary dynamic force to attain the objectives of Article 2'. P. VerLoren van Themaat, 'Some Preliminary Observations on the Intergovernmental Conferences: The Relations between the Concepts of a Common Market, a Monetary Union, an Economic Union, a Political Union and Sovereignty', (1991) 28 CMLR 291, p. 294; Cf. B. Van der Esch, 'E.E.C. Competition Rules: Basic Principles and Policy Aims' (1980) 7 LIEI 75.

Further, in the context of Article 2 EEC, the contribution of competition policy to the operation of economic policy has sometimes been seen as its second objective, since it 'permits the Community authorities to carry out certain positive, though indirect, action with a view to promoting a harmonious development of economic activities within the whole Community'.[35] By virtue of the same logic, all general goals of European integration under Article 2 EC, and their instruments, can be considered to form objectives of EC competition policy. Thus, competition Commissioner Van Miert has emphasised that:

Competition policy has so long been a central Community policy that it is often forgotten that it is not an end in itself but rather one of the instruments towards the fundamental goals laid out in the Treaty—namely the establishment of a common market, the approximation of economic policy, the promotion of harmonious development and economic expansion, the increase of living standards and the bringing about of closer relationship between Member States. Competition policy therefore cannot be understood or applied without reference to this legal, economic, political and social context.[36]

This confirms the role of competition policy as an element of the general economic policy of the Community; by comparison the assertion that establishing the internal market forms its first priority seems timid. In academic discussion it is often assumed as self-evident that the influence of political considerations on competition policy is unwarranted. Whatever the truth of this assertion may be, it can hardly be based on the constitutional framework of the Community, the case law of the Court of Justice, or the policy statements of the Commission.

The dominant role of the integration objective does not mean that the more traditional arguments for competition policy (such as ensuring the diffusion of economic power, and promoting consumer welfare, or efficiency) are ignored. The Commission clearly considers efficiency as a goal of competition policy in its own right:

Competition is the best stimulant of economic activity since it guarantees the widest possible freedom of action to all. An active competition policy pursued in accordance with the provisions of the Treaties establishing the Communities makes it easier for the supply and demand structures continually to adjust to technological development. Through the interplay of decentralised decision-making machinery, competition enables enterprises continuously to improve their efficiency, which is the *sine qua non* for a

---

[35] Case 14/68 *Walt Wilhelm v Bundeskartellamt* [1969] ECR 1, paras. 4–5. At issue was the supremacy of Community law under the parallel application of national and Community competition rules. Cf. J.-F. Verstrynge, 'Current Antitrust Policy Issues in the EEC: Some Reflections on the Second Generation of Competition Policy', in B. Hawk (ed.), *Annual Proceedings of the Fordham Corporate Law Institute 1984: Antitrust and Trade Policies in International Trade* (New York, 1985); J.-F. Verstrynge, 'The System of EEC Competition Rules', in P. J. Slot and M. H. Van der Woude (eds.), *Exploiting the Internal Market: Co-operation and Competition Toward 1992* (Deventer, 1988).

[36] K. Van Miert, 'Competition Policy in the 90s', speech for the Royal Institute of International Affairs (Chatham House, London), 11 May 1993.

steady improvement in living standards and employment prospects within the countries of the Community. From this point of view, competition policy is an essential means for satisfying to a great extent the individual and collective needs of our society.[37]

The competition policy of the Community has not failed to pay its due to the merits of competition per se either:

It should also be understood that although the Treaty speaks of the establishment of (a) system of undistorted competition, competition policy has never been seen as a narrow economic concept linked solely to the promotion of efficiency but is intimately linked to our concept of democracy. We can have no meaningful democracy if economic power is concentrated in the hands of a few powerful individuals or corporations. (. . .) Neither can we have a meaningful pluralist democracy if the State controls all or very large part of the means of production as we have seen demonstrated so vividly in East Europe.[38]

Hence, the competition policy of the Community covers all three types of goals:

The Member States of the European Community share a common commitment to individual rights, to democratic values and to free institutions. It is those rights, values and institutions at the European and national levels that provide the necessary checks and balances in our political systems. Effective competition provides a set of similar checks and balances in the market economy system. It preserves the freedom and right of initiative of the individual economic operator and it fosters the sprit of enterprise. It creates an environment in which European industry can grow and develop in the most efficient manner and at the same time take account of social goals. Competition policy should ensure that abusive use of market power by a few does not undermine the rights of the many; it should prevent artificial distortions and enable the market to stimulate European enterprise to innovate and to remain competitive on a global scale.[39]

This is not to say that the objectives of competition policy of the Community are hereby exhausted. The efficiency objective is not only secondary to that of market integration, but has also been overridden by objectives such as fairness and the interests of small and medium-sized enterprises.[40] The Court of Justice

---

[37] *First Report on Competition Policy*, above, n. 22, p. 11.   [38] Van Miert, above, n. 36.

[39] *Fifteenth Report on Competition Policy*, above, n. 24, p. 11.

[40] The principle of fairness, comprising equality of opportunity, special regard for small and medium-sized enterprises, and equity ('the legitimate interests of workers, users and consumers') has been identified as a third fundamental objective of competition policy, after that of an open and unified common market, and 'ensuring that at all stages of the common market's development there exists the right amount of competition in order for the Treaty's requirements to be met and its aims attained'. Commission of the EEC, *Ninth Report on Competition Policy* (Brussels, 1980), pp. 9–11. Critical: Korah, above, n. 28; V. Korah, 'EEC Competition Policy: Legal Form or Economic Efficiency', (1986) 39 *Current Legal Problems* 85. For a more positive evaluation: 'the Community rules on competition seem to fulfil three broad functions: (i) to prevent barriers to trade being erected by private agreements between undertakings, abuse of monopoly power, or state subsidies; (ii) to preserve effective competition as the spur to the creation of the single market; and (iii) to encourage efficiency, innovation and lower prices'. C. Bellamy and G. D. Child, *Common Market Law of Competition* (3rd ed., London, 1987), p. 14.

has further suggested that restraints of competition in the pursuit of yet other policy objectives can be justified, so long as 'workable competition' is maintained.[41] The legal constraints imposed on the pursuit of various public policy objectives under Community competition policy are thus very similar to those imposed by the principle of free competition on the pursuit of public policy objectives in general.[42] In both cases the Court exercises limited judicial review.

In sum, it appears that the competition policy of the Community does not have a limited number of objectives. Rather, the competition policy of the EC has a primary objective, which is that of market integration, and a number of economic justifications, in part pure efficiency arguments, in part efficiency arguments derived from the economic theory of market integration. Competition policy aims to reconcile these with other policy objectives (or indeed the objectives of other policies) both in the various sectoral contexts and against the background of general economic policy. These secondary objectives of competition policy can include industrial policy in general, and specific horizontal aspects thereof (such as policy on R&D and SMEs), as well as sectoral considerations of industrial policy (such as restructuring). This underlines the fact that Community competition policy can serve both the process of competition per se and (sectoral) structural objectives.

III. EC COMPETITION POLICY AND THE COMPETITIVENESS OF PRIVATE UNDERTAKINGS

A. The Legal Framework of EC Competition Policy

Beside the general principle of Community law of free competition in open markets, the constitution of the EC provides for a system ensuring that

---

[41] 'The requirement contained in Articles 3 and 85 of the EEC Treaty that competition shall not be distorted implies the existence on the market of workable competition, that is to say the degree of competition necessary to ensure the observance of the basic requirements and the attainment of the objectives of the Treaty, in particular the creation of a single market achieving conditions similar to those of a domestic market. In accordance with this requirement, the nature and intensiveness of competition may vary to an extent dictated by the products or services in question and the economic structure of the relevant market sectors'. Case 26/76 *Metro SB-Großmärkte GmbH & Co KG v Commission* [1977] ECR 1875, para. 20. 'The powers conferred upon the Commission under Article 85(3) show that the requirements for the maintenance of workable competition may be reconciled with the safeguarding of objectives of a different nature and that to this end certain restrictions on competition are permissible, provided that they are essential to the attainment of those objectives and that they do not result in the elimination of competition for a substantial part of the Common Market'. ibid., para. 21. Cf. Van der Esch, above, n. 34, p. 82; Case 85/76 *Hoffmann-La Roche & Co AG v Commission* [1979] ECR 461.

[42] Case 139/79 *Maizena v Council* [1980] ECR 3393; Case 240/83 *Procureur de la République v Association de défense des brûleurs d'huiles usagées (ADBHU)* [1985] ECR 531. Cf. B. Van der Esch, 'Dérégulation, autorégulation et le régime de concurrence nonfaussée dans la CEE', (1990) 26 CDE 499.

competition on the internal market is not distorted. The system of rules on which the competition policy of the Community is based is laid down in Articles 3(g), 5(2), 85–90 and 92–94 EC.[43] Together with the other general principles of Community law (such as the principles of subsidiarity, proportionality and non-discrimination), and the substantive provisions setting out the duties and procedures for the institutions of the Community, as interpreted by the European Court of Justice, these form the constitutional framework for EC competition policy.

The competition rules of the Treaty are directly effective and are regularly enforced by national courts. Formally the national competition authorities are free to apply the EC competition rules as well.[44] However, after an initial period of uncertainty, the implementation of the competition rules under the EC Treaty has been concentrated in the hands of the Commission.[45] This is now a dominant feature of EC competition law. The main reason for this centralisation lies in the fact that, although the first two paragraphs of Article 85 EC are directly effective, the possibility to exempt agreements otherwise caught by the pro-hibition rests with the Commission alone.[46] The high degree of centralisation of competition policy is not without problems. The implementing rules cast the scope of the prohibitions in the Treaty widely, leading to mass notification of agreements requiring individual decisions for exemption. As a result, the Com-mission has been overloaded with cases, and has resorted to dealing with the bulk of them by informal means, which in turn raises problems of transparency and effective legal protection.[47]

Although a form of spontaneous harmonisation has taken place, whereby most of the Member States have modelled their national antitrust legislation on that of the Community, the competition authorities of the Member States have been reluctant and ill-equipped to apply the Community competition rules. Most national competition authorities are not sufficiently independent, and no adequate mechanism for co-ordination between the national authorities and the Com-mission currently exists. The result has been an uneven level of legal protec-tion and fragmented policy, in spite of superficial similarities between rules.

---

[43] Article 91 EC on dumping (which applies only to undertakings from third countries) can be regarded either as part of the competition rules or of the common commercial policy. In practice, whereas the other competition rules are applied by DG IV, antidumping actions are pursued by DG I, which is concerned with foreign trade.

[44] So long as the precedence and supremacy of Community law are respected; the power of national competition authorities to apply Articles 85 and 86 so long as the Commission has not initiated a procedure is stated in Article 9(3) of Regulation 17/1962. Cf. Case 14/68 *Walt Wilhelm and Others v Bundeskartellamt* [1969] ECR 1, para. 4 pp. 13–14; and Article 88 EC.

[45] Although it was originally intended (in contrast to the ECSC Treaty) that its implementation would require co-operation between the Commission and national authorities, rather than enforce-ment action by the Commission alone. Goyder, above, n. 27, p. 30.

[46] Case 127/73 *BRT v SABAM* [1974] ECR 51.

[47] Critical: I. Van Bael, 'The Antitrust Settlement Practice of the EEC Commission', (1986) 23 CMLR 61.

Proposals for improving decentralised enforcement of the EC competition rules in national courts and by national competition authorities are once again under discussion.[48] This debate has been encouraged particularly by the experience gained with the application of subsidiarity in the Merger Regulation, and the inclusion of the subsidiarity principle in the EC Treaty.

The Treaty basis of the executive duties of the Commission concerning the implementation of competition policy under Articles 85 and 86 EC is formed by Articles 87 and 155 EC (both directly and in the exercise of delegated powers). Under Article 87 EC the procedural framework for the application of the competition rules was worked out in Council Regulation 17 of 1962.[49] Regulation 17 defines the scope and implications of Articles 85 and 86 EC and the procedures to be followed by the Commission. On the one hand, it spells out that prohibitions entailed in the first two paragraphs of Article 85 and Article 86 EC are directly effective, rendering them enforceable by individuals before national courts. On the other hand, Regulation 17 gives an extensive definition of the powers of the Commission, concerning both investigation and adjudication. The Commission may initiate inquiries on its own initiative, as well as at the instigation of Member States or persons claiming a legitimate interest. It may request information from firms, and also enter their premises to inspect documents and conduct further investigations.[50]

Once opened, cases may be resolved by the Commission in various ways, which range from formal exemptions under Article 85(3) EC and negative clearances under Articles 85(1) and 86 EC to informal 'comfort letters'. The degree to which these solutions are legally binding bears an inverse relationship to the frequency with which they are applied.[51] Infringements are mostly resolved by negotiated settlement, but in exemplary cases formal decisions are issued, which are taken by the Commission as a collegiate body, under the general terms of

[48] An exhaustive discussion is found in J. Temple Lang, 'European Community Constitutional Law and the Enforcement of Community Antitrust Law', in B. Hawk (ed.), *Annual Proceedings of the Fordham Corporate Law Institute 1993: Antitrust in a Global Economy* (New York, 1994) especially at pp. 539–541. The Court has confirmed that the Commission can decline to pursue competition complaints where an adequate remedy is available at the national level. Joined Cases T-24/90 and T-28/90 *Automec Srl v Commission* [1992] ECR II-2223 ('Automec II'). Cf. COM(94) 161, *23rd Competition Report from the Commission: 1993*, paras. 189–191.

[49] Council Regulation 17/62 ((1962) OJ 204), amended by Council Regulation 59/62 ((1962) OJ 1655); Council Regulation 118/63 ((1963) OJ 2696); and Council Regulation 2822/71 ((1971) OJ L285). On the background and contents of Regulation 17 see Goyder, above, n. 27, ch. 4: 'Early Years of DG IV'.

[50] Indeed many authors doubt that the Council, if it had the power to reconsider, would ever again delegate such significant powers to the Commission. Goyder, above, n. 27, p. 26.

[51] Although they are not binding on the Commission or the national courts, comfort letters nevertheless convey a presumption of legality and may give rise to legitimate expectations enforceable in a court of law. The same presumably holds for general notices issued by the Commission regarding its application of the competition rules. Cf. S. Weatherill and P. Beaumont, *EC Law* (London, 1994), pp. 618, 687.

Article 163 EC. Under the terms of Regulation 17, the Commission may further impose specific conditions (including time-limits), interim measures, and substantial fines.[52] These powers are without parallel in any other area of Community law. They are supplemented by considerable delegated as well as original powers of legislation.

Since this legislation is for the main part focused on the application of the competition rules by the Commission, national procedural rules and remedies (notably the possibility of obtaining the award of damages and costs) have not been harmonised.[53] The implementing legislation adopted to date, apart from Council Regulations dealing with specialised areas such as anti-dumping and mergers,[54] consists of a number of Commission Directives (adopted recently under Article 90(3) EC),[55] as well as Commission Regulations dealing with group exemptions for specific sectors and types of agreement.[56] The latter are based on the Commission's authority to issue block exemptions under Article

[52] Under Article 15(2) of Council Regulation 17/62 fines may amount up to 1 million ECU or 10 per cent of global turnover (whichever is highest). More recently, very high fines have been used by the Commission as a deterrent, a policy tool aimed at increasing the efficiency of enforcement. Fines must nevertheless be proportional to the individual violation concerned.

[53] This in turn promotes further reliance of private parties on enforcement by the Commission and presents a further barrier to decentralised implementation. Under Community law remedies remain the exclusive province of the national systems. However, under Article 5 EC national courts must ensure that remedies are indeed available, and that these are not less favourable than those for comparable actions under national law: Case 33/76 *Rewe Zentralfinanz et al v Landwirtschaftskammer für das Saarland* [1976] ECR 1989; Case 45/76 *Comet BV v Produktschap voor Siergewassen* [1976] ECR 2043; Case 61/79 *Amministrazione delle Finanze dello Stato v Denkavit Italia Srl* [1980] ECR 1205. Recently, there may be a general development toward more uniform remedies: A. Ward, 'Effective Sanctions in EC Law: A Moving Boundary in the Division of Competence', (1995) 1 *European Law Journal* 205. For competition law in general, explicit guidelines might be adopted. Temple Lang, above, n. 48.

[54] Council Regulation 4064/89/EEC on the control of concentrations between undertakings ((1989) OJ L393/1; corrected version in (1990) OJ L257/14) (hereafter 'Merger Regulation'). Council Regulation 2423/88/EEC on protection against dumped or subsidized imports from countries not members of the European Economic Community ((1988) OJ L209/1).

[55] Commission Directive 80/723/EEC on the transparency of financial relations between Member States and public undertakings ((1980) OJ L195/35); Commission Directive 88/301/EEC on competition in the market for telecommunications terminal equipment ((1988) OJ L131/72); Commission Directive 90/388/EEC on competition in the markets for telecommunications services ((1990) OJ L192/10); Commission Directive on the Application of Articles 92 and 93 of the EEC Treaty and of Article 5 of the Commission Directive 80/723 EEC to Public Undertakings in the Manufacturing Sector ((1993) OJ L254/16); Commission Directive 94/46/EC amending Directive 88/301/EC and Directive 90/388/EEC in particular with regard to satellite communications ((1994) OJ L268/15).

[56] For example Commission Regulation 1983/83 on exclusive distribution agreements ((1983) OJ L173/1); Commission Regulation 1984/83 on exclusive purchasing agreements ((1983) OJ L173/5); Commission Regulation 2349/84 on patent licensing agreements ((1984) OJ L219/15); Commission Regulation 123/85 on motor vehicle distribution agreements ((1985) OJ L53/1); Commission Regulation 417/85 on specialization agreements ((1985) OJ L53/1); Commission Regulation 418/85 on research and development agreements ((1985) OJ L53/5); Commission Regulation 4087/88 on franchising agreements ((1988) OJ L359/46); Commission Regulation 556/89 on know-how licensing agreements ((1989) OJ L61/1).

85(3) EC, which was laid down in Council Regulation 19 of 1965.[57] The purpose of these exemptions is to provide clear guidance to firms and to reduce
the workload of the Commission. After the extensive procedural powers laid
down in Council Regulation 17 of 1962, this power of delegated legislation
forms the second main pillar of the independent competition policy powers of
the Commission. It is this combination which has given rise to the complaint
that the Commission unites the function of legislator, prosecutor and administrative judge.[58] Further, a number of notices and guidelines has been published,
which are intended to provide parties with information on the competition policy of the Commission but are not as such legally binding.[59] This use of 'soft
law' has grown recently, and serves to relieve the capacity problems of the
Commission.[60]

For the main part, the competition policy of the Community is behavioural
rather than structural. This is illustrated, for example, by the fact that under
Article 86 EC abuse of dominant position, rather than dominant position per
se, is prohibited, and by the fact that throughout competition policy the 'effects
doctrine' is followed. This does not mean that structural problems cannot be
addressed. For example, although there are no provisions for divestiture, undertakings to this effect as part of the negotiation of individual exemptions are
neither unknown, nor unusual. This can be linked to the overriding importance of the integration objective, which requires wide-ranging discretion on the
part of the Commission to allow behaviour compatible with long term benefits favouring the internal market, and to restrict behaviour which may enhance

---

[57] Council Regulation 19/65 ((1965) OJ 533) originally gave the Commission this power regarding distribution agreements and patent licenses. Council Regulation 2821/71 ((1971) OJ L285/46;
modified by Regulation 2743/72, (1972) OJ L291/144) gave the Commission similar powers regarding specialisation agreements; Council Regulation 3976/87 did the same for air transport ((1987)
OJ L374/9; amended by Regulation 2344/90, (1990) OJ L217/13; and by Regulation 2411/92,
(1992) OJ l240/19); and Council Regulation 1534/91 ((1991) OJ L143/1) for the insurance sector.
For the adoption of the delegated legislation concerned, the normal advisory committee procedures
apply. Atypically, Council Regulation 4056/86 on maritime transport ((1986) OJ L378/14) provides
its own group exemption. Cf. Goyder, *EC Competition Law* (2nd ed., Oxford, 1993) ch. 8: 'Article
85(3): Conditions for Exemption'.

[58] As a result, the function of individual officials of DG IV has been described as 'quasi-
judicial' and as concerned with policy initiation. S. Wilks, 'The Metamorphosis of European
Competition Law', in F. Snyder (ed.), *European Community Law* Vol. I (Aldershot, 1993), p. 282.
Wilks argues that the tensions between discretion and accountability have been resolved through
(1) strict bureaucratic procedure, and (2) the reliance on tight legal reasoning. Both obviously
provide checks on the use of administrative discretion to pursue industrial policy goals. Cf. the
critique by Van Bael, above, n. 47.

[59] Cf. Commision Guidelines on the application of the EEC competition rules in the telecommunications sector ((1991) OJ C233/2); Commission Notice on the assessment of cooperative joint
ventures pursuant to Article 84 of the EEC Treaty ((1993) OJ C43/02).

[60] Cf., in general, F. Snyder, 'Soft Law and Institutional Practice in the European Community',
in S. Martin (ed.), *The Construction of Europe: Essays in Honour of Emile Nöel* (Deventer, 1994);
G. Della Cananea, 'Administration by Guidelines: The Policy Guidelines of the Commission in the
Field of State Aids', in G. Darecker (ed.), *Schriftenreihe der Europäischen Rechtsakademie Trier
3: Combatting Subsidy Fraud in the EC Area* (Cologne, 1993).

economic efficiency, but has adverse effects on patterns of trade between the Member States.

There are two main sets of Treaty provisions regarding competition which are not covered by the implementing rules of Regulations 17/62 and 19/65. Under Article 90 EC, the Commission can issue both Directives and Decisions in individual cases, to ensure the application of the Treaty rules on competition and free movement to undertakings granted special and exclusive rights. In particular the ability to enact original legislation is unique to the Treaty, although it has long been rendered impractical by the lack of detailed provisions on the scope of such legislation and the procedures for its adoption.

Articles 92–94 EC on state aids provide a second category of enforcement procedures which are not covered by Regulation 17/62. In contrast to the prohibition system of Articles 85 and 86 EC, state aids are not as such illegal. Article 92(2) EC provides a list of types of aid which *are compatible* with the common market, Article 92(3) EC a list of aids which *may be considered compatible*, thereby conferring considerable discretionary power upon the Commission.[61] The list of Article 92(3) EC can be extended by the Council on a proposal by the Commission. Under the terms of Article 93 EC, the aid systems of the Member States are under constant review by the Commission, and subject to a strict notification requirement.[62] Although under Article 93(2) EC the Commission is entitled to take decisions requiring aid to be abolished or altered, and can refer alleged infringements of the state aid rules directly to the Court of Justice (in derogation of the standard procedures under Articles 169 and 170 EC), the Council may decide by unanimity that the contested aid is to be considered compatible with the common market.[63] Under Article 94 EC the Council is authorised to lay down procedural requirements for the Commission's state aid decisions. To avoid Council interference, the Commission has so far refrained from making proposals under this head.[64] Unusually for the competition rules, the state aids regime of the Treaty is itself both relatively detailed, and establishes a clear institutional balance at the Community level, albeit by derogation from normal procedures.[65]

---

[61] L. Hancher, T. Ottervanger and P. J. Slot, *EC State Aids* (London, 1993).

[62] Note that reporting arrangements in the areas of state aids and financial transparency in the relations between the Member States and undertakings granted special and exclusive rights were adopted under Article 90. Cf. Commission Directive 80/723/EEC on the transparency of financial relations between Member States and public undertakings ((1980) OJ L195/35).

[63] Since the early 1960s this clause has not been used outside the agricultural sector. C.-D. Ehlermann, 'State Aid Control in the European Union: Success of Failure?', (1995) 18 *Fordham International Law Journal* 1212, p. 1216.

[64] ibid., p. 1215.

[65] It should be noted however that whereas the Community exercises control over state aids, it does not control the aid budgets of the Member states. This leads to distortions of competition, and hampers the Community's effort to promote economic cohesion through the structural funds and selective state aid approvals. T. Frazer, 'The New Structural Funds, State Aids and Interventions on the Single Market', (1995) 30 ELR 3.

The European Court of Justice exercises judicial supervision over the Commission's application of the competition rules, and protects the rights of parties and persons claiming a legitimate interest, under Articles 173, 175, 186 and 178 *juncto* 215 EC. In these cases the Court of Justice exercises minimal judicial control similar to that of an administrative court, focused on procedure.[66] Under Article 173 EC the Court is, moreover, limited to the specific grounds provided there.[67] The Court further rules on competition questions raised as prejudicial references under Article 177 EC by national courts. Finally, the Court has decided important cases concerning the competence of the Commission under the competition rules in proceedings under Article 170 EC, as well as cases regarding alleged Treaty infringements concerning free competition by the Member States, brought by the Commission under Article 169 EC. Criticism of the lack of full judicial review by the Court, and occasional charges of unsophisticated economic analysis were met at least in part by the establishment of the Court of First Instance in October 1988, which brings more specialised and extensive resources to the judicial control of competition policy.[68] Parties before the Court of First Instance may appeal, on points of law, to the European Court of Justice.

The role of the European Parliament with regard to competition policy is negligible. Under Articles 87 and 94 EC it is to be consulted before Council Regulations are adopted. More notable is the fact that since the adoption of Regulations 17/62 and 19/65 the formal influence of the Council on the Commission's conduct of competition policy has likewise been minimal. The practical effects of this have long been limited by restrictions on the application of the competition rules. In some sectors, such as sea and air transport, the Council has withheld the necessary implementing powers from the Commission. In other fields, notably the utilities (energy, telecommunications and transport), the competition rules were not applied until after the adoption of the Single Act, under the general consensus that these industries formed natural monopolies. Further, the Commission hesitated to act with determination against state aids, although here the Treaty itself provided relatively clear guidance. In practice, in all these areas, the Commission bowed not so much to legitimate public policy concerns of the Member States, as to their political sensitivities, even where the evident distortions of competition were concerned. Instead, it has long

[66] For an expression of the Court's own conception of its role in these terms, see Case 42/85 *Remia BV v Verenigde Bedrijven Nutricia NV* [1985] ECR 2545, p. 2575, para. 34 (judicial review limited to verification of statement of reasons, manifest error, or misuse of power). Cf. D. J. Gerber, 'The Transformation of European Community Competition Law?', (1994) 35 *Harvard International Law Journal* 97, pp. 126ff.

[67] Cf. Case 78/76 *Steinike and Weinlig v Germany* [1977] ECR 593; Case C-303/88 *Italy v Commission* [1991] ECR I-1433.

[68] Created by Council Decision 88/591 ((1988) OJ L319; corrected by (1989) OJ C215/1). Cf. Articles 168a EEC, 168a EC.

concentrated on private infringements perpetuating market segmentation, which by comparison sometimes appeared almost trivial in nature.[69]

The only formal input of the Member States takes place through an advisory committee (introduced by Regulation 17/62), the views of which are not in any way binding on the Commission.[70] Hereby, the independent decision making powers of the Commission concerning competition policy (state aids excepted) are arguably the strongest under any provisions of the Treaty. In this sense, competition policy may be regarded as one of the rare areas of EC law where the Council acts as a true legislative, the Commission as an executive branch. Given the fundamental importance of competition policy, these powers form one of the main sources of strength which enable the Commission to sustain the dynamism of European integration without prior consent from (or consensus among) the Member States.

The possibilities of influencing other policy areas through the use of competition policy instruments (or the threat thereof) may be considerable. This is one of the most important reasons why the Commission has so far resisted the creation of an independent European cartel office as an encroachment on its institutional position, and as a significant shift in the constitutional balance which is potentially disfavourable to further integration.[71] However, the engrained suspicion that any change to the current system of competition policy enforcement will provide the Council with an opportunity to clip the Commission's wings has compromised the possibilities for reform of what is widely acknowledged to be a structurally overloaded system.[72]

B. EC Competition Policy towards Private Undertakings

The Commission has significant independent powers under the competition rules. It has painstakingly built up its extensive system of case law and administrative procedures in the enforcement of Article 85 EC against private parties.

---

[69] Gerber describes this as 'the effort to establish community-building norms at low economic cost and with minimal political risk'. D. J. Gerber, 'Constitutionalizing the Economy: German neo-liberalism, Competition Law and the "New" Europe', (1994) 42 *American Journal of Comparative Law* 25, p. 121. Cf. Wilks, above, n. 58.

[70] Apparently, France initially desired that the Member States would have a collective veto under Article 10(3) of Regulation 17, but backed down to strenuous opposition from the Commission and Germany. The Commission has apparently not hesitated to override unanimous opinions of the advisory committee. Under the Merger regulation, this committee can request that its opinions on draft decisions be published, opening the road to informed public debate of competition policy. Goyder, above, n. 57, pp. 45–46.

[71] Cf. C.-D. Ehlermann, 'Reflections on a European Cartel Office', (1995) 32 CMLR 471.

[72] Cf. A. J. Riley, 'More Radicalism, Please: The Notice on Co-operation between National Courts and the Commission in Applying Articles 85 and 86 of the EEC Treaty', (1993) 14 ECLR 91. An earlier critique which has not lost its force is I. S. Forrester and Ch. Norall, 'The Laicization of Community Law: Self-Help and the Rule of Reason: How Competition Law is and could be Applied', (1984) 21 CMLR 11.

The policies on horizontal and vertical agreements which are by now, long-established, are rarely challenged by the Member States; the main outstanding issue in this area is the demand for more effective implementation. Early fears (and hopes) that the Commission would succumb to pressures from the Member States in favour of private parties have, at least in this area, been proven to be unfounded. If the Commission pursues industrial policy goals in its policy toward private undertakings, it does so largely independently of the Member States.

The impact of industrial policy considerations in the competition policy of the EC can be distinguished between its role in defining general lines of policy and the margin for administrative discretion in individual cases. Concerning competition policy in general, the priority of the integration objective must be recalled. This is of importance in particular in the context of the internal market programme. The perceived need for the restructuring of European industry has been one of the main motives for (as well as a driving factor behind) the internal market programme, which was strongly supported by major European firms precisely for this reason.[73] The efficiency benefits of scale, improvements in production and distribution, and trans-national collaboration, notably in R&D, have motivated specific competition legislation by the Commission. This can be seen as a general trend in European competition policy, driven by industrial policy considerations: structural adjustment forms the essence of the Community approach to industrial policy.

The relevant block exemptions and related competition law are all squarely based on the criteria of Article 85(3) EC and as such are not widely contested.[74] The impact of the administrative discretion of the Commission is perhaps more contentious. Issues which are relevant to the balance between competition and industrial policy seem to arise:

(i) where the Commission takes industrial policy arguments into account under Article 85(1) and 85(3) EC,[75] and under Article 2(1) of the Merger Regulation;[76]

(ii) where the Commission controls the application by the Member States of specific public policy exceptions under Art 92 EC, and Article 22 of the Merger Regulation; and

(iii) where both the Commission and the national courts control the application of otherwise unspecified public policy objectives by the Member States under Article 90(2) EC.

[73] Cf. COM(85) 310, Completing the Internal Market, White Paper, pp. 34ff.

[74] 'It is ... to be expected that the power to grant group exemptions will become one of the major instruments by which the European Commission steers its competition policy in coordination with the other policies of the European Communities. Competition policy thus becomes part of the overall economic policy the Commission is pursuing'. Verstrynge, above, n. 35 [1988], p. 6.

[75] Cf. R. Bouterse, *Competition and Integration: What Goals Count? EEC Competition Law and Goals of Industrial, Monetary and Cultural Policy*, Ph.D. thesis (Florence 1992).

[76] Council Regulation 4064/89, above, n. 54.

Administrative discretion within the Community system of competition policy operates at many levels, both within and outside the margins of appreciation allowed to the Commission under Article 85(3) EC and other. There is widespread evidence that advice and informal opinions play an important role, even where formal procedures are never started. Within the competition procedures themselves, the definition of the relevant product and geographical markets allows the Commission relatively broad discretion in finding anticompetitive behaviour, which is not generally subject to strict judicial review by the Court of Justice. The criteria of prevention, restriction and distortion of competition, the definitions of dominant position and abuse thereof, and the effect on trade between the Member States likewise allow discretion at the hands of the Commission. Finally, there is political discretion at the level of the Commission taking decisions as a collegiate body, and of the Council in the area of state aids.

It is often held that its wide margins of administrative discretion make Community competition policy less effective. In their criticism of the administrative practice of the Commission, lawyers tend to advocate restricting competition policy to a strict 'effects on competition' test; economists on the other hand (following the influential Chicago school of antitrust) favour a strict test of 'effects on efficiency' instead.[77] Needless to say, these two approaches are logically opposed, and concur only on the need to reduce the margins for discretionary policy making.

However, much of the discussion on administrative discretion of the Commission is misconceived.[78] The general issue is that of the role non-competition public interest objectives should play in competition policy. In the final analysis, competition policy is economic policy (or, more accurately perhaps, economic regulation), not law or economics. First, so long as economic integration forms the primary objective of EC competition policy, there will be an intrinsic need for a flexible approach. Second, it is dubious that the consensus necessary to allow straightforward application of strict legal or economic criteria exists in the Community in the same way as is often argued to be the case in the German Federal Republic. The German system of competition law, which is often held up as a model of depoliticised and strictly rule-based policy, is itself not without room for political influence and administrative discretion, and arguably under pressure.[79]

---

[77] S. Wilks and L. McGowan, 'Discretion in European Merger Control: The German Regime in Context', (1995) 2 *Journal of European Public Policy* 41, p. 42.

[78] Wilks and McGowan argue that '. . . over-reliance on the law is destructive of the substance of policy and only succeeds in marginalising the policy area'. Instead, they plead in favour of an emphasis on 'the limitations of legal and economic tests and the importance of institutional design, public service ethics, and processes of checks, balances and transparencies'. ibid., pp. 42–43.

[79] ibid., pp. 60ff; Gerber, above, n. 66, p. 75. Bulmer likewise discusses the German negotiating position concerning the EC Merger Control regulation as an attempt of the German economics ministry to seek reconciliation with the *Bundeskartellamt* after the damaging conflict between the

Moreover, denying administrative discretion may be counterproductive. Already the Commission has been criticised for shrouding discretionary decisions in opportunistic legal motivations which serve mainly to satisfy pro forma judicial control. This occurs both due to systemic overload, and in order to camouflage potentially contentious decisions, such as those involving considerations of industrial policy. Hence, neither the 'real reasons' for Commission decisions nor their 'industrial policy content' can be established on the basis of the *Official Journal*. At the level of individual decisions, the issue of whether or not industrial and competition policy are compatible is less fundamental than are the problems of decisions, and the nature of judicial and political control.

C. The Case of Merger Control

The need for an EC merger policy has long been contested. Recently, merger policy has become a central issue in the context of the debate on industrial policy.[80] Atypically for EC competition policy, merger control is by definition concerned with market structure rather than firm behaviour. Since mergers and acquisitions do not as such constitute anti-competitive behaviour, they do not fit very well into the prohibition system of EC law. Moreover, the drive to increase the scale of national and European companies has traditionally been seen, first, as the prerogative of national industrial policy, and more recently as a logical result of, or even a prerequisite for, the creation of an internal market. Merger control thus takes place on the threshold of industrial policy. Finally, merger control is a relative novelty at the national level. Even today, most of the Member States do not have a system of merger control, and where they do, their evaluation criteria and procedures vary widely.[81]

Considering merger control, problems of institutional design and political considerations are intertwined, focused on the dimensions of effective implementation and subsidiarity.[82] Because of these considerations, merger control has been at the heart of recent demands for the creation of a European Cartel Office.

---

two over the Daimler-Benz/MBB affair, albeit in a setting where the record of the latter on prohibiting mergers (and finding these prohibitions upheld in the courts) is remarkably poor. S. Bulmer, 'Institutions and Policy Change: The Case of Merger Control', (1994) 72 *Public Administration* 423, pp. 437–439.

[80] Cf. E.-J. Mestmäcker, 'Fusionskontrolle im Gemeinsamen Markt zwischen Wettbewerbspolitik und Industriepolitik' (1988) 23 EuR 349; and 'Merger control in the Common Market: Between Competition Policy and Industrial Policy', in B. Hawk (ed.), *Annual Proceedings of the Fordham Corporate Law Institute: 1988* (New York, 1989).

[81] The United Kingdom introduced merger control in its 1965 Monopolies and Mergers Act, incorporated into the 1973 Fair Trading Act. Germany and France followed suit in 1973 and 1977, respectively.

[82] H. C. Overbury, 'Politics or Policy? The Demystification of EC Merger Control', in B. Hawk (ed.), *Annual Proceedings of the Fordham Corporate Law Institute 1992: International Antitrust Law and Policy* (New York, 1993).

Although the EEC Treaty did not provide for merger control,[83] the issue has been under discussion in the Community at least since 1965.[84] The gestation of Community merger control lasted from 1972, when the Council first requested legislative proposals from the Commission under this head, until 1989, when the Merger Regulation was finally adopted, entering into force in 1990.[85] The main reason for this long delay on an important issue of competition policy was that the Member States opposed ceding competence to the Commission over changes in industrial structure. This was motivated both by national industrial policy concerns, and by a general desire to protect economic sovereignty. Against this background, the broad Community interest criterion for exemption which was originally proposed by the Commission was particularly unhelpful, as it would have given the Commission the widest possible discretionary power.[86]

Hence, merger control languished near the bottom of the Council's legislative agenda. This changed, first, when the Commission successfully applied Articles 86 and 85 EC to mergers (which led to increasing notification, but left important gaps),[87] and, second, when in anticipation of the internal market

[83] Unlike the ECSC Treaty, which in its Article 66(1) and 66(5) gave detailed provisions extending far-reaching discretionary powers to the High Authority concerning concentrations, 'whether the transaction concerns a single product or a group of products, and whether it is effected by merger, acquisition of shares or parts of the undertaking or assets, loan, contract or any other means of control'. This included (conditional) prior authorisation, or exemption, on a series of grounds. The general objectives of the ECSC Treaty and of merger control in that setting, notably the French desire for constraints on the German war industry and the absence of national controls, at the high-water mark of supranationalism, explain the different regimes. Bulmer, above, n. 79, pp. 427–428.

[84] Overbury, above, n. 82, p. 561, with reference to a seminal 1966 Commission Memorandum on concentrations.

[85] Council Regulation 4064/89/EEC on the control of concentrations between undertakings (1989) OJ L393/1.

[86] Colin Overbury (first head of the merger task-force within DG IV) suggests that the plurality of objectives of European competition policy was itself the most complicating factor. Above, n. 82, p. 561.

[87] In response to the evident need for some form of merger control the Commission and Court of Justice have in turn resorted to Article 86 and 85 EC, with mixed results. For the application of Article 86 EC to mergers (based on the inclusion of a merger among the possible interpretations of 'abuse' of dominant position) see Case 6/72 *Continental Can v Commission* [1973] ECR 215; Case T-51/89 *Tetra-Pak Rausing v Commission* [1990] ECR II-309. For the more recent application of Article 85 EC see Joined Cases 142 and 156/84 *British American Tobacco Ltd and R.J. Reynolds Inc v Commission* [1987] ECR 4487 ('Philip Morris'), where the criterion of investment agreements leading to 'legal or *de facto* control' over another undertaking was introduced; Commission Decision 87/1 ((1987) OJ L3/17) 'Irish Distillers Group'; as well as Commission Decision 89/93 ((1989) OJ L33/44) 'Italian Flat Glass'; and the ensuing Joined Cases T-68, T-77 and T-78/89 *Italiana Vetro v Commission* [1992] ECR II-1403.

It is worth noting that the first draft of the Merger Regulation was submitted in the aftermath of Case 6/72, *Continental Can*; the version which was ultimately adopted after Joined Cases 142 and 156/84 *Philip Morris*. The dual legal basis of the regulation was found in Articles 87 and 235 EC in order to allow the control of types of concentrations not foreseen under the EC Treaty. This would, for instance, apply to mergers creating joint dominance, as was found to be the case in Case IV/M190 *Nestlé/Perrier* ((1992) OJ L356/1). Yet this argument appears to contradict the (admittedly scarce) existing case law of the Court applying Article 85 EC to joint dominance, as in the *Philip Morris* Case.

programme the number of mergers and acquisitions increased dramatically.[88] Merger control did not form part of the original 1992 programme.[89] However, confronted with the uncertainty of multiple notifications under national and Community rules, undertakings came to strongly support the introduction of a one-stop system of merger control.[90] Ultimately, merger control was presented as a necessary complement to the 1992 programme, in the context of the pervasive need for restructuring of European industry. Facilitating cross-country mergers and collaboration would promote Community integration since 'external growth by means of mergers and acquisitions can be a means of quickly realizing potential cost savings and integration gains offered by the internal market'.[91]

On the one hand, the Commission promoted the Merger Regulation as a necessary part of a strict system of antitrust rules, in the absence both of effective national controls and of co-ordination mechanisms for mergers with a Community dimension. On the other hand, it courted the business community with the promise of one-stop shopping and legal certainty, avoiding multiple procedures involving possibly contradicting demands. The Commission offered a coherent package of regulations which met the concerns of multiple constituencies: the support for the Merger Regulation may thus be explained by the combination

[88] K. George and A. Jacquemin, 'Dominant Firms and Mergers', (1992) 102 *The Economic Journal* 148, p. 154; L. Tsoukalis, *The New European Economy: The Politics and Economics of Integration* (Oxford, 1991), pp. 91ff.

[89] Remarkably, merger control was not mentioned in the *1985 White Paper*, above, n. 73, where the emphasis was on the need for rigorous discipline on state aids instead. ibid., pp. 39–40. The question seemed to be whether European competition policy should be tightened or relaxed in order to better achieve the internal market. 'Economies of scale that bulk large relative to any national market, and would therefore lead inevitably to highly concentrated industries at the national level, may be much smaller relative to the EC market as a whole. Thus economic integration may in effect serve as an anti-trust policy, curbing what would otherwise be problematic levels of monopoly power'. P. R. Krugman, 'Economic Integration in Europe: Some Conceptual Issues', in T. Padoa-Schioppa *et al*, *Efficiency, Stability and Equity: A Strategy for the Evolution of the Economic System of the European Community* (Oxford, 1987), p. 120.

[90] The classic case was the GEC-Siemens bid for control of Plessey, which was notified to the Commission, the authorities of four Member States, as well as four authorities outside the EC. Bulmer, above, n. 79, pp. 432–433.

[91] Summarising the discussion which took place in the 1980s: 'Competition and Integration: Community Merger Control Policy', (1994) 57 *European Economy*, p. vii. The thesis that merger control was a necessary corollary of the 1992 programme (given acceleration of the rate of mergers and the need for industrial restructuring) was put forward inter alia in P. Buigues, A. Jacquemin and F. Ilkovitz, 'Horizontal Mergers and Competition Policy in the European Community', (1989) 40 *European Economy*; and the Commission's Reports on Competition Policy for 1988 and 1989.

The logic of the reasoning involved has been contested both on legal and on economic grounds: J. Davidow, 'Competition Policy, Merger Control and the European Community's 1992 Program', (1991) 29 *Columbia Journal of Transnational Law* 11; N. Kay, 'Industrial Collaborative Activity and the Completion of the Internal Market', (1991) 29 JCMS 347; N. Kay, 'Mergers, Acquisitions and the Completion of the Internal Market', in K. Hughes (ed.), *European Competitiveness* (Cambridge, 1993). It is not evident that the 1992 merger wave was motivated by a search for synenergy and efficieny rather than self-preservation: '. . . where 1992 is successful, its direct effect should be to switch the emphasis in corporate strategies from cooperation to competition'. ibid., p. 177. It is suggested that political and bureaucratic reasons may have motivated this extension of Commission authority, rather than the needs of competition law enforcement.

of industry pressure, the general momentum provided by the internal market programme, the particular need for merger control given the resulting market developments, and the carefully crafted compromise of the text, which provided a new model for competition legislation. After a seventeen-year delay, the Merger Regulation was finally adopted in 1989, at the height of the initial 1992 euphoria and of the merger wave which accompanied it. The Merger Regulation has become emblematic as a compromise between effective enforcement and subsidiarity, true to the new balance of powers embodied in the Single Act.

The Merger Regulation fulfils three functions:

   (i) it establishes and allocates jurisdiction on mergers;
  (ii) it provides substantive criteria for their assessment;
 (iii) it provides a timetable and administrative procedures.

The most remarkable feature of the Merger Regulation is that it allocates responsibility for merger control between the national and Community levels by reference to a turnover threshold, albeit with three possible exceptions. According to its Article 1, mergers involving a combined aggregate worldwide turnover of five billion ECU, and an aggregate Community turnover of at least two of the undertakings involved of more than 250 million ECU each, are deemed to have a Community dimension. Such mergers require prior notification to and assessment by the Commission, unless each of the undertakings involved achieves more than two-thirds of its aggregate Community turnover within one Member State.

There are three exceptions to this general attribution of competence. First, under Article 9 of the Merger Regulation, a Member State may request the Commission to decide that the State may itself investigate a merger which creates an anti-competitive situation in a market within that Member State, and one which presents all the characteristics of a 'distinct market'. Second, Article 22 of the Merger Regulation provides for the inverse situation, where a Member State may request the Commission to act against a concentration which falls below the general threshold, but significantly impedes effective competition within that Member State and affects trade between the Member States.[92] Third, Article 21 provides that Member States may, in derogation of the general rules, take appropriate measures to protect certain legitimate interests other than those taken into account by the Merger Regulation, notably concerning public security, plurality of the media, and prudential rules.[93]

---

[92] Over 1990–1993, only one such request was received, from the Belgian government: Commission Decision IV/M.278, *British Airways/Dan Air* ((1993) OJ C68/5). COM(93) 385, Community Merger Control: Report from the Commission on the implementation of the Merger Regulation.

[93] The Commission also reserves the right to act under Articles 85, 86 and 89 EC against concentrations which do not have a Community dimension under the terms of the Merger Regulation but do exceed the 2 billion ECU worldwide turnover and 100 million ECU Community turnover thresholds which it had originally proposed. 'Commission Declaration: Notes on Council Regulation (EEC) No 4064/89', in Community Merger Control Law, *EC Bull* Supplement 2/90.

The complex allocation of jurisdiction established by the Merger Regulation can be explained as a balance between the objectives of competition at the European level and wider national public interest considerations, which was shaped by the institutional dynamics in the Council under conditions of unanimous decision making.[94] Thus the introduction of the threshold mechanism has been traced to the United Kingdom, the possibility of referral to the national competition authorities to Germany, and that of mergers below the thresholds to the Commission to The Netherlands. Further, the high thresholds assured some Member States (such as France and the Mediterranean countries) that their national industrial and regional policies designs would not necessarily be frustrated. As a result, the Merger Regulation forms the most sophisticated application of the principle of subsidiarity in competition law.[95]

The content of the Merger Regulation has been as contested, as has its allocation of competence. The starting point for the appraisal of concentrations is a substantive test based on the combination of the criteria of dominant position (familiar from Article 86 EC),[96] and that of impeding effective competition, in Article 2(3) of the Merger Regulation.[97] Further, in its Article 2(1), the Merger Regulation lists the criteria relevant for assessing the compatibility of a merger with the common market. Under Article 2(1)b, alongside the more familiar criteria of market position, economic and financial power, the alternatives available for suppliers and users, the existence of barriers to entry, trends of supply and demand, and the interests of intermediate and ultimate consumers, 'the development of technical and economic progress' is to be taken into account, 'provided that it is to consumers' advantage and does not form an obstacle to

[94] The most convincing explanation of the adoption of the Merger Regulation after 17 years of negotiation is provided by Bulmer, above, n. 79.

[95] The draft regulation was submitted simultaneously with a Commission Notice containing a de minimis exemption for SMEs ((1986) OJ C231/2). For a detailed account of how subsidiarity has always been a guiding principle of competition policy see Temple Lang, 'European Community Constitutional Law and the Enforcement of Community Antitrust Law', in B. Hawk (ed.), *Annual Proceedings of the Fordham Corporate Law Institute 1993: Antitrust in a Global Economy* (New York, 1994). The Merger Regulation itself has been criticised as an abdication by the Commission, and as an illegal redistribution of powers. Criticism was generated especially by the apparent threat to legal certainty due to the weakening of standing for interested third parties, and the fact the Merger Regulation appeared to relinquish Community control over all mergers which fell below the thresholds. 'Constitutional' objections were raised against primary reliance on Article 235 EEC as its legal basis. Cf. J. S. Venit, 'The "Merger" Control Regulation: Europe comes of Age . . . or Caliban's Dinner', (1990) 27 CMLR 7; on the rights of third parties cf. Editorial, 'Judicial Review and Merger Control', (1992) 29 CMLR 1.

[96] Cf. Case 27/76 *United Brands v Commission* [1978] ECR 207; Case 85/76 *Hoffmann-LaRoche v Commission* [1979] ECR 461; Case 322/81 *NV Nederlandsche Bandenindustrie Michelin v Commission* [1983] ECR 3461.

[97] The emphasis in the Commission's practice is on establishing whether a position of dominance exists rather than whether effective competition is impeded. As a result, although a dominant position is not as such illegal, nor does its existence demonstrate a significant impediment to effective competition, the creation or strengthening of dominant position carries a presumption of illegality. Cf. T. A. Downes and D. S. MacDougall, 'Significantly Impeding Effective Competition', (1994) 19 ELR 286.

competition'. On the basis of these provisions, a three-step test is involved: the determination (i) of the relevant product market; (ii) of the relevant geographic market, and (iii) of the compatibility of the merger with the common market.[98]

The tension between industrial and competition policy within the merger regulation centres on the clause concerning 'technical and economic progress'.[99] Compared to the wide efficiency defence foreseen in earlier drafts, the technical and economic progress clause is relatively limited.[100] There is no agreement as to whether or not this clause in fact constitutes an efficiency defence; to date, Commission decisions are not motivated in efficiency terms.[101]

Under a purely competition oriented system of merger control the main objective would be to maintain effective competition by blocking mergers which create or strengthen a dominant position. Industrial policy, understood as the promotion of structural adjustment, would require a more lenient approach in a number of cases. Concentration may form an instrument of industrial restructuring where increased scale is perceived as related to efficiency, or as necessary for survival in global markets (strategic mergers).[102] Here, the main direct conflict between industrial and competition policy occurs where significant economies of scale favour industrial restructuring, but the resulting concentration increases market power. This situation could be covered by the economic progress clause of Article 2(1)b. Other industrial policy arguments which can be accommodated under Article 2(1)b are the need to promote cross-border concentrations (as instruments of integration) and technological progress.[103]

[98] D. Neven, S. Nuttall and P. Seabright, *Merger in Daylight: The Politics and Economics of European Merger Control* (London, 1993), p. 91.

[99] Cf. also Recital 13 of the Merger Regulation, with reference to the objectives of Article 2 EEC, economic and social cohesion.

[100] An earlier draft stated that '. . . the competitiveness of the sectors concerned with regard to international competition and the interests of consumers shall be taken into account'. (1989) OJ C22/16, cited in Bulmer, above, n. 79, p. 437. Kay argues that since mergers should generally be associated with efficiency losses rather than gains, there would have been stronger grounds for an efficiency objection instead. Above, n. 91 [1993], p. 178.

[101] Buiges, Jacquemin and Ilkovitz, above, n. 91, pp. 52–53; Bulmer, above, n. 79, p. 440; Neven *et al*, above, n. 98, consider that in Commission Decision IV/M.050, *AT&T/NCR* ((1991) OJ C16/20) efficiency arguments appear to have played a role, whereas in Commission Decision IV/M.053, *Aerospatiale/Alenia/de Havilland* ((1991) OJ L334/42), where the parties pleaded cost savings of 0.5 per cent of combined turnover, they were dismissed by the Commission as 'negligible', and apparently did not affect the final decision. A confusing feature of the Commission's approach is that it is not consistent, and at times seems to regard cost savings as a negative factor which can lead to the strengthening of dominant position. ibid., pp. 116–117.

[102] Cf. P. Buigues and A. Jacquemin, 'Strategies of Firms and Structural Environments in the Large Internal Market', (1989) 28 JCMS 53; L. Tsoukalis, above, n. 88. The evidence on the existence of strategic motives for mergers is mixed: R. Caves, 'Corporate Mergers in International Economic Integration', in A. Giovannini and C. Mayer, *European Financial Integration* (Cambridge, 1991).

[103] Recent arguments appear to indicate that any policy to stimulate Euro-mergers and acquisitions is fundamentally flawed. First, there is ample evidence that co-operation between European firms can at best be complementary for firms' strategies, and a bias towards co-operation with United States and Japanese firms is therefore likely to persist. Cf. Kay, above, n. 91 [1993]; R. van Tulder and G. Junne, *European Multinationals in Core Technologies* (Chichester, 1988). Cf. P. A. Geroski,

Critics of industrial policy fear that the fact that the regulation was based primarily on Article 235 EC could facilitate the pursuit of such objectives under Article 2(1)b.[104] They also point out that so far the Commission has only moved to block two mergers (out of a total of more than 200 notifications), and note that in general mergers result in efficiency losses rather than gains. The conclusion which is usually drawn is that merger control should be exercised on competition criteria alone, preferably by an independent agency isolated from political pressure; or, as a second best solution, under procedures where the political nature of merger decisions is transparent, possibly explicitly modelled on the German system.[105]

The Commission maintains that the merger decisions taken so far demonstrate clearly that the application of the merger regulation is based on competition principles, although it is also in conformity with the industrial policy of the Community. Further, it points out that (as under Article 85(3) EC), the need to consider economic and technological progress under Article 2(1)b of the Merger Regulation is limited by the requirements that consumers benefit, and that competition not be eliminated. More fundamentally, the Commission holds that 'prohibition is not the aim of merger control and that it is only as a matter of the last resort that the regulatory authorities will oppose a permanent structural change in the market'.[106] Instead:

... the Commission has aimed to apply the Regulation in conformity with its fundamental objectives: allowing concentrations which bring about necessary corporate reorganisations in the Community as a result of the opening of national markets to Community and world markets, while prohibiting or modifying concentrations which are likely to

'Vertical Relations Between Firms and Industrial Policy', (1992) 102 *The Economic Journal* 138; P. A. Geroski and A. Jacquemin, 'Industrial Change, Barriers to Mobility and European Industrial Policy', in A. Jacquemin and A. Sapir (eds.), *The European Internal Market: Trade and Competition —Selected Readings* (Oxford, 1983); A. Jacquemin and D. Wright, 'Corporate Strategies and European Challenges Post-1992', (1993) 31 JCMS 525; A. Jacquemin, 'European Industrial Policy and Competition', in P. Coffey (ed.), *Economic Policies of the Internal Market* (London, 1979).

Second, in many areas European firms have now attained the size of their United States competitors (and far exceeded that of the largest Japanese firms) without this having brought the desired benefits of scale in terms of costs and competitiveness. New developments in trade theory and industrial economics have pointed out that economies of scale are only significant in a limited number of industrial sectors, and that even these may not necessarily be the ones on which a modern economy may wish to focus. Cf. P. A. Geroski and A. Jacquemin, 'Large Firms in the European Corporate Economy and Industrial Policy in the 1980s', in A. Jacquemin (ed.), *European Industry: Public Policy and Corporate Strategy* (Oxford, 1984); P. A. Buigues and A. Jacquemin, 'Strategies of Firms and Structural Environments in the Large Internal Market', (1989) 28 JCMS 53. Evidence that efficiency and returns decrease rather than increase with size, especially when the latter is the result of conglomerate mergers, has been a recurrent theme in economic literature: Cf. B. Dankbaar, J. Groenewegen and H. Schenk (eds.), *Perspectives in Industrial Organization* (Dordrecht, 1990).

[104] Mestmäcker, above, n. 80 [1989], pp. 8–9. Cf. considerations 8 and 13 of the Merger Regulation.

[105] Monopolkommission, *Sondergutachten 17—Konzeption einer europäischen Fusionskontrolle* (Baden-Baden, 1989).

[106] Overbury, above, n. 82, pp. 583–585. Cf. considerations 2–4 of the Merger Regulation.

result in lasting damage to effective competition in the common market or a substantial part of it.[107]

On institutional reform, it retorts that the Commission is actually more independent than existing Community agencies, and can be taken to court if its decisions are found to exceed its powers or are unacceptable on other grounds.

The increasingly numerous evaluations of the Commission's decisions in this area indicate that the Commission has not overtly allowed industrial policy criteria to prevail over competition.[108] The evidence does suggest that mergers are facilitated rather than obstructed. Generally, the Commission attempts to find solutions which will permit the merger to proceed, in consultation with the parties involved, and through imposing conditions and obligations in its decisions accordingly.[109] Firms perceive the possibilities for bargaining at various levels as pervasive, and their influence on the outcome of the process as strong.[110] Although no formal efficiency defence exists, practice suggests that efficiency considerations are taken into account, and enter into the process through such diverse mechanisms as inter-service consultation within the Commission, and private hearings with the responsible Commissioner during the negotiation of remedies. Favourable assessments of dominance and lenient remedies often appear to accommodate efficiency concerns. In the interest of transparency, it seems preferable that efficiency considerations should explicitly be taken into account, and that claims by firms to this effect should be independently verified.[111]

---

[107] COM(93) 385, above, n. 92, p. 4.

[108] Cf. M. Bishop and J. Kay (eds.), *European Mergers and Merger Policy* (Oxford, 1993); Downes and MacDougall, above, n. 97; J. T. Halverson, 'EC Merger Control: Competition Policy of Industrial Policy? Views of a US Practitioner', (1993) 19 LIEI 49; A. Hughes, 'Competition Policy and the Competitive Process: Europe in the 1990s', (1992) 43 *Metroeconomica* 1; A. Jacquemin *et al*, *Merger and Competition Policy in the European Community* (Oxford, 1990) P. H. Admiraal (ed.); Neven *et al*, above, n. 98; A. S. Pathak, 'EEC Merger Regulation Enforcement During 1992', (1992) 17 ELR *Competition Checklist* 132. M. Siragusa and R. Subiotto, 'The EEC Merger Control Regulation: The Commission's Evolving Case Law', (1991) 28 CMLR 877; J. S. Venit, 'Review of the 1993 Decisions under the Merger Regulation', (1993) 18 ELR *Competition Checklist* 133.

[109] The Commission has focused on three types of remedies: (1) the removal of barriers to entry, cf. Commission Decision IV/M.157, *Air France/Sabena* ((1992) OJ C272/5); Commission Decision IV/M.259, *British Airways/TAT* ((1992) OJ C326/16); and Commission Decision IV/M.042, *Alcatel Telettra* ((1991) OJ L122/48); (2) the ending of capital, personal and contractual links in oligopolistic markets, cf. Commission Decision IV/M.113, *Courtaulds/SNIA* ((1991) OJ C333/16), Commission Decision IV/M.012, *Varta/Bosch* ((1991) OJ L320/26), and Commission Decision IV/M.190, *Nestlé/Perrier*, above n. 87; and (3) the divestiture of assets and shares both in order to reduce market share and facilitate entry: cf. Commission Decision IV/M.043, *Magneti Marelli/CEAC* ((1991) OJ L222/38), Commission Decision IV/M126, *Accor/Wagons-Lits* ((1992) OJ L204/1), Commission Decision IV/M.019, *Nestlé-Perrier*, above, n. 87, Commission Decision *Du Pont/ICI* ((1992) OJ C7/13), and Commission Decision IV/M291, *KNP/BT/VRG* ((1993) OJ L217/35). Cf. COM(93) 385, above, n. 92, p. 5.

[110] Neven *et al*, above, n. 98, ch. Four: 'The Reactions of Firms', and pp. 215ff.

[111] ibid., pp. 12–13; 239–240.

Although the vast majority of mergers is approved it is difficult to establish whether political motives play an important role.[112] In the infamous *Aerospatiale/Alenia/DeHavilland* case, the first merger to be blocked, the Commission was subjected to intense political pressure and publicly vented outrage by the French and Italian governments, to such an extent that the discussion carried over into the mass media.[113] This has generally been read as a test-case demonstrating that the Commission's merger policy is competition-driven. It may, however, have compromised the willingness of the Member States to lower the Merger Regulation thresholds, and it has given rise to various proposals promoting wider public interest criteria.[114]

Even where such external political pressures can be resisted, the political nature of decision making within the Commission remains, and much depends on the political weight and effectiveness of the responsible Commissioner. Although DG IV recently blocked the *Bertelsmann/Kirch/Deutsche Telekom* concentrative joint venture *MSG-Media Service*,[115] another merger which DG IV had proposed to block, *Mannesmann/Valourec/ILVA*, was instead passed narrowly by the Commission.[116]

These observations confirm that the industrial policy issue may be less important than the danger of 'agency capture'.[117] If the need for some form of administrative discretion is accepted, the general problem of wider public interest considerations, legitimacy, and the risks of capture of competition policy by government or industry take on greater importance. In general, three possible remedies have been proposed. These are: increasing (i) the accountability; (ii) the independence; and (iii) the transparency of merger control, and of competition policy in general.

[112] However, substantial circumstantial evidence of the importance of political bargaining at the Commission level is available. For an account of Commissioner Brittan's efforts to find a first merger case that could be blocked, against the efforts by the other Commissioners, representing their national interests see G. Ross, *Jacques Delors and European Integration* (Cambridge, 1995), pp. 177ff.

[113] Commission Decision IV/M.053, above, n. 101. Apparently, the Commission itself was badly split on the decision, with Commissioner Brittan carrying a majority of one vote over a block around Commissioners Bangemann and Van Miert, and, more importantly, President Delors (who ultimately abstained). The Advisory Committee on Concentrations was likewise split. Cf. Opinion 91/C341/07 ((1991) OJ C314/7).

[114] L. Hawkes, 'The EC Merger Regulation: Not an Industrial Policy Instrument: The De Havilland Decision', (1992) 13 ECLR 44.

[115] Case IV/M.469 ((1994) OJ L364/1). The fact that around the same time the *BT-MCI* joint venture was cleared also suggests that collaboration in global markets with partners from third countries is now more acceptable than before, in contrast to attempts at foreclosure of large domestic markets as in the case of MGM.

[116] ((1994) OJ L102/15). Cf. the commentary in (1994) 15 ECLR R-103.

[117] Cf. Bulmer, 'Institutions and Policy Change: The Case of Merger Control', (1994) 72 *Public Administration* 423, pp. 437–439; Neven *et al*, above, n. 98; P. Seabright, 'Regulatory Capture, Subsidiarity and European Community Merger Control', (1994) 57 *European Economy* 109; Wilks and McGowan, 'Discretion in European Merger Control: The German Regime in Context', (1995) 2 *Journal of European Public Policy* 41, p. 42 and S. L. Wilks and McGowan, 'Disarming the Commission: The Debate over a European Cartel Office', (1995) 32 JCMS 259.

In this context, it should be noted that the 1993 review of the functioning of Articles 9 and 22, and of the height of the threshold values, foreseen in Article 1(3) of the Merger Regulation has failed.[118] Requests by national competition authorities under Article 9 of the Merger Regulation are turned down regularly. This can be explained by the fact that the Commission believes that the thresholds which determine its own competence are already too high.[119] The Commission argues in favour of centralised control, where a Community dimension is present, both to provide one-stop shopping and protection of the Community interest where spill-over effects occur which are external to national control.[120] The Commission had hoped to see the thresholds lowered to 2 billion ECU world-wide, and 100 million Community-wide turnover. It predicted this would double the current level of fifty notifications yearly. Given strong resistance by the Member States and the national competition authorities,[121] the Commission has opted for a further review in the course of 1996 instead.[122] Several Member States (notably Germany and the United Kingdom) have linked revision of the thresholds to the creation of an independent European Cartel Office, which was discussed at the Intergovernmental Conference which started in 1996.

IV. COMPETITION AND PUBLIC POLICY

A. The Application of EC Competition Rules to the Member States

Although the fact that the Member States might distort competition was acknowledged from the earliest beginnings of the Community, until recently they were largely excluded from the application of the competition rules. The Commission concentrated on establishing procedural and legislative powers, and a functioning system of enforcement aimed foremost at abuse by private undertakings. The

---

[118] M. Siragusa, 'The Lowering of the Thresholds: An Opportunity to Harmonise Merger Control', (1993) 14 ECLR 139.

[119] Between 1990 and 1993 there were five such requests. Four originated from the German *Bundeskartellamt*: Commission Decision IV/M.012, *Varta/Bosch*, above, n. 109; Commission Decision IV/M.222, *Mannesmann/Hoesch* ((1993) OJ C114/34); Commission Decision IV/M.238, *Siemens/Philips* ((1993) OJ C11/5); Commission Decision IV/M.165, *Alcatel/AEG Kabel* ((1992) OJ C6/23). One came from the UK Monopolies and Merger Commission: Commission Decision IV/M.180, *Steetley Tarmac* ((1992) OJ C50/11). COM(93) 385, Community Merger Control: Report from the Commission to the Council on the Implementation of the Merger Regulation. All four requests from the *Bundeskartellamt* were refused, which has not helped the at times tense relations between this body and DG IV. Recently however, the first case was passed to Berlin: Case IV/M.330, *CPC/McCormick/Rabobank/Ostmann*. Cf. COM(94) 161, *23rd Competition Policy Report from the Commission: 1993*.

[120] ibid., pp. 7–14.   [121] Wilks and McGowan, above, n. 117, p. 268.

[122] COM(93) 385, Community Merger Control: Report from the Commission on the implementation of the Merger Regulation.

overriding objective of competition policy was 'to establish community-building norms at low economic cost and with minimum political risk'.[123]

Although market oriented, the economic systems of the Member States were guided by a political logic of intervention. Active national industrial policies were pursued by various means, such as state aids, discriminatory public procurement, and extensive state holdings. In general, the Member States enjoyed broad discretionary powers in economic policy. The direction of economic policy was determined by corporatist arrangements which favoured risk aversion, the concentration of benefits on cartel type interest groups, and the diffusion of the costs incurred over unorganised general interests. As a result, mercantilist policies prevailed, which focused on sectoral particularities, strategic sectors and a general assumption of pervasive economies of scale, and comprised notions of competition as potentially wasteful or harmful, and at odds with equity.

Obviously, this type of economic policy was predisposed towards capture by private interests. Yet the opaque nature of the decision making processes involved and the potential for extensive income redistribution under conditions of rapid economic growth, provided a broad consensus underpinning the corporatist model. In this context national competition policy was generally subordinated to economic policy (including widespread price and production controls), public interest exceptions, and political discretion generally. Industry agreements were often not considered anti-competitive per se, and were often used as instruments of public policy.[124] Although this system left room for economic integration, there were political limits to the extent to which such integration could encroach on national economic sovereignty.

During the 1970s, the national corporatist systems came under increasing pressure. Following exogenous economic shocks, economic growth ground to a halt. The initial reaction of the Member States was to treat this as a temporary adjustment problem, to be resolved by increasing, rather than reducing, state intervention. As public enterprises were forced to come to the rescue of an increasing number of struggling private firms, the share of direct state ownership in the economy rose dramatically during the crisis years.[125] Private firms were tempted (and encouraged) to engage in various forms of anti-competitive behaviour in order to weather the crisis, while subsidies and aids of various

[123] Gerber, above, n. 26, pp. 121–122.

[124] Given widespread state intervention and the impact of private interests on public policy, undertakings looked to their national governments for guidance, rather than to the Community, where interest-representation was underdeveloped. W. Streeck and Ph. C. Schmitter, 'From National Corporatism to Transnational Pluralism: Organised Interests in the Single European Market', (1991) 19 *Politics and Society* 209.

[125] J. Vickers and V. Wright (eds.), *The Politics of Privatisation in Europe* (London, 1989); V. Wright (ed.), *Privatization in Western Europe: Pressures, Problems, Paradoxes* (London, 1994). Other motives were economic nationalism, regime consolidation (especially in the new democracies of Greece, Portugal and Spain), political patronage (Italy), and appeasement of regional tensions (Belgium). Wright, ibid., pp. 21–22.

forms multiplied. Retrenching however, failed, and led to a debilitating drain both on public enterprise as such (which up to this point had performed reasonably well), and on public finances in general.

With some exceptions, such as the Davignon plan for the rationalisation of the steel sector, the role of the Community was clearly undermined by these trends. The Commission came under pressure to accept increasing numbers of 'short term' anti-competitive measures in the interest of the weakened Member States' economies, notably in the area of state aids.[126] The Commission reacted by concentrating on securing compliance in a limited number of areas, thus maintaining the momentum of integration, while avoiding direct conflict over national crisis management.

From the early 1980s onward, the Member States began to withdraw from direct intervention in the economy.[127] Their broad reversal of policy towards liberalisation, deregulation, and privatisation was motivated by economic necessity and more subtle changes in the prevalent ideological and economic paradigm.[128] To allow restructuring of the national economies, previously sheltered sectors were exposed to the market, and arms' length regulation on the basis of general rules increasingly came to replace political management of the economy. In the process, the opportunities for a more active competition policy increased, both at the national and the Community level.

One aspect of this was the strengthening of competition rules in the majority of the Member States, often modelled on EC competition law.[129] This added further incentives to increase competition, as political discretion was gradually replaced by the rule of economic law. For the Community, a major shift

[126] Cf. Jacquemin, above, n. 103 [1979], pp. 22–34; J.-L. Cadieux, 'Restructuration industrielle et politique communautaire vis-à-vis des aides nationales', in J. Dutheil de la Rochère and J. Vandamme (eds.), *Intervention Publiques et Droit Communautaire* (Paris, 1988).

[127] Various specific rationales offered for privatisation include the need for a revitalisation of the national economy; to increase efficiency; to facilitate tough labour policies (after workers lose their privileged public sector status); the rationalisation of production and of group holdings; to increase access to market capital; to reduce governments' commercial risk; the improvement of public sector liquidity; and short-term government budget considerations. Wright, above, n. 125.

[128] This broad systemic change has been defined variously as the transition from the 'welfare state' to the 'competition state', from the 'Fordist' mode of production to 'Post-Fordism', from 'économie politique de marché' to 'état de droit économique', as the demise of corporatism, and others, with various ideological connotations. Cf. P. G. Cerny, 'The Limits of Deregulation: Transnational Interpenetration and Policy Change', (1991) 19 *European Journal of Political Research* 173; P. G. Cerny, *The Changing Architecture of Politics: Structure, Agency and the Future of the State* (London, 1990); H. Dumez and A. Jeunemaître, 'L'État et le Marché en Europe. Vers un État de droit économique?', (1992) 42 *Revue Française de Science Politique* 263; H. Dumez and A. Jeunemaître, *La concurrence en Europe: De nouvelles règles du jeu pour les entreprises* (Paris, 1991); B. Rosamond, 'Mapping the European Condition: The Theory of Integration and the Integration of Theory', (1995) 1 *European Journal of International Relations* 391; Streeck and Schmitter, above, n. 124.

[129] Temple Lang, 'European Community Constitutional Law and the Enforcement of Community Antitrust Law', in B. Hawk (ed.), *Annual Proceedings of the Fordham Corporate Law Institute 1993: Antitrust in a Global Economy* (New York, 1994), pp. 536–537.

coincided with the adoption of the 1992 programme.[130] As both the Member States and industry increasingly turned to European solutions, the competition policy of the Community came to manifest a new assertiveness. This assertiveness applied to both new areas, and new general types of agreements to which the competition rules were now applied.[131]

Most importantly, barriers due to state regulation and intervention have become the focus of the competition policy of the European Community.[132] The Commission has been increasingly active both concerning the enforcement of the rules on state aids, and in enforcing the provisions of Articles 85, 86 and 90 EC against the Member States and privileged undertakings.

Three priorities dominate recent Commission policy on state aids:[133]

(i) the strict examination of existing aid schemes, including the repayment of past aids;[134]

(ii) supplementing and updating of the general principles which the Commission has attempted to establish since the early 1980s, including the

---

[130] The possible deregulatory effects of harmonisation and competition among rules as part of the internal market programme will not be considered here. Cf. R. Dehousse, C. Joerges, G. Majone and F. Snyder, with M. Everson, *Europe After 1992: New Regulatory Strategies*, EUI Working Paper Law 92/31 (Florence, 1992); C.-D. Ehlermann, 'Ökonomische Aspekte des Subsidiaritätsprinzips: Harmonisierung versus Wettbewerb der Systeme', (1995) 18 *Integration* 11; N. Reich, 'Competition Among Legal Orders: A New Paradigm of EC Law?', (1992) 29 CMLR 861; H. Siebert and M. J. Koop, 'Institutional Competition Versus Centralization: *Quo Vadis* Europe?', (1993) 9 *Oxford Review of Economic Policy* 15; J.-M. Sun and J. Pelkmans, 'Regulatory Competition in the Single Market', (1995) 33 JCMS 67; J. P. Trachtman, 'International Regulatory Competition, Externalization and Jurisdiction', (1993) 34 *Harvard International Law Journal* 47.

[131] The explanatory factors have been divided into five external factors and two internal ones. The external factors are: (1) the continuing support of the Court of Justice; (2) and the European Parliament; (3) the elevation of the market integration objective (which is also the primary objective of competition policy) under the 1992 programme, boosting the importance of DG IV and its morale; (4) the general support for the 1992 programme, providing further legitimacy; (5) the 'philosophical endorsement of the market' as the dominant ideological feature of the 1980s. The two factors internal to DG IV are (1) the rise of a 'third generation' of highly motivated officials; and (2) the consecutive leadership of two strong Commissioners, Peter Sutherland and Sir Leon Brittan. Cf. Wilks, 'The Metamorphosis of European Competition Law', in F. Snyder (ed.), *European Community Law* Vol. I (Aldershot, 1993), pp. 276ff: 'A Conspiracy of Events: Competition Policy Comes of Age'.

[132] Thus '. . . it is felt that at the present stage of economic integration in the Community the barriers are greatest in markets currently subject to state regulation'. Commission of the EC, *Twentieth Report on Competition Policy* (Brussels-Luxembourg, 1990) p. 50. Cf. Gerber, 'Constitutionalizing the Economy: German neo-liberalism, Competition Law and the "New" Europe', (1994) *American Journal of Comparative Law* 25, pp. 137–138.

[133] C.-D. Ehlermann, 'The Contribution of EC Competition Policy to the Single Market', (1992) 29 CMLR 257, p. 274. Cf. Ehlermann, 'State Aid Control in the European Union: Success of Failure?', (1995) 18 *Fordham International Law Journal* 1212, p. 1216; Hancher, Ottervanger and Slot, *EC State Aids* (London, 1993); L. Hancher, 'State Aids and Judicial Control in the European Community', (1994) 15 ECLR 134; F. G. Wishlade, 'Competition Policy, Cohesion and the Co-ordination of Regional Aids in the European Community', (1993) 14 ECLR 143.

[134] Cf. Case C-310/87 *France v Commission* [1990] ECR I-307 ('Boussac').

application of the 'market investor test' to state investment in public enterprises;[135]

(iii) tighter control of new aid cases.

The strict enforcement of the Treaty rules on state aids imposes important constraints on the ability of the Member States to conduct autonomous industrial policy, of which such aids have traditionally been the privileged instrument.[136] Moreover, now the state aids rules are applied with equal force to public undertakings, the latter have become unattractive as industrial policy tools, encouraging privatisation.[137]

As national economic intervention came under pressure from competition policy, the Court was called to clarify the remaining scope for the exercise of public authority by the Member States. It has made clear that the concept of undertaking used under the competition rules applies to any entities engaged in economic activity (regardless of their statute), but not to bodies engaged in the exercise of public authority.[138] The relation between national regulatory powers

---

[135] Case C-305/89 *Italy v Commission* [1991] ECR I-1635 ('Alfa-Romeo'); Case C-303/88 *Italy v Commission* [1991] ECR I-1433 ('ENI-Lanerossi'). Commission Directive 80/723/EEC on the transparency of financial relations between Member States and public undertakings (1980) OJ L195/35, which established reporting requirements and a system of Commission supervision, gave rise to Joined Cases 188–190/80 *French Republic et al v Commission* [1982] ECR 2545 ('Transparency Directive'), in which the regulatory powers of the Commission under Article 90(3) were first confirmed by the Court. The Commission attempted to extend the terms of the transparency directive in its Communication on the application of Articles 92 and 93 of the EEC Treaty and of Article 5 of the Commission Directive 80/723 EEC to public undertakings in the manufacturing sector ((1991) OJ C273/2). This communication was challenged by France in an Article 173 procedure, and struck down by the Court of Justice as an attempt to introduce additional obligations on the Member States which lacked a legal basis. The Court remarked that the use of Article 90(3) would have been appropriate in this case, and the Commission duly re-enacted the directive on this basis ((1993) OJ L254/16). Case C-325/91 *France v Commission* [1993] ECR I-3283, noted by Pappaioannou (1994) 31 CMLR 155.

[136] Consequently, state aids policy has been described as an '. . . encroachment into the economic sovereignty of the Member States' since '(T)he ability to establish, finance, subsidise and fiscally influence industrial and commercial undertakings . . . is historically fundamental to the integrity of the modern industrialised state'. Wilks, above, n. 131, p. 282.

[137] A. Abate, 'Droit communautaire, privatisations, déréglementations', (1994) 4 *Revue du Marché Unique Européen* 11, p. 35.

[138] In Case C-41/83 *Italy v Commission* [1985] ECR 873 ('British Telecom'), the Court found that a body holding regulatory powers, such as British Telecom, could be considered an undertaking under Article 86 EEC concerning the exercise of those functions. In Case C-41/90 *Höfner v Macrotron* [1991] ECR I-1979, the Court stated that 'in the context of competition law . . . the concept of an undertaking encompasses every entity engaged in an economic activity regardless of the legal status of the entity and the way in which it is financed', para. 21 p. 2016. In Case C-92/91 *Ministère Public v Taillandier* [1993] ECR I-5383 the Court applied the concept of undertaking to a branch of the French telecommunications ministry. However, in Joined Cases C-159 and C-160/91 *Poucet et Pistre* [1993] ECR I-637 the Court considered that the operation of a public social security service does not constitute an 'economic activity'; and in Case C-364–92 *SAT-Fluggesellschaft* [1994] ECR I-43, that activities related to the control and supervision of air space did not constitute economic activities in the sense of Article 90 juncto Article 86 EC. Cf. *23rd Competition Report from the Commission*, above, n. 119, p. 211.

and the Community competition rules was addressed in particular in the case law on the joint application of Articles 3(f), 5(2), and 85 and 86 EEC.[139]

Originally, the Court appeared to be developing a doctrine which would impose severe constraints on economic policy of the Member States.[140] In 1977, the Court ruled that the Member States were barred from depriving the competition rules of the Treaty from their *effet utile*, or effectiveness.[141] In Case 229/83 *Au Blé Vert*, the Court appeared to suggest that legislation which makes anti-competitive behaviour redundant by itself restricting competition could fall foul of the *effet utile* rule.[142] The scope of the *effet utile* case law was gradually expanded until, in 1988, four categories of state measures infringing the obligations of the Member States under Article 5(2) in combination with Article 3(f) EEC were defined, divided into two branches.[143] State measures amounted to an illegal distortion of competition, first, where the state imposed, facilitated the conclusion, or reinforced the effects of restrictive agreements,[144] and, second, where it delegated to undertakings the responsibility to take measures of economic policy.[145]

[139] Article 5 EC, which contains the constitutional principle of loyal co-operation, has long been at the centre of debate on the limits to the economic sovereignty of the Member States. Cf. M. Blanquet, *L'article 5 du traité CEE: Recherche sur les obligations de fidélité des états membres de la Communauté* (Paris, 1994); J. Temple Lang, 'Article 5 of the EEC Treaty: The emergence of constitutional principles in the Case Law of the Court of Justice', (1987) 10 *Fordham International Law Journal* 503; J. Temple Lang, 'Community Constitutional Law: Article 5 EEC Treaty', (1990) 27 CMLR 645.

[140] Cf. L. Gyselen, 'State Action and the Effectiveness of the EEC Treaty's Competition Provisions', (1989) 26 CMLR 33; R. Joliet, 'Réglementations étatiques anticoncurrentielles et droit communautaire', (1988) 24 CDE 363; P. Pescatore, 'Public and Private Aspects of European Community Competition Law', (1987) 10 *Fordham Internation Law Journal* 373. Some commentators held high hopes for wholesale deregulation and liberalisation on this basis. Cf. A. Bach, *Wettbewerbsrechtliche Schranken für staatliche Maßnahmen nach europäischem Gemeinschaftsrecht* (Tübingen, 1992); P. Behrens, 'Die Wirtschaftsverfassung der EG', in G. Brüggemeier (ed.), *Verfassungen für ein ziviles Europa* (Baden-Baden, 1994); E.-J. Mestmäcker, 'Zur Anwendbarkeit der Wettbewerbsregeln auf die Mitgliedstaaten und die Europäischen Gemeinschaften', in J. Baur, P.-Ch. Müller-Graf and M. Zuleeg (eds.), *Europarecht, Energierecht, Wirtschaftsrecht: Festschrift für Bodo Börner zum 70. Geburtstag* (Cologne, 1992); Monopolkommission, *Hauptgutachten 1988/ 1989: Wettbewerbspolitk vor neuen Herausforderungen* (Baden-Baden, 1990); B. Van der Esch, 'Die Artikel 5, 3f, 85/86 und 90 EWGV als Grundlage der wettbewerbsrechtlichen Verpflichtungen der Mitgliedstaaten', (1991) 155 ZHR 274.

[141] Case 13/77 *GB-INNO-BM v ATAB* [1977] ECR 2115.

[142] Cf. Case 229/83 *Leclerc v Au Blé Vert* [1985] ECR 1.

[143] Case 267/86 *Van Eycke v ASPA* [1988] ECR 4769. Cf. L. Gyselen, 'Anti-Competitive State Measures under the EC Treaty: Towards a Substantive Legality Standard', (1993) 18 ELR *Competition Checklist* 55. *Van Eycke* remains the judicial standard for determining the anticompetitive nature of state measures. Gyselen advocates the introduction of a threefold filter for the prohibition of state measures as anticompetitive: (1) determining whether the measure distorts competition within the meaning of Article 85 EC; (2) whether it is aimed at achieving genuine economic or monetary policy objectives; or (3) any other legitimate objectives capable of overriding competition policy concerns. ibid., pp. 66–73.

[144] Cf. Case 123/83 *BNIC v Clair* [1985] ECR 402; Joined Cases 209–213/84 *Ministère Public v Asjes et al* [1986] ECR 1425 ('Nouvelles Frontieres'); Case 311/85 *Vereniging van Vlaamse Reisbureaus v Sociale Dienst* [1987] ECR 3801; Case 136/86 *BNIC v Aubert* [1987] ECR 4789.

[145] Case 231/83 *Cullet v Leclerc* [1985] ECR 305; Case 267/86 *Van Eycke*, above, n. 143, para. 15: 'to deprive its own legislation of its official character by delegating to private traders responsibility for taking decisions affecting the economic sphere'.

Recently, the Court has adopted a formal approach to these categories, which allowed it to uphold various price control measures which might have been abolished had the earlier 'effects' approach been applied.[146] Henceforth, a clear link between the state regulation concerned and the alleged anti-competitive agreement will be required for the application of Articles 5(2) and 85 or 86 EC to such regulations.[147] The Court will declare illegal restrictions of competition by means of cartel, whereas legislative or regulatory solutions of the same content are acceptable, in so far as they respect the principles of non-discrimination and proportionality (restrictively applied).[148]

This results in a more narrow concept of the internal market similar to that established in the *Keck* line of case law on Articles 30–36 EC.[149] The European Court of Justice has sketched the borderline between the principles of Community loyalty and subsidiarity in a manner that forecloses further dramatic encroachments on national economic sovereignty.[150] As the application of the competition rules and of the rules on the market freedoms converges, the formal approach taken by the Court of Justice is nevertheless fatal to corporatism. In order to benefit from the protection of national economic sovereignty, economic policy must take clear form as public law, independent from private agreements. This will lead to further juridification and proceduralisation of economic policy.

[146] Case C-185/91 *Bundesanstalt für den Güterfernverkehr v Gebrüder Reiff GmbH & Co KG* [1993] ECR I-5801; Case C-2/91 *Wolf W. Meng* [1993] ECR I-5751; Case C-245/91 *OHRA Schadeverzekeringen NV* [1993] ECR I-5851, noted by Bach (1994) 31 CMLR 1357; Hancher and du Pré (1994) 42 SEW 686; Van der Esch (1994) 30 CDE 523. This approach was confirmed in Case C-18/93 *Corsica Ferries* [1994] ECR I-1783; and Case C-153/93 *Delta Schiffahrts- und Speditions-Gesellschaft* [1994] ECR I-2517.

[147] Advocate General Darmon considered bringing vertical price fixing under Articles 5(2) and 85 EC to be the thin end of the wedge, which would lead to a general presumption of illegality of economic measures by the Member States; and leave the Court as self-appointed legislature. Case C-185/91 *Reiff*, above, n. 146, paras. 73, 77.

[148] The proportionality principle is at the heart of Article 5 EC. It is further laid down in Articles 3b, 90(2), 92(3)c, 223(1)b and 226(3) EC.

[149] Cf. Joined Cases C-267 and C-268/91 *Keck and Mithouard* [1993] ECR I-6097; Case C-292/92 *Ruth Hünermund et al v Landesapothekerkammer Baden-Württemberg* [1993] ECR I-6787, noted by Roth (1994) 31 CMLR 845. Following this case law, Article 30 EC does not apply to state measures where these do not discriminate in law or fact against imports. 'The "home State control" principle provides not just an institutional structure for the internal market but also delimits the scope of the internal market, or at least what activities should be regulated by the Community institutions'. D. Chalmers, 'Repackaging the Internal Market—The Ramifications of the *Keck* Judgement', (1994) 19 ELR 384, p. 402; M. Poiares Maduro, '*Keck*: The End? The Beginning of the End? Or just the End of the Beginning?', (1994) 1 *Irish Journal of European Law* 30. The similarities between these two lines of case law are developed by N. Reich, 'The "November Revolution" of the European Court of Justice: *Keck, Meng* and *Audi* Revisited', (1994) 31 CMLR 459.

[150] For services, a similar development may be taking shape. Cf. Case C-288/89 *Stichting Collectieve Antenne Voorziening Gouda* [1991] ECR I-4007; Case C-353/89 *Commission v The Netherlands* [1991] ECR I-4069, noted by Feenstra (1993) 30 CMLR 424; Case C-384/93 *Alpine Investments BV v Minister van Financiën* [1995] I-1141. Cf. J. M. Fernández Martín and S. O'Leary, 'Judicial Exceptions to the Free Provision of Services', (1995) 1 *European Law Journal* 308. The Court has exercised restraint concerning economic sovereignty in external trade as well. Cf. Joined Cases C-181/91 and C-248/91 *Parliament v Council and Commission* [1993] ECR I-3685.

B. The Case of Article 90 EC

The balance between the application of the competition rules and national economic sovereignty, public ownership, and regulation, has further been developed in relation to Article 90 EC.[151] This article forms a more detailed articulation of Article 5(2) EC, which is more specific in two respects: it indicates the particular area concerned (undertakings granted special and exclusive rights, or legal monopolies), and specifies the provisions of the Treaty which are concerned.[152] Article 90 is meant to reconcile the fundamental freedoms and competition rules of the Treaty, and the system of undistorted competition of Article 3f EEC (3g EC) with the existence of a public sector. The latter is guaranteed by Article 222 EC, and by a public interest exemption in Article 90(2) EC.[153]

The enforcement of this long obscure provision of the EC Treaty has in recent years become one of the priorities of Community competition policy.[154] The open questions on the application of Article 90 EC concern:

  (i) the legality of state monopolies under Article 90(1) EC;
  (ii) the competence of the EC to enact directives and decisions under Article 90(3) EC;

---

[151] Cf. Ch. Bright, 'Article 90, Economic Policy and the Duties of the Member States', (1993) 4 ECLR 263; D. Edward and M. Hoskins, 'Article 90: Deregulation and EC Law: Reflections Arising From the XVI FIDE Conference', (1995) 32 CMLR 157; C.-D. Ehlermann, 'Managing Monopolies: The Role of the State in Controlling Market Dominance in the European Community', (1993) 4 ECLR 61; L. Hancher, 'Artikel 90 EEG—Minder troebel, maar nog niet helder', (1993) 41 SEW 328; Ph. Lowe, 'Telecommunications Services and Competition Law in Europe', (1994) 5 EBLR 139; J. M. Naftel, 'The Natural Death of a Natural Monopoly: Competition in EC Telecommunications after the Telecommunications Terminals Judgment', (1993) 14 ECLR 105; A. Pappalardo, 'State Measures and Public Undertakings: Article 90 of the Treaty Revisited', (1991) 12 ECLR 29.

[152] In Case 13/77 *GB-INNO-BM v ATAB*, referring to Article 5(2) EC, the Court stated that 'Article 90 is only a particular application of certain general principles which bind the Member States'. Above, n. 141, para. 42 p. 2146. However, in his opinion on Cases C-2/91 *Meng*, above, n. 146, and C-254–91 *OHRA*, above, n. 146, Advocate General Tesauro rejected a strict relationship between Article 90 and 5(2) EC. In the first case, the very structure of the market is affected, in the second only the relatively minor issue of restriction of price-competition, which leaves the number of competitors unaffected.

[153] Article 90(1) EC states the rule that Member States are not allowed to enact or maintain in force concerning public undertakings or undertakings to which they have granted special or exclusive rights, any measures contrary to the rules contained in the Treaty, in particular the rules provided for in Article 6 and Articles 85 to 94 EC. This refers especially to the anti-discrimination provisions of Articles 30 and 59 EC, the competition rules, and the rules on state aids. Article 90(2) EC gives a limited derogation from the application of the Treaty rules to services of a general economic interest and revenue-producing monopolies, in so far as these rules would obstruct the performance of the tasks of such enterprises, and to the extent that this would not be contrary to the Community interest. Article 90(3) EC charges the Commission with observing the application of Article 90 EC, where necessary by way of directives and decisions addressed to the Member States.

[154] C.-D. Ehlermann, 'Neuere Entwicklungen im europäischen Wettbewerbsrecht', (1991) 26 EuR 307, p. 319.

(iii) the scope of the derogation of Article 90(2) EC, especially in regard to services in the public interest.

The legality of state monopolies has long been at issue. Until recently, the main statement of the law was found in Case 155/73 *Sacchi*, concerning the compatibility of the Italian state monopoly on television broadcasting with the freedom to provide services and Article 86 EEC.[155] Here the Court indicated that although television broadcasting falls under the provision of services, and hence under the scope of the direct application of Article 59 EEC, Article 90(1) EEC permits the Member States to grant special and exclusive rights to undertakings.[156] The fact that the grant of an exclusive right entailed the creation of a monopoly was not regarded as incompatible with Article 86 EEC (nor was the extension of this monopoly), although the behaviour of the undertaking in question remained subject to the prohibitions against discrimination and the competition rules.[157]

Case 41/83 *Italy v Commission*[158] concerned the power of the Commission to apply Article 86 EEC to a (formerly public) undertaking charged with rule making duties, such as British Telecom (BT). The Court held that Article 86 EEC applied, since the activities of BT which were involved were commercial in nature.[159] This confirmed that public undertakings were not as such exempted from observing the competition rules. Most importantly, the Court observed that the application of Article 90(2) EEC was not left to the discretion of the Member State which had charged the undertaking involved with a task of general economic interest. In Case 311/84 *Télé-Marketing*, the Court confirmed that Article 86 EEC applied to state monopolies and undertakings granted special and exclusive rights.[160] Moreover, it now held that an abuse in the sense

---

[155] Case 155/73 *Sacchi* [1974] ECR 409.

[156] Since '... nothing in the Treaty prevents Member States, for considerations of public interest, of a non-economic nature, from removing radio and television transmissions ... from the field of competition, by conferring on one or more establishments an exclusive right to conduct them'. ibid., para. 14 pp. 429–430.

[157] Where the undertakings were '... entrusted with the operation of services of general economic interest, the same prohibitions apply, as regards their behaviour within the market, by reason of Article 90(2), so long as it is not shown that said prohibitions are incompatible with the performance of their task'. ibid., para. 15 p. 430.

[158] Case 41/83 *British Telecom*, above, n. 138, noted by Ross (1985) 10 ELR 457. Italy had intervened under Article 173(1) to challenge the validity of a Commission decision addressed to British Telecom (BT), the first time a Member State used its privileged position to challenge a decision directed at an undertaking in another Member State. The British Government, pursuing a comprehensive programme of liberalisation and privatisation, intervened on behalf of the Commission.

[159] Where the United Kingdom Government had abetted BT's infringements, BT would not be exempted, but rather the United Kingdom would be liable as well (following the *effet utile* reasoning in Case 13/77 *GB INNO v ATAB*, above, n. 141).

[160] Case 311/84 *Télé-Marketing* [1985] ECR 3261. 'Article 86 of the Treaty must be interpreted as applying to an undertaking holding a dominant position on a particular market, even where that position is not due to the activities of the undertaking itself but to the fact that by reason of the provisions laid down by law there can be no competition or only limited competition on that market'. Para. 18 p. 3276.

of Article 86 EEC might be committed if the undertaking concerned sought to extend its monopoly.[161]

In Case C-202/88 *Terminal Directive*,[162] the Court repeated that although special and exclusive rights were mentioned in Article 90 EEC, this did not mean they were compatible with the Treaty under all circumstances. Nor was abuse of the special and exclusive rights a precondition for the exercise by the Commission of its powers under Article 90(3) EEC. Since the Commission was entitled to interpret the obligations following from the Treaty under Article 90(1) EEC, the scope of these powers depended on that of the specific Treaty provisions which were to be upheld in this manner. Article 90(1) EEC could therefore be seen as a reference clause.

The judgement in *Terminal Directive* was criticised for its narrow legal basis in Article 30 EEC, since many commentators believed that Articles 59 and 86 EEC should have been relied on instead. The Court subsequently adopted this path when dealing with special and exclusive rights in a series of cases concerning the *effet utile* of Article 90 EEC in combination with Article 86 EEC. First, in Case C-41/90 *Macrotron*, concerning a state employment agency, the Court ruled that Article 90(1) *juncto* 86 EEC applied to situations '*where the undertaking in question*, merely by exercising the exclusive rights granted to it, cannot avoid abusing its dominant position'.[163] Moreover, the Court held that an enterprise granted a legal monopoly by definition has a dominant position.[164]

Second, in Case C-260/89 *ERT*, concerning a cumulation of exclusive rights on television broadcasting and retransmission, Article 90(1) EEC was applied in combination with Articles 59 and 86 EEC.[165] Even in the absence of evidence of abuse, the Court held that Article 90(1) EEC prohibited the granting of exclusive rights where such rights are liable to create a situation where the undertaking is led to infringe Article 86 EEC. This indicated that Articles 90(1) and 90(2) EEC were directly effective.[166] Third, in Case C-179/90 *Porto di Genova*, on docking services, where abundant evidence of a range of violations of Article 86 EC existed, Articles 30, 86 and 90(1) EEC were applied jointly,

---

[161] The Court stated that 'an abuse within the meaning of Article 86 is committed where, without any objective necessity, an undertaking holding a dominant position on a particular market reserves to itself or to an undertaking belonging to the same group an ancillary activity which might be carried out by another undertaking as part of its activities on a neighbouring but separate market with the possibility of eliminating all competition from such undertaking'. ibid., para. 23 p. 3278.

[162] Case C-202/88 *French Republic v Commission* [1991] ECR I-1223 ('Terminal Directive'), noted by Slot (1991) 28 CMLR 964; Wheeler (1992) 17 ELR 67.

[163] Case C-41/90, above, n. 138, para. 29 p. 2018, noted by Slot (1991) 28 CMLR 964.

[164] The Court stated that 'an undertaking with a legal monopoly may be regarded as occupying a dominant position within the meaning of Article 86 of the Treaty'. ibid., para. 28 p. 2018. *In casu* the beneficiary could not avoid infringing Article 86 EEC (even although, in violation of German law, it allowed competition), due to manifest failure to meet demand.

[165] Case C-260/89 *ERT v Dimotiki* [1991] ECR I-2925, noted by Slot, above, n. 163.

[166] ibid., para. 37 p. 2962.

as the granting of the exclusive right in question induced its beneficiary to commit abuses.[167]

Fourth, in its preliminary ruling in Case C-18/88, *RTT v GB INNO*[168] (concerning the Belgian telecommunications monopoly) the Court of Justice again applied Article 90(1) EEC in combination with Article 86 EEC. Here it went beyond the position taken in *Macrotron*, to state that the granting of exclusive rights which extend an existing dominant position may in itself constitute an infringement of the provisions of Article 86 EEC.[169] Recently, the Court has suggested that monopolies which lack a public interest justification are contrary to Community law. In Case C-320/91 *Corbeau*, the Court was asked, under an Article 177 EEC reference, to rule on the legality of the Belgian postal monopoly under Article 90 EEC.[170] It considered that an exclusive right, conferred on an undertaking entrusted with the operation of services of general economic interest, which goes beyond what can be justified under Article 90(2) EEC, is at odds with Article 90(1) EEC, since it impairs the *effet utile* of Article 86 EEC.[171]

This completes the development of Article 90(1) EC from a provision which added little to the general principle of Community loyalty in Article 5(2) EC in *Sacchi*, first to be read as reference clause (*Terminal Directive*), the content of which depended on the Articles it was used to apply, and subsequently to an independent norm (*Corbeau*). It remains unclear whether the grant or existence of any exclusive right which is not justified by Article 90(2) is per se illegal. On the one hand, this is the case since any exclusive right which is not covered by Article 90(2) breaches Article 90(1) EC *juncto* Article 86 EC.[172] On the other hand, the granting of exclusive rights is not illegal per se, a breach of Articles 90(1) and 86 can result from failure to ensure that they remain within the bounds set by Article 90(2).[173] A third interpretation sees Article 90(2) itself

---

[167] Case C-179/90 *Merci Convenzionali Porto di Genóva SpA v Siderurgica Gabrielli SpA* [1991] ECR I-5889, noted by Gyselen (1992) 29 CMLR 1229.

[168] Case C-18/88 *Régie des Télégraphes et des Téléphones v SA GB-INNO-BM* [1991] ECR I-5951, noted by Gyselen (1992) 29 CMLR 1229.

[169] The Court held that 'where the extension of the dominant position of a public undertaking or undertaking to which the states have granted special or exclusive rights results from a state measure, such a measure constitutes an infringement of Article 90 in conjunction with Article 86 of the Treaty'. ibid., para. 21 p. 5980. Here, the extension of the dominant position of RTT into the market for telephone equipment was regarded as an infringement, confirming the earlier case law on the extension of a dominant position by reserving ancillary activities in another market. Case 311/84 *Télé-Marketing*, above, n. 160.

[170] Case C-320/91, *Procureur du Roi v Paul Corbeau* [1993] ECR I-2533, noted by Gilliams (1994) 42 SEW 515; Hancher (1994) 31 CMLR 105. Cf. A. Wachsmann and F. Berrod, 'Les critères de justification des monopoles: un premier bilan après l'affaire *Corbeau*', (1994) 30 RTDE 39.

[171] ibid., paras. 11–13; 21 pp. 2567–2568; p. 2570.

[172] Gyselen, 'Anti-Competitive State Measures under the EC Treaty: Towards a Substantive Legality Standard', (1993) 18 ELR *Competition Checklist* 55.

[173] Hancher, above, n. 151. These positions are classified by Edward and Hoskins as: (1) the absolute competition approach; (2) the limited competition approach; (3) the limited sovereignty approach; and (4) the absolute sovereignty approach. Above, n. 151, pp. 159ff. In their view the Court in *Corbeau* tends toward limited competition. The position of Advocate General Tesauro is more clearly on this line.

form an independent norm, which applies to services of general economic interest.[174] Other exclusive and special rights would then be approached under Article 90(1) EC in combination with Article 86 EC (where the behaviour of the undertaking would play a role), or under Articles 30 or 59 EC.[175]

Pending further guidance by the Court of Justice, the last reading appears to be the more convincing one. This means that exclusive and special rights which involve distortions of competition are illegal, barring the exceptions provided in Article 90(2) EC, and elsewhere in the Treaty. Under Article 90(2) EC both economic and non-economic defences are admissible. This amounts to a special regime for services of general economic interest and revenue producing monopolies. Notably, where this is necessary to ensure a public service task, cross-subsidisation is permissible, subject to a proportionality test. Where exclusive and special rights are contested under Article 90(1) *juncto* 86 EC in other cases, no public interest derogations exist. Neither the extension nor the creation of national monopolies are likely to pass the Article 86 EC test. Where Article 90(1) is applied in combination with Article 59 EC, only non-economic justifications in the general interest may be considered. After *Keck*, where Article 90(1) is applied together with Article 30 EC, distortions of competition by state regulations which do not discriminate between undertakings by nationality will be allowed.

The drawback of this position is that the outcome depends on the head under which the exclusive rights in question are challenged. This is problematic especially since the direct effect of Article 90 EC has become firmly established,[176] and in Case C-320/91 *Corbeau* and Case C-393/92 *Almelo*,[177] the national judiciary was charged with balancing the Community interest and the national public interest under Article 90(2) EC. In order to apply the Article 90(2) justification to an exclusive right, a court must determine its necessary scope in order to meet the public service objectives involved. Since *Corbeau*, the application of Article 90(2) EC requires, first, a justification of the granting of the exclusive right on public interest grounds, and, second, a proportionality

---

[174] Gilliams, above, n. 170.

[175] Two variants are possible. If the rights are considered illegal *per se*, the public interest exceptions to the free movement rules could yet provide protection. Under Article 90(1) *juncto* 86 EC, no derogation would be available. If they are considered legal, some violation of these Treaty Articles would have to be proven. Under Articles 30 and 59 EC, the usual non-economic justifications would apply.

[176] The question of the direct effect of Article 90 EC was resolved in a series of preliminary rulings under Article 177, which came about as private parties claimed to rely on the directly effective provisions of Terminal Directive 301/88 before national courts: Joined Cases C-46 and C-93/91 *Procureur du Roi v Lagauche et al, Evrard* [1993] ECR I-5267; Case C-69/91 *Ministère Public v Decoster*, [1993] ECR I-5335; and Case C-92/91 *Ministère Public v Taillandier* [1993] ECR I-5383, noted by Hancher (1994) 31 CMLR 857.

[177] Case C-393/92 *Almelo v Energiebedrijf Ijsselmij* [1994] ECR I-1477, noted by Hancher (1995) 32 CMLR 305. The legal problem involved gave rise to a series of challenges: Case T-16/91 *Rendo* [1992] ECR II-2417; appealed as Case C-19/93 P, *Rendo et al v Commission* [1995] ECR I-3336; Case T-2/92 *Rendo v Commission*, order of 29 March 1993, (1993) OJ C123/13.

test.[178] In most cases more market-conform solutions which are less onerous than imposing monopoly provision will be available. Conflict between the principles of proportionality and subsidiarity will be unavoidable, unless the national courts restrict themselves to control of 'manifest errors' in applying the proportionality test.[179]

The third issue concerning Article 90 EC is that of the Commission's competence to enact directives and decisions under Article 90(3), which has long been contested. Article 90 EC formed the legal basis for the adoption of two Commission Directives, which abolished special and exclusive rights concerning the provision of telecommunications, terminal equipment, and services.[180] Both Article 90 EC Directives were challenged by a number of Member States. In Case C-202/88 *Terminal Directive*,[181] the Court defined the Commission's power to issue directives under Article 90(3) EEC, the application of the Treaty to legal monopolies, and in particular the power of the Commission to suppress them under Article 90 EEC. The general issue at stake was the blurring of the distinction between the surveillance and legislative powers of the Commission.[182]

The Commission was held to have the power to determine the obligations of the Member States under Article 90(1) EEC in a general way, without any obligation to use Article 169 EEC (which applies only to specific infringements).[183] Regarding the exercise of powers otherwise attributed to the Council under Articles 87 and 100a EEC, the Court ruled that it was possible for the Commission and the Council to hold concurrent rule making powers.[184] Moreover, since the powers of the Commission under Article 90(3) EEC were held to be more specific than the general powers of the Council, the Commission was not barred from exercising them concurrently.

The Court reaffirmed the power of the Commission to specify the obligations of the Member States regarding public undertaking in Joined Cases

[178] Thus, Article 90(2) of the Treaty '. . . provides that undertakings entrusted with the operation of services of general economic interest may be exempted from the application of the competition rules contained in the Treaty in so far as it is necessary to impose restrictions on competition, or even to exclude all competition from other economic operators in order to ensure the performance of the particular tasks assigned to them'. ibid. para. 14 p. 2568.

[179] This is the solution proposed by Edwards and Hoskins, above, n. 151, pp. 171–172.

[180] Commission Directive 88/301/EEC on competition in the market for telecommunications terminal equipment ((1988) OJ L131/72); and Commission Directive 90/388/EEC on competition in the markets for telecommunications services ((1990) OJ L192/10). At this point, the single precedent for the Article 90(3) directives on telecommunications liberalisation was Commission Directive 80/723/EEC on the transparency of financial relations between Member States and public undertakings (1980) OJ L195/35, which merely established reporting requirements.

[181] Case C-202/88 *Terminal Directive*, above, n. 162.

[182] Articles 2 and 7 of the directive required the Member States to withdraw all special and exclusive rights. Articles 6 and 9 dealt with the duty to establish an independent body for monitoring equipment specifications and type approval, and the provision to the Commission of reports on compliance with the terms of the directive, respectively.

[183] Joined Cases 188–190/80, above, n. 135. Note however, that the Commission, in the case on non-compliance, will still have to take action under Article 169. Slot, above, n. 162.

[184] Repeating its earlier finding in Cases 188–190/80 *Transparency Directive*, ibid.

C-271/90, C-281/90 and C-289/90 *Services Directive*.[185] This time, rather than their existence, the scope of the legislative powers of the Commission under Article 90(3) EEC was at stake. The Court ruled that Article 90(3) EEC confers upon the Commission the power to make general regulations specifying obligations resulting from the Treaty, and that its authority is therefore not restricted to supervising existing Community regulations. Likewise it confirmed that the Commission had correctly used its more specific powers under Article 90(3) EEC rather than deferring to the more general powers of the Council under Articles 100 and 87 EEC.[186]

The Commission's power to issue decisions under Article 90(3) EC was clarified in Joined Cases C-48 and C-66/90 *Dutch Couriers*,[187] concerning a contested decision on competition in postal services. The Court ruled that Article 90(3) EEC empowered the Commission to issue decisions aimed at ending specific violations of the competition rules, rather than having to resort to the more onerous procedure of Article 169 EEC. The Court held that denying the right of the Commission to adopt individual decisions under Article 90(3) EEC would deprive this provision of its *effet utile*. However, violation of the rights of the defence (in particular the right to be heard) as exemplified under Articles 93(2) and 169 EEC caused the Court to throw out the challenged Article 90(3) EEC decision.

Immediately after the ruling in *Terminal Directive*, it was suggested that Article 90(3) EEC directives could be enacted for the postal services, gas, electricity, insurance, and transport markets.[188] Yet although the Commission threatened the use of Article 90(3) EEC directives in the electricity and gas sectors unless exclusive import rights were abolished, it has since chosen to initiate Article 169 EC proceedings instead, while proposing traditional harmonisation measures under Article 100a EC.

The problem of using Article 90(3) EC for enforcement purposes is threefold. First, the use of Article 90(3) EC directives is not subject to approval by the Council and the European Parliament, and upsets the institutional balance

---

[185] Joined Cases C-271/90, C-281/90 and C-289/90 *Spain, Belgium and Italy v Commission* [1992] ECR I-5833, noted by Emiliou (1993) 18 ELR 306.

[186] Finally, since the free provision of services under Article 59 EEC has become unconditional and directly effective, the Commission can specify the obligations arising from this, without prior Council legislation. Case 33/74 *Van Binsbergen* [1974] ECR 1299; Case 279/80 *Webb* [1981] ECR 3305. Moreover, in Case 352/85 *Bond van Adverteerders et al v The Netherlands* [1988] ECR 2085, the Court held that in relation to Article 56 economic objectives are not included under the public policy exception. Hereby the freedom to provide services of Article 59 is subject in the first place to the exceptions contained in Articles 55 and 56, in the second place to the 'public interest' exception developed in the case law, and finally to the derogation of Article 90(2).

[187] Joined Cases C-48 and C-66/90 *Netherlands, Koninklijke PTT Nederland NV and PTT Post BV v Commission* [1992] ECR I-565, noted by Flynn and Turnbull (1993) 30 CMLR 396.

[188] Cf. Ehlermann, 'The Contribution of EC Competition Policy to the Single Market', (1992) 29 CMLR 257, p. 272: 'The Court's most recent case law on Article 90 will stimulate and facilitate DG IV's activities with regard to energy, postal services, telecommunications and the audiovisual sphere. The judgment on telecommunications terminal equipment could provide a guide for dealing with exclusive rights in the electricity and gas industries'.

of the Community. This is of particular importance in the aftermath of the laborious ratification process of the Maastricht Treaty, and given the judicial restraint shown by the Court of Justice in its recent case law on *effet utile* and the remaining margins for national economic regulation. Second, the Member States must still be relied on to implement Article 90 EC directives. The widening implementation gap even regarding measures approved by the Member States is not encouraging in this regard. Third, Article 90(3) EC does not cover the rights of the defence for affected Member States, unlike other alternatives to Article 169 EC, such as Article 93(2). Adopting the procedural rules of Article 93(2) will make the use of decisions under Article 90(3) little more attractive than the Article 169 EC procedure.[189]

For these reasons, the Commission has exercised restraint in its use of Article 90(3) EC, and has emphasised the benefits of a consensual approach and gradual liberalisation instead.[190] The development involving Article 90 EC has nevertheless added an important instrument to the Commission's arsenal. Article 90 directives may be used to break deadlocks in decision making between the Council and European Parliament where the Commission considers that the political cost involved is sustainable, or to fill gaps in regulation where its competence is not contested. Together with the developments concerning state aids and the *effet utile* of Articles 85 and 86 EC, the case law on Article 90 EC indicates that a new balance between national economic sovereignty and the requirements of Community law is being established.

C. Policy Convergence and the Reorganisation of EC Competition Policy

The Member States have become aware not only that traditional industrial policies are counterproductive, but that Community competition policy is making them increasingly difficult to pursue. At the same time, national competition policy has become more important, as part of the overall reorientation of national economic policy away from corporatist arrangements and intervention, toward economic regulation. Most Member States have not only adopted competition laws (often modelled on those of the EC Treaty), but encouraged national

---

[189] Article 90(3) decisions are immediately effective, and an appeal against them does not suspend their effect, as is the case in an Article 169 procedure. In joined Cases C-48 and 66/90 *Dutch Couriers*, the Court held regarding Article 90(3) decisions that, where Article 90(3) itself does not provide for procedural rules, the rights of the defence were guaranteed by the general principle of Community law of the right to be heard. Following this judgment however, it seems that regarding Article 90(3) decisions, in principle the consultative procedures of Article 92(3) are to be followed. Finally, it may be noted that an infringement procedure under Article 169 EC may result in the imposition of a lump sum or penalty payment ex Article 171 EC, but an Article 92(3) procedure may not. Slot, above, n. 162.

[190] *23rd Competition Report*, above, n. 10, p. 13. Only two further directives of relatively minor importance have been adopted under this article. Both merely aim at a comparatively modest extension of the scope of the existing three Article 90 directives: first, a Commission Directive to replace the communication extending the terms of the transparency directive (above, n. 135); second, an essentially uncontested directive extending the provisions of Directives 88/301/EEC and 90/388/EC to the satellite sector: Commission Directive 94/46/EC ((1994) OJ L268/15).

regulators to actually apply these rules independently from more immediate political considerations.

As a result, the distribution of competence regarding competition policy in the Community has come under discussion. This became evident with the Merger Regulation, and its complex system of attributing jurisdiction: the reluctance to agree to further centralisation was demonstrated by the refusal to review the merger turnover thresholds in 1993. Of course the Member States have long begrudged the Commission its sweeping powers under Regulations 17/62 and 19/65. Recently, the Member States (in particular Germany) have revived the more radical idea of creating a European Cartel Office to deal with competition cases. National regulators and industry groups have added further demands for change.[191]

This is not to say that the direction of reform is clearly defined. The various demands for reform of competition policy have different motives, and the reform proposals go in different directions. Some Member States mainly wish to limit Commission intrusion on national economic sovereignty, with the avowed aim of preserving wide sway for their industrial and regional policies. The mere suspicion of industrial and regional policy considerations filtering through to the Commission level motivates others to wish to seal off their more strict national competition policies. Hence, whereas France and Italy have proposed reforms allowing considerations of national or European industrial policy to override competition criteria, and to give the Council a voice in competition decisions, the United Kingdom and Germany advocate transferring competition policy competence to a politically independent body restricted to applying competition criteria.

The Member States appear to concur mainly on the general need for subsidiarity. The interest in this varies from a concern for the survival of the state as an independent economic actor, to projects aimed at directing European integration away from political and economic union toward a free trade track. Finally, the self-interest of competing institutions at the national level (notably the *Bundeskartellamt*) plays an important role.[192] With criticism so widespread, and the opportunity for institutional reform provided by the Intergovernmental Conferences,[193] the issue of reorganisation of competition policy is firmly on the agenda.

[191] Cf. Ehlermann, 'Reflections on a European Cartel Office', (1995) 32 CMLR 471; Wilks and McGowan, above, n. 117.

[192] Merger control forms 70 per cent of the BKA's workload. Lowering the merger threshold for example would further undermine a body which is already under pressure from increasingly independent-minded courts and the Economics Ministry. Wilks and McGowan, 'Discretion in European Merger Control: The German Regime in Context', (1995) 2 *Journal of European Public Policy* 41, p. 48.

[193] Since the enunciation of the 'Meroni Doctrine' by the Court of Justice in 1958, it has been clear that only a revision of the Treaty will allow for the creation of true independent agencies. Case 9/56 *Meroni v High Authority* [1957–1958] ECR 133 and Case 10/56 *Meroni v High Authority* [1957–1958] ECR 157. Cf. Lenaerts, 'Regulating the Regulatory Process: "Delegation of Powers" in the European Community', (1993) 18 ELR 23. Ehlermann, above, n. 71, has suggested including a generic provision in the Treaty which enables such bodies to be established.

The paradox of recent developments is therefore that, on the one hand, widespread spontaneous harmonisation of competition policy has occurred, and that the Member States are pursuing converging macroeconomic policies as well, but that on the other hand, a backlash against the Commission may be undermining its competition policy competence. Reform proposals should be seen more in the light of the general struggle over the division of powers between the Community and the Member States, rather than just as an issue concerning the merits of European competition policy. In this struggle over economic sovereignty, the Member States are threatening to avail themselves of their prerogatives as masters of the Treaty. The result is likely to be an attempt to limit the influence of the Commission, rather than one to reorient competition policy toward strict competition goals.

The criticism of existing arrangements at the Community level can be reduced to four points: (i) a lack of independence; (ii) a lack of accountability; (iii) a lack of subsidiarity; and (iv) a lack of transparency.[194] Various models for resolving the first problem exist, mainly based on separating the political and the 'factual' application of competition policy. DG IV, or an independent agency (presumably hived off from DG IV), would prepare decisions based on competition criteria only, to be approved by the Commissioner responsible for Competition, or by the Commission advised by an expert Monopolies Commission.[195] The accountability problem could be addressed jointly with that of independence by increasing access to procedures for interested parties, strengthening judicial control, and clearly separating the political and technical stages.

The subsidiarity problem could be resolved by a redistribution of current competences, by limiting further expansion of current Commission competence, or by a trade-off between the two. The changes proposed under this head range from the introduction of a rule of reason approach under Article 83(1) EC to allowing national authorities to apply Article 85(3) EC.[196] Increasing transparency, finally, would be relatively easy to implement and address all three other problems as well. This could be achieved by establishing clear criteria for assessment, publishing proposals, soliciting comments and promoting debate, and publishing decisions together with the undertakings (remedies) by the firms involved. Like increasing independence or accountability, this would reduce the danger of industry or government 'capture' of competition policy.[197]

---

[194] Neven, Nuttall and Seabright, *Merger in Daylight: The Politics and Economics of European Merger Control* (London, 1993), p. 166.

[195] Cf. ibid., pp. 229ff for four models of revising merger control, based on various distributions of the tasks of notification; investigation; negotiation; decision; political review; and judicial review.

[196] Note that '. . . the Commission's reluctance to introduce a "rule of reason" in the application of Article 85(1) and its preference for formalistic analysis under Article 85(1), which has been touched on above, might be perceived as reluctance to surrender an instrument for developing other Commission policy aspirations within the context of Article 85(3)'. S. B. Hornsby, 'Competition Policy in the 80's: More Policy Less Competition', (1987) ELR 79, p. 99. The rule of reason approach might also be consistent with the recent *Keck* case law.

[197] 'The task for public policy is not somehow to prevent interest group pressures form affecting regulation, but rather to ensure that the pressures to which regulatory authorities respond are reasonably representative of society at large'. Neven *et al*, above, n. 194, p. 166.

The most important proposal to have been tabled by the Member States is that of creating an independent European Cartel Office, an idea which is fiercely resisted by the Commission (notably DG IV) as a threat to its institutional independence.[198] The agency model would introduce a major element of constitutional change, not only affecting competition and industrial policy but economic regulation in Europe in general. Currently, the European Central Bank (ECB) provides a model of transfer of economic policy making to (quasi) independent bodies, and the European System of Central Banks (ESCB) an example of policy making networks of such bodies.[199] Unlike the ECB and ESCB, a European Cartel Office would involve judicial control and the protection of individual economic rights. This would further promote the trend toward the depoliticisation and juridification of the economic policy, regulated by non-majoritarian rule-based institutions.

Since the Member States are divided, the drive to create a European Cartel Office could yet be defeated. However, as has been noted, the Merger Regulation thresholds have been taken hostage in this debate. More broadly, competition policy as such has been taken hostage by the proposals to alter the institutional design which has been so fundamental to its dynamic development. In building a system of norms, the Commission was able to work in tandem with the European Court of Justice. In order to influence the institutional design of competition policy the Commission may have to cultivate different constituencies, perhaps primarily the national regulatory authorities.

At various times, the Commission itself has promoted the idea of decentralised application of the competition rules (by the national courts and national competition authorities respectively), although it has been reluctant to discuss reduction or reform of its own discretionary powers.[200] The relations between the Commission and the national competition authorities may be seen as determined by the risk of an implementation deficit versus the potential fragmentation of policy inherent in demands for increased subsidiarity.[201] A centralised competition policy (as at present) is likely to pay more regard to competition considerations, but lacks the means for effective implementation. Decentralised

---

[198] Wilks and McGowan, 'Disarming the Commission: The Debate over a European Cartel Office', (1995) 32 JCMS 259. Note that Article 3 of the 1965 Decision of the Representatives of the Governments of the Member States on the provisional location of certain institutions and departments of the Communities provides that '(T)here shall also be located in Luxembourg the judicial and quasi-judicial bodies, including those competent to apply the rules on competition, already existing or yet to be set up pursuant to the Treaties ...'.

[199] Cf. F. Snyder, 'EMU—Metaphor for European Union? Institutions, Rules and Types of Regulation', in R. Dehousse (ed.), *Europe After Maastricht: An Ever Closer Union* (München, 1994).

[200] Notice on cooperation between the National Courts and the Commission in Applying Articles 85 and 86 of the EEC Treaty ((1993) OJ C39/6). Cf. Riley, 'More Radicalism, Please: The Notice on Co-operation between National Courts and the Commission in Applying Articles 85 and 86 of the EEC Treaty', (1993) 14 ECLR 91.

[201] Wilks, 'The Metamorphosis of European Competition Law', in F. Snyder (ed.), *European Community Law* Vol. I (Aldershot, 1993), p. 288.

application entails the risk of fragmentation, especially where the use of public interest exemptions is involved. This problem is particularly serious for the balance between industrial and competition policy. The solution to these contradictory demands and the co-ordination problem between the different levels of government may be sought in establishing effective intermediate structures.[202] For the Commission, the challenge will be that of using the de facto harmonisation of competition rules in the Member States to promote convergence in the area of implementation, while avoiding dramatic institutional change.

V. Conclusion

The link between competition and industrial policy has two dimensions. First, the competition policy of the Community has imposed limits on national industrial policy in ways which were not foreseen when the EEC Treaty was concluded. In particular the recent developments concerning state aids, the constitutional comity clause of Article 5(2) EC and undertakings granted exclusive and special rights, demonstrate that competition policy places constraints on national economic sovereignty.

In addition the main recent elements of competition policy (the creation of a vigourous merger policy; the reduction of government-created barriers; and policies to promote co-operative ventures and technological development), are all in line with the new industrial policy of the Community, focused on promoting structural adjustment. Thus, rationalisation through mergers is controlled, but promoted by the Commission. The pursuit of public policy by means of state aids and undertakings granted special and exclusive rights has been brought under strict Community control, although a margin of national discretion remains.

According to the thesis of complementarity between industrial and competition policy, the latter forms an instrument of industrial policy (with almost exclusively pro-competitive effects). This complementarity is not particular to the new approach to industrial policy. From the beginning, Community proposals for industrial policy emphasised the completion of the internal market. Both industrial and competition policy are horizontal policies which form part of the general economic policy of the Community, and the Community approach to both policies is simultaneously market-oriented, and aimed at market integration. Moreover, the industrial policy of the Community regards the process of competition in free markets as a precondition for effective structural adjustment. The objectives and the instruments of Community competition policy go beyond the protection of the *process* of competition. It may give priority to considerations of market *structure*, if the fundamental requirements of competition law (and Community law in general) are respected.

---

[202] Such as policy networks, or epistemic communities. Cf. E. B. Haas, *When Knowledge is Power: Learning and Adaptation of International Organisations* (Berkeley, 1990).

These characteristics emerge clearly from the competition rules, the case law, and the policy statements of the Commission. It is, however, difficult to examine just how the Commission uses its administrative discretion in individual cases, since its decisions are merely subject to restricted judicial review, not a fundamental policy reappraisal. Nevertheless, the process whereby the scope for national industrial policy is restricted by means of Community competition policy, which itself forms an instrument of a Community industrial policy aimed at promoting structural adjustment, provides a prima facie case for the complementarity between industrial and competition policy at the Community level in practice, to be tested at the sectoral level.

The emphasis of competition policy is shifting. Strengthened by the consensus underpinning the internal market programme, the competition policy of the Community has gained momentum. It has evolved beyond its initial focus on constructing a centralised system to combat market segmentation by private agreements, to controlling distortions of competition by the Member States, with increasing emphasis on decentralised enforcement.

As a result, the economic sovereignty of the Member States has come under pressure. The Member States are retreating from direct economic intervention, leaving more space for competition in the market. The Community is not in a position to take over this interventionist role (as redistributive policies remain beyond its scope), and appears committed to a liberal industrial policy. However, after a long slide of (at least formal) economic sovereignty toward the Community, a backlash is taking place. The problem is that of finding the necessary degree of consensus on the orientation of economic regulation, to establish the necessary degree of public intervention and the level at which it should be exercised, and the appropriate institutional design.

For the competition policy of the EC, the following solutions have so far been sought: (i) judicial restraint *vis-à-vis* the Member States; (ii) internalisation of the balancing between various objectives within Community competition policy; (iii) decentralisation, differentiated allocation of competence, and proposals for establishing an independent Community competition authority.

Once fundamental principles had been established, the Court of Justice has demonstrated increasing judicial restraint in testing the application of public interest criteria by the Member States. A formal approach is replacing the previous, more dynamic, application of the *effet utile* doctrine: the needs of economic regulation may legitimise public policy exceptions, but must take due legal form. In the absence of common or co-ordinated policies, the Court will enforce the rule of law, but otherwise takes a deferential approach to national regulation which pursues legitimate public policy goals.

The Member States have found a new consensus on the merits of market oriented economic policies. This does not mean they will lightly surrender economic sovereignty to the Community. For competition policy, the adoption of the Merger Regulation seems to have formed the turning point. Although the

Merger Regulation extended the Commission's powers, it placed strict limits on its competence to enforce subsidiarity. Further, the Member States have established and strengthened their own competition authorities, and have proposed to resolve the co-ordination problem by the creation of an independent European Cartel Office. By exercising their prerogatives as parties to the Treaty, they may yet impose this solution upon a reluctant Commission.

Given its wide powers and independent role in competition policy, the Commission has been able to make the theory that the industrial and competition policies of the EC are complementary a credible one. The competition policy of the Community has always had wide objectives. From the outset therefore, the task of balancing the promotion of integration, efficiency, the competitiveness of European industry, and other potentially contradictory objectives has been internalised by competition policy. However, the implementation deficit which was the result of the centralisation has placed practical limits on the implementation of competition policy, and the Member States and the Court have placed political and legal limits on its further expansion. This has forced the Commission to propose co-ordinated but decentralised implementation as an alternative to the creation of a European Cartel Office. It remains to be seen whether the ultimate solution will balance the objectives of industrial and competition policy with equal success.

5

The Compatibility of Industrial and Competition Policy: The Case of Telecommunications

I. INTRODUCTION

After almost three decades of stagnation, the telecommunications policy of the European Community has seen a dramatic expansion over the past years. EC telecommunications policy has aimed at joint liberalisation of the industry and harmonisation of the regulatory framework. First, the use of the Commission's competition policy powers has been instrumental in forcing liberalisation and deregulation at the national level. As a result, public ownership and monopoly are making way for privatisation and competition. Second, the Community has pursued a programme of harmonisation of national legislation, which aims to enable competition to unfold, and has introduced regulations to replace state ownership as a means of protecting the public interest. The full liberalisation of both telecommunications services and infrastructure is scheduled for 1998. A paradigmatic change with widespread implications is in the process of completion.

By extending the internal market to telecommunications, the Community has sought to promote the competitiveness of European industry. Telecommunications liberalisation is intended to promote the economies of scale and scope, and other benefits of competition, which will provide general welfare benefits, through lower prices and improved services, with an accelerator effect on the European economy as a whole. This reasoning is in line with the 'horizontal approach' to industrial policy which has been advocated by the Commission, and is required by Article 130 EC.

Further, the R&D programmes of the Community have, since their outset, had an emphasis on telecommunications (notably through the Research and Development in Advanced Communication Technologies for Europe (RACE) programme). Regional goals are pursued both through funding for telecommunications infrastructure in the peripheral areas of the Community, and by longer transition phases for liberalisation for the benefit of Member States with small and less developed networks. Even under the application of the competition rules to private parties, the need to strengthen the competitiveness of the European industry versus their international competitors is taken into account. These various strands of telecommunications policy aimed at improving the competitiveness of European industry come together in the promotion of trans-European networks (TENs) under Article 129b EC. TENs form a major component of the drive to launch the European economy outlined in the 1993 Delors White Paper on Growth, Competitiveness and Employment, which described them as 'the lifeblood of the competitiveness of European industry'.[1]

The main reasons for selecting telecommunications as a sectoral case-study to clarify the relationship between the competition and industrial policies of the EC are the following three. First, telecommunications is considered to be a crucial, or strategic, economic sector by the Commission and the Member States of the Community since it is the only one of the four main sectors into which information technology (IT) is traditionally subdivided (with computing, consumer electronics and components) in which the Community is truly internationally competitive and has a trade surplus.[2] With the convergence of the four industries into a single IT industry strong competitors from the other sectors will 'cross over' into telecommunications, increasing pressure on European producers. However, a position of strength in telecommunications may give Community industry another opportunity to move back into the computer and components markets, which had previously seemed lost.

Hence, telecommunications is considered to be the key to the Community's future position in high-technology. On the employment side this corresponds to the hope that it will provide 'the basis of the future service economy', or 'information society', aimed at halving European unemployment by the year 2000.[3] The economic importance of the sector is underlined by the emphasis it has received in the internal organisation of the EC, with its 'own' DG XIII. The example of telecommunications may have wide application, since telecommunications policy forms a learning experience both for other network industries which currently have a public utility character, and the broadcasting, electronics, entertainment, and information technology sectors, with which it is converging.

A second reason for selecting telecommunications is that the use of competition policy to liberalise this area has been both extensive in scope, and novel in form. The effect of the application of the competition rules on the telecommunications sector far exceeds that achieved in any other regulated industry, in particular through the use of Article 90(3) EC Commission Directives.[4] Arguably, this involved a shift of constitutional significance in the institutional balance of the Community.

Third, telecommunications liberalisation gives rise to a number of regulatory issues of wider relevance. As the national public monopolies make place for

---

[1] COM(93) 700, 'Growth, Competitiveness, Employment. The Challenges and Ways Forward into the 21st Century', (hereafter: '1993 White Paper'), p. 82.

[2] Cf. H. Ungerer and N. Costello, *Telecommunications in Europe: Free Choice for the User in Europe's 1992 Market. The Challenge for the European Community*, European Perspectives Series (Brussels, 1988), pp. 92ff.

[3] The estimates for information-based jobs in the Community by the year 2000, upon which the Commission bases its policy, predict that 'by the year 2000 more than 60% of Community employment will be strongly information-related—and will therefore depend on telecommunications'. ibid., p. 89. The 1993 White Paper further worked out these predictions. Above, n. 1.

[4] Cf. COM(94) 161 final, *23rd Competition Report from the Commission—1993*, p. 3.

private undertakings competing in European and global markets, a new regulatory framework is required. This has to take into account the various objectives (and underlying interests) involved, which range from safeguarding the rights of individual consumers, the efficiency of national economies, and the promotion of European industry, to guiding the convergence between the entertainment, broadcasting, information technology, and telecommunications sectors. Further, the appropriate balance between European and national regulation remains to be established. Constitutional, technical, and practical problems are thus intertwined. They may inform the thesis that beyond the debate on the conflict or complementarity of industrial and competition policy lie more pertinent issues concerning the politics of institutional design.

In sum, the telecommunications policy of the EC at present forms one of the best examples of how integration, technical, and regulatory change affect the economic order of the Member States, and their interaction within the framework of the EC Treaty. This chapter gives an overview of the development of EC telecommunications policy as an example of the compatibility of industrial and competition policy at the Community level, and an attempt to construct a new regulatory system which reconciles the two.

II. THE GLOBAL TELECOMMUNICATIONS REVOLUTION AND THE EMERGENCE OF EC POLICY

A. Telecommunications as a Natural Monopoly

Telecommunications was originally based on a stable technology that was developed in the last quarter of the nineteenth century (analog and copper-wire).[5] Since this technology required large investments in infrastructure, and the service provided was a basic one, the industry was characterised by economies of scale and scope, and by the positive externalities generated by the large numbers of interconnected users (network effect). Given the high ratio of fixed versus variable costs a single network was perceived as optimal both from the perspective of the provider and the users of services involved (since with each additional user the value of the service increases for all other users, and its cost is reduced). Hence, the provision of telecommunications infrastructure and services was generally considered to be a natural monopoly, and the rapid geographic and social spread of network connections led to actual monopolisation.[6]

---

[5] The natural monopoly argument presupposes the existence of a stable technology (or at least of a predictable trajectory of technological development), which limits the number of fundamental choices to be made.

[6] Cf. G. Dang Nguyen, 'Telecommunications: A Challenge to the Old Order', in M. Sharp (ed.), *Europe and the New Technologies: Six Case Studies in Innovation and Adjustment* (London, 1985), p. 89. Private, regulated monopolies, however, persisted in a number of European countries, including Spain and Sweden.

The natural monopoly argument in itself did not necessary entail public owner-ship of the network. However, for reasons including military security, network integrity, and the politically motivated desire to provide universal coverage of the national territory, formal public monopolies soon became the norm in West-ern Europe (although in the United States similar results were achieved by the closely regulated private monopoly of AT&T).[7] The obligation to provide uni-versal service (provision of basic services on demand and at a standardised price within a certain territory, irrespective of actual cost—not always honoured in practice) introduced an argument of social justice in favour of monopoly, and required a system of extensive cross-subsidisation between profitable (inner-city, long-distance, and international) and unprofitable (local and rural) calls.

Until the late 1980s therefore, the provision of telecommunications in the Member States was typically entrusted to national Post, Telegraph and Tele-phone Ministries (PTTs). Beyond the exclusive provision of network and ser-vices, these PTTs were generally charged with extensive rule-making powers.[8] Furthermore, the PTTs' activities often extended beyond those related to their public service task, such as banking and insurance. As a matter of course, tele-communications monopolies were extended to cover new types of services and technologies. Where a monopoly was not directly involved in the manufacture of switching and terminal equipment, it would cultivate privileged supplier rela-tionships, which were used to prop up national champions in the consumer elec-tronics and information technology. Finally, the tariff structure was not only biased in favour of domestic and rural users, but the PTTs were often expected to generate revenues towards the national budget as well.[9]

Under these conditions, the PTTs' strategies tended to rely on technical and political considerations rather than market demand. Beyond the economics of natural monopoly, entrenched national political interests can therefore be read into the monopoly-based organisation of the industry. Rural constituencies, which are generally overrepresented politically, and voters in general, stood to

---

[7] K.-H. Ladeur, 'Die Neuordnung der Telekommunikation. Zur Funktion eines öffentlichen Unternehmens in hochkomplexer Umwelt', (1991) 74 *Kritische Vierteljahresschrift für Gesetzgebung und Rechtswissenschaft* 176.

[8] Thus: 'under national legislation, telecommunications organisations are generally given the function of regulating telecommunications services, particularly as regards licensing, control of type approval and mandatory interface specifications, frequency allocation and monitoring the condi-tions of use. In some cases, the legislation lays down only general principles governing the opera-tion of the licensed services and leaves it to the telecommunications organisations to determine specific operating conditions'. Commission Directive 90/388/EEC on competition in the market for telecommunications services ((1990) OJ L192/10), recital 28.

[9] Cf. P. F. Cowhey, 'The International Telecommunications Regime: The Political Roots of Regimes for High Technology', (1990) 44 *International Organization* 169; J. Hills, 'Dependency Theory and its Relevance Today: International Institutions in Telecommunications and Struc-tural Power', (1994) 20 *Review of International Studies* 169; Ch. Hüttig, 'Die Deregulierung des internationalen Telekommunikationssektors: Zum Verhältnis von technischer Entwicklung und ordnungspolitischem Wandel', (1989) Sonderheft 10 *Leviathan* 144. Greater detail in E. Noam, *Telecommunications in Europe* (New York, 1992).

gain from these arrangements, as did the labour force of the PTTs which was generally highly unionised, and enjoyed special public sector employment status (which might not include the right to strike, but usually restricted lay-offs and included other privileges). Together with privileged suppliers, these groups formed a strong domestic coalition in support of monopoly provision.[10] Competing interests, primarily those of business users, non-privileged equipment producers, and foreign providers of equipment and services, were shut out of the market and the decision-making process. The consumer interest (which in principle covers not only individual residential users with limited requirements, but also high volume corporate users with an interest in advanced services) was undifferentiated and usually ignored, except for the universal service guarantee.

Given the vested interests at stake, and the consensus on the validity of the natural monopoly argument for telecommunications, the PTTs were (under Community law) excluded *de jure* from the liberalisation of public procurement (with water, transport and energy), and de facto from the application of competition policy.[11] In a formal sense, this should be seen as an application of Article 90(2) EC, since the PTTs were both revenue producing monopolies and provided services in the general interest. Further, since most telecommunications operators were publicly owned, Article 222 EC was generally held to (indirectly) protect their monopoly status. Finally, since they were constituted as government ministries and combined rule-making and operating functions, the PTTs appeared to be covered by the general sovereign powers of the Member States.

The international telecommunications regime likewise rested on the principle that monopolies of services and equipment were required to provide optimal service both domestically and internationally.[12] In general, the principle of self-financing of telecommunications investment (from service revenue, rather than investment through financial intermediaries) was accepted not only domestically, but also in specialised international bodies such as the International Telecommunications Union (ITU), and the International Consultative Committee for Telephones and Telegraph (CCITT). Within these UN subsidiaries, organised as classic international organisations, the views of telecommunications engineers from the national PTTs, with an emphasis on 'network integrity' over commercial considerations, prevailed. Hence international rules and rates were established in a telephone cartel of PTTs, supplemented by further bilateral bargains between monopolists. Costs were thus established on the basis of 'technological requirements', a package of cross-subsidies, and restrictive international agreements.

[10] Cf. Cowhey, ibid.
[11] Representing 6 per cent of Community GDP, the utilities were exempted from the public procurement rules. Council Directive 71/305/EEC concerning the coordination of procedures for the award of public works contracts ((1971) OJ L185/5); and Council Directive 77/62/EEC coordinating procedures for the award of public supply contracts ((1977) OJ L13/1). Cf. A. Brown, 'The Extension of the Community Public Procurement Rules to Utilities', (1993) 30 CMLR 721.
[12] Cowhey, above, n. 9, p. 177.

When technological advances first began to reduce the cost in particular of long-distance and international calls, the resulting growth in profit was used for further cross-subsidisation of local calls, to fund network upgrading, siphoned off by the treasury, or in a variety of other ways (in the French case including cash subsidies to the struggling national electronics industry). This widening gap between actual costs and prices led, as it had in the United States, to the phenomenon of by-pass: attempts by businesses to avoid the public network and construct their own infrastructure or message forwarding routes. Increasingly, the most well-heeled consumers were defecting from the system.

Until the 1980s, the 'postal-industrial complex' (PTTs combining posts and telecommunications—and in some countries postal savings banks—and their suppliers) fended off any challenges to the existing system.[13] Ultimately however, monopoly provision of telecommunications was undermined worldwide by a combination of technological change, regulatory change stimulated by a shifting balance between the economic interests involved, and spill-over of regulatory change. The attack on the coalitions of the national monopolies and their suppliers came in three 'waves'. First, as early as the 1950s sharply rising demand for equipment led to the entry of alternative suppliers. Second, in the 1960s and 1970s developments in microwave technology gave rise to the possibility of competing networks. Whereas these challenges were still fairly effectively preempted and absorbed by most monopolies, in the United States, as a private company facing multiple regulators, AT&T faced greater difficulties, and was continuously subjected to antitrust suits and investigations.[14]

The third challenge, based on technical convergence between the information technology and computer industries (notably the introduction of fibre-optic cables, digital switching, and data compression systems, which allowed the transmission of packaged data and vastly improved transmission speed, thus removing previous capacity constraints), was finally successful. With the introduction of digital technology and the development of advanced services, new and powerful competitors sought entry, the 'natural monopoly' argument for the monopoly provision of telecommunications was eroded, and regulatory change became all but inevitable. The watershed is generally considered to have been the conclusion of the famously long-drawn AT&T de-investiture case, which

[13] The privileged manufacturers were able to corner their national markets where (given the long life of equipment) initial technological choices were perpetuated. The only time when the PTTs had the opportunity to cultivate new suppliers was when a new generation of equipment was introduced (i.e. once every twenty to thirty years). Dang Nguyen, above, n. 6, p. 101.

[14] Cf. J. A. K. Huntley and D. C. Pitt, 'Divestiture and Market Structure: Competition and Deregulation in US Telecommunications', (1989) 10 ECLR 407. For a critical survey of the various investigations and their effects on price and competition see R.W. Crandall, *After the Breakup: U.S. Telecommunications in a More Competitive Era* (Washington DC, 1991). Cf. *United States v Western Electric Co, Inc, and American Telephone and Telegraph Company, Civil Action 17–49* (D.N.J., 1949); *Microwave Communications, Inc,* 18 FCC 2d 953 (1963); *Specialized Common Carrier Service,* 29 FCC 2d 870 (1971); *Second Computer Inquiry,* 77 FCC 2d 384 (1980).

resulted not merely in splitting up AT&T but also in substantial deregulation and liberalisation of the market, with the exception of local networks.[15]

The Modified Final Judgement (MFJ) of 1982 forced AT&T to divest itself of its twenty-two regional operating companies, which were merged into seven holding companies (Regional Bell Operating Companies, or RBOCs), and opened up competition in long-distance and international services.[16] However, AT&T was allowed to move into information technology. The creation of the RBOCs served to eliminate cross-subsidies from monopoly services and vertical fore-closure, the most important abuses with which AT&T had been charged. Several further operating restraints were imposed upon the RBOCs: the MFJ required non-discriminatory services to long distance companies, and barred the RBOCs from providing long-distance services, manufacturing, and from providing cable television and information services. While the RBOCs retained *de jure* local monopolies, they were excluded from advanced services. This combination of open terminal and long-distance services markets and restrictions on local tele-phony led to further technical advances, and the entry of the RBOCs into over-seas markets, in an attempt both to follow their 'domestic' customers and to remain active in the development of the advanced services from which they had been excluded in the United States.[17] The RBOCs were thus preparing to re-enter United States markets closed under the terms of the MFJ, in anticipa-tion of the relaxation of regulations while constraints in those markets after competition took root there.

Henceforward, the American market was to be a competitive and lightly regu-lated one, with liberal conditions of entry for foreign terminal equipment, and increasing cross-penetration between telecommunications and information tech-nology firms. A situation of unbalanced market opening and rapid technical change resulted. In particular the EC Member States and Japan, which benefitted from access to the United States terminal market, but lagged in other areas (especially in information technology and advanced services), found themselves subject to United States pressures to match the opening of the American mar-ket. This demand for reciprocity was expressed both bilaterally and in inter-national fora, foremost the General Agreement on Tariffs and Trade (GATT). Pressures on the European telecommunications sector thus became institutional,

[15] *United States v American Telephone and Telegraph Co*, 552 F. Supp. 131 (D.D.C. 1982), *aff'd sub nom., Maryland v United States*, 460 US 1001, 103 S. Ct. 1240, 75 L. Ed. 2d 472 (1983).
[16] The agreement between the Department of Justice and AT&T (a consent decree dependent on a 'public interest evaluation' of the terms of the settlement, was announced on 8 January 1982). The MFJ, which formed the modification and approval of the settlement by a US District Judge (Harold Green), was read on 24 August 1982, and came into effect in January 1984. Cf. J. A. K. Huntley and D. C. Pitt, 'Judicial Policy Making: The Greeneing of US Telecommunications', (1990) 10 *International Review of Law and Economics* 77.
[17] A. Metraux, *European Telecommunications Policy and the Regional Bell Operating Companies* (Geneva, 1991).

as well as technological.[18] At the same time, in Europe, user and electronics industries (especially those that competed internationally) demanded liberalisation and market opening within the Community, in order to provide them with a home market of adequate size.

Radical reform followed in the United Kingdom, albeit without much pressure from the United States.[19] The continental EC Member States chose various mixtures of retrenching and reform, the latter to be largely driven by the European Community, where the internal market drive had begun. The 1992 programme required limited liberalisation in the sector in all Member States. Moreover, the information technology and telecommunications industries were converging into 'telematics', just as the computer and electronics industries in the Community floundered. The Commission, supported by segments of industry, began to explore avenues for a more active involvement of the EC, in the support of R&D and otherwise. The resulting combination of liberalisation, harmonisation and industrial policy initiatives began to take shape from 1983 onward.

B. Telecommunications and Industrial Policy

Telecommunications liberalisation in the EC can be seen as the expression of a new economic policy consensus. This consensus was based on technical developments, the interests of transnational economic actors, and a new approach to industrial policy by the Member States, all of which favoured extending the internal market to the telecommunications sector.[20] Although the liberalisation process as such has been shaped by the application of the Treaty rules on free movement and competition, its occurrence can be explained by the importance assigned to liberalisation of telecommunications as an industrial policy measure.

All nations recognise the importance of telecommunications for economic growth, and the international competitiveness of their national industries. First, the telecommunications sector as such generates a large and growing share of GDP.[21] Second, telecommunications provides the general electronic infrastructure on which modern economies increasingly rely. Third, advanced telecom-

---

[18] G. Majone, 'Cross-National Sources of Regulatory Policy-Making in Europe and the United States', (1991) 11 *Journal of Public Policy* 79.

[19] In the United Kingdom the Conservative Thatcher government was ideologically predisposed toward privatisation of British Telecom (BT), to complete halting reforms which had started as early as 1969. BT was privatised in 1984, after a new operator (Mercury Plc) was licensed to construct a fibre optic city service network in 1983. Hereby monopoly was replaced with a duopoly, regulated by OFTEL. It should be noted that a variety of motives lay behind liberalisation in Britain. Among these were the promotion of BT as a 'national champion', relatively free from union pressure, and subject to light-handed regulation instead of political control.

[20] Hüttig, above, n. 9, p. 146.

[21] It was predicted that the telecommunications share of Community GDP would rise from 2 to 7 per cent between 1984 and 2000. COM(87) 290, *Towards a Dynamic European Economy: Green Paper on the Development of a Common Market for Telecommunications Services and Equipment* (hereafter: '1987 Green paper'), p. 2.

munications services not only form a source of competitive advantage for firms, but these advanced services themselves are thought to be one of the most attractive growth markets in high technology.[22] The relative priority placed on promoting competition as a process or the competitiveness of national industry, however, varies from country to country. Thus, the American and British systems of telecommunications policy are generally considered to rely primarily on market forces, whereas the continental European systems tend to rely on 'industrial policy' considerations.[23] In Community policy both elements are found.

In this context, it is important to note the general characteristics of the European position in telecommunications trade. This trade balance is negative with the United States and Japan, but positive with third countries, adding up to a net surplus in telecommunications trade. Although the picture is one of successful exports to the former Comecon states and developing countries, these markets are vulnerable to competition from the United States, Japan and other Pacific Rim countries. Moreover, a further loss of its share of the highly competitive advanced markets and future growth markets which drive new developments would be most harmful to the competitiveness of European telecommunications industry.[24] The Community telecommunications equipment industry is at risk of the 'scissors of competition' from advanced technology produced by the United States and Japan at the high end of the market, and from price competition by the newly industrialised countries at the low end.[25]

Consequently, introducing competition in the internal market was presented as a first step to improving the competitiveness of the European equipment industry. This meant that one type of industrial policy, based on national monopoly and protectionism, was to be replaced by another, based on the realisation of the internal market, that sought to reconcile international trade and competition with promoting the competitiveness of European industry.

[22] Cf. W. Sandholtz, 'Institutions and Collective Action: The New Telecommunications in Western Europe', (1993) 43 *World Politics* 242, p. 243.

[23] E.-J. Mestmäcker, 'Competing Goals of National Telecommunications Policy', in E.-J. Mestmäcker (ed.), *The Law and Economics of Transborder Telecommunications* (Baden-Baden, 1987), pp. 21–23.

[24] For the equipment industry a 296 million ECU trade surplus existed in 1990, over exports worth 4558 million ECU and imports totalling 4262 million ECU. The principal trading partners were, in order of importance, EFTA, the United States and Japan. This, however, conceals a dependence on exports to developing countries (facilitated by soft loans or grants) to offset a significant trade deficit with industrialised nations. SEC(92) 1049, The European telecommunications equipment industry—the state of play, issues at stake and proposals for action, pp. 17–19. Running a small and declining surplus on trade with EFTA, the Community ran a trade deficit with the United States of 439 million ECU, on imports of 1001 million ECU and exports of 563 million ECU; a trade deficit with Japan of 1134 million ECU, with imports of 1204 million ECU and exports of merely 70 million ECU; a trade deficit with Hong Kong, South Korea, Singapore and Taiwan of 180 million ECU on imports of 441 million ECU and exports of 261 million ECU. The trade surplus with countries other than EFTA, Japan, the US and the Asian NICs amounted to 2060 million ECU on exports of 2591 million ECU and imports of 532 million ECU. ibid.

[25] Cf. U. Hilpert (ed.), *State Policies and Techno-Industrial Innovation* (London, 1991), Introduction, p. xii.

Under the old industrial policy around the 'postal industrial complex' of the 1960s and 1970s, the monopolies' economies of scale were harnessed both in the pursuit of social objectives, and in sustaining national champions in electronics and information technology through monopoly procurement.[26] However, European telecommunications technology was stagnant, and fragmented markets led to high 'costs of non-Europe' in inefficiencies.[27] Yet even the suggestion of an EC telecommunications policy was absent, and telecommunications was excluded from the early liberalisation of public procurement. The privileged relationships supporting the postal industrial complex were not contested, and the natural monopoly argument rarely even made explicit: the sector was de facto excluded from the application of Community law.

In the late 1970s, with technical convergence, the availability of advanced and competitively priced telecommunications became a structural precondition for economic exchange as the carrier for financial and data communications. The introduction of information technology revolutionised both telecommunications networks and services, leading to diversification of the market of telecommunications products. Consequently, the information technology industry started pushing for entry into the telecommunications equipment market, and industrialised nations began to see 'telematics' as part of a technological competition which would determine the new international division of labour.

Initially however, the Member States continued to pursue parallel national (and mutually defeating) policies intended to gain strategic advantages in this area. Ultimately however, technological developments and the demand for the efficiency of the invisible hand reinforced each other. Slowly, the dominant paradigm of monopoly provision, market segmentation along national lines and reliance on 'mature' technology was rendered obsolete, providing opportunities and demand for Community involvement.

First, the internationalisation of the market combined with the size of the minimum share needed for survival led the more competitive European telecom

---

[26] Considering the investment volumes of the TOs it is not surprising their procurement policies should be seen as useful tools for stimulating the information technology, electronics, and component sectors. The 1987 Green Paper cites investment at 17 billion ECU for 1985. Above, n. 21. By the estimate of a consultancy report prepared for SEC (92) 1048, 1992 Review of the Situation in the Telecommunications Services Sector, annual investment in the EC under the scenario of complete liberalisation is expected to rise from 33 billion ECU in 1990 to 140 billion ECU in 2010 (a cumulative total of 1200 billion ECU over 20 years). Analysis ltd, *Performance of the Telecommunications Sector up to 2010 under Different Regulatory and Market Options: Final Report to the Commission of the European Communities* (Executive report; Cambridge, 1992), pp. 44–45. The more conservative figure used in the *1992 Review* for the funds necessary for infrastructural investment is that of 400 Billion ECU before the year 2000.

[27] In 1986 public procurement in the Community was worth 15 per cent of GDP, and more than intra-Community trade. Yet only a few percent of public procurement tenders were awarded to firms based in other Member States. The total yearly cost of non-Europe in public procurement was calculated at 21.5 billion ECU. Telecommunications equipment accounted for a large part of this. P. Cecchini, M. Catinat and A. Jacquemin, *The European Challenge 1992: The Benefits of a Single Market* (Aldershot, 1989), pp. 16ff. According to the same report, reform of telecommunications services could lead to further savings of around 4 billion ECU yearly. ibid., p. 46.

firms to favour liberalisation. This would increase their business options, through concentration, diversification, or expansion abroad. Market opening and privatisation in Asia, the Pacific, Latin America, and ultimately Central and Eastern Europe raised the stakes yet further. Given exponentially rising costs of upgrading networks and developing new products, strategies based on even the largest national European markets were bound to fail.[28]

Second, the Member States (as the OECD members in general) began to take a positive view of the trend toward competitive telecommunications markets, since they hoped it would bolster their relative position in the global economic competition (off-setting the comparative advantage of Newly Industrialised Countries (NICs) in lower labour cost).[29] In particular, liberalisation came to be seen as a necessary condition for success in the competition for telecommunications hubs of multinational companies and foreign direct investment, as well as the development of high technology products.[30] It thus became part of policies aimed to steer structural adjustment towards growth sectors, and services in general.

Third, the Commission did much to promote, jointly, the case for liberalisation and the promotion of European industry. Accordingly, it identified telecommunications as representing the most important civil investment in new technologies and services in the Community for the foreseeable future.[31] At first, this approach focused in particular on the equipment industry. In a context of structural adjustment to the global redivision of labour, telecommunications equipment formed the only high technology sector in which the Community retained a positive trade balance.[32] Due to its convergence with the high technology sectors of electronics, components, and information technology, the European position in terminal equipment was often presented as a last chance to expand its lead in this sector into other areas, and remedy earlier failures.

[28] The best illustration of this argument is that in the mid-1980s a global market share of 8 per cent was regarded as the minimum necessary to sustain a viable telematics industry. The largest individual European TO accounted for only 6 per cent of the world market, the United States and Japanese markets for 35 per cent and 11 per cent respectively. 1987 Green Paper, above, n. 21, foreword.

[29] Hüttig, above, n. 9, p. 156. However, Member States have been concerned that with international competition domestic service and employment levels might suffer, and that they might end up underwriting costly, yet uncertain, commercial ventures.

[30] The inefficiency that resulted from protectionism was considerable. Price differentials which were estimated at 20 per cent between Europe and the United States in the 1970s had grown to between 60 and 100 per cent by the early 1980s. Dang Nguyen, above, n. 6, p. 98. This widening gap resulted as prices in the United States were driven down by competition.

[31] Ungerer and Costello, above, n. 2, p. 83.

[32] The balance is negative for (1) computing; (2) consumer electronics; and (3) components (notably semi conductors). This is repeated in a number of reports, including the 1987 Green Paper. The global value of the four sectors in the mid-1980s was: computing 170 billion ECU (of which equipment 120, computing services 50 billion ECU); components 30 billion ECU; consumer electronics 105 billion ECU (equipment 55, services 50 billion ECU); telecommunications 390 billion ECU (equipment 90, services 300 billion ECU). Telecommunications services thus account for more than 40 per cent of the aggregate value of the four sectors. Ungerer and Costello, above, n. 2, pp. 92ff.

More recently, telecommunications have been at the heart of the transition to the 'service economy'. It is this area on which the 1993 Delors White Paper on Growth, Competitiveness and Employment focused in its strategy to reinvigorate the European economy, and inspire the public by translating European integration into job creation and regional development.[33] Although traditional voice telephony still accounts for the bulk of the telecommunications services market, a clear shift is occurring towards advanced, and 'multimedia' services. In the most optimistic projections this will transform the role of telecom from a basic infrastructure for private users to the nervous system of the information economy, the information highways of the 'Information Society', held out as a model of the post-industrial future. Accordingly, the focus for industrial policy has shifted from the promotion of equipment manufacturing to facilitating the take-off of multimedia services.

C. The Emergence of EC Telecommunications Policy

A first sign of a shift in the position of the Member States was the positive reaction in the Industry Council to a Commission Communication on the emergence and importance of telematics in 1979.[34] Community industry in information technology, components (semi-conductors) and electronics, was losing ground, and the failure of national industrial policies was becoming painfully apparent. Second, the deregulation and privatisation efforts of the Thatcher government, although contested, brought home the practical possibility of introducing alternative forms of market organisation. Finally, early efforts at establishing a telecommunications policy for the EC were caught in the momentum building for the internal market programme, initially in particular its R&D dimension.

Change began in 1983 with the formation of a Task Force on information technology and telecommunications in Industry DG III.[35] Since the competitiveness of the European information technology industry was held to be at risk, common R&D programmes were seen as an opportunity to bolster this sector. With the backing of a roundtable of leading European industrialists first organised by Industry Commissioner Davignon in 1979, the Community research

[33] COM(93) 700, Growth, Competitiveness, Employment: The Challenges and Ways Forward into the 21st Century.

[34] COM(79) 650, European Society faced with the Challenge of new Information technology: A Community Response. The concept of telematics was introduced in Europe by the report to the French President by S. Nora and A. Minc, *L'informatisation de la société* (Paris, 1978).

[35] This Task Force produced a stream of communications intended to put telecommunications firmly on the agenda of the Council: COM(83) 329, Communication concerning telecommunications in the Community; COM(83) 371, Communication on prospects for the development of new policies; COM(83) 547, Discussion paper for the special Council meeting of 20–21 September on the question of improving the international competitive position of European firms; COM(83) 573, Communication on lines of action in the field of telecommunications. The Task Force became the core of the new DG XIII for Telecommunications, Information Industries and Innovation, created in 1986.

programme for information technology (ESPRIT) was started in 1984.[36] In the same year a senior telecommunications officials group (SOG-T) was established, with an Analysis and Forecasting Group (GAP, a sub-group of the SOG-T) to identify medium and long term objectives, in particular concerning R&D efforts.[37]

As a result, telecommunications (which had been identified as a 'strategic industry') appeared on the agenda both as part of the R&D programme in the form of the RACE initiative, and as an area to which the liberalisation effort of the 1992 programme was to be extended. Telecommunications policy and the various industrial policy strands of the internal market programme (R&D, standardisation, mutual recognition, liberalisation of public procurement) thus share a common history.[38] It was the Industry Council which approved the creation of SOG-T and the lines of action it proposed,[39] and Telecommunications DG XIII originated as a hive-off from Industry DG III.

With these foundations in place, co-ordinated activity at the Community level started in 1984 with Council approval of an action plan for implementing a common telecommunications policy.[40] The goals of this action programme were:

(i) promoting the creation of an advanced European telecommunications infrastructure;

(ii) contributing to the creation of a Community-wide market for services and equipment;

(iii) contributing to the competitiveness of European industry and service providers.[41]

---

[36] Council Decision 82/878/EEC on a preparatory phase for a Community research and development programme in the field of information technologies ((1982) OJ L369/37); Council Decision 84/130/EEC concerning a European programme for research and development in information technologies (ESPRIT) ((1984) OJ L67/54); Council Decision 88/279/EEC concerning the European strategic programme for research and development in information technologies (ESPRIT) ((1988) OJ L118/32). In 1985 ESPRIT was followed by RACE, a specific programme for R&D co-operation in telecommunications. Arguments for Community action in telecommunications have never failed to address the competitiveness of the European electronics industry.

[37] The GAP was composed of representatives of the PTTs, the ministries of economic affairs, industry and science, and the Commission. 1987 Green Paper, above, n. 21, p. 114.

[38] Cf. Sandholtz, above, n. 22, pp. 256ff.   [39] COM(83) 573, above, n. 35.

[40] COM(84) 277, Progress report on the thinking and work done in the field, and initial proposals for an action programme; Conclusions of the Telecommunications Council of 17 December 1984 (Minutes of 979th Meeting of the Council, 17 December 1984).

[41] More accurately, in following the Action Programme, the Commission, in 1985 and 1986 made proposals along the following five main lines: (1) co-ordination regarding the future development of telecommunications in the Community and common infrastructure projects (ISDN, digital mobile communications, IBC); (2) creation of a Community wide market for terminals and equipment, and promotion of common standards; (3) the launch of a programme of pre competitive and pre normative R&D (RACE); (4) promoting the introduction and development of advanced services and networks in peripheral regions; (5) building common positions for international telecommunications negotiations. 1987 Green Paper, above, n. 21, at 98. A review of the progress made was given in COM(86) 325, Communication from the Commission to the Council on European Telecommunications Policy.

From 1984 onwards the Telecommunications Council met twice yearly, and in 1986 DG XIII, responsible for telecommunications, information industries and innovation, was established. While a more detailed sectoral policy was being developed, the activities of the Commission focused on harmonisation and standardisation.[42] Thus, the Council approved the first initiatives concerning Integrated Service Digital Networks (ISDN), the co-ordination of the introduction of mobile communications systems, and mutual recognition of type approval.[43]

In particular, the EC's early efforts in R&D were of great importance for putting telecommunications on the Community agenda, and building a coalition of interests to support the position of the Commission. Telecommunications featured prominently in the EC's R&D programme as a crucial market for high technology industry, with the telecommunications administrations as the largest civil investors in high technology. The high development costs for new products and services in telecommunications and information technology led to a need for large markets.[44] The particular purpose of the focus on telecommunications was to stimulate the (weak) information technology and electronics industry by consolidating what was perceived as a strong European position in

---

[42] Essential to harmonisation of telecommunications standards was the 'new approach' to standardisation, introduced by Council Resolution of May 7 1985 on a new approach to technical harmonisation and standards ((1985) OJ C161/1). Cf. J. Pelkmans, 'The new approach to technical harmonisation and standardisation', (1987) 25 JCMS 249; Ch. Joerges, 'Markt ohne Staat? Die Wirtschafts-Verfassung der Gemeinschaft und die Renaissance der regulativen Politik', in R. Wildenmann (ed.), *Staatswerdung Europas? Optionen für eine politische Union* (Baden-Baden, 1991). Within the 'new approach' two phases of telecommunications standardisation can be distinguished. During the first phase mutual recognition of conformity test results in accordance with common conformity specifications drawn up by the European Conference of Postal and Telecommunications Administrations (CEPT), on the basis of the work of specialised bodies such as the European Committee for Standardisation (CEN), and the European Committee for Electrotechnical Standardisation (CENELEC) was relied on. The second phase saw creation of a new mechanism for producing common standards with the creation of the European Telecommunications Standardisation Institute (ETSI) on the basis of a memorandum of understanding of 15 January 1988 by the Member States. Cf. Council Resolution of 27 April 1989 on standardization in the field of information technology and telecommunications ((1989) OJ C117/1). ETSI draws up standards at the request of the Commission, which must then be accepted by the Commission and published in the *Official Journal* in order to enter into force. This procedure was conceived by the Commission in a political move intended to sidestep the CEPT, which was seen as too closed and dominated by the PTTs. Cf. Sandholtz, above, n. 22, p. 260.

[43] Cf. Council Recommendation 84/549/EEC concerning the implementation of harmonisation in the field of telecommunications ((1984) OJ L298/49); Council Directive 86/361/EEC on the initial stage of mutual recognition of type approval for telecommunications terminal equipment ((1986) OJ L217/21); which modified and extended Council Directive 83/189/EEC on laying down a procedure for the provision of information in the field of information of technical standards and regulations ((1983) OJ L109/8); Council Directive 86/529/EEC on the adoption of common technical specifications on the MAC/packet family of standards for direct satellite television broadcasting ((1986) OJ L311/28); Council Decision 87/95/EEC on standardisation in the field of information technology and telecommunications ((1987) OJ L36/31); Council Recommendation 86/659/EEC on the coordinated introduction of the Integrated Services Digital Network (ISDN) in the European Community ((1988) OJ L382/36); Council Recommendation 87/371/EEC on the coordinated introduction of public pan-European cellular digital landbased mobile communications in the Community ((1987) OJ L196/81).

[44] 1987 Green Paper, above, n. 21, pp. 137–138.

telecommunications. The period leading up to the Single European Act saw the successive launch of: ESPRIT (1984); RACE (1985); STAR (1986) and the first framework programme of 1987.[45]

The primary goal of RACE (Research and Development in Advanced Communication Technologies for Europe), was the Community-wide introduction of Integrated Broadband Communications (IBC) by 1995, taking into account the evolving ISDN.[46] RACE (1987–1991) and ESPRIT were the main R&D programmes for promoting Community competitiveness ('strategic and market-responsive') with a total EC budget contribution of 1100 million ECU.[47] STAR (1987–1991), co-ordinated by DG XVI, surpassed even this[48], with a budget of 1300 million ECU.[49] As a result, the telecommunications-related research

[45] Council Decision 87/516/Euratom-EEC concerning the framework programme for Community activities in the field of research and technological development (1987 to 1991) ((1987) OJ L302/1); as amended by Council Decision 88/193/Euratom-EEC supplementing Decision 87/516/Euratom-EEC concerning the framework programme for Community activities in the field of research and technological development (1987 to 1991) ((1988) OJ L89/35). The framework programme was adopted under Article 130I, introduced by the Single Act.

[46] Council Decision of 14 December 1987 on a Community programme in the field of telecommunications technologies—research and development (R&D) in advanced communications technologies in Europe (RACE program) (88/28/EEC; (1988) OJ L16/35).

[47] Participants were obliged to match EC funding. More accurately, the figures were as follows: the 'definition phase' of RACE, proposed in March 1985, was slated for 22.1 million ECU over eighteen months; the first five year phase of RACE (1987–1991), proposed in October 1986, was approved in December 1987 by the Council with EC funding of 550 million ECU (involving 294 participants in 92 projects). The second phase of RACE (1990–1994), was proposed in May 1990, and approved by the Council in June 1991, with an EC participation of 484 million ECU over five years. Cf. (1) COM(85) 113, Proposal for a Council Decision on a Preparatory Action for a Community Research and Development Programme in the Field of Telecommunications Technologies: R&D in Advanced Communications Technologies for Europe (RACE), Definition Phase; Council Decision 85/372/EEC on a definition phase for a Community action in the field of telecommunications technologies: R&D in advanced communications technologies for Europe (RACE) ((1985) OJ L210/24); (2) COM(86) 547, Proposal for a Council Regulation on a Community action in the field of Telecommunications Technologies RACE; Council Decision 88/28/EEC on a Community programme in the field of telecommunications technologies—research and development (R&D) in advanced communications technologies in Europe (RACE program) ((1988) OJ L16/35); Council Decision 91/352/EEC adopting a specific research and technological development programme in the field of communications technologies (1990 to 1994) ((1991) OJ L192/8), Annex II.
The second phase of RACE listed eight priority areas: (1) IBC (111 million ECU); (2) Intelligence in networks/Flexible communications resource management (43 million ECU); (3) Mobile and personal communications (53 million ECU); (4) Image and data communications (68 million ECU); (5) Integrated services technologies (39 million ECU); (6) Information security technologies (29 million ECU); (7) Advanced communications experiments (121 million ECU); (8) Test infrastructures and interworking (20 million ECU). Cf. Annex I and II to Council Decision 91/352/EEC; Sandholtz, above, n. 22, p. 259.

[48] Council Regulation 3300/86/EEC instituting a Community programme for the development of certain less-favoured regions of the Community by improving access to advanced telecommunications services (STAR programme) ((1986) OJ L305/1). Financing for STAR drew on the European Regional Development Fund, as a Community programme within the meaning of Article 7 of Council Regulation 1787/84/EEC on the European Regional Development Fund ((1984) OJ L169/1).

[49] Ungerers and Costello, *Telecommunications in Europe: Free Choice for the User in Europe's 1992 Market. The Challenge for the European Community*, European Perspectives Series (Brussels, 1988), pp. 153–158.

programmes of the Community for this period accounted for the largest part of expenditure in the EC budget after the CAP.[50] It bears emphasising, therefore, that the major financial commitments to the telecommunications sector were independent of any transfer of competence in this sector to the Community, and preceded the Single Act.

These were not the only telecommunications related R&D efforts sponsored by the Community. First, the Community sponsored projects intended to stimulate European co-operation in electronic data interchange.[51] In total, R&D in telecommunications and information technology accounted for 40 per cent of the allocation of total Community R&D expenditure under the first framework programme.[52] Second, a specific R&D programme concerning telematics systems in 'areas of general interest', was adopted under the third framework programme.[53] Third, the Community participated in a number of EUREKA projects in information technology and telecommunications.[54] Finally, investment in telecommunications was undertaken through the European Investment Bank, the New Community Lending Instrument, and the European Regional Fund.[55]

This massive stimulus package was accompanied by first efforts toward liberalisation. In line with the overall extension of Community action in the field, the Commission lifted its moratorium on the application of the competition

[50] A. Cawson, 'Interests, Groups and Public Policy-Making: The Case of the European Consumer Electronics Industry', in J. Greenwood, J. Grote and K. Ronit (eds.), *Organised Interests and the European Community* (London, 1992), p. 112.

[51] Council Decision 87/499/EEC introducing a communications network Community programme on trade electronic data interchange systems (TEDIS) ((1989) OJ L285/35); Council Decision 98/241/EEC amending Decision 87/499/EEC introducing a communications network Community program on trade electronic data interchange systems (TEDIS) ((1989) OJ L97/46). Related initiatives were the 1984 Interinstitutional Integrated Services Information System (INSIS) and 1985 Cooperation in automation of data and documentation for imports/exports and agriculture (CADDIA) programmes. Cf. Council Resolution of 9 June 1986 on the use of videoconference and videophone techniques for intergovernmental applications ((1986) OJ C160/1); COM(87) 360, The establishment of a policy and a plan of priority actions for the development of an information services market.

[52] 1987 Green Paper, above, n. 21, p. 138. On the predominance of IT-Telecommunications in the R&D framework programme, cf. L. K. Mytelka and M. Delapierre, 'The Alliance Strategies of European Firms in the Information Technology Industry and the Role of ESPRIT', (1987) 24 JCMS 231; J. Peterson, 'Technology Policy in Europe: Explaining the Framework Programme and Eureka in Theory and Practice', (1991) 29 JCMS 269.

[53] Council Decision 91/353/EEC adopting a specific programme of research and technological development in the field of telematic systems in areas of general interest (1990 to 1994) ((1991) OJ L192/18). The areas supported by this programme, for a total of 376,2 million ECU were: (1) the establishment of TENs between administrations (41,3 million ECU); (2) transport services— including Dedicated Road Infrastructure for Vehicle Safety in Europe (DRIVE) (124,4 million ECU); (3) health care—Advanced Informatics in Medicine in Europe (AIM) (97 million ECU); (4) flexible and distance learning—Developing European Learning Through Technological Advance (DELTA) (54 million ECU); (5) libraries (22,5 million ECU); (6) linguistic research and engineering (22,5 million ECU); (7) rural areas (14 million ECU).

[54] Cf. COM(86) 664, EUREKA and the Community Technology Community. The most important of these as an industrial policy issue that involved the Community concerned high definition television (HDTV).

[55] 1987 Green Paper, above, n. 21, p. 114.

rules to the telecommunications sector. Although no systematic approach to the introduction of competition had yet been developed, actions were taken under Articles 37 and 90 EEC against the Member States, and under Articles 85 and 86 against various undertakings, including public network operators. Most importantly, the Court confirmed the Commission's view that the competition rules of the Treaty applied to telecommunications administrations, and that the extension of existing public monopolies into new areas (such as modems and cordless telephones) would not be tolerated.[56]

Based on the action programme of 1984, the standardisation and R&D efforts around the internal market programme, extensive consultation and discussion with a wide rang of interested parties, and the results obtained in the first important telecommunications case before the Court of Justice,[57] the Commission in 1987 issued its Green Paper on telecommunications.[58] This document established consensus around the central aim of extending the internal market programme to telecommunications, which has since guided Community policy. On this basis, a distinct Community regime for the sector was established.

III. THE CURRENT TELECOMMUNICATIONS LAW AND POLICY OF THE EC

A. The Legal and Policy Framework

The general framework of Community telecommunications law and policy is formed by the EC Treaty as amended by the Treaty on European Union. It provides the general objectives and the legal basis for telecommunications law and policy, as well as the institutional structure within which it is to function. Although stable (since rarely amended), the Treaty framework is not static. A first major break was formed by the coming into force of the Treaty

---

[56] In (1) *British Telecommunications*: Commission Decision of 10 December 1982 ((1982) OJ L 360/36); Case 41/83, *Italy v Commission* [1985] ECR 873. (2) *International Courier Services*: Germany: *Bull EC* 1-1985, para. 2.1.10; France: *Bull EC* 12-1985, para. 2.1.79; (3) *Cordless telephones in Germany*: *Bull EC* 3-1985, para. 2.1.43 (4) Case 311/84 *Centre Belge d'études de marché Télémarketing (CBEM) S.A. v Compagnie Luxembourgeoise de Télédiffusion S.A. and Information Publicité S.A.* [1985] ECR 3261; (5) *Modems*: Germany: *Bull EC* 7/8-1986, para. 2.1.85. Cases that did not directly involve the Member States or their TOs: (1) *IBM undertaking on SNA interfaces: Bull EC* 10-1984, para. 3.4.1; (2) *SWIFT* (Society for Worldwide Interbank Financial Telecommunications) and *SITA* (Airprices Worldwide Telecommunications Network): Article 85 inquiries into the pricing of international leased lines by the CEPT (not reported); (4) *Corning Glass Works*: Commission Decision of 14 July 1986 ((1986) OJ L236/30).

[57] Case 41/83 *Italy v Commission*, above, n. 56.

[58] 1987 Green Paper, above, n. 21; COM(88) 48, Towards a Competitive Community-wide telecommunications Market in 1992. Implementing the Green Paper on the Development of the Common Market for Telecommunications Services and Equipment. These proposals have been described as a 'mixture of neo-liberal infrastructural policy and neo-mercantilist industrial policy'. V. Schneider and R. Werle, 'Vom Regime zum korporativen Akteur: Zur institutionellen Dynamik der Europäischen Gemeinschaft', in B. Kohler-Koch (ed.), *Regime in den internationalen Beziehungen* (Baden-Baden, 1989), p. 428.

on European Union in November 1993. A second break may yet be formed by the outcome of the 1996 Intergovernmental Conference which is to review the Treaty structure.

The EEC Treaty did not include any provisions with particular reference to telecommunications. Originally therefore, the framework for telecommunications law and policy was formed by the general obligation to establish an internal market, laid down in Articles 2 and 8a EEC: the liberal core of the economic constitution of the Community. Hence, the main provisions of the Treaty relevant to telecommunications liberalisation were Articles 30 to 37 (free movement of goods), and Article 52 to 66 EEC (freedom to provide services; and freedom of establishment). Further, given the obligation of Article 3(f) EEC concerning the institution of a system of undistorted competition in the internal market, the competition law provisions of Article 85 (control of anti-competitive agreements), Article 86 (abuse of monopoly power), and Article 90 EEC (application of the Treaty rules to the public sector), were applied to break up the public telecommunications monopolies.[59] Article 90 EEC was of particular importance, since the application of the public interest exception of Article 90(2) to special and exclusive rights on voice telephony and infrastructure enabled the phased liberalisation of the telecommunications sector, and Article 90(3) EEC was used to specify the application of the competition rules.[60]

Prior to the Single European Act, and before a coherent policy for the sector had been developed, some early legislative measures concerning telecommunications were based on Articles 100 and 235 EEC (notably concerning the mutual recognition of type approval and R&D). Since the Single Act, an extensive body of European telecommunication legislation has come to rest on two pillars: harmonisation under Article 100a EEC, and (more unusually) liberalisation under Article 90 EEC. As is well known, Article 100a EEC (designed to facilitate the completion of the internal market) provided for qualified majority decision making by the Council, in co-operation with the European Parliament under the procedure of Article 149 EEC.

Article 90 EC straddles the two categories. It is meant to reconcile the competition rules of the Treaty and the system of undistorted competition of Article 3f EEC (3g EC) on the one hand, and Article 222 EC on the other (which states that the Treaty does not prejudice the rules in the Member States governing property ownership). As such, it is at the heart of the balance struck between

[59] Articles 85 and 86 concern the conduct of undertakings and not the law or regulations of the Member States. Yet by virtue of Articles 3g and 5(2) EC, the latter are barred from adopting or maintaining in force any measures which deprive the competition rules of their effectiveness. Further, where such state measures concern public undertakings or undertakings which have been granted special or exclusive rights, Article 90 EC applies. Cf. above, ch. 3, in particular section IV B.

[60] Cf. C. Esteva Mosso, 'La compatibilité des monopoles de droit du secteur des télécommunications avec les normes de concurrence du traité CEE', (1993) 29 CDE 445; C.-D. Ehlermann, 'Managing Monopolies: The Role of the State in Controlling Market Dominance in the European Community', (1993) 14 ECLR 61, pp. 67–68.

the liberal economic constitution, legitimate national public interest exceptions, and the neutrality of the Treaty in regard to the system of property ownership in the Member States. When the internal market was extended to the telecommunications sector, conflict between the Commission and the Member States focused on the interpretation of Article 90 EC. Therefore, EC policy for the sector can be seen as a process of progressively re-defining the balance of rights and interests that is required by this Article.[61] In the course of this process, the practical meaning of Article 222 EC has been much reduced: although the formal economic neutrality of the Treaty has been retained, the increasing constraints on the Member States' freedom of action imposed by EC law have de facto promoted not only liberalisation and deregulation, but privatisation.[62]

The entry into force of the Treaty on European Union on 1 November 1993 modified the constitutional framework. Among the general changes to the Treaty, the most important were the introduction of the principle of subsidiarity for areas of concurrent competence in Article 3b EC, and the co-decision procedure of Article 189b EC. The former requires that telecommunications legislation at the level of the EU be limited to topics with a Community dimension, which could not effectively be achieved by the Member States acting independently. The latter means that for all legislation under Article 100a EC, the approval of the European Parliament is now required on equal footing with that of the Council, under a complex procedure involving multiple rounds of negotiation between the two legislative bodies. By virtue of these two general changes, the residual regulatory powers of the Member States (albeit exercised through independent national regulators), and the influence of Parliament on telecommunications legislation were reinforced.

The specific changes to the EC Treaty affecting telecommunications were the introduction of Articles 3(n) and 3(s) EC, and the corresponding Titles regarding trans-European networks (TENs), and consumer protection. Telecommunications

---

[61] Article 90(1) states the rule that Member States are not allowed to enact or maintain in force, concerning public undertakings or undertakings to which they have granted special or exclusive rights, acts contrary to the rules contained in the treaty, in particular the competition rules. Article 90(2) gives a limited derogation from the application of the Treaty rules to services of a general economic interest and revenue-producing monopolies, in so far as these rules would obstruct the performance of the tasks of such enterprises, and to the extent that this would not be contrary to the Community interest. Article 90(3) charges the Commission with observing the application of Article 90, where necessary by way of directives and decisions addressed to the Member States.

[62] Regarding liberalisation and privatisation of undertakings (formerly) granted special and exclusive rights, notably in telecommunications: '. . . the EC Treaty does not in any way prejudice the ownership of such undertakings. Nevertheless, the fact remains that the entry of new competitors onto the market, combined with the limited growth for public expenditure in the Member States, will probably result in some privatisation of these sectors, particularly if private enterprise can hope to benefit from an open environment'. COM(94) 161, *23rd Competition Report from the Commission—1993*, para. 41. On the relationship between liberalisation, deregulation and privatisation see C.-D. Ehlermann, 'Libéralisation et privatisation' (editorial); and A. Abate, 'Droit communautaire, privatisations, déréglementations', (1994) 4 *Revue du Marché Unique Européen* 5, p. 11.

was first explicitly mentioned in the Treaty in Title XII EC (Articles 129b–d) on TENs.[63] The importance of this Title is that although it presumes 'the framework of a system of open and competitive markets', it establishes objectives for telecommunications policy which go beyond liberalisation per se, notably: (i) the interconnection; and (ii) interoperability of national networks; as well as (iii) access to such networks. In the context of subsidiarity, these three objectives are to be regarded as the priorities of the future harmonisation efforts under EC law. This change reflects the general shift in focus of the economic constitution toward structural adjustment. However, given the existence of this specific basis in the Treaty for an active industrial policy on network infrastructure, Industry Title XIII itself may be expected to be of less relevance to telecommunications.

Title XI EC (Article 129a) commits the Community to contribute to the protection of the health, safety and economic interests of consumers, and to keep them adequately informed. Perhaps less obviously, this is nevertheless relevant to Community telecommunications law and policy, given the importance of providing guarantees for the public interest in a liberalised environment (especially regarding universal service). This is not merely in line with the new emphasis on consumers' rights, but should also be seen as an extension of individual economic rights, and indeed citizens' rights.[64] Under the Treaty on European Union therefore, the constitutional framework of telecommunications law and policy has been enlarged well beyond the internal market objective of negative integration by achieving the free movement of services and goods and a system of undistorted competition: the Titles regarding TENs and consumer protection now provide specific positive objectives for telecommunications legislation.

Two phases of EC telecommunications specific law and policy can be identified. The first phase, which ran from 1987 to 1992, following the publication of the 1987 Green Paper, was that of partial liberalisation.[65] The second and current phase is that following the 1992 review of the sector, during which full liberalisation of the telecommunications was agreed (although questions remain on the appropriate regulatory framework).[66] By coincidence, the reform of the

---

[63] Title XII aims to promote both the internal market and economic and social cohesion. It involves both co-operation and codecision procedures, and requires consultation of the Committee of the Regions. Title XII specifically provides for the adoption, in accordance with Article 189b EC, of guidelines which identify projects of common interest that may be supported by the Community through feasibility studies, loan guarantees and interest-rate subsidies. Other measures may be adopted under Article 189c EC, in particular regarding the standardisation required for the interoperability of networks. Title XII has not so far been used as a basis for legislation.

[64] This is demonstrated also by the great interest the European Parliament takes in this issue, in the case of telecommunications especially in relation to universal service.

[65] COM(87) 290, above, n. 21; Council Resolution 88/257/EEC on the development of the common market for telecommunications services and equipment up to 1992 ((1988) OJ C257/1).

[66] SEC(92) 1048, 1992 Review of the Situation in the Telecommunications Services Sector; and the Council Resolution of 22 July 1993 on the review of the situation in the telecommunications sector ((1993) OJ C213/1).

Treaty and beginning of the most recent phase of telecommunications law and policy occurred in the final months of 1993.

The framework of Community policy for the telecommunications sector was developed in four Commission Green Papers, and the Council Resolutions on their conclusions. These Green Papers were designed to establish consensus around central issues prior to drawing up a detailed legislative programme. Extensively researched by external consultants and national expert groups, and accompanied by multiple rounds of consultation, they formed the centrepieces of policy debate at the European level. It is noteworthy that this process was deliberately used to involve interested parties (many of which had previously been denied institutionalised access at the national level) in policy making at the Community level.[67]

On the basis of the 1987 Green Paper, the Council reached consensus on the creation of an open common market for telecommunications equipment and services through a combination of liberalisation and harmonisation. The acceptance of reform by the Member States was based on a compromise regarding its initial scope, which reflected the gradual adjustment of the balance between national public interest and the competition rules of the Treaty as required by Article 90(2) EC.

This compromise was the following. On the one hand, the principle of progressively establishing the internal market for telecommunications by 31 December 1992 was accepted, in line with the general 1992 objective. On the other hand, it was agreed that the extension of the internal market would be compatible with the continued exclusive provision and special rights of telecommunications administrations (TOs) regarding the supply and operation of network infrastructure and the provision of a limited number of essential services, where this was essential for safeguarding the public service role, as well as the financial stability of the TOs. This public service role consisted mainly (but not exclusively) of providing universal service. Further, as the TOs were of vital importance for the economies of all Member States (in many cases forming the largest single national undertakings) their future was of obvious political concern. Since both universal service and the financial stability of the telecommunications operators (TOs) depended on pervasive cross-subsidies, competition and cost-based tariffs would be phased in over time.[68]

---

[67] Cf. G. Fuchs, 'Policy-Making in a System of Multi-Level Governance—The Commission of the European Community and the Restructuring of the Telecommunications Sector' (1994) 1 *Journal of European Public Policy* 177; E. Grande and V. Schneider, 'Reformstrategien und staatliche Handlungskapazitäten. Eine vergleichende Analyse institutionellen Wandels in der Telekommunikation in Westeuropa', (1991) 32 *Politische Vierteljahresschrift* 452; Sandholtz, 'Institutions and Collective Action: The New Telecommunications in Western Europe', (1993) 43 *World Politics* 242, p. 243. V. Schneider, G. Dang-Nguyen and R. Werle, 'Corporate Actor Networks in European Policy-Making: Harmonizing Telecommunications Policy', (1994) 32 JCMS 473; V. Schneider, 'Organised Interests in the European Telecommunications Market', in Greenwood, Grote and Ronit, above, n. 50.

[68] Commission Directive 90/388/EEC on competition in the market for telecommunications services (1990) OJ L192/9, consideration 18.

Hence, a distinction was introduced between non-reserved services on the one hand, and a limited number of reserved services and infrastructure on the other.[69] Exclusive or special rights for the national telecommunications administrations on the operation of network infrastructure and the provision of basic services (that is reserved services) were accepted subject to certain conditions, in particular their monitoring and periodic review by independent national regulators, supervised by the Commission. The markets for non-reserved (that is value added) services and terminal equipment were to be opened immediately, with guarantees of interoperability and open network provision (ONP) in order to enable competition. The implementation of liberalisation was to be guaranteed by the separation of the regulatory and operational tasks of the national TOs, and strict scrutiny of both public and private undertakings under the competition rules.

The direction of reform was reviewed in 1992 with a round of consultations on future telecommunications regulation.[70] This formed an attempt to take the liberalisation process a decisive step further by lifting the exception which had previously been made for public voice telephony under Article 90(2) EC. During the review, the Commission emphasised the competitive disadvantage of European users due to segmented national markets, the remaining monopoly on voice services, and concomitant distortions in prices and tariff structures.[71] A number of potential responses were set out, among which the full liberalisation of telecommunications services.

The review coincided with the resolution of a legal conflict between the Commission and a number of Member States over the instruments to be used for market opening. Although the Member States co-operated in enacting harmonisation legislation under Article 100a EC, they generally continued to resist and delay liberalisation. The Commission had responded by issuing directives on the application of Article 90 EC to public undertakings and undertakings to which the Member States granted exclusive or special rights in telecommunications, in 1988 and 1990 respectively.[72] After decisions of the Court of Justice on the contested Article 90 EC directives essentially confirmed the Commission's position,[73] the way was cleared for reform, and the Council reached consensus on the need to move towards full services liberalisation.

[69] The reserved services, including voice telephony, accounted for the vast bulk of the market. In practice, the non-reserved services were mainly new value-added services (although not formally defined as such).

[70] SEC(92) 1048, above, n. 26; and COM(93) 159, Communication on the Consultation on the Review of the situation in the telecommunications services sector.

[71] SEC(92) 1050, *Towards Cost Orientation and the Adjustment in Pricing Structures—Telecommunications Tariffs in the Community*.

[72] Commission Directive 88/301/EEC on competition in the markets in telecommunications terminal equipment ((1988) OJ L131/72); and Commission Directive 90/388/EEC, above, n. 68. Hereafter: 'Terminal Directive' and 'Services Directive'.

[73] Case 202/88 *French Republic v Commission* [1991] ECR I-1223; and Joined Cases C-271/90, C-281/90 and C-289/90 *Spain, France, Belgium and Italy v Commission* [1992] ECR I-5833. Cf. P. Ravaioli and P. Sandler, 'The European Union and Telecommunications: Recent Developments

Consequently, in Council Resolution 93/C213/EEC[74] a new balance was struck between liberalisation, harmonisation, and the need to guarantee universal service. Full liberalisation of public voice telephony services was set for 1998 to allow for structural adjustment (notably tariff rebalancing), with additional adjustment periods up to 2003 for Member States with less developed or very small networks. A package of proposals for reform of the Community regulatory framework in order to achieve this liberalisation was to be presented in 1995, after the publication of Green Papers on mobile and personal communications, and on a policy for telecommunications infrastructure and cable television networks.

The Satellite Green Paper, which played on fears of flagging European competitiveness in the space segment sector, formed the first instalment of this package.[75] The subsequent Mobile Green Paper established a link between services and infrastructure liberalisation, and emphasised decentralised regulation.[76] Finally, the Green Paper on Infrastructure (published in two instalments, in 1994 and 1995) set an agenda and a timetable for full infrastructure liberalisation. Most important, the Green Paper on Infrastructure linked, as a general principle, infrastructure and services liberalisation.[77] Hence, it proposed the immediate removal of all restrictions on the use of infrastructure for the provision of satellite, mobile, and other liberalised services, with the exception of the use of infrastructure for the provision of voice telephony to the general public. The networks over which voice telephony was delivered were to be liberalised in step with the service itself, and Community standards of universal service were to be defined and guaranteed through mechanisms compatible with services and infrastructure competition.[78]

The Green Paper on Infrastructure received strong industry support, and was not resisted by the dominant TOs, which had concluded that rapid liberalisation would also provide opportunities to get rid of burdensome government regulation and establish themselves as European (and global) players at an early stage. The recent acceptance of these proposals by the Council will lead to the full liberalisation of telecommunications by 1998, wholesale privatisation, as

in the Field of Competition', (1994) 2 *The International Computer Lawyer* 2 (Part I); 20 (Part II); W. Sauter, 'The Telecommunications Law of the European Union', (1995) 1 *European Law Journal* 92.

[74] Above, n. 66.

[75] COM(90) 490, Towards Europe-wide systems and services: Green Paper on a common approach in the field of satellite communications in the European Community.

[76] COM(94) 145, Towards the Personal Communications Environment: Green Paper on a Common Approach in the Field of Mobile and Personal Communications in the European Union.

[77] COM(94) 440, Green Paper on the liberalisation of telecommunications infrastructure and cable television networks. Part One: Principles and Timetable; and COM(94) 682, the Green Paper on the liberalisation of telecommunications infrastructure and cable television networks. Part Two: A common approach to the provision of infrastructure for telecommunications in the European Union.

[78] Cf. Council Resolution of 7 February 1994 on universal service principles in the telecommunications sector ((1994) OJ C48/1); and the Commission Statement concerning Council resolution on universal service in the telecommunications sector ((1994) OJ C48/8).

well as market entry by (and strategic alliances with) numerous new competitors from within and outside the Community.[79]

B. Liberalisation: Competition Policy

The implementation of EC telecommunications policy has relied on the parallel application of the competition rules of the Treaty by the Commission, and harmonisation legislation by the Council. Directives, based on Articles 100a and 90(3) EC, have been the legislative instrument of choice (so far, no regulations have been adopted). Generally, the application of competition policy has preceded (and enabled) harmonisation legislation. As competition is taking off, the number of Commission decisions in individual competition cases is increasing rapidly. It is difficult to overestimate the importance of the application of the competition rules for telecommunications liberalisation: there is no single economic sector where the impact of competition policy has had a comparable impact on the transformation of national policy, and indeed Community competences. More recently, a debate has taken shape on whether the competition rules could be relied on primarily, or exclusively.

Two novelties should be pointed out. First, regarding telecommunications terminal equipment, and services, the Commission has used its competence under Article 90 EC to issue directives requiring the abolition of exclusive and special rights. This meant a significant extension of the exercise of its (implicit, but contested) powers under this Article. The scope of Article 90 EC has still not been settled decisively. Yet potentially, the precedent set for telecommunications could be used to attack special and exclusive rights in other sectors dominated by (public) monopolies, notably broadcasting, energy, water, and transport. Second, the Commission has made an innovative use of 'soft competition law', in the form of guidelines on the application of the competition rules to the telecommunications sector.[80]

The Commission first spelled out the principles for the application of Article 90 EEC to the telecommunications monopolies in two directives it adopted under Article 90(3) EEC. These directives aimed to implement the positions regarding the liberalisation of non-reserved activities taken in the 1987 Green Paper. To this end, Commission Directives 88/301/EEC and 90/388/EEC[81] extended the application of the fundamental freedoms and the competition rules

---

[79] Council Resolution of 22 December 1994 on the timetable and principles for the liberalisation of telecommunications infrastructure ((1994) OJ C379/04). This Resolution closely follows the policy proposals set out by the Commission in its Green Paper on Infrastructure, above, n. 77; and COM(95) 158, Consultation on the Green Paper on the Liberalisation of Telecommunications Infrastructure and Cable Television Networks.

[80] Guidelines on the Application of the EEC Competition Rules in the Telecommunications Sector ((1991) OJ C233/2). Hereafter: 'Competition Guidelines'. The unusual feature is that these are *sectoral* guidelines, covering all types of behaviour.

[81] Above, n. 68 and n. 72.

of the Treaty to the telecommunications undertakings to which the Member States had granted special and exclusive rights by abolishing these rights, with certain exceptions. Hereby the Commission gave a new and contested reading to Article 90 EC.[82]

Commission Directive 88/301/EEC ('Terminal Directive') formed the first concrete measure aiming at the liberalisation of telecommunications in the Community. It was based on Articles 3, 30, 37, and 86 EC *juncto* Article 90(3) EEC, and concerned the market for terminal equipment. The Terminal Directive stated that the grant of special and exclusive rights in this area led to both potential and actual restrictions on imports from other Member States, and was therefore interdicted by Article 30 EEC. Likewise, the non-discrimination requirement of Article 37 EEC had been violated. Article 86 EEC applied to the telecommunications monopolies where they imposed tying clauses, limited outlets and inhibited technological progress. Taken together, this was considered contrary to the objective of Article 3(f) EEC and the Member States' obligations under Article 5 EEC (*effet utile*).

Consequently, the Terminal Directive stated that the grant and maintenance of such special and exclusive rights was prohibited under Article 90(1) EEC, and that Article 90(3) EEC provided the only instrument by which the Commission could efficiently carry out its task of monitoring the Member States. The derogation of Article 90(2) EEC did not apply since type-approval procedures would have sufficed to ensure that terminal equipment was in conformity with essential requirements. Therefore, the Terminal Directive ordered the withdrawal of special and exclusive rights, and required termination of existing contracts.[83] This was the first time the Commission used its powers to suppress public monopolies as such, rather than the abuse of monopoly powers by such entities. Article 6 of the Directive required the Member States to entrust type approval to an independent body.

Second, Commission Directive 90/388/EEC on telecommunications services ('Services Directive') restated and extended the claims of the Terminal Directive. Directive 90/388/EC was based on Articles 59 and 86 EEC. Like the Terminal Directive it sought the abolition of special and exclusive rights, and required the Member States to take the necessary measures to enable other operators to provide telecommunications services. Unlike the Terminal Directive, it applied the derogation of Article 90(2) in line with the compromise position of

---

[82] The single precedent for the Article 90(3) EEC directives on telecommunications liberalisation was Commission Directive 80/723/EEC on the transparency of financial relations between Member States and public undertakings ((1980) OJ L195/35). Directive 80/723/EEC, which established reporting requirements and a system of Commission supervision, gave rise to Cases 188–190/80 *French Republic et al v Commission* [1982] ECR 2545 (*Transparency Directive*), in which the regulatory powers of the Commission under Article 90(3) were first defined. The legal problems involved concerning the interpretation of Article 90 EC are discussed in detail above in ch. 3, section IV B.

[83] Commission Directive 88/301/EEC, above, n. 72, arts 2 and 7 respectively.

the 1987 Green Paper: subject to a general review of policy by 1992, a number of services (notably voice telephony)[84] were excepted from liberalisation.

This derogation from the application of Articles 59 and 86 EEC was brought under 90(2) EEC as concerning the performance of a public task (the provision of a universal network) which could only be guaranteed on the basis of the financial resources derived from the monopoly provision of voice telephony services.[85] Given the pace of technological change, the exception was to be a temporary one, subject to review. Article 10 of the Services Directive called for an overall assessment of the situation in the telecommunications sector in relation to the aims of the Directive. This formed the Commission's foothold for reviewing the justification of the Article 90(2) exception for the monopolies on voice telephony by 1992.

Another important provision of the Services Directive was its Article 7, which required the Member States to separate the operating and regulatory functions of their telecommunications operators. Supplemented by the committee procedures of the open network provision legislation (ONP, see below), this created a network of national regulators. The latter provides the basis for the co-ordination of surveillance and in effect a new regulatory regime for the sector. Article 8 of the Services Directive required that, after the exclusive or special rights had been withdrawn, all contracts with the undertakings involved for the supply of telecommunications services with more than one year to run, would be terminated at six months' notice.

Predictably, both Article 90 EC Directives were immediately challenged by the Member States. It is remarkable that, although the Court largely confirmed their legality (boosting the Commission's liberalisation effort), there have been no further independent Article 90(3) EC directives. While the Commission initially threatened their use to liberalise the gas and electricity sectors, so far these threats have remained just that. There are good reasons for the reticence of the Commission to use this new legal instrument. Beyond objections on grounds of accountability and legitimacy (not to mention the working relations between the institutions), the Member States must still be relied on to implement Article 90 EC directives.[86]

Competition legislation under Article 90 EC has served as a formidable tool to break the deadlock on liberalisation in Council, but the future balance of

[84] At the time, the 'exception' of voice telephony concerned 90 per cent of sector revenue, albeit expected to fall to 80 per cent within about 15 years. Also excluded from the application of the Services Directive were broadcasting, telex and mobile telephony, destined for specific regulation.

[85] This public task was defined as 'the provision and exploitation of a universal network, i.e. one having general geographical coverage, and being provided to any service provider upon request over a reasonable period of time'. Commission Directive 90/388/EEC, above, n. 68, consideration 18.

[86] For telecommunications, an intermediate solution was found. Instead of adopting new Commission directives under Article 90 EC, the Commission has subsequently resorted to Directives extending the provisions of Directives 88/301/EEC and 90/388/EC.

sectoral regulation and application of (general) competition rules remains to be established. Meanwhile, the Commission is confronted by the results of its liberalisation efforts in the form of increasing numbers of notifications as (would-be) telecommunications firms engage in strategic alliances. Further, it is required to police what may be expected to be a prolonged phase of market opening, during which the former TOs remain de facto oligopolists. Finally, the convergence of the media, information technology, and entertainment sectors with telecommunications raises complex competition issues involving copyright, intellectual property, data and privacy protection, and plurality of media ownership.

The application of competition policy to telecommunications is complicated by fears for the future of European undertakings, and the threat of market dominance in some sectors by United States companies in particular. The politicisation of competition decisions looms where many of the more formidable entrants will be non EU giants, and ownership in the various economic sectors involved is being reshuffled worldwide. In particular, the balance to be struck is that between co-operation, necessary to establish advanced services as well as networks, and competition.[87] These issues were first addressed in the 1991 guidelines for the application of EC competition policy to the telecommunications sector.[88]

The Competition Guidelines are unique as an exegesis of competition policy for a particular economic sector. They were expressly intended to introduce an element of stability in the liberalisation process.[89] The first reason for the particular need for guidance is that the TOs, emerging from a long tradition of legal protection, now have to take into account the requirements of competition policy while making large investments in a fast moving environment.[90] The second reason is that particular forms of co-operation are to be promoted: the Competition Guidelines explicitly define the role of the application of the competition rules within the context of overall Community telecommunications policy, and specify that the Commission's proposals for the telecommunications industry must be taken into account for their application.[91]

---

[87] 'The objective is, *inter alia*, to contribute to more certainty of conditions for investment in the sector and the development of Europe-wide services'. Competition Guidelines, above, n. 80, para. 2.

[88] ibid. Concerning the relationship between the competition rules applicable to undertakings and those applicable to the Member States, the Competition Guidelines complement the Article 90 Directives where they cover the principles governing the application of Articles 85 and 86 on the one hand, and Article 90 on the other. ibid., para. 14.

[89] In principle they concern the direct application of Articles 85 and 86 EC to undertakings. Nevertheless, the provisions of the Competition Guidelines are relevant for the application of Article 90 to the extent that they concern the behaviour of undertakings which are the beneficiaries of special or exclusive rights, or fall under the *effet utile* rules. Cf. Ehlermann, above, n. 60.

[90] Cf. *21st Report on Competition Policy from the Commission—1991* (Brussels, 1991), point 20.

[91] This is illustrated by the reference in the preface to the Competition Guidelines to the industrial policy document SEC(91) 565, The European Electronic and Information Technology Industry: State of Play, Issues at Stake and Proposals for Action, as an example of the proposals to be taken into consideration.

The Competition Guidelines provide an outline of the relevant product and geographic market definitions for telecommunications equipment and services. They discuss the application of Articles 85 and 86, and the measure in which Article 90(2) and the essential requirements introduced by the Services Directive[92] justify restrictions of competition, restructuring and the impact of international conventions on the application of EEC competition rules to the sector.

Concerning the definition of the geographic market it is observed that although within the EEC national markets still appear to form distinct geographic markets, 'it is expected that the geographic market will progressively extend to the EEC territory at the pace of the progressive realization of a single market'.[93] In the course of this process, the competitiveness of the undertakings operating in EC markets could be affected to the extent that in the long run they would not survive as independent operators. Therefore the market power of the undertakings concerned, their interrelated activities and interaction between the EC and world markets are taken into consideration.[94] Increasingly, world markets will form the appropriate frame of reference.

First, the TOs' monopolies in reserved services and infrastructure up to 1998 will raise problems since they are not excluded from competing in non-reserved services (that is there are no 'lines of business restrictions'). Their dominant position retained in voice and data transmission, as well as de facto dominant positions in other services complicate the provision of equitable access guarantees. Conflict of interests obviously arises where the network operator has to provide competing service suppliers access to network, with problems of illegal usage restrictions (including discrimination, limiting the provision of services in free competition and tying contracts) and cross-subsidisation.[95] Infringements of Article 86 EC may also be the result of the abusive exercise of industrial property rights over standards,[96] abuses of dominant purchasing position, and abuse of 'essential' (or 'bottleneck') facilities. On the one hand therefore, the TOs are to be controlled, since they remain in a position to frustrate liberalisation.

---

[92] Competition Guidelines, above, n. 80, paras. 21–24. In para. 23 the Commission correctly inferred from the case law of the Court 'that it has exclusive competence, under control of the Court, to decide that the exception of Article 90(2) applies', citing Case 10/71, *Mueller-Hein* [1971] ECR 723, and Case 66/86 *Ahmed Saeed* [1989] ECR 803. This position was subsequently confirmed by the Court in Case 202/88 (*Terminal Directive*), and joined Cases C-271/90, C281/90 and C-289/90 *Services Directive*, above, n. 73.

[93] Competition Guidelines, above, n. 80, para. 32.   [94] ibid., para. 35.

[95] Cross-subsidies by operators outside the EC may be deemed abusive in terms of Article 86 EC, confirming the extraterritorial application of EC competition law, especially if the operator in question holds a dominant position for equipment or non-reserved services within the EC (confirming the extratrerritorial application of EC competition law). Cf. Commission Decision IV32.737 *Eirpage* ((1991) OJ L306/22).

[96] The abuse of proprietary standards is most relevant in relation to convergence with the information industry, although the current trend seems to one towards open standards. The most celebrated case is *IBM undertaking on SNA interfaces Bull EC* 10-1984, para. 3.4.1. Cf. Commission press release No IP(88) 814 of 15 December 1988. Competition Guidelines, above, n. 80, paras. 111–115.

On the other hand however, the telecommunications market is developing rapidly, and co-operation may be necessary to address new customer needs, and to overcome the segmentation of the internal market.[97] Agreements between TOs are held to be necessary in particular to provide for the interoperability of networks.[98] Second, co-operation between providers of services and network operators may likewise restrict competition from third parties, or lead to an extension of dominant position. Among the prospective economic benefits from such co-operation are 'the rationalization of the production and distribution of telecommunication services, in improvements in existing services or developments of new services, or transfer of technology which improves the efficiency and the competitiveness of European industrial structures'.[99] Third, regarding agreements between service providers other than TOs, the threat of cross-subsidisation and discrimination is held to be especially serious in the case of vertical integration 'whether within or outside the Community'.[100]

The Competition Guidelines' emphasis on innovation and restructuring is pervasive. Although in general R&D agreements would have to fall under the general block exemption for such agreements under Article 85(3),[101] 'full range co-operation', or joint distribution agreements linked to joint R&D not covered by that Regulation, can be exempted, 'even between large firms' where this would 'lead to improving the structure of European industry and thus enable it to meet strong competition in the world market place'.[102] Restructuring moves, through mergers or joint ventures, are seen as in general beneficial to the industry, since '(T)hey may enable the companies to rationalize and to reach the critical mass necessary to obtain the economies of scale needed to make important investments in research and development' that are held 'necessary to develop new technologies and to remain competitive in the world market'.[103] This will affect the application of the pre-existing regulation on mergers and concentrative joint ventures.[104] Similarly, where co-operative joint ventures between

---

[97] Benefits of agreements between TOs that might merit exemptions could be 'one-stop shopping', cost reductions, improvements in the quality of the network and standardisation of services.
[98] Competition Guidelines, paras. 2 and 36.   [99] ibid., para. 68.
[100] Competition Guidelines, para. 72.
[101] Commission Regulation 415/85/EEC on research and development agreements ((1985) OJ L53/5).
[102] Competition Guidelines, para. 77.   [103] ibid., para. 131.
[104] Cf. Case IV/M.042 *Alcatel/Telettra* (Decision of 12 April 1991); Case IV/34.768 *International Private Satellite Partners* ((1994) OJ L354/75); Case IV/M.468 *Siemens/Italtel* ((1994) OJ C264/4); Case IV/34.792 *CMC-Talkline* ((1994) OJ C221/9); Case IV/34.422 *Aérospace/Alcatel Espace* ((1994) OJ C47/6). A negative decision was taken in Case IV/M469 *MSG Media Service* (94/292/EC; (1994) OJ L364/1) when a joint venture between Bertelsmann, Deutsche Bundespost Telekom and Taurus (the leading German publishing company; dominant TO as well as dominant cable TV operator; and dominant provider of programming and pay-TV, respectively) for the provision of digital pay-TV was blocked under the Merger Regulation. Only the second concentration to be blocked ever, this joint venture was held to lead the creation of a 'durable' dominant position, foreclosing the largest national Community market, which would otherwise become part of a (highly competitive) emerging global market.

Community undertakings and undertakings from third countries are concerned, the Commission will take technology transfer and aid industrial restructuring into account when granting an exemption.[105]

More recently a distinct approach to 'strategic alliances' has been developed.[106] Such alliances stop short of full mergers and takeovers, but go beyond more traditional forms of co-operation in particular in their attempt to allow evolution of the co-operation involved in line with (largely unpredictable) market developments.[107] As such they are typical of the telecommunications sector. Since strategic alliances are aimed at emerging markets, they are likely to fall under Article 85 EC and the Merger Regulation, rather than Article 86 EC. The Commission decisions on strategic alliances are important, since they have a direct impact on which actors will have access to these markets. Interestingly, the Commission has tended to make its approval of strategic alliances conditional upon the existence of open markets in the Member States (and third countries) concerned.[108] This involves such factors as the existence and independence of the national regulators, their instruments to guarantee open access and interconnection and control cross-subsidisation, the ownership of (alternative) infrastructure, the number of domestic competitors and the buying power of consumers.[109] In particular where the future of the dominant TOs is concerned, it is clear that the application of these criteria may have a strong liberalising influence on regulatory reform in the Member States.

---

[105] In the *Optical Fibres* case, the Commission considered that the joint venture enabled European companies to produce a high technology product, promoted technical progress, and facilitated technology transfer. (86/405/EEC; (1986) OJ L236/30). 'Therefore, the joint venture permits European companies to withstand competition from non-Community producers, especially in the USA and Japan, in an area of fast-moving technology characterised by international markets'. The Commission acted likewise in *Canon/Olivetti* (88/88/EEC; (1988) OJ L52/51); *GEC-Finmeccanica* (Press Release IP/94/815).

[106] Cf. M. Peña Castellot, 'The Application of Competition Rules in the Telecommunications Sector: Strategic Alliances', (1995) 1:4 *DG IV Competition Policy Newsletter* 1.

[107] Cf. Commission Decision IV/33.3361, *Infonet* (OJ 1992 C7/3); Commission Decision IV/34.768, *International Private Satellite Partners*, above, n. 104, and n. 108, below.

[108] A recent example is provided by Commission Decision 94/579/EC in Case IV/34.857 *BT-MCI* ((1994) OJ L223/36). Here, the Commission granted an exemption for seven years to Newco (a joint venture between BT and MCI), considering the relevant market as the developing and global one of value-added and enhanced services ('Concert') to multinational corporations and other advanced users. Most important, the Commission motivated its decision, *inter alia*, with the consideration that the home markets of both companies were truly open to competition. Cf. A. Van Liederkerke, 'Developments in EC Competition Law in 1994—An Overview', (1995) 32 CMLR 921, pp. 956ff. In ATLAS (a joint venture between France Télécom and Deutsche Bundespost Telekom operating in the same market) the Commission indicated that its approval would require further market opening in France and Germany ((1994) OJ C377/9). Hence, the Commission appears to be reconsidering its long-standing policy in favour of collaboration between European undertakings in favour of companies based in open markets. Cf. however Case IV/M394 *REW-Mannesmann-Deutsche Bank* (clearance; IP/93/1241). Other prospective competitors in this market awaiting Commission clearance include AT&T's Worldsource/Unisource (with Swedish Telia, and the Dutch and Swiss TOs) and the recently announced IBM-STET joint venture.

[109] Peña Castellot, above, n. 106, p. 5.

In short, the Competition Guidelines indicate that application of the competition rules of the Treaty in the telecommunications sector leaves space for the introduction of industrial policy considerations in the conduct of competition policy. Given the multiple objectives of EC competition policy, this is not unusual, and remains within the margin of discretion of the Commission. What is unusual is that the considerations involved are made public, and explicit. Paradoxically, by this increased transparency, the possibility of informed (public) debate of individual decisions is increased, and the margins for industrial policy are reduced.

C. Harmonisation: ONP Council Legislation

The harmonisation of telecommunications legislation in the EC can be seen both as an instrument of deregulation (complementing the negative integration achieved by competition policy), and as a tool of re-regulation at the European level (or positive integration through harmonisation). Harmonisation legislation concerning telecommunications included that on standardisation, R&D, and public procurement, which extended the general principles of the internal market programme to the sector.[110] This legislation, partly adopted before the Single Act, did not address the particular features of the telecommunications markets as dominated by public undertakings subject to public interest obligations.

Of greater interest therefore is, second, the body of sector-specific harmonisation legislation concerning Open Network Provision (ONP). Based on Article 100a EC, the ONP rules currently provide the basic framework for Community telecommunications regulation. Two phases of ONP legislation can be identified: (i) that for the partially liberalised environment, where the TOs retained (partial) monopolies; and (ii) that for the fully liberalised environment. Proposals concerning the latter remain, in large part, to be approved.

The concept of ONP was first introduced in the 1987 Green Paper.[111] The decision to develop a competitive market for non-reserved services alongside

---

[110] Cf. section IIC, above, and Council Directive 90/531/EEC on procurement procedures of entities operating in the water, energy, transport and telecommunications sectors ((1990) OJ L297/1); Council Directive 92/13/EEC coordinating the laws, regulations and administrative provisions relating to the application of community rules on the procurement procedures of entities operating in the water, energy and telecommunications sectors ((1992) OJ L76/14); and Council Directive 93/38/EEC coordinating the procurement procedures of entities operating in the water, energy, transport and telecommunications sectors ((1993) OJ L199/84). Brown, 'The Extension of the Community Public Procurement Rules to Utilities', (1993) 30 CMLR 721.

[111] In effect, the 1987 Green Paper adopted the concept of 'workable competition', as pioneered in Case 26/76 *Metro v Commission* [1977] ECR 1875; V. Hatzopoulos, 'l'"Open Network Provision" (ONP) moyen de la dérégulation', (1994) 30 RTDE 63, p. 66. This explains the difference between the concepts of ONP in the EC and open network architecture (ONA) in the United States, which imposed unbundling between local and long-distance telephony. Cf. R. Mansell, *The New Telecommunications: A Political Economy of Network Evolution* (London, 1993), p. 74. The ONP vision was that 'Network infrastructure providers were effectively to become "common carriers" with no rights to give special favours to anyone, even divisions within their own companies'. N. Higham, 'Open Network Provision in the EC: A Step-by-Step Approach to Competition', (1993) 17 *Telecommunications Policy* 242, p. 243.

the dominant TOs (which were not barred from competing for the provision of such services) led to the need for ONP legislation. This was intended to allow the new providers of non-reserved service to reach their customers and develop into viable competitors, and to ensure that the provision of liberalised services would be implemented in a harmonised manner, facilitating the establishment of a Community-wide market.[112] Designed as asymmetric regulation substituting for (and over time itself to be substituted by) competition, ONP thus formed a crucial element of the compromise solution to telecommunications liberalisation.

Originally therefore, ONP was in the first place intended to form an interface between the providers of reserved services and infrastructure and those of non-reserved services. Since the ONP rules were designed to compensate for unequal bargaining power, their scope was limited to those TOs which have been granted special or exclusive rights by the Member States. ONP legislation was to provide the framework for the definition of technical conditions, usage conditions, and tariff principles, which would allow new competitive service providers open access to the networks owned by the telecommunications administrations. In this way anti-competitive cross-subsidies, and discrimination of competing service providers by the dominant TOs were to be precluded. In the second place, ONP set rules designed to protect the public interest under conditions of competition, guaranteed by a network of independent national regulators (NRAs, which the Member States were required to establish under the Terminal and Services Directives), co-ordinated by the Commission.[113]

Directive 90/387/EEC provided the framework for all ONP legislation.[114] It concerns the harmonisation of open and efficient access to (and use of) public networks and services, in particular technical interfaces, usage and

---

[112] Hereby the conflicts and delays that would result from enforcing the internal market for liberalised telecommunications services by resorting to the Treaty rules on competition and the freedom to provide services were to be avoided. 1987 Green Paper, above, n. 21, p. 69.

[113] Cf. Joined Cases C-46 and C-93/91, *Procureur du Roi v Lagauche et al, Evrard* [1993] ECR I-5267; Case C-69/91, *Ministère Public v Decoster*, [1993] ECR I-5335; and Case C-92/91, *Ministère Public v Taillandier* [1993] ECR I-5383, noted by Hancher (1994) 31 CMLR 857. Case C-18/88, *RTT v GB-INNO* [1991] ECR I-5951 indicated that the cumulation of regulatory and commercial functions is as such incompatible with the competition rules. Annotation Gyselen (1992) 29 CMLR 1229, p. 1237. In *Lagauche* and *Evrard*, the Belgian legislation implementing Commission Directive 88/301/EEC was struck down for failing to meet its requirement that drawing up technical specifications and type approval should be carried out by an independent body. In *Decoster* and *Taillandier*, the French implementation of Directive 88/301/EEC was likewise found wanting. The French ministry for posts and telecommunications at the time fulfilled both regulatory and commercial functions. It was found not to be sufficiently independent under the terms of the directive, although the different functions had been entrusted to separate departments within the administration. This seems to indicate that nothing short of complete separation will satisfy the requirement of independence. These rulings boosted the establishment of independent regulators, as desired by the Commission. They also indicated that Articles 90 and 86 jointly might be applied in a similar manner in other situations where public undertakings fulfil regulatory functions.

[114] Council Directive 90/387/EEC on the establishment of the internal market for telecommunications services through the implementation of open network provision ((1990) OJ L192/1). (Hereafter: 'ONP Framework Directive').

tariff conditions. Most importantly, the ONP Framework Directive established the fundamental principles and essential requirements for the system of ONP legislation. The three basic principles of ONP are *objectivity*, *transparency* and *non-discrimination*. The essential requirements which may justify restrictions of open access in the public interest are limited to security of network operations and integrity, interoperability of services, and data protection.[115]

The ONP Framework Directive further deals with the creation of standards suitable for ONP. The procedure for the definition of ONP conditions provides for mandates to the European Telecommunications Standardisation Institute (ETSI), and public consultation.[116] For this purpose (among others), it creates a committee of representatives of the Member States (ONP Committee) which is to consult a Consultative and Co-ordination Platform (CCP) of telecommunications operators, users, consumers, manufacturers, and service providers. In practice, the ONP Committee is drawn from the national regulatory authorities.[117] The annexes of the Directive provide a list of the areas for which ONP conditions will be developed, as well as a reference framework for future Commission proposals.[118]

---

[115] Under Article 90(2) limitations on the scope of ONP are possible, justified by the general economic interest. The main example of this is obviously the exception applied to public voice telephony by Commission Directive 90/388/EEC and Council Resolution 93/C213/EEC.

[116] Drafting of these conditions occurs under the auspices of the Commission. ETSI draws up standards at the request of the Commission, which must then be accepted by the latter and published in the *Official Journal* in order to enter into force. Standards adopted under ONP carry the presumption (subject to rebuttal) that they fulfil the requirement of open and efficient access. The direct involvement of users, manufacturers and services providers other than TOs in the standardisation process (as well as licensing of alternative manufacturers) may be necessary for granting an exemption under Article 85(3) to agreements that impose technical and quality standards for access to the public network. *Competition Guidelines*, above, n. 80, paras. 49–52.

[117] The ONP Committee functions as an advisory committee except concerning the adoption of the rules on the application of the essential requirements and standardisation decisions regarding services across national frontiers (to ensure the inter-operability of cross-border services). Here the procedures are those of a regulatory committee type 'a'. Cf. Council Decision 87/373/EEC, laying down the procedures for the exercise of implementing powers delegated to the Commission under Article 145 EEC ((1987) OJ L197/33).

[118] The areas listed are leased lines, packet switched data services, integrated services digital network (ISDN), voice telephony, telex, and mobile services. Cf. Council Directive 92/44/EEC on the application of ONP to leased lines ((1992) OJ L165/27); Council Recommendation 92/382/EEC on the application of open network provision to public packet switched data services ((1992) OJ L200/1); Council Recommendation 92/383/EEC on the application of open network provision to ISDN ((1992) OJ L200/10); Proposal for a European Parliament and Council Directive on the application of open network provision (ONP) to voice telephony COM(92) 247 (Council Directive)/ COM(94) 689 (Council and European Parliament Directive) ((1995) OJ C122/4); Amended Proposal for a European Parliament and Council Directive on the mutual recognition of licenses and other national authorisations to operate telecommunications services (COM(92) 254/COM(94) 41); COM(95) 379, Proposal for a European Parliament and Council Directive on Interconnection in Telecommunications: Ensuring Universal Service and Interoperability through Application of the Principles of Open Network Provision; ONP Analysis report on intelligent network functions; network management; local loop; and broadband communications ((1994) OJ C215/18). ONP lists of standards (leased lines; packet-switched data services; ISDN and candidate interfaces for switched broad band networks); and ETSI mandates are published regularly.

Council Directive 92/44/EEC on the application of open network provision to leased lines is the main piece of specific ONP legislation that has been adopted to date.[119] Leased lines were singled out in Council Resolution 88/C257/01 as being of particular importance:[120] the availability of high-capacity leased lines in particular was considered essential to the development of advanced value-added services, necessary to maintain the technological edge of the Community in telecommunications industry, and to promote the competitiveness of European industry as a whole.

To this end, the Leased Lines Directive defines the minimum set of leased lines to be provided by the Member States and the way in which the essential requirements are to be applied. The Directive further introduces a number of innovations of wider relevance. These concern the way in which the NRAs exercise their authority, including notification and reporting arrangements, the application of tariffing and cost accounting principles, common ordering and billing procedures, as well as the introduction of appeal and conciliation procedures. Hereby, both procedural and substantive terms for the operation of the NRAs are spelled out.[121]

The ONP Committee features in the conciliation procedure of the Leased Lines Directive, as well as in the evaluation of the implementation of the Directive by the Member States, and (as regulatory committee) in modification of the minimum set of lines in accordance with technological developments.[122] Since the members of this committee are in practice drawn from the NRAs, it is clear that the Leased Lines Directive, beyond setting standards of Community law for the functioning of the NRAs, also increases the co-ordination between the regulatory authorities in question.

Thus, Article 8 of the Leased Lines Directive requires that the Member States provide a dispute settlement procedure which respects due process, and its Article 12 establishes a conciliation procedure by a working group of the ONP committee. The Directive provides non-binding arbitration for disputes which cannot be resolved at the national level, or involve operators in more than one Member State.[123] Although this procedure does not prejudice legal action under the Treaty or national law, it is nevertheless a significant development toward centralised (or at least co-ordinated) conflict resolution.[124]

---

[119] Above, n. 118, (hereafter: 'Leased Lines Directive').

[120] Council Resolution 88/257/EEC on the development of the common market for telecommunications services and equipment up to 1992 (1988) OJ C257/1.

[121] This is necessary since there has been no codification of Community rules of administrative law which might otherwise be referred to.

[122] According to the regulatory committee procedure this list was amended by Commission Decision of 15 June 1994 on amendment of Council Directive 92/44/EEC ((1994) OJ L181/40).

[123] The ONP Leased Lines Directive Conciliation Procedure was first applied on 26 July 1994, leading to an agreement to deliver a leased line by Telefonica (the Spanish TO) to Esprit Telecom.

[124] Alternative legal recourse for denial of access or discrimination can be sought: (1) before national courts based on EC competition law; (2) under national implementing legislation; or (3) directly effective EC legislation after the implementation deadlines have passed; (4) by a complaint with the Commission under the competition rules. Higham, above, n. 111, p. 248.

The trend toward strengthening the functioning of the NRAs and the introduction of appeal and centralised review procedures is reinforced by the proposal for a Directive on the application of ONP to voice telephony.[125] This is already indicated by the fact that in this proposed directive the majority of the individual provisions is addressed directly to the NRAs, and that it introduces more detailed obligations in regard to their supervisory duties—aiming to increase the independence and effectiveness of the national regulators.

The aims of the proposed Directive on voice telephony are: (i) to establish the rights of users; (ii) to ensure open and non-discriminatory access to the telephone networks for all users (including competing service providers); and (iii) to enhance Community-wide provision of voice telephony services.[126] The basic contribution of the Directive is that it sets out a clear regulatory hierarchy which consists of three tiers. The first tier is formed by commercial agreements, and the primary regulatory responsibility of the NRAs as a second tier is confirmed. The Commission (assisted by the ONP Committee) forms a third tier, intended to guarantee the Community dimension with minimal intervention. This market based system can be seen as a horizontal and vertical application of the principles of subsidiarity: not only is public intervention exercised at the lowest effective level, but public intervention in the private sphere is also to be limited to a minimum as such.[127]

The proposed Directive on voice telephony sets out a framework for access and interconnection to the public networks. The right to access is extended to all users and can only be restricted with prior agreement of the NRAs, based on the essential requirements.[128] In accordance with the priority given to commercial agreements, the NRAs should normally rely on the negotiation of access and interconnection between the parties involved. However, they may intervene on their own initiative at any time, and must do so if requested by either party. The NRAs are obliged to ensure that the conditions in the agreements are non-discriminatory, fair and reasonable for both parties, and offer the greatest benefit to all users.[129] The NRAs may require that details of interconnection agreements

---

[125] COM(92) 247/COM(94) 689 (revised version), above, n. 118 (hereafter: 'proposed Directive on voice telephony').

[126] ibid., explanatory memorandum, p. 2.

[127] The principle of subsidiarity applied since the entry into force of the Treaty on European Union on 1 November 1993. Meanwhile, Council Resolution of 22 July 1993 on the review of the situation in the telecommunications sector (1993) OJ C213/93 had likewise called for 'the development of a clear and stable regulatory framework based on subsidiarity'.

[128] Telecommunications operators providing fixed public networks in other Member States, and operators providing public mobile telephony services in the same Member States excepted. The latter two categories have a right to interconnect. Proposed Directive on voice telephony, above, n. 118, Articles 10 and 11.

[129] They are also to ensure that the agreements are entered into and implemented in an efficient and timely manner, and include conditions regarding compliance with relevant standards, essential requirements and end-to-end quality. Cost-oriented, non-discriminatory and fully justified access charges may be included in interconnection agreements, but are to be applied only after approval by the NRA.

be made available to them, but prior approval is not required for agreements to take effect.

The proposal further includes a number of substantive rules relevant to universal service.[130] Elements of universal service, which has become a basic objective of European telecommunications policy, have also been identified in earlier ONP implementing legislation. The concept of universal service adopted by the Community is dynamic, and will over time come to include advanced services.[131] Given, however, that at present universal service and voice telephony are still practically synonymous, and given the level of detail paid to the elements of universal service in the proposed Directive, the proposed Directive on voice telephony forms the core piece of legislation in this regard.

The proposed Directive on voice telephony exemplifies a new type of regulation for a demand-driven market, in which users' rights play a central role. Its substantive innovations, concerning transparent accounting rules, more detailed dispute settlements and conciliation procedures are in line with this development, which will lead to further juridification of telecommunications policy.

So far the proposed Directive has not been adopted due to wider problems over the inter-institutional balance in the context of the implementation of Community legislation. Whereas the Commission proposal had provided for a so-called advisory committee which was acceptable to Parliament, the Council (by confirming its common position under Article 189b(6) EC, after two rounds of conciliation procedures had failed) had entered a regulatory committee type 'A' instead (enabling implementing decisions to be referred back to the Council, but not the Parliament).[132] The proposed ONP Directive thus became the first piece of Community legislation, contested on the comitology issue, to be blocked by the European Parliament under the new decision making rules.[133]

---

[130] In particular concerning: (1) the provision of basic telephone service; (2) the quality of service; (3) tariff policy; (4) publication of information about the service; (5) subscriber directories; (6) operator assistance and directory inquiry services; (7) public pay phones; (8) access to emergency services; and (9) specific conditions for disabled users and persons with special needs.

[131] Council Resolution of 7 February 1994 on universal service principles in the telecommunications sector ((1994) OJ C48/1); and the Commission Statement Concerning Council resolution on universal service in the telecommunications sector ((1994) OJ C48/8).

[132] Under the two earlier ONP Directives the ONP Committee had, for some types of decisions, been set up as a regulatory committee in a similar manner. However, these directives were adopted under the co-operation procedure of Article 149 EEC, by which a unanimous Council by definition had the final word on comitology. On the comitology issue and procedures: K. Bradley, 'Comitology and the Law: Through a Glass, Darkly', (1992) 29 CMLR 693; A. Dashwood, 'Community Legislative Procedures in the Era of the Treaty on European Union', (1994) 19 ELR 343; G. Della Cananea, 'Cooperazione e integrazione nel sistema amministrativo delle Communità europee: la questione della "comitologia"', (1990) 40 *Rivista Trimestriale di Diritto Pubblico* 655.

[133] In February 1995 the Commission adopted a new proposal for the application of ONP to voice telephony, above, n. 118. This text replaced a proposal of August 1992 which had originally been submitted under the co-operation procedure. This earlier proposal was caught by the co-decision rules of Art 189b EC after the coming into force of the Treaty on European Union, and duly rejected by the newly elected European Parliament in a vote on 19 July 1994. Cf. W. Sauter,

This widely predicted demonstration of assertiveness under the new decision-making rules immediately increased the voice of Parliament in legislation (and thereby in telecommunications harmonisation). Rather than risking a stalemate on all Article 189b EC legislation containing comitology provisions (including all such internal market legislation by virtue of Article 100a EC), Parliament and Council have meanwhile reached a *modus vivendi* under which they will have an equal voice in legislative decisions.[134] The main changes introduced to the proposed Directive on voice telephony relate to this compromise on committee procedures, and it is expected the legislative hurdles will now be cleared soon.[135]

To complete the discussion of the first phase of telecommunications harmonisation, the proposal which aims to establish the mutual recognition of licensing procedures for telecommunications services (as called for by Article 7 of the ONP Framework Directive) must be mentioned.[136] Strictly speaking, this proposal falls outside the scope of ONP, as it sets up a separate committee structure. It sets out harmonised conditions for the mutual recognition of licenses (to be elaborated by the European Committee of Telecommunications Regulatory Affairs: ECTRA),[137] one-stop shopping procedures, a conciliation procedure analogous to that of ONP, and an advisory Community Telecommunications Committee (CTC) composed of representatives of the NRAs.[138] Obviously, the

'The Rejection of the ONP Voice Telephony Directive by the European Parliament: The Entry of a New Player in European Telecommunications and its Effects on the Future of ONP', (1994) 5 ULR 176.

[134] SEC(94) 645, Draft Inter-Institutional Agreement on Comitology. Under this solution, for acts adopted under 189b EC, advisory or management committee procedures will be followed for non-legislative measures. Proposed legislative measures will be submitted simultaneously to an advisory committee and the European Parliament (or the relevant parliamentary committee), but are adopted by the Commission alone. Parliament and Council may agree to repeal the measure, with retroactive effect, within one month. In such cases the Commission may repeat this procedure, or re-submit a proposal according to the procedures of Article 189b EC. Although this procedure may seem impractical, it should be noted that only in about 2 per cent of cases do regulatory committees refer decisions back to the Council.

[135] Article 27(5) of the original proposal had referred decisions which could not be resolved in the conciliation procedure to the regulatory committee procedure. Under the new proposal, there is no provision for resolving a deadlock in the conciliation procedure. In practice, recourse will be taken to normal legal proceedings.

[136] COM(94) 41, Amended proposal for a European Parliament and Council directive on the mutual recognition of licenses for telecommunications services. Like the proposal for the application of ONP to voice telephony, this proposed directive has had a tortured history. The original proposal was submitted as COM(92) 254 in July 1992, but was upstaged by Council Resolution C213/93, which supported mutual recognition and an interim 'one-stop shopping' procedure rather than the dual procedure of mutual recognition and Single European Telecommunications Licenses which had originally been foreseen. Cf. COM(93) 652, Proposal for a directive on a policy for the mutual recognition of licenses for the provision of satellite network and communications services.

[137] Set up in the context of the CEPT, the regional organisation of the International Telecommunications Union (ITU)—the specialised UN body for international co-operation in telecommunications.

[138] The main principle is that licensing will remain with the Member States, subject to a number of rules: (i) the award of licenses may not create special or exclusive rights; (ii) the number of licenses may only be restricted on the basis of the essential requirement, or in the case of public

mutual recognition of licences and co-ordination of national authorisation procedures is of the greatest importance for establishing an internal market for
telecommunications.

Since the membership of the CTC is likely to be identical to that of the ONP
Committee, and given Article 7 of the ONP Framework Directive, licensing
might have been brought under the scope of ONP instead. The mandatory consultation by the ONP Committee of the CCP of users, TOs and manufacturers'
organisations provided for in the ONP Framework Directive was, however, irre-
concilable with the confidential nature of the licensing process, and a separate
structure was therefore preferred. With representatives of the NRAs represented
on the ONP Committee as well as ECTRA, the CTC forms another element of a
system of overlapping networks of regulators which has developed as a result
of the need for international co-ordination, and the assertion of the supremacy
of Community law.[139]

Hereby, the basic regulatory structure for the era of partial liberalisation and
harmonisation of Community telecommunications, as based on Commission
Directive 388/90/EEC (Services Directive) and Council Directive 387/90/EEC
(ONP Framework Directive) has been given. When the deadline for full liberalisation of public voice telephony services was set for 1998, it was clear that
this required the lifting of the exceptions under Article 90(2) EC provided in
the Services Directive, and adaptation of the regulatory framework. Hence in
the transition to a liberalised environment, liberalisation could be managed by
an extension of the first phase of telecommunications regulation.[140]

IV. INDUSTRIAL POLICY AND THE FUTURE OF
TELECOMMUNICATIONS REGULATION

A. Current Issues of Telecommunications Regulation

The original objective of Community telecommunications regulation was to
create the conditions under which a competitive market structure could develop

networks, public service requirements in the form of trade regulations; (iii) licensing requirements
must clearly distinguish between infrastructure and services, whereas the latter may not be subject
to individual licensing.

[139] The Services Directive, the ONP measures and the two Directives ensuring the mutual recognition of type approvals for terminal equipment established the overall framework for national
licensing by identifying the limited range of restrictions which may be imposed within national
authorisations for telecommunications or equipment intended for use by the general public. COM(94)
682, Green Paper on the liberalisation of telecommunications infrastructure and cable television
networks. Part Two: A common approach to the provision of infrastructure for telecommunications
in the European Union, pp. 59ff.

[140] Proposals for the amendments to the regulatory framework necessary to achieve liberalisation of all public voice telephony services were to be presented by 1 January 1996. At the end of
1994 the principle of full services liberalisation was extended to simultaneous liberalisation of the
underlying infrastructure: again, ONP was identified as the basic regulatory framework.

in a situation where dominant carriers continued to enjoy legal monopolies on infrastructure and voice telephony under the exception of Article 90(2) EC. With agreement on the introduction of full competition for telecommunications services and infrastructure by 1998, the need for a revision of the regulatory framework became evident. At issue were: (i) the objectives, (ii) the scope, and (iii) the level and methods of regulation.

First, in Council Resolution C213/93, which confirmed the acceptance of services liberalisation by the Council, the preparation of amendments to the Community regulatory framework necessary in order to achieve full liberalisation of all public voice telephony services by 1 January 1998 was requested. This Resolution recognised as key factors for the development of future regulatory policy for telecommunications the application of ONP measures as the basis for the definition of universal service, and as the appropriate framework for network regulation, notably interconnection. This indicated that the decentralised system of policy implementation by the NRAs, co-ordinated by the Commission, was favoured.

Second, the importance of interconnection and interoperability of trans-European services as central policy objectives was further underlined by Article 129b EC (introduced by the Treaty on European Union) and the 1993 Delors White Paper. The latter made creation of trans-European networks (TENs) a central plank of its drive to stimulate the competitiveness of European industry, and identified them as the 'lifeblood of competitiveness'.[141] In response to the 1993 White Paper, the Council charged the so-called Bangemann Group of prominent industrialists with reporting on specific measures concerning information infrastructure.[142]

The resulting *Bangemann Report* held out the promise of an 'Information Society', the product of a third industrial revolution based on information and communications technology. As fundamental preconditions for this development, the report signalled the need for the abolition of monopoly (including

---

[141] COM(93) 700, Growth, Competitiveness, Employment: The Challenges and Ways Forward into the 21st Century, p. 82. For TENs in general, the main objective of the White Paper was to remove obstacles to private investment. For trans-European telecommunications networks, the specific objectives were: (1) overcoming the existing state of fragmentation to complete the Single Market; and (2), the creation of new markets for (multi-media) services, which was expected to have an accelerator effect upon the European economy as a whole.

[142] Cf. especially 'Europe and the Global Information Society: Recommendations to the European Council', in *EC Bull* Supplement 2/94, the so-called *Bangemann Report*. This report was prepared by a roundtable of leading European industrialists, in consultation with the National Information Initiative/Information Infrastructure Task Force promoted by United States Vice-President Al Gore. The roundtable represented the leading European multinationals interested in the multimedia convergence between the information technology and media industries, (many of which had been involved in earlier similar efforts), including CLT, DT-Mobilfunk, ICL, IBM-Europe, IRI, Olivetti, Philips, Siemens, Reed Elsevier and Volvo. The group was co-ordinated by Viscount Davignon of the Belgian *Société Genérale* and former Commissioner of DG III, who as such had been responsible for setting up the early Community R&D programmes as well as Telecommunications DG XIII itself.

infrastructure), and the establishment of a European regulatory authority, to be charged with licensing, network interconnection, the management of scarce resources, and general advice to the NRAs (a 'Euro-FCC').[143] Further, it stressed the need for adjustment of tariffs toward cost, the removal of political constraints on the TOs, and an equitable division of the burdens of universal service and equal access.[144] In line with Article 129b EC, the importance of interconnection and interoperability was highlighted: 'Two features are essential to the deployment of the information infrastructure needed by the Information Society: one is a seamless interconnection of networks and the other that the services and applications which build on them should be able to work together (interoperability). (...) Interconnection of networks and interoperability of services and applications are recommended as primary Union objectives'.[145]

The *Bangemann Report* was endorsed by the Corfu European Council of June 1994. Taking up the first recommendation of the *Bangemann Report*, the Green Paper on Infrastructure maintained, as a 'general principle', the existence of a link between infrastructure and services liberalisation. This was based on the concerns over a bottleneck in infrastructure provision, especially for high capacity lines, regarding both prohibitively high pricing and availability.[146] This was presented as harmful to the competitiveness of European industry, delaying the development of advanced services and pan-European networks, and thereby of the information society. These arguments, supported by leading European industrialists, had a decisive impact upon the adoption of Council Resolution C379/94, which recognised the general principle of infrastructure liberalisation by 1 January 1998.[147]

These developments indicated clear political and market support for reform. Moreover, they demonstrated that under the new constitutional framework telecommunications policy was to promote structural adjustment by freeing market forces. With the exception of establishing a single European regulatory authority, most of the issues identified by the *Bangemann Report* could, in principle, be dealt with by removing the remaining exceptions under the Services Directive

---

[143] i.e. the creation of a single regulatory framework for all operators, based on the principles of transparency and non-discrimination, and complemented by practical rules for dispute resolution and remedies against the abuse of market dominance.

[144] Many of these points were standing Commission policy; their importance lies in the fact that they were adopted by a powerful private advisory group to the Council, representing the 'market response'.

[145] 'Europe and the Global Information Society', above, n. 142, p. 17. Cf. Part II of the Green Paper on Infrastructure, above, n. 139, p. 70.

[146] The key statistic quoted was that even after the entry into force of the Leased Lines Directive, 2Mbit leased lines in the EU remain on average ten times more expensive than in the United States.

[147] Cf. Council Resolution of 22 December 1994 on the timetable and principles for the liberalisation of telecommunications infrastructure ((1994) OJ C379/04). This Resolution closely follows the policy proposals set out by the Commission in its Green Paper on the Liberalisation of Telecommunications Infrastructure and Cable Television Networks. Part One: Principles and Timetable (COM(94) 440).

and extending the ONP system.[148] In reaction, the Commission has outlined its joint telecommunications and industrial policy (which largely follows the line taken in the *Bangemann Report*)[149] and worked out the regulatory agenda in Part II of its Green Paper on the liberalisation of telecommunications infrastructure.[150]

Autonomously, but after voluntary consultation of Council and European Parliament,[151] the Commission extended the scope of Article 90 EC by progressive modifications of the Services Directive, thereby sidestepping the institutional conflict which might have resulted from further independent Article 90 EC legislation.[152] First, the Article 90(2) EC exceptions for telecommunications will be fully removed by 1998. Second, a skeleton framework for the measures to be taken by the Member States is given, to be supplemented by more detailed rules under Council harmonisation directives.

Concerning harmonisation, the Green Paper on Infrastructure identified the two key issues to be addressed under ONP as interconnection and universal service.[153] Given existing asymmetries, '(I)nterconnection is the key for transforming the former monopolistic market structure in telecommunications into a competitive one';[154] it is also crucial for the development of trans-European networks and services. The approach to interconnection in the liberalised environment combines market opening and subsidiarity. It requires the removal of current

---

[148] In addition, the *Bangemann Report* pleaded for co-ordinated regulatory action in the areas of intellectual property rights, privacy and media ownership, necessary to create the stable framework for investment required for the emergence of multimedia services. Above, n. 142.

[149] COM(94) 347, Action Plan on Europe's Way to the Information Society (*EC Bull* Supplement 2/94). The link between telecommunication and industrial policy (summed up by the Information Society objective) was further developed in COM(94) 319, An Industrial Competitiveness Policy for the Community (*EC Bull* Supplement 3/94); Cf. Council Resolution of 21 November 1994 on the strengthening of the competitiveness of Community industry ((1994) OJ C343/1).

[150] Part II of the Infrastructure Green Paper on Infrastructure, above, n. 139; COM(95) 158, Consultation on the Green Paper on the Liberalisation of Telecommunications Infrastructure and Cable Television Networks; COM(94) 513, Present Status and Future Approach for Open Access to Telecommunications Networks and Services (Open Network Provision).

[151] The Commission has adopted the practice of presenting Article 90(3) EC Directives to Council and Parliament for consultation, as well as publishing them for public comment (after inter-service consultation within the Commission, and prior to their final adoption by the Commission acting as a collegiate body). Formally, the Commission alone remains responsible.

[152] A Commission Directive covering the satellite sector, and three recent proposals concerning cable TV, mobile telephony, and the preparation of full services liberalisation: (1) Commission Directive 94/46/EC amending Directive 88/301/EEC and Directive 90/388/EEC in particular with regard to satellite communications ((1994) OJ L268/15); (2) SEC(95) 308, Draft Commission Directive amending Commission Directive 90/388/EEC regarding the abolition of the restrictions on the use of cable television networks for the provision of telecommunications services; (3) Draft Commission Directive amending Directive 90/388/EEC with regard to mobile and personal communications ((1995) OJ C197/5); and (4) Draft Commission Directive amending Commission Directive 90/388/EEC regarding the implementation of full competition in telecommunications markets (not yet reported).

[153] The other fundamental regulatory issues identified in the Green Paper are ensuring a fair competitive environment and ensuring comparable and effective access to global markets; and 'broader societal issues' (generated by multi-media convergence).

[154] Wissenschaftliches Institut für Kommunikationsdienst GmbH (WIK), 'Network Interconnection in the Domain of ONP', (Study for DG XIII, 1994), p. 49.

barriers, and the extension of the three tier regulatory framework to (i) commercial negotiations of interconnection agreements; (ii) provision of dispute resolution procedures and supervision by the NRAs; and (iii) the formulation of common principles at the European level.

The Green Paper on Infrastructure defined universal service as 'access to a defined minimum service of specified quality to all users at an affordable price based on the principles of universality, equality and continuity'.[155] Whereas at present universal service obligations rest on the dominant TOs alone (as the primary justification of the special and exclusive rights they enjoy), in the future all market participants should, in principle, participate in the funding of uneconomic universal service, or its provision.[156] The NRAs will supervise the revision of the financing of universal service as part of a process in which the present general subsidies of local access are to be replaced by tariff rebalancing and the introduction of special tariffs aimed at needy or uneconomic customers. It should be noted, however, that universal service has also been placed in the context of citizens' rights.[157]

Given these priorities, the Commission identified two stages for the transition of harmonised telecommunications regulation to a fully competitive environment.[158] First, the existing package of legislation and regulatory measures is to be implemented, notably by the adoption of the proposed Directive on voice telephony and the full implementation of the Leased Lines Directive. The second stage of harmonisation was to deal in particular with the objectives of interconnection and universal service.[159] The fundamental question was that of the

[155] Part II of the Green Paper on Infrastructure, above, n. 139, p. xv. This regards the provision of the basic telephone service, quality of service and tariff policy. Secondary objectives are access to information about the service, dispute resolution procedures for users, subscriber directories, operator assistance and directory inquiry services, public pay phones, access to emergency services, and specific conditions for disabled users and persons with special needs. Further, targets or recommendations are proposed for advanced features, such as itemised billing, touch-tone dialling, call-forwarding, calling line identification, green number or 'freephone' services, call transfer and access to directory and operator services in other Member States. ibid., pp. 81–82. Specific elements of universal service had already been developed in the proposed Directive on voice telephony. Cf. Council Resolution 94/C379/03, above, n. 147.

[156] Concerning the financing of universal service, a preference is expressed for the use of universal service funds over access charges, although the decision for one or the other is to be taken at the national level. Universal service funds would allow all market participants to provide service rather than pay into the fund, and exert downward pressure on the cost. The funds would be independently administered. The system of access charges on the contrary presupposes that universal service is provided by the dominant TO, which also administers the system.

[157] The dual aim of this process 'should be to provide consumers and business with a diverse offering of quality telecommunications at competitive prices whilst guaranteeing universal access to basic telecommunications services for all citizens'. Part II of the Green Paper on Infrastructure, above, n. 139, p. 43. Over time, the benefits of reduced cost and improved quality over a widening range of services should be extended to all users.

[158] COM(94) 513, above, n. 150.

[159] Further, interoperability (for which interconnection is a precondition) will be pursued primarily through standardisation. The objective on standardisation is the development of market-led interface standards to ensure open markets and protect users' interests. However, the objectives of

future scope of regulation: whether, with the abolition of all exclusive and special rights, ONP should be extended to cover all operators, or merely those in
a position of market dominance.[160]

In the recent Commission proposal for an Article 100a EC Directive which
sets out a harmonised framework for interconnection under ONP, a differentiated system of rights and duties for various types of operators is introduced.[161]
This Directive is to come into effect on 1 January 1998 and will form the main
plank of the revision of the regulatory framework. Similar to the Leased Lines
Directive and the proposed Directive on voice telephony, a three tier system of
regulation is proposed, with reliance on market agreements, supervised by the
NRAs and supplemented by legal review, and a dispute resolution procedure
to facilitate the creation of TENs.

Public telecommunications networks operators and service providers would
have the right to be granted interconnection, and a corresponding obligation
to grant requests of interconnection by others.[162] Operators and providers of
services with more limited ambitions would have neither an automatic right to
interconnection, nor a corresponding obligation to interconnect. Public operators
and service providers in a position to control essential facilities would be obliged
to interconnect with each other on a non-discriminatory basis, in order to ensure
the availability of national and trans-European services. Finally, organisations
with significant market power would be subject to additional obligations, notably concerning accounting and functional separation of their activities, in order
to facilitate regulatory supervision.[163]

The definition of market power combines a double threshold with an element
of administrative discretion. First, all TOs with a market share in excess of 25

market-led standards, and standards which guarantee open markets and users' interests are in fact
contradictory. For interconnection, instead of the voluntary standardisation of article 5(1), the ultimate remedy of mandatory standards defined in article 5(3) of the ONP Framework Directive may
well be applied (in particular in order to develop Pan-European standards for mobile networks).

[160] The redefinition of regulation currently based on the existence of exclusive and special rights
is a horizontal issue which also involves Council Directives 90/531/EEC; 92/13/EEC; and 93/
38/EEC (on public procurement); and Council Directive 91/263/EEC (terminal equipment; mutual
recognition). In principle, striking the reference to 'special and exclusive rights' in the existing ONP
directives would suffice to make them applicable to all TOs licensed to provide public networks
and (or) services. Public telephony remains to be adequately defined. Cf. SEC(95) 545, Communication on the Status and Implementation of Directive 90/388/EEC on Competition in the Markets
for Telecommunications Services.

[161] Above, n. 118 (hereafter: 'proposed Interconnection Directive'). The proposed interconnection Directive is to establish: (i) general principles for interconnection; (ii) a framework for commercial negotiations; (iii) a common approach and ceilings on that part of the interconnection charge
related to universal service; and (iv) a mechanism for dispute resolution.

[162] The definitions of public networks and services, and those of the organisations with rights
and obligations to interconnect as set out in Article 4 of the proposed Interconnection Directive,
are set out in Annexes I and II of the proposed interconnection Directive, ibid.

[163] These include requirements to publish interconnection price lists, to introduce cost-oriented
interconnection tariffs and transparent cost-accounting systems, as well as accounting separation,
and to meet all reasonable requests for interconnection.

per cent of a particular telecommunications market will be presumed to enjoy such power. Second, the proposed Directive sets an annual turnover threshold of 50 million ECU for the certain accounting separation obligations, intended to facilitate regulatory control. Third, the NRAs may determine the existence or absence of significant market power in derogation from these two standard criteria, based on other factors such as size, degree of vertical integration, and ability to act independently of competitors.[164]

Since the Treaty provisions on abuse of dominant position are not affected by the ONP rules, the Commission will supplement the control exercised by the NRAs.[165] The most problematic feature of the parallel systems under ONP and the competition rules is that they establish overlapping jurisdictions (with different powers) based on similar but different criteria ('market power' versus 'dominant position'). The Commission has floated the idea of proposing an Article 87 EC Council Regulation to specify the application of Articles 85 and 86 EC to access in the telecommunications sector. This is intended to provide the TOs involved with a stable and predictable perspective on the application of the competition rules by the Commission, the national competition authorities, and the national courts.[166]

Finally, it is noteworthy that the Commission (in consultation with the ONP committee) may issue further guidelines concerning the implementation of the proposed interconnection Directive.[167] On the one hand (since under the inter-institutional agreement on comitology the ONP committee will henceforth function as an advisory committee) this means further implementing powers are to be delegated to the Commission. On the other hand, it is worth noting that

---

[164] According to Article 17 of the proposed interconnection Directive, those TOs which have: (1) universal service obligations (exclusively covering the fixed network and services); (2) significant market power; (3) and/or interconnection obligations are to be notified to the Commission by 31 January 1997 (and thereafter). In many cases these categories will obviously overlap. The Commission may request a reasoned statement for the classification of a TO as enjoying significant market power.

[165] The Court of Justice has defined dominant position as a position of economic strength enjoyed by an undertaking which allows it to prevent effective competition from being maintained in the relevant market by giving it the power to behave largely independently of its competitors, customers and consumers. Rather than an abstract measure of market share, the ability of a firm to set or control prices is usually taken as evidence of the existence of such dominance. Case 27/76 *United Brands v Commission* [1978] ECR 207.

[166] Establishing a European policy on interconnection could further require modification of the proposed Directive on voice telephony and amendment of the Leased Lines Directive. In particular, Member States will have to ensure the availability of a minimum level of transmission capacity. It has been proposed that a link should be made between market share and the obligations under ONP to provide a minimum set of harmonised offerings, which will depend on the general revision of the scope of ONP. Finally, proposals for the extension of ONP to mobile telecommunications may be expected following the publication of the consultation on the 1994 Green Paper on mobile telephony COM(94) 145, above, n. 76; and COM(94) 492, Communication on the Consultation on the Green Paper on Mobile and Personal Communications.

[167] Notably on: (1) the costing and financing of universal service; (2) on cost accounting and interconnection charges; (3) on accounting separation; (4) and on the responsibilities of the NRAs as well as the dispute resolution system.

many provisions of the proposed interconnection Directive confer facultative powers on the NRAs, which 'may' decide to impose obligations which go far beyond the minimum harmonisation otherwise provided by the Directive. Further, the individual Member States may opt to provide more specific national rules.[168] Considerable diversity in the intensity of regulation at the national level will therefore be possible.

Hereby a detailed framework for bringing interconnection and universal service under the ONP rules has been proposed, which will form the main element of the revision of the regulatory structure. The system of the twin tracks of liberalisation and harmonisation would thus be retained, although there appears to be a risk of the development of parallel structures. Nevertheless, for the immediate future the objectives and scope, as well as the level and method of regulation, appear to have been settled.

B. Alternative Methods and Levels of Regulation for Telecommunications in the EC

The development of the telecommunications policy of the EC along parallel tracks of liberalisation and harmonisation has been noted. The question remains whether this will continue under full competition, in particular in the light of the earlier hypothesis that beyond the alleged contradiction between the industrial and competition policy of the Community, the allocation of decision making between the different levels of government should be considered. The problem is that of establishing both the minimum degree of regulation necessary and the appropriate level of policy making. This is also relevant in the light of the further hypothesis that there is a general tendency toward depoliticisation of economic policy, with the European Central Bank and System of European Central Banks as the most extreme example of independent expert administration of an important part of the economy.

On the one hand, in the liberalised environment the importance of harmonised ONP regulation seems likely to increase, since it forms the key to the important public interest objectives of universal service, and interconnection. On the other hand, the question of the scope of regulation becomes more contentious, as the TOs progressively lose market share to new competitors, and alternative infrastructure becomes available.[169] In principle, mandatory regulatory obligations could be reduced as competition develops. This raises the question whether ONP could in the future be replaced by competition policy. Since calls for the creation of a European regulatory authority have been heard, a second question is whether the current decentralised system of ONP could be replaced by an independent centralised European telecommunications agency.

---

[168] Notably concerning universal service obligations, collocation and facility sharing, and data protection.
[169] Cf. SEC(95) 308, above, n. 152.

On first sight, competition policy and ONP regulation appear to be substitutes, as was implied by the 1987 Green Paper, which suggested that a fear of delays due to litigation if the competition rules were relied on formed the main reason for introducing harmonisation instead. Over time, a shift of emphasis has occurred, and it would be tempting to conclude that the ultimate outcome would be full competition with minimal regulation, based on enforcement of the competition rules of the Treaty.[170]

Community competition policy should not in general be seen as anti-trust enforcement through prosecution and litigation. Given its highly centralised nature and limited resources, the Commission cannot engage in conflict on too many fronts at once. Although Articles 85 and 86 EC are directly effective, it has been widely noted that the current system is not well suited to decentralised application by the national courts and competition authorities. Therefore, the Commission increasingly relies on rule-making and the use of soft law to make its competition policy more predictable and more easily enforceable. There is thus no question of two clear-cut alternatives in the sense of anti-trust enforcement by litigation versus sectoral regulation by bureaucratic administration. Rather, the fundamental difference with ONP legislation is formed by the terms of implementation: whereas EC competition policy remains highly centralised, the implementation of harmonised legislation is fully decentralised.

Further, the priorities of competition policy and specialised telecommunications legislation are different. Whereas competition policy may be suited to guarantee free competition in open markets, it is much less suited to pursue specific public interest objectives, such as universal service. There may thus, in the long run, be an argument for replacing asymmetric regulation with symmetric regulation, with competition policy as an enforcement mechanism of last resort, rather than for replacing telecommunications regulation by competition policy as such. This indeed appears to be the view of DG IV: 'The overall approach adopted, which combines liberalization and harmonization, shows that the liberalization of an economic sector does not require the removal of all rules but, on the contrary, calls for a regulatory framework so as to avoid harmful distortions'.[171]

Hence, on a closer view, competition policy and detailed telecommunications regulation such as ONP do not form functional equivalents. Indeed, the modifications to the constitutional requirements regarding subsidiarity, TENs and consumer protection appear to have made the competition rules unsuitable as an alternative to ONP.

---

[170] Further, to some observers, competition among rules is inherently superior to harmonisation, and consequently a choice for competition policy would be preferable. Cf. C. Henry, 'Public Service and Competition in the European Community Approach to Communications Networks', (1993) 9 *Oxford Review of Economic Policy* 45; H. Siebert and M. J. Koop, 'Institutional Competition versus Centralization: *Quo Vadis* Europe?', (1993) 9 *Oxford Review of Economic Policy* 15; J.-M. Sun and J. Pelkmans, 'Regulatory Competition in the Single Market', (1995) 33 JCMS 67.

[171] COM(94) 161, *23rd Competition Policy Report from the Commission—1993*, p. 61.

Therefore, for the foreseeable future, the present relationship between the two types of rules appears likely to continue. The ONP and competition rules are complementary, not alternatives. Yet if ONP and competition policy are to be applied side by side, a co-ordination problem arises. Although it is not feasible here to give an exhaustive account of the various ways in which this problem might be resolved, these would seem to include further guidelines for the national competition authorities, the creation of an advisory committee (drawn from these authorities and the NRAs) seconded to DG IV, stricter reporting requirements under the existing ONP rules, an Article 90 EC directive combining several of these solutions, or an Article 87 Council Regulation on access (an idea which was recently floated).[172] Such measures may come to form part of the general rethinking of the implementation and co-ordination of the competition policy of the Community.

In the Community system, co-ordination problems have traditionally been solved by resorting to 'comitology'. Regulatory policy at the Community level has focused on rule-making by the Commission, within the legislative framework established by the Council and the European Parliament, and assisted by committees of national representatives, with implementation at the national level, subject to Community supervision.[173] This comitology mechanism provides the Council with a control mechanism over the Commission at the implementation stage, and involves networks of national sectoral experts in administrative rule making and execution.

On the one hand, comitology (i) supplies the structurally overburdened Commission with expertise; (ii) establishes links between administrations; and (iii) builds up networks of experts; it (iv) provides decision makers with information; (v) helps to support Member States with scarce administrative resources; (vi) monitors implementation; and (vii) helps to develop new regulatory responses.[174] On the other hand, comitology has been criticised for obstructing the integration process and for undermining its democratic legitimacy by allowing the Council, but not the European Parliament, a voice in the implementation of Community legislation.[175] In the case of ONP, where the European Parliament

---

[172] It is noteworthy that co-ordination problems arise even within individual DGs of the Commission. Within DG IV, an 'information society' directorate has recently been established under Temple Lang, responsible not only for posts and telecommunications, but also for the information technology, media and intellectual property rights issues involved.

[173] Della Cananea, 'Cooperazione e integrazione nel sistema amministrativo delle Communità europee: la questione della "comitologia"', (1990) 40 *Rivista Trimestriale di Diritto Pubblico* 655.

[174] For a view which holds that these functions could be more effectively exercised by administrative agencies cf. R. Dehousse, C. Joerges, G. Majone and F. Snyder (with M. Everson), *Europe After 1992: New Regulatory Strategies*, Working Paper Law 92/31 (European University Institute, Florence, 1992), pp. 50ff.

[175] However, the European Court of Justice has consistently upheld the legality of comitology. Case 25/70 *Köster* [1970] ECR 1161, paras. 6–10; Case 23/75 *Rey Soda* [1975] ECR 1279. Further, it has been argued that the voice of the Member States is essential, since they still form the predominant source of democratic legitimacy for the Community. Cf. J. J. H. Weiler, 'Problems of Legitimacy in Post 1992 Europe', (1991) 46 *Aussenwirtschaft* 411. Finally, at the implementation

has actually blocked legislation containing such provisions, this objection need hardly be stressed further.[176] Other objections against comitology include its complexity and the ambiguity of the relevant rules; its lack of transparency; and the ensuing lack of coherence between sectoral policies.[177]

Apart from providing a system of rules, through the creation of the ONP Committee the ONP legislation of the EC has established a network of the national regulators to implement them: the detailed rules of administrative procedure and the network of NRAs established by the ONP legislation provide a 'complex system of institutionalised collective bargaining', which can be used to resolve conflicts of interests with a European dimension.[178] The network of regulators in which the NRAs are involved is wider than ONP, or even than the Community.[179] Yet often, the individual bureaucrats representing the NRAs on a plethora of committees and other bodies, are actually the same persons. Hence, the ONP Committee forms a node in a system of overlapping networks of regulators, and an essential mechanism to integrate the policy making capacities of these various systems.[180]

While participation of the NRAs in wider international networks may enhance their independence *vis-à-vis* the Commission, the ONP framework has introduced a hierarchical element, which places the Commission over the national regulators at least in this context. Further, the independence of these regulators from the TOs and their national governments may be expected to be strengthened by their joint status as experts involved in problem solving. Finally, through

stage of the policy process it may be justified to give preference to alternative sources of legitimacy, such as participation and procedural guarantees (especially if democratic representation has been fully effective at the legislative stage). Cf. G. Winter, 'Drei Arten Gemeinschaftlicher Rechtssetzung und ihre Legitimation', in G. Brüggemeier (ed.), *Verfassungen für ein ziviles Europa* (Baden-Baden, 1994).

[176] Comitology is pervasive in telecommunications: in terms of the number of meetings and participants involved (in particular private sector experts), DG XIII is only narrowly surpassed by the directorates-general responsible for agriculture and social policy. Cf. G. J. Buitendijk and M. P. C. M. Van Schendelen, 'Brussels Advisory Committees: A Channel for Influence?', (1995) 20 ELR 37, pp. 40–41. For an exhaustive overview M. C. Biéla, 'Étude sur les comités et les télécommunications', (unpublished paper, Institut National des Télécommunications, December 1992).

[177] Cf. Dehousse *et al*, above, n. 174.

[178] M. T. Austin, 'Europe's ONP Bargain: What's in it for the User?', (1994) 18 *Telecommunications Policy* 97, p. 97.

[179] First, the ONP Committee will overlap the Community Telecommunications Committee that is envisaged by the directive on the mutual recognition of licenses. Hereby, functional integration of rule making and implementation of the Community policy on services and infrastructure liberalisation, universal service, interconnection, tariffing and licensing is provided. Second, the members of the ONP Committee are in practice often also the national experts for the specialised Council working groups which prepare telecommunications legislation for discussion in the Coreper and adoption by the Council. By this informal mechanism, the legislative and implementation phases are co-ordinated at an early stage. Third, the comitology representation of the National Regulatory Authorities serves to internalise links to international sectoral arrangements which are formally outside the institutional structure of the EC such as the CEPT.

[180] Hereby, trends toward divergence and discrepancy which might otherwise undermine the effectiveness and legitimacy of European telecommunications policy are contained.

the Co-ordination and Consultation Platform created by the ONP Framework Directive, the participation of the various social and economic interests is guaranteed. The resulting strength of the ONP system is that it provides a venue for wide participation in the policy formulation process, and mediates the various interests involved in a consensus-building effort which can be argued to increase the legitimacy of Community policy making.[181]

More recently, the establishment of European regulatory agencies has been proposed as a solution to the co-ordination problems which were hitherto solved by recourse to comitology arrangements.[182] The *Bangemann Report* called for the creation of a European telecommunications agency, and the Commission appears to be considering the merits of such a move.[183] Consequently, the remaining alternatives appear to be that of a loosely coupled system of NRAs, involved in the implementation of harmonised legislation on the one hand, and an independent centralised European telecommunications agency on the other.

A necessary requirement for the creation of independent regulatory agencies is agreement on their objectives, a condition which currently appears to have been met for telecommunications policy. Further, it has been observed that the general role of a regulator has three aspects: (i) that of an independent administrator; (ii) that of protector of a defined public interest; and (iii) that of facilitator of private interests.[184] In particular, independent agencies can perform the functions of administrative rule-making, adjudication, arbitration, conciliation, mediation and facilitation of negotiation. These functions overlap with those of the current ONP system.[185] The main strengths of independent agencies, in contrast with comitology, are efficiency and transparency. The main problem with the use of such agencies is that of ensuring accountability, which in the Community is further complicated by the subsidiarity requirement.

However, under European law, there are severe constraints to the possibility of creating independent agencies. Indeed, since the enunciation of the 'Meroni Doctrine' by the Court of Justice in 1958, it has been clear that only a revision of the Treaty will allow for the creation of truly independent agencies.[186]

---

[181] 'ONP must be viewed as a dynamic and evolutionary process of finding agreement and an institutionalised collective bargaining system operating between the diverse interests of telecommunications organisations (TOs), end users, service providers, manufacturers, Member States, and the Commission itself'. Austin, above, n. 178, p. 98.

[182] Cf. G. Majone, 'Independence vs. Accountability? Non-Majoritarian Institutions and Democratic Government in Europe', in J. J. Hesse (ed.), *European Yearbook of Public Administration* (Oxford, 1994).

[183] Cf. former Director General of DG IV C.-D. Ehlermann: 'Telekommunikation und Europäisches Wettbewerbsrecht', (1993) 28 EuR 134; 'Reflections on a European Cartel Office', (1995) 32 CMLR 471; and 'Ökonomische Aspekte des Subsidiaritätsprinzips: Harmonisierung versus Wettbewerb der Systeme', (1995) 18 *Integration* 11.

[184] Cf. WIK report, above, n. 154, pp. 40ff.

[185] M. Everson, 'Independent Agencies: Hierarchy Beaters?', (1995) 1 *European Law Journal* 180.

[186] Case 9/56 *Meroni v High Authority* [1957–1958] ECR 133 and Case 10/56 *Meroni v High Authority* [1957–1958] ECR 157. Cf. K. Lenaerts, 'Regulating the Regulatory Process: "Delegation of Powers" in the European Community', (1993) 18 ELR 23.

Although specialised administrative bodies with autonomous legal personality have, in fact, been created, they have always remained under the ultimate control of the Commission of the EC.[187] These bodies should therefore be ranked as 'quasi-agencies' instead of as independent agencies. Hence, an independent telecommunications agency would require Treaty amendment, at least in the form of a generic provision which enables such bodies to be established.[188]

In practice, existing bodies such as the European Agency for the Evaluation of Medical Products greatly resemble comitology arrangements.[189] This quasi-agency is based on committees of national experts appointed by the Member States, co-ordinated by the Commission, and under supervision of a Management Board. This Board is composed of representatives of the Member States, the Commission, as well as, it is worth underlining, the European Parliament. Decisions on product authorisation and supervision are taken by the Commission, assisted by standing committees which may refer decisions back to the Council.

The evident similarities with the system of ONP suggest that a European Telecommunications Agency could be created along these lines without upsetting the present institutional balance, or requiring Treaty amendment.[190] The inter-institutional agreement on comitology could provide an example of the way in which democratic legitimacy could be guaranteed.[191] The precise objectives of such a body would have to be defined by application of the subsidiarity principle. In practice such an agency would take over the centralised functions foreseen in the ONP and mutual recognition directives. The advantages might be sought in efficiency and transparency, and raising the profile of the issues involved.

Even if a Treaty revision were feasible, the Member States would presumably be reluctant to grant full independence before some working experience had been gained with the functioning of a European regulator under a more familiar format. Either solution might have advantages over present comitology in terms of transparency, which could further be guaranteed by disclosure arrangements. Given the application of the subsidiarity principle however, neither a fully independent agency nor a quasi-agency would obviate the need for the NRAs, functioning according to ONP rules, and for some form of co-ordination between them. Hence, like the application of competition policy the

---

[187] There is some disagreement whether the legal basis for the creation of such bodies should be sought in Article 100a or 235 EC. Cf. Lenaerts, ibid.

[188] Cf. Ehlermann, above, n. 183 [1995].

[189] Cf. Council Regulation 1210/90/EEC on the establishment of the European Environment Agency and the European environment information and observation network ((1990) OJ L120/1); Council Regulation 2309/93/EEC laying down Community procedures for the authorization and supervision of medicinal products for human and veterinary use and establishing a European Agency for the Evaluation of Medicinal Products ((1993) OJ L214/1).

[190] Ehlermann, above, n. 183 [1993]; W. Sauter, 'The ONP Framework: Towards a European Telecommunications Agency', (1994) 5 ULR 140.

[191] SEC(94) 645, Draft Inter-Institutional Agreement on Comitology. Above, n. 134.

establishment of a regulatory agency does not form a clear-cut alternative to the present system.

For the foreseeable future therefore, the ONP system will remain the basic framework for European telecommunications regulation, in particular regarding universal service, interconnection, and trans-European networks and services. Evidently, the application of the competition rules will continue, and may be facilitated by further guidelines and improved co-ordination between the Commission and national regulators. Finally, the creation of a quasi-agency (but not an independent agency) with a limited responsibility appears feasible. EC telecommunications policy will thus continue to rely on harmonisation legislation and competition policy, and on parallel competences, but perhaps with an increasing role for a specialised European regulator.

C. Telecommunications Policy as a Case Study of EC Industrial Policy

It is clear that liberalisation and harmonisation were used in tandem, first, to extend the internal market to telecommunications, and next, to establish a regulation which pursues sector-specific aims going beyond this general objective. What remains to be clarified is the role industrial policy considerations played in this process. Although this role has been pervasive throughout, it has not always been explicit. Immediately before, but especially after the adoption of the Single European Act, telecommunications and industrial policy met under the various heads of the internal market programme, including:

  (i) public procurement liberalisation;
 (ii) the promotion of Community R&D;
(iii) standardisation;
 (iv) infrastructure;
  (v) protection of telecommunication interests under the common commercial policy.

Under the EC Treaty as amended by the Treaty on European Union, a second phase has begun. An industrial policy based on information technology and communications has become central to the attempt to relaunch the European economy as an 'organized European space', to supplement the internal market and economic and monetary union. Although the linkages established under the internal market programme remain, the main current concerns are the establishment of TENs and the promotion of multimedia services (involving the co-ordination of initiatives concerning data and privacy protection, intellectual property rights, and pluralism in media ownership), and stimulating private investment. During both phases there has been tension between the goals of promoting the competitiveness of the European telecommunications equipment and services industry, and European industry as a whole.[192] The balance is held by Community competition policy.

If the definition of industrial policy used is to include R&D promotion, and other elements of the internal market programme, a parallel emergence of policies on telecommunications and electronics and data technology can be observed at the heart of the early industrial policy initiatives of the Community. After the adoption of the 1990 Industrial Policy Guidelines (which expressed the consensus view on industrial policy on which Industry Title XIII of the Treaty on European Union was based) industrial policy arguments have become ever more explicit.[193]

First, a decisive step was taken with the presentation of industrial policy proposals for the electronics and information technology industry,[194] and the (closely related) telecommunications equipment industry.[195] These proposals formed the first examples of sectoral application of the EC's new horizontal industrial policy, and in reaction to them the May 1993 Telecommunications Council made its first formal declaration on industrial policy for the sector.[196]

---

[192] The industrial policy dimension of telecommunications is meant to be centred on its leverage effect on the economy at large. The crucial question is whether the emphasis will be on promoting the EC telecommunications industry, or the telecommunications user industries (which affects *inter alia* the reciprocal market access issue for third countries). Whereas EC producers have recently performed poorly in the equipment market, it is hoped they may do better in services when networks are liberalised. According to the White Paper, in 1994 the EC terminal equipment market was valued at 26 billion ECU, with an annual growth rate of 4 per cent; the EC telecommunications service sector at 84 billion ECU, at a growth rate of 8 per cent. The telecommunications sector was expected to account for 6 per cent of GDP by the year 2000. Above, n. 171, p. 87.

[193] 'The Commission, in its Communication of November 1990 on industrial policy, made market orientation an essential component of any policy for sectoral development. The Commission considers, on the basis of an industry wide consultation, that market orientation and public service in the telecommunications sector are complementary'. In the same context the Community's R&D programmes are praised for having 'made a substantial contribution to the promotion of the European telecommunications industry'. COM(93) 159, Communication on the Consultation on the Review of the situation in the telecommunications services sector, in reference to COM(90) 556, Industrial policy in an open and competitive environment: Guidelines for a Community approach.

[194] SEC(91) 565, The European Electronic and Information Technology Industry: State of Play, Issues at Stake and Proposals for Action. This document was requested in the Council Resolution which approved the guidelines on industrial policy of COM(90) 556. *Bull EC* 11-1990, para. 1.3.110. In SEC(91) 565 the focus is especially on telecommunications as a source of demand, or market creation. In this context it addresses TENs, the creation of computerised telecommunications links between administrations (CADDIA, TEDIS, INSIS etc), Broadband services (IBC) networks, pan-European HDTV, and the Community initiatives in the field of learning (DELTA), public health (AIM) and transport (DRIVE), and joint efforts to disseminate and exploit the results of R&D work.

[195] SEC(92) 1049, The European telecommunications equipment industry—the state of play, issues at stake and proposals for action, pp. 17–19. The four objectives identified were: (1) the establishment of the internal market; (2) the support of technological development; (3) the improvement of the position of terminal equipment manufacturers; (4) and the search for fair conditions of competition in the world market.

[196] *Bull EC* 5-1993, para. 1.2.78. The Council adopted conclusions which confirmed the four objectives, and called for the strengthening of Community action, and new measures where necessary. In its commentary, the ECOSOC requested the implementation of reciprocity in trade, with equivalent market access in non-European countries. Cf. IND/478 Opinion of the Economic and

With their emphasis on market opening and promotion of structural adjustment, these sectoral documents clearly followed the line set out in the 1990 Industrial Policy Guidelines.[197] Second, the Competition Guidelines concerning the application of competition rules to the telecommunications sector explicitly stated that these industrial policy proposals would be taken into account in the conduct of competition policy.[198] Hereby the Competition Guidelines provided the first practical example of how the industrial and competition policy of the Community might be reconciled.

The first phase of industrial policy and telecommunications was dominated by Community efforts concerning public procurement, joint R&D, and standardisation. Whereas the public procurement policies of the Member States' PTTs had served to boost privileged equipment producers, such strategies were not wholly abandoned for the internal market as a whole.[199] Structural adjustment towards 'telematics' was seen as an opportunity to transform the nature (and the value) of more traditional economic activities, and consequently promoted by the Community's R&D framework programme. Community support for co-operative R&D on broadband communications infrastructure under the RACE programme (notably concerning ISDN[200] and TENs[201]) was even more

Social Committee on SEC(92) 1049 final, 28 April 1993 (CES 472/93), with reference to Opinion on the Commission communication on industrial policy in an open and competitive environment ((1992) OJ C40/31), on COM(90) 556, above, n. 193.

[197] By some accounts however, the proposals on information and technology industry indeed preceded the 1990 Industrial Policy Guidelines. Cf. G. Ross, 'Sidling into industrial policy: Inside the European Commission', (1993) 11 *French Politics and Society* 20; G. Ross, *Jacques Delors and European Integration* (Cambridge, 1995), pp. 115ff.

[198] SEC(91) 565, above, n. 194, was cited in the Competition Guidelines as an example of the type of Community actions to be taken into account in competition policy. Above, n. 80. The Competition Guidelines indicated that exploitation of joint R&D results, for example through joint distribution, may be acceptable even between large firms, where this aids structural adjustment aimed at meeting global competition. ibid., para. 77.

[199] Cf. Council Directive 90/531/EEC, on procurement procedures of entities operating in the water, energy, transport and telecommunications sectors ((1990) OJ L297/1). Utilities are allowed and sometimes even obliged to reject non-Community tenders, even where they may be the cheapest or economically most advantageous (the normal criteria for awarding tenders under Article 27(1) of the Directive), if the products originate in countries which have not concluded agreements to ensure comparable and effective access to Community undertakings. Article 29(2) of the Directive allows the rejection of tenders where their content of third country products exceeds 50 per cent of total value. According to Article 29(3) preference *must* be given to equivalent tenders which cannot be rejected under the 50 per cent rule, where tenders shall be considered equivalent if the price difference between tenders does not exceed 3 per cent.

[200] Cf. Proposal for a Council Decision on a series of guidelines for the development of ISDN as trans-European network (93/C 259/05; (1993) OJ C259/5); Proposal for a Council Decision adopting a multi-annual Community action concerning the development of ISDN as a trans-European network (TEN-ISDN) (93/C 259/06; (1993) OJ C259/7); G. Fuchs, 'ISDN: "The Telecommunications Highway for Europe after 1992" or "Paving a Dead-End Street?": The Politics of Pan-European Telecommunications Network Development', MPIFG Discussion Paper 93/6 (Cologne, 1993).

[201] COM(90) 585 final, Towards trans-European Networks—for a Community action programme; SEC(91) 565, above, n. 194, lists TENs, computerised telecommunications links between administrations, as well as other infrastructure projects, under the 'proposals for action' necessary to stimulate demand, presaging the linkages made by the 1993 White Paper, above, n. 171.

important. Since the quality of telecommunications infrastructure is relevant for the investment and location decisions of firms this involved social and economic cohesion. Connected both with infrastructure provision and Community R&D is the issue of standardisation.[202] Standardisation brings out the tendency to favour harmonisation at the Community level, not merely as a goal in its own right, or to complete the internal market, but also to preempt international standardisation and attempt to lock in markets, to secure competitive advantages for European firms.[203]

The second phase of the industrial policy dimension of telecommunications policy can be identified with Title XII EC on TENs, introduced by the Treaty on European Union, in particular the context of the 1993 Delors White Paper and its follow-up documents.[204] The White Paper used the concept of TENs to link the Community's industrial policy initiatives in electronics, informatics, and telecommunications. It sought to break a vicious circle of lagging growth, competitiveness, and employment through establishing a catalytic role for European public authorities: that of identifying and creating new markets through strategic TEN projects. Stimulating investment in infrastructure was intended to boost business confidence, create jobs, and help revive growth directly. The perceived benefits from investment of this nature range from supporting the European electronics and information technology industry, to promoting social and economic cohesion.

---

[202] Cf. COM(91) 521, Standardization in the European Economy: Green Paper on the development of European Standardization; Council Resolution of 27 April 1989 concerning standardization in the fields of information technology and telecommunications ((1989) OJ C117/1). In the 1990 Industrial Policy Guidelines, the Commission (in a clear reference to telecommunications) ranks standardisation as an element in accelerating the development of the technological capacity of the Community 'the positive effect that a high level of standards, the implementation of technologically advanced trans-European networks and public procurement open to the most sophisticated technologies can have on demand'. Above, n. 193, p. 17. At 19, telecommunications reappears as one of the sectors 'that can play a key role for the development of the European industry and the European economy as a whole'. Cf. Council Resolution of 18 November 1991 concerning electronics, information and communication technologies ((1992) OJ C325/2).

[203] This accounts in particular for the ill-fated HDTV effort of the Community. Cf. COM(84) 300, Green Paper on the establishment of the Common Market for Broadcasting, especially by Satellite and Cable; Council Directive 86/529/EEC, above, n. 43; Council Directive 89/552/EEC on the coordination of certain provisions laid down by law, regulation or administrative action in the Member States concerning the pursuit of television broadcasting activities, ((1989) OJ L298/23); Council Directive 92/38/EEC on the adoption of standards for satellite broadcasting of television standards ((1992) OJ L137/17). Cf. J. Farrell and C. Shapiro, 'Standard setting in High-Definition Television', in M. N. Baily and C. Winston (eds.), *Brookings Papers on Economic Activity: Microeconomics* (Brookings Institution, 1992); Monopolkommission, *Wettbewerbspolitik oder Industriepolitik: Hauptgutachten 1990/1991* (Baden-Baden, 1992), ch. 6: 'Wettbewerbswirkungen von Standards in der Telekommunikation'; L. McKnight, 'The international standardization of telecommunications services and equipment', in Mestmäcker (ed.), *The Law and Economics of Transborder Telecommunications* (Baden-Baden, 1987), pp. 423ff; J. Peterson, 'Towards a Common European Industrial Policy? The Case of High Definition Television', (1992) 28 *Government and Opposition* 496.

[204] COM(93) 700, Growth, Competitiveness, Employment: The Challenges and Ways Forward into the 21st Century.

The infrastructure proposals of the 1993 White Paper met with a mixed reaction in the Brussels European Council of December 1993.[205] Reluctant especially to sanction public investment by the Community, the Council charged the so-called Bangemann Group of prominent industrialists with reporting on specific measures concerning information infrastructure. Wholehearted support by private industry in the resulting *Bangemann Report*, however, made an important contribution towards making infrastructure liberalisation acceptable to the Member States. The link between the industrial (or competitiveness) and telecommunications policies of the Community was further developed by Commission documents on competitiveness and the information society.[206] First, in a communication of 19 July 1994, the Commission outlined an action plan for a joint telecommunications and industrial policy,[207] which presented telecommunications liberalisation as a step on the way to the so-called information society. In this document the Commission rearranged its telecommunications policy proposals and priorities to reflect the recommendations of the Bangemann group, in an attempt to maintain the momentum established since the publication of the 1993 White Paper.[208]

The Action Plan repeats the calls of the *Bangemann Report* for infrastructure liberalisation, reform of the regulatory framework, and establishing a European authority, as well as the importance of ongoing efforts concerning standardisation, tariffs, external trade, and a number of issues introduced by multimedia convergence. The worldwide dimension will be pursued, in the context of the GATS negotiations, the new World Trade Organization, and the World Intellectual Property Organization.[209] Concerning the potential legal obstacles to the

[205] Cf. Editorial, 'Growth, Competitiveness and Unemployment: The Challenges Facing the European Union', (1995) 31 CMLR 1.

[206] Cf. 'Growth, Competitiveness and Employment: White Paper Follow-Up', *Bull EC* 2-94.

[207] COM(94) 347, Action Plan on Europe's Way to the Information Society (*EC Bull* Supplement 2/94). The action plan covers four areas: (1) the legal and regulatory framework; (2) networks, basic services, applications and content; (3) social and cultural aspects; and (4) public promotion of the information society concept. The action plan, adopted in response to the Delors White Paper was appropriately discussed (along with a wider action programme on industrial competitiveness) by the first joint session of the Telecommunications and Industry Councils on 28 September 1994.

[208] The concept of the 'information society' has become central to Industry Commissioner Bangemann's contribution to the relaunch of the European economy projected by the 1993 White Paper. The Commissioner, who presently combines the industry and telecommunications portfolios of DGs III and XIII, has backed the idea of creating an 'Information Society Council' and an 'Information Society DG'. The former is likely to be the present Telecommunications Council. The latter would combine parts of DGs III and XIII, possibly with the media and intellectual property directorates of DGs X and XV.

[209] The relevance of this project is illustrated by the fact that the first G7 Summit hosted by the Commission of February 1995 focused on the information society. Echoing the Action Plan, the G7 conference covered co-operation on infrastructure development, a regulatory framework balancing competition, property rights and privacy, and finally, the applications and the general consequences for society. The agenda was largely set by the information technology industries in the United States, Japan and Europe, which jointly released a white paper aiming at establishing a global information infrastructure characterised by the free movement of products and services (Source: 'G7-live', on-line information service provided during the summit by IBM-Europe).

development of multimedia services in related areas, the Council is encouraged to review the protection of intellectual property rights and privacy, as well as the rules on media concentration and broadcasting.[210] Regarding networks, basic services, applications and content, the Commission stressed the role of private sector co-operation and initiatives.[211]

Second, the link between telecommunication and industrial policy was emphasised by An Industrial Competitiveness Policy for the Community, which claimed a coherent legal basis for a policy to promote the competitiveness of European industry in Titles XII to XV and VIII EC.[212] However, aside from references to the importance of the information society in general, and TENs in particular, this document contains no new substantive proposals concerning telecommunications. No doubt this is largely due to the fact that telecommunications reform is by far the most fully developed item on the agenda, and to some extent its inclusion in the context of the information society and competitiveness policy follows *post hoc* logic.

The 1994 Council Resolution on industrial policy linked: (i) the 1990 Industrial Policy Guidelines; (ii) the 1993 White Paper; (iii) the 1994 Action Plan; and (iv) the 1994 document on Industrial Competitiveness Policy.[213] This is significant, first, as a demonstration of Council approval of the continuity of the 1990 approach, and second, because it consolidates the linkages proposed by the Commission between industrial policy, telecommunications liberalisation, and the Information Society project.

---

[210] The former include proposals in the field of private copying, and the legal protection of databases, data privacy, personal data and privacy in the context of digital networks, and on the use of standards for the transmission of TV signals. Concerning the latter, Green Papers on intellectual property rights in the information society, and on the legal protection of encrypted broadcasts were foreseen, along with efforts on encryption. Finally, the Commission promised a follow-up to COM(92) 480, the Green Paper on Pluralism and media concentration in the internal market, and a review of the 'television without frontiers' Directive 89/552/EEC, above, n. 203. Cf. COM(93) 464, Proposal for a Council Directive on the legal protection of databases; COM(92) 433, Data privacy framework directive; COM(94) 128, Amended proposal for a European Parliament and Council Directive concerning the protection of personal data and privacy in the context of digital telecommunications networks, in particular the integrated services digital network (ISDN) and digital mobile networks; COM(93) 556, Proposal for a Directive of the European Parliament and the Council on the use of standards for the transmission of television signals.

[211] This regards, among others, the follow-up to the Satellite (COM(90) 490), Mobile (COM(94) 145) and Audiovisual (COM(94) 96) Green Papers. In particular, an information society 'project office' is established to promote initiatives and maximise the use of existing instruments, including those of the 4th framework programme, the TEN-ISDN and TEN-IBC initiatives, and the Structural Funds. The projects on which public-private partnership will be stimulated include in particular those identified by the *Bangemann Report* (such as telematic services for SMEs, transport telematics, public administration TENs, electronic tendering, and urban information highways).

[212] COM(94) 319, An Industrial Competitiveness Policy for the Community (*EC Bull* Supplement 3/94).

[213] Council Resolution of 21 November 1994 on the strengthening of the competitiveness of Community Industry ((1994) OJ C343/1).

It is obvious that promotion of the information society has not only become one of the most important general objectives of telecommunications policy, but also forms part of an agenda setting effort by the Commission, aimed at spreading the gains from its success at liberalising this sector. However, in concrete terms, apart from establishing issue-linkages (such as those between telecommunications liberalisation, broadcasting, and guarantees for plurality of media ownership, or data, consumer, and privacy protection) the main substantive proposals still appear to be those of telecommunications reform. The speed and direction of further change will in large part depend on private sector initiatives—and perhaps not primarily those currently sponsored by benevolent administrations.

V. Conclusion

The development of a Community policy on telecommunications may be recapitulated as a three phase process. The first phase, prior to the Single Act, was characterised by extensive state regulation and public monopolies charged with providing services in the general interest, accompanied by protectionist public procurement practices aimed at nurturing 'national champions'. In this phase telecommunications was largely non-competitive, standardisation was limited to the individual Member States, and the relevant non-municipal law was restricted to international agreements and the internal rules of organisations such as the PTT-based CEPT. The Rome Treaty did not mention telecommunications and Articles 222 and 90(2) EC seemed to imply that the Member States were acting within their rights when excluding telecommunications form the common market. However, the early R&D initiatives of the Community helped to mobilise a private industry coalition for change.

In the second phase, change swept through the telecommunications sectors in the Member States as the existing rules on the free circulation of goods and services and on competition were applied to the sector with renewed vigour, supplemented by harmonisation directives. Both external factors—notably the United States push for inclusion of telecommunications services in the GATT Uruguay Round—and factors internal to the EC—the 1992 programme and the SEA—were instrumental here.

The third and current phase will see the remaining special and exclusive rights abolished. The Member States have already begun to 'opt out' of the system of public telecommunications operators (and for privatisation), establishing rules to guarantee the public interest within the framework of open markets instead. As a result, by 1998 the sector will be fully liberalised, telecommunications will have moved to the centre of the Community agenda for structural adjustment, and the Commission will have established itself as a primary actor in the field, both as the initiator of legislation, and at the centre of a network of regulators.

In sum, the Community regime for telecommunications has changed due to a combination of factors, including technological advances, the spill-over of international regulatory change, the internal market programme, reform in the Member States, and the pressure of industrial lobbies:

1. Technological change undermined the natural monopoly argument. Digitalisation led to convergence of telecommunications and information technology, and the number of potential market entrants multiplied accordingly.

2. The internationalisation of the telecommunications sector led to both external and internal pressure for liberalisation. As the combined result of technological developments and constant legal challenges to the lucrative monopoly, regulatory change started in the United States, and subsequently spilled over to other countries. Telecommunications operators based in the newly liberalised markets aimed to gain equivalent access to markets abroad, with the support of their respective governments and large users in continental Europe.

3. The internal market programme exposed the inefficiency of the national PTTs as a source of competitive disadvantage for European industry.

4. Also, with the Single European Act, the methods and strategies of integration changed. The new approach to harmonisation (under Article 100a) and standardisation made positive integration in telecommunications easier to achieve.

5. The failure of national high-technology programmes and the launching of joint R&D programmes (Title VI EEC) in tandem with the internal market added to a perception of telecommunications reform as capable of reanimating the moribund European computer industry.

6. A number of the Member States had begun reform of their telecommunications sectors as a result of these pressures.

7. The Commission mobilised powerful industrial lobbies in favour of deregulation.

8. It used the four freedoms and competition rules of the Treaty to force the hand of the Member States, relying in particular on Article 90 EC.

9. Simultaneously, a market oriented system of harmonisation legislation was introduced by Council Directives.

10. The new Titles on Industry, TENs, and Consumer Protection constitutionalised the objectives of Community telecommunications policy, and provided the basis for a communications-technology based policy to promote the competitiveness of European industry.

Although a range of factors played a role in transforming the sector, there can be thus no doubt of the relevance of EC telecommunications policy to the links between the industrial and competition policies of the Community. In the first place telecommunications shows how other policies, such as standardisation and R&D collaboration, have been used for industrial policy purposes.

Second, the proposed investment in telecommunications infrastructure to develop trans-European networks for an 'information society' shows how horizontal industrial policy might work through the stimulation of demand, creating markets and infrastructure networks designed to enhance the competitiveness of European industry in general. In the third place, telecommunications shows how competition policy forms the framework (at least in a formal sense) within which these activities occur, and imposes limits on them. This control will increase further now the Commission will increasingly be dealing with private competitors, rather than public monopolies.

More importantly perhaps, the case of telecommunications shows how the requirements of competition policy restricted the industrial policies of the Member States (the attack on state monopolies, the separation of regulatory and operating functions, the liberalisation of public procurement, and European standardisation efforts), and thereby placed industrial policy on the agenda at the Community level. So far, European multinationals have both stimulated and benefitted from this process at the cost of national monopolies (and with as yet uncertain results for citizen-consumers, and society at large), which provides evidence of a paradigm shift in favour of the market process. This confirms both the market orientation and the compatibility of EC industrial and competition policy.

Further, the case of telecommunications illustrates the relevance of the need to develop new regulatory solutions to address the problems of the horizontal and vertical distribution of power which follow from the progress of European integration. Telecommunications is an especially cogent example, since the industry formed a part of the state administration, and the process of liberalisation and harmonisation involved explicit rolling back of sovereignty. The liberal ideology that prevailed in the Commission has led to proposals for liberalisation that went further than was envisaged in any of the Member States. In order to overcome resistance from the Member States (either on grounds of principle, or representing the interests of the 'postal-industrial complex'), the Commission has mobilised a coalition of interests which supported its position, and was capable of effective 'reverse lobbying' with the Member States. The new regulatory structure has not only reduced political control at the level of the Member States, but created independent national authorities, and institutionalised the influence of diverse economic interests.

From a rights or constitutionally oriented viewpoint administration by network seems to have problematic features. This applies *a fortiori* to a perspective of democratic control or accountability. Procedural guarantees, the right to be heard, legal recourse against administrative acts, and balanced representation of various interests may be required to give the emerging structures a semblance of legitimacy. Transparency of decision making will make procedural guarantees more meaningful, while they enhance the possibility that contentious issues find their way to the political arena. Such guarantees can be identified in the system of ONP legislation and the creation of independent regulators (at the national level, and perhaps at the Community level in the future).

The competition and industrial policies of the Community have so far proven to be compatible in the telecommunications sector. The real issues are not the possible contradictions between competition and industrial policy, or models of free trade and state intervention, but concern rather the pursuit of public policy goals in free markets. A combination of centralisation of power at the Community level and devolution of power towards specialised national authorities, linked together in fairly loose structures, at the expense of the Member States, and with economic actors reorienting themselves towards the Community level, seems to occur in a process of which the net sum is market oriented reform and increased liberalisation.

The remaining question is whether on the basis of the observations concerning the telecommunications sector there is room for general statements on the relationship between the competition and industrial policies of the EC. Such generalisation does appear to be justified. In the first place the emergence of telecommunications policy demonstrates the success of the internal market programme and the transition from negative to positive integration. Liberalisation was combined with harmonisation aimed at market opening and providing a basic regulatory framework. Industrial policy (including R&D and standardisation policy), was one of the policies that was reasserted at the Community level, but as 'horizontal' in nature, and as such compatible with competition policy. This demonstrates the practical limitations of the 'original' neo-liberal economic constitution of the EEC Treaty. Although liberal in wording, this text was without practical significance for the telecommunications sector. The Single European Act and Treaty on European Union have not replaced national intervention by Community intervention, so much as a rationalised public policy toward more precise objectives, including industrial policy objectives, but within an overall context dominated by liberalisation.

Likewise, the observations based on the case of telecommunications appear to have wider sectoral application. First, by convergence in technology and ownership, the telecommunications sector is moving across economic boundaries. This creates a wide range of economic sectors (information technology; entertainment; broadcasting) across which the telecommunications experience may be regarded as relevant. Second, the new 'multimedia' sector is expanding across national boundaries. As a result, telecommunications provides a good example of the convergence of international economic and technological developments forcing a European reaction which involved a transfer of power to the EC level as the Member States found themselves incapable of effective action. In line with the concept of spill-over a transfer of competence has occurred, as individual national systems were unable to provide adequate response to global systemic pressure.

The case of telecommunications is, of course, especially instructive in regard to the other network industries which were (or still are) public utilities. This mainly means transport and energy, which are moreover, also covered by the infrastructure title of the Treaty on European Union. Finally, telecommunications is both a high technology and service industry, which further increases the scope of the conclusions drawn from this example.

Only economic sectors which have a longer and more distinct tradition of Community industrial policy (such as agriculture and steel), or which have been consciously removed from the sphere of influence of the EC (such as aerospace and defence) would seem to be largely exempt from the lessons to be learned from the telecommunications experience. In all cases however, the twin tracks of liberalisation and harmonisation, or establishing the internal market through introducing competition, while defining the areas where regulation in the public interest is required, can be found. Likewise, the attention for the competitiveness of European industry will become increasingly explicit, and the shift to market based regimes, and a minimum level of regulation is clear. Finally, attempts at policy co-ordination through comitology structures and network arrangements, backed up by the Commission's competition policy competence, are pervasive. Thus, the direction of the horizontal and vertical division of competences (although complex and riddled with exceptions) will be determined.

6
Conclusion

The findings can be summarised as follows. The EC Treaty as elaborated by the European Court of Justice forms the economic constitution of the European Community, which governs the relations between the various levels of government and the market. Under this economic constitution the Community has limited competences, and no particular economic order is prescribed for the Member States: the Treaty remains neutral regarding the economic order at the national level. National measures in the public interest, which take due legal form and respect the basic principles of Community law, may legitimise exceptions to the internal market. This leaves the Member States an autonomous sphere within the general constraints imposed by Community law.

The economic order at the Community level is that of a market system which guarantees individual economic rights. However, this market orientation is not absolute: legitimate public policy goals can justify exceptions from market policies at the Community level as well, subject to limited judicial review. Whether industrial policy considerations can override the principle of free competition depends on whether the legal basis for the measures involved allows administrative discretion. In this sense, there is no hierarchical order between the various intermediate objectives of the Treaty set out in Article 3 EC.

The economic constitution of the Community has evolved over time, both through its interpretation by the European Court of Justice, and by successive Treaty amendments. The original Rome Treaty focused on achieving the common market, mainly through negative integration by means of the four freedoms and competition. Policy co-ordination, even in the interest of realising the internal market, remained relatively underdeveloped: harmonisation under Article 100 EEC was ineffective under de facto unanimity decision making. With some exceptions, notably in competition policy, the implementation of Community law remained under the political control of the Council. The role of the European parliament was mainly a consultative one, and the Community remained dependent on indirect (national) democratic legitimation through the Council.

Nevertheless, the case law of the Court, which introduced the doctrines of the supremacy and direct effect of Community law, made it possible for negative integration to proceed in the absence of political agreement. The doctrines of supremacy and direct effect, and the protection of human rights under Community law, enabled the Court to attribute the status of constitutional charter to the Treaty. Given the diminutive role of the European Parliament, this constitutional charter guaranteed the rule of law at the Community level, but not democratic government.

The Single Act added new competences which required policy co-ordination, such as those on R&D, and modified the decision making rules. Notably, it enhanced the role of the European Parliament and facilitated decision making by qualified majority. Inspired by the vision of the 1992 programme, the Rome Treaty, after the Single Act, remained focused on completing the internal market. With the Treaty on European Union, the objectives of integration and the scope of Community competence were widened, and the power of the European Parliament was extended further. The co-ordination of policy became increasingly important in a number of fields, in particular in the context of the preparation for economic and monetary union. Although the Member States retain freedom regarding the means they choose, their economic and monetary policies are bound to commonly agreed objectives, laid down in the Treaty. Hereby, the economic constitution was extended well beyond the internal market. It was at this point that the Community received, for the first time, a concurrent competence regarding the promotion of the competitiveness of European industry.

With the introduction of the principles of stability, free competition in open markets, the convergence criteria, and the relevant procedures for policy coordination in the EC Treaty, the European Union now has a fully-fledged economic constitution. However, as a political constitution the Treaty remains incomplete. This casts doubt on the legitimacy of transfer and the pooling of competences in the economic realm. The Member States, as parties to the Treaty on European Union, attempted to bar a further creeping expansion of Community competence, such as had occurred under the EEC Treaty. Hence, the new competences introduced, (such as those concerning industrial policy, health, consumer protection, education, and culture) were restrictively defined. For the same reasons, a general principle of subsidiarity was introduced into the Treaty in Article 3b EC, the practical application of which remains unclear.

In the context of the tortuous ratification process of the Maastricht Treaty, serious political differences in the relations between the Community and the Member States have surfaced. At their most extreme, these cast doubt on the most fundamental principles of European law, including supremacy and direct effect. Meanwhile, the Court of Justice has taken the road of judicial restraint in recent cases on the free movement of goods and the application of the competition rules of the Treaty to state measures. In the absence of clear political guidance on the appropriate level for public policy making, the Court is framing limits to the scope of Community law.

The central paradox which results is that, on the one hand, the Union has widened its charter, whereas on the other hand, the Member States are in theory allowed an autonomous sphere in economic regulation which is wider than was often thought. The Member States are not restricted to particular methods to reach the economic objectives set by the Treaty. Yet in spite of the judicial restraint recently displayed by the Court, the margin of discretion for national policy making has narrowed over time, and the economic objectives have become increasingly precise. In practice there is a bias toward liberal market policies, and the liberalisation required by the integration process has been accompanied by deregulation, and, increasingly, privatisation. Although the Community condones the mixed economy, the realities of the integration process render the former impracticable. Consequently, the political debate is shifting from the scope of negative integration to the methods and legitimacy of positive integration. The democratic quality of decision making and the possibility of the emergence of a pan-European polity play an important part in this discussion.

Against this setting, the emergence of industrial policy competence for the Community must be explained. Industrial policy deals with the problems inherent in market economies (market failures) that the Member States traditionally preferred to deal with in the context of their national economic policies and were reluctant to entrust to the Community. More recently, consensus has developed on the general merits of measures aimed at promoting industrial restructuring. The definition of industrial policy finally adopted by the Community in 1990 was '. . . the effective and coherent implementation of all those policies which impinge on the structural adjustment of industry'. It perceives competition policy both as a precondition for, and as an instrument of, industrial policy. This is also true for the internal market and commercial policy. Hence, Community industrial policy attributes a positive value to the process of competition in open markets as a factor promoting the competitiveness of European industry. Overall, the Community concept of industrial policy is clearly a liberal market-based one, in line with current economic theory.

Although the Council only approved this approach in 1990, the Industrial Policy Guidelines did not form a break with earlier proposals for a Community industrial policy, which likewise aimed at the completion of the internal market and facilitating the interplay of market forces. Hence, the Community approach to industrial policy is the result of a lengthy development which is continuous. Industrial policy has always formed an integral part of the integration strategy of the Commission. The success of the industrial policy of the Community has been piecemeal, but increased over time as the scope of European integration widened.

Nevertheless, a change in emphasis of the industrial policy proposals of the Community has occurred, which reflects a negative view of direct intervention in the market by the Member States. Such intervention, which prevailed until recently and reached its apex during the economic crises of the 1970s, is now widely perceived as counterproductive, and at odds with Community law. Community industrial policy has become acceptable in so far as the Member States are now unable to effectively promote industrial competitiveness individually, and where a unified response is required. Therefore, the main change in perspective regarding industrial policy occurred at the national level, rather than at the Community level. A horizontal industrial policy competence for the Community emerged once consensus was achieved on the fact that national industrial policies of sectoral intervention had failed. The most important innovation of the 1990 Industrial Policy Guidelines was that they limited the role of public authorities to providing a stable economic and regulatory framework for market developments, and a 'catalytic' function of stimulating structural adjustment. This forms a step away from the mixed economy at the national level.

The Industry Title introduced by the Treaty on European Union seeks to reconcile the objectives of free competition in open markets and the promotion of the competitiveness of European industry. As such, it forms a reassertion of the open texture of the constitution of the Community regarding the orientation of economic policy. This does not mean that Title XIII EC should be seen as the 'linchpin' for co-ordinated Community intervention. With decision making by unanimity, and subject to the principle of subsidiarity, Article 130 EC does not provide effective means for co-ordination of the industrial policies of the Member States. Nor does it facilitate co-ordination of the various other policy competences of the Community itself in the pursuit of industrial policy initiatives. The competition safeguards of Article 130(1) and 130(3) EC limit the scope of the application of the Industry Title: Article 130 EC does not provide a legal basis for the administrative discretion required to allow exceptions to the principle of free competition.

Further, the limited financial resources of the Community restrict its ability to conduct industrial policy through public investment. Therefore, if the interventionist industrial policies of the Member States are abandoned for lack of success, and the ability to pursue them is limited by Community competition policy, the reduction of public intervention at the national level will not be replaced by Community intervention. This makes it more likely that providing a coherent regulatory environment conducive to structural adjustment by private parties will be the focus of Community industrial policy. This regulatory framework will be co-determined by considerations other than the competitiveness of European industry. Market opening as such is a priority of industrial policy, and other sectoral objectives will have to be considered. Article 130 EC can serve as a basis for general agenda setting efforts, but the balance between competition and competitiveness will be struck under the individual provisions of the Treaty on which specific measures are based. Therefore, the industrial policy powers of the Community, such as they are, remain fragmented in nature.

More recently, the Commission has linked the main industrial policy initiatives to its proposals aimed at increasing social and economic cohesion in the context of economic policy co-ordination. The 1993 White Paper on growth, competitiveness and employment cast industrial policy as a central element of the growth strategy of the Community, and as a flanking policy of the co-ordination of economic policy toward economic and monetary union. As the Community moves from negative to positive integration, its industrial policy has become part of a general strategy which seeks to harness structural adjustment in the pursuit of wider social and economic goals. Industrial policy is therefore one of the pillars of a general effort to set the agenda for integration beyond the internal market programme.

Hereby the hypothesis that the new industrial policy competence of the Community must be seen in the context of the transition from negative integration to positive integration, policy co-ordination, and, in particular, economic and monetary union is confirmed. This observation confirms the acceptance of this competence on account of the Member States, rather than the orientation of Community industrial policy. The latter has been long established, and requires measures of negative and positive integration alike. Further, the change in perspective of the Member States and their willingness to proceed to a limited pooling of competence on industrial policy is the result of a new balance between state and market.

This is underlined by the findings regarding competition policy. Initially, the Commission focused on developing the main instruments and principles of competition policy in fighting private distortions of competition. More recently, strengthened by the consensus on the internal market programme, the competition policy of the Community has imposed increasingly strict limits on state intervention in the economy. Hereby, it promoted a general trend away from national corporatism, which had relied on state aids, public ownership, and restrictive private agreements to pursue public interest objectives. After broadly supporting the Commission during its institution building phase, and in pursuit of the internal market objective, the Court of Justice now seeks a new balance between the requirements of competition and national economic sovereignty. Although public constraints on competition remain possible, they are now subject to control under Community law, and must take due legal form. This has made public ownership unattractive, leading to privatisation, and will generally promote the introduction of new forms of economic regulation at arm's length.

Hence, the Member States have come under pressure, leading to attempts to limit further encroachment on their national economic sovereignty and find acceptable forms of economic regulation. The Member States are retreating from direct economic intervention, and are developing their own competition policies, parallel to those of the Community. However, the co-ordination between competition policy at the two levels is inadequate. Although its main principles and procedures have now been firmly established, the competition policy of the Community remains highly centralised in the hands of the Commission. This has caused capacity problems and an implementation deficit. While the Commission seeks to improve multi-level policy co-ordination, the Member States are now seeking ways to combine reform of Community competition policy with the introduction of provisions protecting their economic sovereignty. The Merger Regulation, which introduced a complex system to attribute competence between the Community and national level, based on subsidiarity, provides the foremost example of how the two may be balanced.

Apart from placing limits on the industrial policies of the Member States, EC competition policy forms an instrument of industrial policy at the Community level. This is possible since the competition policy of the Community has wide goals. Competition policy has therefore been able to internalise the task of balancing potentially contradictory objectives, including the promotion of integration, of efficiency, and of the competitiveness of European industry. The competition rules thus leave room to accommodate industrial policy considerations. In line with the Community industrial policy, specific instruments of competition policy (such as the Merger Regulation) aim to promote structural adjustment, R&D collaboration, and the dissemination of new technology and know-how. In sum, the competition policy of the Community goes beyond the protection of the *process* of competition, and may on occasion give preference to considerations of market *structure*, so long as the fundamental requirements of competition law (and Community law in general) are respected.

It is, however, difficult to trace the role industrial policy considerations play in individual Commission decisions. This is so because these decisions are merely subject to restricted judicial review, not to a fundamental policy reappraisal. Consequently, there are concerns over the lack of transparency and the danger of government and industry capture of Community competition policy. Among the proposed solutions to these problems, that of creating an independent European Cartel Office is of more general interest. It would point to further depoliticisation and juridification of economic policy, or regulation. Unlike the European Central Bank and the European System of Central Banks, a European Cartel Office would take account of individual economic rights, and be subject to judicial control.

Hereby, the hypothesis that Community industrial and competition policy are in principle compatible has been confirmed. This complementarity is possible due to the market orientation of the Community approach to industrial policy, and the open texture of the Community competition policy. The various characteristics which define the ideal-typical opposite forms of industrial and competition policy sketched in the general introduction do not apply to the Community. This is illustrated by the case study on telecommunications.

The Community regime for telecommunications has changed fundamentally over recent years. The explanatory factors identified are:

   (i) technological change;
   (ii) internationalisation;
   (iii) the impetus to expand the internal market programme to telecommunications;

(iv) the new methods and strategies of integration introduced by the Single European Act;

(v) the failure of national high-technology programmes, and concern over the international competitiveness of the European information technology, components and consumer electronics industries;

(vi) reform in the Member States;

(vii) the mobilisation of powerful industrial lobbies in favour of liberalisation by the Commission;

(viii) a concerted and novel application of the four freedoms and competition rules of the Treaty;

(ix) the introduction of a market oriented system of harmonisation legislation;

(x) the constitutionalisation of the objectives of Community telecommunications policy by the Treaty on European Union.

EC telecommunications policy developed along the twin tracks of liberalisation and harmonisation. When individual national systems were unable to provide an adequate response to global systemic pressure, powerful private interests and the Commission united to exploit the direct effect of the market freedoms and the competition rules, and to force liberalisation. These initiatives drew on the general support for the internal market programme. Yet effective liberalisation could not be achieved without harmonisation, the introduction of common procedures, objectives, and methods of co-ordination. Although there is no clear general Treaty basis for a Community telecommunications policy, there clearly is a fully-fledged Community policy in this area. Under harmonisation legislation wider considerations (such as those of consumer protection) are now institutionalised, and the European Parliament is carving out a role for itself.

The relevance of EC telecommunications policy to the links between the industrial and competition policies of the Community is clear. The requirements of competition policy have restricted the national industrial policies in this sector, 'rolling back' the Member States. The argument that telecommunications liberalisation was of fundamental importance to the competitiveness of European industry provided a basis for consensus on reform, and the guiding motive for harmonisation. Telecommunications standardisation and R&D collaboration at the Community level were used for industrial policy purposes. Hence, the competition and industrial policies of the Community have been proven to be compatible at the sectoral level as well. The twin tracks of liberalisation and harmonisation have established the internal market by introducing competition, while defining the areas where regulation in the public interest is required.

The result is a new concept of the internal market, which includes broader social and economic goals. Industrial and competition policy arguments were freely mixed when private multinationals persuaded the Member States to dismantle their telecommunications monopolies to enable the creation of an

'information society'. The proposals to develop trans-European telecommunications networks (TENs) for this information society provide an example of
how horizontal industrial policy can promote the competitiveness of European
industry in general by stimulating demand, creating markets and infrastructure.
The development of TENs further illustrates the importance of providing a
coherent regulatory framework in order to harness structural adjustment, in particular where this is to be based on the mobilisation of private rather than of
public capital.

The new regulatory structure which is emerging for the telecommunications
sector has reduced the scope of political control at the level of the Member
States. Independent regulatory authorities were created to implement harmonised rules in national markets, linked by loose structures based on comitology.
Comitology was also used to encourage and institutionalise the participation of
diverse economic interests in policy making at the Community level. Parallel
to telecommunications specific regulation the competition rules form a general
safeguard. In particular the establishment of independent national telecommunications regulators and the general trend toward privatisation of the telecommunications operators point to changes both in market structure and methods
of economic regulation.

As has been seen, the emergence of the industrial policy of the Community,
or the promotion of structural adjustment, forms part of the development of the
socio-economic dimension of integration, and the extension of the economic
constitution. Although liberal in wording, the original economic constitution of
the EEC Treaty was without practical significance for large sections of the economy. The amendments introduced by the Single European Act and the Treaty
on European Union have not replaced national intervention by co-ordinated Community intervention. Instead they have promoted the rationalisation of public
policy toward more precise objectives, including industrial policy objectives, but
within an overall context of liberalisation. Seen in the context of economic
growth and international competitiveness, the industrial policy of the Community forms an important part of the post-1992 agenda for European integration.
Attention for the competitiveness of European industry will become increasingly explicit, but as part of a trend towards market based regulation.

Instead of the hypothetical contradiction between competition and industrial
policy, the more serious problem is finding consensus on the necessary degree
of public intervention, the level at which it should be exercised, and the appropriate institutional design under conditions of multi-level policy co-ordination. Or,
with a slightly different emphasis, a clear link should be established between the
legitimation of public intervention in the economy and the distribution of power
in the Community system. Ideally, the political constitution should be modified
to address systematically the horizontal and vertical division of power in the
Community and the appropriate legal form of policy co-ordination. Since the

Member States have so far been reluctant to engage in a revision of the Treaty along these lines, intermediate structures have emerged in an ad hoc manner.

Policy co-ordination takes various forms, usually based on the well-known comitology structures which derive democratic legitimation from the Member States, but compromise the role of the European Parliament. With the changing demands of European law and the new economic constraints, new methods of pursuing public interest objectives are evolving. In the telecommunications sector, a shift of competence toward the EC level was accompanied by devolution of power towards specialised national authorities, at the expense of political control by the Member States. For competition policy, the creation of a European Cartel Office has been proposed, which might become the first independent Community agency and would provide a new model of economic regulation. The modalities for proceeding toward economic and monetary union likewise seek to isolate monetary policy from political interference. In all three cases, a constitutional form of legitimation is chosen, based on the rule of European law.

Hence, the Member States appear to favour the rule of law over democracy at the European level, leading to the juridification (in particular proceduralisation and constitutionalisation) of economic policy. This process is by no means complete: further procedural guarantees including the right to be heard, broader scope for legal recourse against administrative acts, and balanced interest representation will be required if the rule of economic law is to function. The transparency of (discretionary) decision making must be improved, both to make these procedural guarantees effective, and in order to ensure that contentious issues reach the political arena.

However, the advent of democratic control at the European level is by no means entirely dependent on the wishes of the Member States or the eventual emergence of European polity. The demand of the European Parliament for democratic control over industrial policy at the Community level was denied, whereas strict constitutional limits were put in place. However, for all legislation with an internal market dimension, including most of the legislation affecting the information society project, the European Parliament already enjoys significant powers under the codecision procedure. It has further used these powers to force at least a partial solution to the comitology conflict by means of an inter-institutional agreement. The independent dynamics of the democratic process, like the dynamics of negative integration through law, may have been underestimated.

Bibliography

Abate, A., 'Droit communautaire, privatisations, déréglementations', (1994) 4 *Revue du Marché Unique Européen* 11.

Ackerman, B. A., *The Future of Liberal Revolution* (New Haven, 1992).

Arnull, A., *The General Principles of EEC Law and the Individual* (Leicester, 1990).

'A Constitution for Europe?', EUI Working Paper RSC 95/9 (Florence, 1995).

Audretsch, D. B., 'Industrial Policy and International Competitiveness', in Nicolaides, Ph. (ed.), *Industrial Policy in the European Community: A Necessary Response to Economic Integration?* (Maastricht, 1993).

—— 'Divergent Views in Antitrust Economics', (1988) 33 *The Antitrust Bulletin* 135.

Austin, M. T., 'Europe's ONP Bargain: What's in it for the User?', (1994) 18 *Telecommunications Policy* 97.

Bach, A., *Wettbewerbsrechtliche Schranken für staatliche Maßnahmen nach europäischem Gemeinschaftsrecht* (Tübingen, 1992).

Baker, J. B., 'Recent Developments in Economics that Challenge Chicago School Views', (1989) 58 *Antitrust Law Journal* 645.

Balassa, B., *The Theory of Economic Integration* (New York, 1961).

Bangemann, M., *Meeting the Global Challenge: Establishing a Successful European Industrial Policy* (London, 1992).

—— 'Pour une politique industrielle européenne', (1992) 35 RdMC 367.

Barents, R., 'The Community and the Unity of the Common Market', (1990) 33 *German Yearbook of International Law* 9.

Bayliss, B. T., and El-Agraa, A. M., 'Competition and Industrial Policies with an Emphasis on Competition Policy', in El-Agraa, A. M. (ed.), *The Economics of the European Community* (3rd ed., New York, 1990).

Behrens, P., 'Die Wirtschaftsverfassung der Europäischen Gemeinschaft', in Brüggemeier, G. (ed.), *Verfassungen für ein ziviles Europa* (Baden-Baden, 1994).

Bellamy, C., and Child, G. D., *Common Market Law of Competition* (3rd ed., London, 1987).

Bellamy, R., Bufacchi, V., and Castiglione, D. (eds.), *Democracy and Constitutional Culture in the Union of Europe* (London, 1995).

Bermann, G. A., 'The Single European Act: A New Constitution for the Community?', (1989) 27 *Columbia Journal of Transnational Law* 528.

Biéla, M. C., 'Étude sur les comités et les télécommunications', unpublished paper (Institut National des Télécommunications, December 1992).

Bishop, M., and Kay, J. (eds.), *European Mergers and Merger Policy* (Oxford, 1993).

Blanquet, M., *L'article 5 du traité CEE: Recherche sur les obligations de fidélité des états membres de la Communauté* (Paris, 1994).

Bletschacher, G., and Klodt, H., *Strategische Handels- und Industriepolitik: Theoretische Grundlagen, Branchenanalysen und wettbewerbspolitische Implikationen*, Kieler Studien No. 244 (Tübingen, 1992).

—— 'Braucht Europa eine neue Industriepolitik?', *Kiel Discussion Paper* No. 177 (Kiel, 1991).

Bork, R. H., *The Antitrust Paradox* (Chicago, 1978).

Bouterse, R., *Competition and Integration: What Goals Count? EEC Competition Law and Goals of Industrial, Monetary and Cultural Policy*, Ph.D. thesis, (Florence 1992).

Bradley, K., 'Comitology and the Law: Through a Glass, Darkly', (1992) 29 CMLR 693.

Bribosia, H., 'Subsidiarité et répartition des compétences entre la Communauté et ses États membres', (1992) 4 *Revue du Marché Unique Européen* 165.

Bright, Ch., 'Article 90, Economic Policy and the Duties of the Member States', (1993) 4 ECLR 263.

Brown, A., 'The Extension of the Community Public Procurement Rules to Utilities', (1993) 30 CMLR 721.

Buigues, P., and Sapir, A., 'Community Industrial Policies', in Nicolaides, Ph. (ed.), *Industrial Policy in the European Community: A Necessary Response to Economic Integration?* (Maastricht, 1993).

Buigues, P., and Jacquemin, A., 'Strategies of Firms and Structural Environments in the Large Internal Market', (1989) 28 JCMS 53.

Buigues, P., Jacquemin, A., and Ilkovitz, F., 'Horizontal Mergers and Competition Policy in the European Community', (1989) 40 *European Economy*.

Buitendijk, G. J., and Van Schendelen, M. P. C. M., 'Brussels Advisory Committees: A Channel for Influence?', (1995) 20 ELR 37.

Bulmer, S., 'Institutions and Policy Change: The Case of Merger Control', (1994) 72 *Public Administration* 423.

Cadieux, J.-L., 'Restructuration industrielle et politique communautaire vis-à-vis des aides nationales', in Dutheil de la Rochère, J., and Vandamme, J. (eds.), *Intervention Publique et Droit Communautaire* (Paris, 1988).

Caporaso, J., and Keeler, J., 'The EC and Regional Integration Theory', Plenary address at the Third Biennial International Conference of the European Community Studies Association 1993.

Cassese, S., 'Oltre lo Stato: i limiti dei governi nazionali nel controllo dell'economia', in Galgano, F., Cassese, S., Tremonti, G., and Treu, T., *Nazioni senza ricchezza, ricchezze senza nazione* (Bologna, 1993).

—— 'La Costituzione Europea', (1991) 11 *Quaderni Costituzionali* 187.

Caves, R., 'Corporate Mergers in International Economic Integration', in Giovannini, A., and Mayer, C., *European Financial Integration* (Cambridge, 1991).

Cawson, A., 'Interests, Groups and Public Policy-Making: The Case of the European Consumer Electronics Industry', in Greenwood, J., Grote, J., and Ronit, K. (eds.), *Organized Interests and the European Community* (London, 1992).

Cecchini, P., Catinat, M., and, Jacquemin, A., *The European Challenge 1992: The Benefits of a Single Market* (Aldershot, 1989).

Cerny, P. G., *The Changing Architecture of Politics: Structure, Agency and the Future of the State* (London, 1990).

—— 'The Limits of Deregulation: Transnational Interpenetration and Policy Change', (1991) 19 *European Journal of Political Research* 173.

Chalmers, D., 'Repackaging the Internal Market—The Ramifications of the *Keck* Judgement', (1994) 19 ELR 384.

Cohen, S. S., and Zysman, J., *Manufacturing matters: The Myth of the Post-Industrial Economy* (New York, 1987).

Constantine, L., 'An Antitrust Enforcer Confronts the New Economics', (1989) 58 *Antitrust Law Journal* 661.

Constantinesco, L.-J., 'La constitution économique de la C.E.E.', (1977) 13 RTDE 244.

Constantinesco, V., 'La subsidiarité comme principe constitutionel de l'Integration Européenne', (1991) 46 *Aussenwirtschaft* 439.

—— 'La structure du traité instituant l'Union européenne—Les dispositions communes et finales des nouvelles compétences', (1993) 29 CDE 251.

Cowhey, P. F., 'The International Telecommunications Regime: The Political Roots of Regimes for High Technology', (1990) 44 *International Organization* 169.

Crandall, R. W., *After the Breakup: U.S. Telecommunications in a More Competitive Era* (Washington DC, 1991).

Curtin, D., 'The Constitutional Structure of the Union: A Europe of Bits and Pieces', (1993) 30 CMLR 17.

Curzon-Price, V., 'Competition and industrial policies with an emphasis on industrial policy', in El-Agraa, A. M. (ed.), *The Economics of the European Community* (3rd ed., New York, 1990).

D'Andrea Tyson, L., *Who's Bashing Whom: Trade Conflict in High-Technology Industries* (Washington DC, 1992).

Dang Nguyen, G., 'Telecommunications: A Challenge to the Old Order', in Sharp, M. (ed.), *Europe and the New Technologies: Six Case Studies in Innovation and Adjustment* (London, 1985).

Dankbaar, B., Groenewegen, J., and Schenk, H. (eds.), *Perspectives in Industrial Organization* (Dordrecht, 1990).

Dashwood, A., 'Community Legislative Procedures in the Era of the Treaty on European Union', (1994) 19 ELR 343.

Davidow, J., 'Competition Policy, Merger Control and the European Community's 1992 Program', (1991) 29 *Columbia Journal of Transnational Law* 11.

De Búrca, G., 'Proportionality in EC Law', (1993) 13 YEL 105.

De Ghellinck, E., 'European industrial policy against the background of the Single European Act', in Coffey, P. (ed.), *Main Economic Areas of the EEC—Towards 1992* (Deventer, 1988).

De Grauwe, P., 'Economic Policy and Political Democracy', (1989) 3 *European Affairs* 66.

Dehousse, R., '1992 and Beyond: The Institutional Dimension of the Internal Market Programme', (1989) 16 LIEI 109.

—— 'Does Subsidiarity Really Matter?', EUI Working Paper LAW 92/32 (Florence, 1993).

Dehousse, R., Joerges, Ch., Majone, G., and Snyder, F. (with Everson, M.), *Europe After 1992: New Regulatory Strategies* Working Paper Law 92/31 (Florence, 1992).

De Jong, H., 'Competition Policy in Europe: Stimulus, Nuisance, or Drawback?', in Groeneveld, K., and Maks, G. (eds.), *Economic Policy and the Market Process* (Amsterdam, 1990).

Della Cananea, G., 'Cooperazione e integrazione nel sistema amministrativo delle Communità europee: la questione della "comitologia"', (1990) 40 *Rivista Trimestriale di Diritto Pubblico* 655.

—— 'Administration by Guidelines: The Policy Guidelines of the Commisssion in the Field of State Aids', in Darecker, G. (ed.), *Schriftenreihe der Europäischen Rechtsakademie Trier 3: Combatting Subsidy Fraud in the EC Area* (Cologne, 1993).

Diez-Picazo, L.-M., 'Reflexiones sobre la Idea de Constitucion Europea', (1993) 20 *Revista de Instituciones Europeas* 533.

Dore, R., *Flexible Rigidities: Industrial Policy and Structural Adjustment in Japan 1970–80* (London, 1986).

Downes, T. A., and MacDougall, D. S., 'Significantly Impeding Effective Competition', (1994) 19 ELR 286.

Dumez, H., and Jeunemaître, A., *La concurrence en Europe: De nouvelles règles du jeu pour les entreprises* (Paris, 1991).

—— 'L'État et le Marché en Europe. Vers un État de droit économique?', (1992) 42 *Revue Française de Science Politique* 263.

Dumont, A., 'Technology, Competitiveness and Cooperation in Europe', in Steinberg, M. S. (ed.), *The Technical Challenges and Opportunities of a United Europe* (London, 1990).

Easson, A., 'Legal Approaches to European Legislation: The Role of the Court and Legislator in the Completion of the European Common Market', (1989) 12 *Revue d'Integration Européen* 101.

Editorial, 'After the Maastricht Agreements—What Industrial Policy?', *Agence Europe* (four parts) Nos 5640–5643, 6–10 January 1992.

—— 'Judicial Review and Merger Control', (1992) 29 CMLR 1.

—— 'Growth, Competitiveness and Unemployment: The Challenges Facing the European Union', (1995) 31 CMLR 1.

Edward, D., and Hoskins, M., 'Article 90: Deregulation and EC Law: Reflections Arising From the XVI FIDE Conference', (1995) 32 CMLR 157.

Ehlermann, C.-D., 'The Internal Market Following the Single European Act', (1987) 24 CMLR 361.

—— 'Neuere Entwicklungen im europäischen Wettbewerbsrecht', (1991) 26 EuR 307.

—— 'The Contribution of EC Competition Policy to the Single Market', (1992) 29 CMLR 257.

—— 'Wettbewerbspolitik im Binnenmarkt', (1993) 39 *Recht der Internationalen Wirtschaft* 793.

—— 'Telekommunikation und Europäisches Wettbewerbsrecht', (1993) 28 EuR 134.

—— 'Managing Monopolies: The Role of the State in Controlling Market Dominance in the European Community', (1993) 4 ECLR 61.

—— 'Libéralisation et privatisation', Editorial, (1994) 4 *Revue du Marché Unique Européen* 5.

—— 'State Aid Control in the European Union: Success of Failure?', (1995) 18 *Fordham International Law Journal* 1212.

—— 'Reflections on a European Cartel Office', (1995) 32 CMLR 471.

—— 'Ökonomische Aspekte des Subsidiaritätsprinzips: Harmonisierung versus Wettbewerb der Systeme', (1995) 18 *Integration* 11.

Elizalde, J., 'Legal Aspects of Community Policy on Research and Technological Development', (1992) 29 CMLR 309.

Emiliou, N., 'Subsidiarity: An Effective Barrier Against the Enterprises of Ambition?', (1992) 17 ELR 383.

Esteva Mosso, C., 'La compatibilité des monopoles de droit du secteur des télécommunications avec les normes de concurrence du traité CEE', (1993) 29 CDE 445.

European Institute of Public Administration, *Subsidiarity: The Challenge of Change. Proceedings of the Jacques Delors Colloquium, Maastricht 21–22 March 1991* (Maastricht, 1991).

Everling, U., 'Die Koordinierung der Wirtschaftspolitik in der Europäischen Wirtschafts-gemeinschaft als rechtsproblem' (1964) No. 296/297 *Recht und Staat* 14, reprinted in Everling, U., *Das europäische Wirtschaftsrecht im Spannungsfeld von Politik und Wirtschaft: Ausgewählte Aufsätze 1964–1984* (Baden-Baden, 1985).

—— 'Rechtsfragen einer Industriepolitik im gemeinsamen Markt', (1968) 3 EuR 175.

—— 'Reflections on the Structure of the European Union', (1992) 29 CMLR 1053.

Everson, M., 'Independent Agencies: Hierarchy Beaters?', (1995) 1 *European Law Journal* 180.

Farrell, J., and Shapiro, C., 'Standard setting in High-Definition Television', in Baily, M. N., and Winston, C. (eds.), *Brookings Papers on Economic Activity: Microeconomics* (Brookings Institution, 1992).

Fernández Martín, J. M., and O'Leary, S., 'Judicial Exceptions to the Free Provision of Services', (1995) 1 *European Law Journal* 308.

Forrester, I. S., and Norall, Ch., 'The Laicization of Community Law: Self-Help and the Rule of Reason: How Competition Law is and could be Applied', (1984) 21 CMLR 11.

Fox, E. M., and Sullivan, L. A., 'Antitrust—Retrospective and Prospective: Where Are We Coming From? Where Are We Going?', (1987) 62 *NYU Law Review* 936.

Frazer, T., 'Competition Policy After 1992: The Next Step', (1990) 53 MLR 609.

—— 'The New Structural Funds, State Aids and Interventions on the Single Market', (1995) 30 ELR 3.

Freeman, C., *Technology Policy and Economic Performance—Lessons from Japan* (New York, 1987).

Frees, Ch.-P., 'Das neue industriepolitische Konzept der Europäischen Gemeinschaft, (1991) 26 EuR 281.

Fuchs, G., 'ISDN: "The Telecommunications Highway for Europe after 1992" or "Paving a Dead-End Street?": The Politics of Pan-European Telecommunications Network Development', MPIFG Discussion Paper 93/6 (Cologne, 1993).

—— 'Policy-Making in a System of Multi-Level Governance—The Commission of the European Community and the Restructuring of the Telecommunications Sector' (1994) 1 *Journal of European Public Policy* 177.

Geelhoed, L. A., 'Het subsidiariteitsbeginsel: Een communautair principe?', (1991) 39 SEW 422.

George, K. and Jacquemin, A., 'Dominant Firms and Mergers', (1992) 102 *The Economic Journal* 148.

Gerber, D. J., 'Constitutionalizing the Economy: German Neo-liberalism, Competition Law and the "New" Europe', (1994) 42 *American Journal of Comparative Law* 25.

—— 'The Transformation of European Community Competition Law?', (1994) 35 *Harvard International Law Journal* 97.

Geroski, P. A., 'European Industrial Policy and Industrial Policy in Europe', (1989) 5 *Oxford Review of Economic Policy* 20.

—— 'Vertical Relations Between Firms and Industrial Policy', (1992) 102 *The Economic Journal* 138.

Geroski, P. A., and Jacquemin, A., 'Large Firms in the European Corporate Economy and Industrial Policy in the 1980s', in Jacquemin, A. (ed.), *European Industry: Public Policy and Corporate Strategy* (Oxford, 1984).

—— 'Industrial Change, Barriers to Mobility and European Industrial Policy', in Jacquemin, A., and Sapir, A. (eds.), *The European Internal Market: Trade and Competition—Selected Readings* (Oxford, 1989).

Gibbons, J. J., 'Antitrust, Law & Economics, and the Courts', (1987) 50 *Law and Contemporary Problems* 217.

Giovanni, A., and Mayer, C., *European Financial Integration* (Cambridge, 1991).

Goybet, C., 'La CEE a-t-elle une politique industrielle?', (1991) 34 RdMC 753.

Goyder, D. G., *EC Competition Law* (2nd ed., Oxford, 1993).

Grande, E., and Schneider, V., 'Reformstrategien und staatliche Handlungskapazitäten. Eine vergleichende Analyse institutionellen Wandels in der Telekommunikation in Westeuropa', (1991) 32 *Politische Vierteljahresschrift* 452.

Grant, W., *The Political Economy of Industrial Policy* (London, 1982).

Green, M., 'The Politics of Big Business in the Single Market Program', Paper presented to the European Community Studies Association Third Biennial Conference, May 27, 1993, Washington DC.

Grünsteidl, W., 'An industrial policy for Europe', (1990) 4 *European Affairs* 14.

Guillermin, G., 'Le principe de l'équilibre institutionnel dans la jurisprudence de la Cour de justice des Communautés européennes', (1992) 119 *Journal du droit international* 319.

Gutman, G., *et al* (eds.), *Die Wirtschaftsverfassung der Bundesrepublik Deutschland* (Stuttgart, 1976).

Gyselen, L., 'State Action and the Effectiveness of the EEC Treaty's Competition Provisions', (1989) 26 CMLR 33.

—— 'Anti-Competitive State Measures under the EC Treaty: Towards a Substantive Legality Standard', (1993) 18 ELR *Competition Checklist* 55.

Haas, E. B., *When Knowledge is Power: Learning and Adaptation of International Organisations* (Berkeley, 1990).

Habermas, J., 'Wie ist Legitimität durch Legalität möglich?', (1987) 20 *Kritische Justiz* 1.

Hallstein, W., *Die Europäische Gemeinschaft* (4th ed., Düsseldorf, 1974).

Halverson, J. T., 'EC Merger Control: Competition Policy or Industrial Policy? Views of a US Practitioner', (1993) 19 LIEI 49.

Hancher, L., 'Artikel 90 EEG—Minder troebel, maar nog niet helder', (1993) 41 SEW 328.

—— 'State Aids and Judicial Control in the European Community', (1994) 15 ECLR 134.

Hancher, L. Ottervanger, T., and Slot, P. J., *EC State Aids* (London, 1993).

Hanf, D., 'Le jugement de la Cour constitutionelle fédérale allemande sur la constitutionalité du Traité de Maastricht: Un nouveau chapitre des relations entre le droit communautaire et le droit national', (1994) 30 RTDE 391.

Hart, H. L. A., *The Concept of Law* (Oxford, 1961).

Hartley, T. C., 'Federalism, Courts and Legal Systems: The Emerging Constitution of the European Community', (1986) 34 *American Journal of Comparative Law* 229.

—— 'Constitutional and Institutional Aspects of the Maastricht Agreement', (1993) 43 ICLQ 213.

—— *The Foundations of European Community Law* (3rd ed., Oxford, 1994).

Hatzopoulos, V., 'L'"Open Network Provision" (ONP) moyen de la dérégulation', (1994) 30 RTDE 63.

Hawk, B., 'The American (Anti-trust) Revolution: Lessons for the EEC?', (1988) 9 ECLR 53.

Hawkes, L., 'The EC Merger Regulation: Not an Industrial Policy Instrument: The De Havilland Decision', (1992) 13 ECLR 44.

Hay, D., 'The Assessment: Competition Policy', (1993) 9 *Oxford Review of Economic Policy* 1.

Heintzen, M., 'Hierarchierungsprozesse innerhalb das Primärrechts der Europäischen Gemeinschaft', (1994) 29 EuR 35.

Henry, C., 'Public Service and Competition in the European Community Approach to Communications Networks', (1993) 9 *Oxford Review of Economic Policy* 45.

Hellman, R., 'Industriepolitik', in Von der Groeben, H., Thiesing, J., Ehlermann, C.-D. (eds.), *Kommentar zum EWG-Vertrag*, Vol. 4 (4th ed., Baden-Baden, 1991).

Helpman, E., and Krugman, P., *Trade Policy and Market Structure* (Cambridge, 1986).

Herdegen, M., 'Maastricht and the German Constitutional Court: Constitutional Restraints for an "Ever Closer Union"', (1994) 31 CMLR 235.

Higham, N., 'Open Network Provision in the EC: A Step-by-Step Approach to Competition', (1993) 17 *Telecommunications Policy* 242.

Hills, J., 'Dependency Theory and its Relevance Today: International Institutions in Telecommunications and Structural Power', (1994) 20 *Review of International Studies* 169.

Hilpert, U. (ed.), *State Policies and Techno-Industrial Innovation* (London, 1991).

Hornsby, S. B., 'Competition Policy in the 80's: More Policy Less Competition', (1987) ELR 79.

Hovenkamp, H., 'Antitrust Policy, Federalism, and the Theory of the Firm: A Historical Perspective', (1990) 59 *Antitrust Law Journal* 75.

Hüttig, Ch., 'Die Deregulierung des internationalen Telekommunikationssektors: Zum Verhältnis von technischer Entwicklung und ordnungspolitischem Wandel', (1989) Sonderheft 10 *Leviathan* 144.

Hughes, A., 'Competition Policy and the Competitive Process: Europe in the 1990s', (1992) 43 *Metroeconomica* 1.

Huntley, J. A. K., and Pitt, D. C., 'Judicial Policy Making: The Greeneing of US Telecommunications', (1990) 10 *International Review of Law and Economics* 77.

—— 'Divestiture and Market Structure: Competition and Deregulation in US Telecommunications', (1989) 10 ECLR 407.

Hyde, A., 'The Concept of Legitimation in the Sociology of Law', (1983) 54 *Wisconsin Law Review* 379.

Jacobs, F. G., 'Is the Court of Justice of the European Communities a Constitutional Court?', in Curtin, D., and O'Keeffe, D. (eds.), *Constitutional Adjudication in European Community and National Law* (London, 1992).

Jacquemin, A., 'Introduction: Competition in Market Economies', in Comanor, W. S., *et al*, *Competition Policy in Europe and North America: Economic Issues and Institutions* (London, 1990).

—— 'European Industrial Policies and Competition', in Coffey, P. (ed.), *Economic Policies of the Common Market* (London, 1979).

Jacquemin, A., *et al*, *Merger and Competition Policy in the European Community* (Oxford, 1990) P. H. Admiraal (ed.).

Jacquemin, A., and Marchipont, J.-F., 'De nouveaux enjeux pour la politique industrielle de la Communauté', (1992) 102 *Revue de l'Économie Politique* 69.

Jacquemin, A., and Wright, D., 'Corporate Strategies and European Challenges Post-1992', (1993) 31 JCMS 525.

Jenny, F., 'Competition and Efficiency', in Hawk, B. (ed.), *Annual Proceedings of the Fordham Corporate Law Institute 1993: Antitrust in a Global Economy* (New York, 1994).

Joerges, Ch., 'Markt ohne Staat? Die Wirtschaftsverfassung der Gemeinschaft und die Renaissance der regulativen Politik' in Wildenmann, R. (ed.), *Staatswerdung Europas? Optionen für eine politische Union* (Baden-Baden, 1991).

—— 'Die Europäisierung des Rechts und die rechtliche Kontrolle von Risiken', (1991) 74 *Kritische Vierteljahresschrift für Gesetzgebung und Rechtswissenschaft* 416.

—— 'European Economic Law, the Nation State and the Maastricht Treaty', in Dehousse, R. (ed.), *Europe After Maastricht: An Ever Closer Union* (München, 1994).

—— 'Das Recht im Prozeß der europäischen Integration: Plädoyer für die Beachtung des Rechts durch die Politikwissenschaft', in Jachtenfuchs, M. and Kohler-Koch, B. (eds.), *Europäische Integration* (Opladen, 1995).

Johnson, C., *MITI and the Japanese Miracle* (Stanford, 1982).

—— (ed.), *The Industrial Policy Debate* (San Francisco, 1984).

Joliet, R., 'Réglementations étatiques anticoncurrentielles et droit communautaire', (1988) 24 CDE 363.

Kapteyn, P. J. G., and VerLoren van Themaat, P., *Introduction to the Law of the European Communities* (2nd ed., Deventer, 1990), Gormley, L. W. (ed.).

Kay, N., 'Industrial Collaborative Activity and the Completion of the Internal Market', (1991) 29 JCMS 347.

—— 'Mergers, Acquisitions and the Completion of the Internal Market', in Hughes, K., (ed.), *European Competitiveness* (Cambridge, 1993).

Kenis, P., and Schneider, V., 'Policy Networks and Policy Analysis. Scrutinizing a New Analytical Toolbox', in Marin, B., and Mayntz, R. (eds.), *Policy Networks: Empirical Evidence and Theoretical Considerations* (Frankfurt, 1991).

Keohane, R. O., and Hoffmann, S., 'Institutional Change in Europe in the 1980s', in Keohane, R. O., and Hoffmann, S. (eds.), *The New European Community: Decision-Making and Institutional Change* (Boulder, 1991).

Koopmans, T., 'The Role of Law in the Next Stage of European Integration', (1986) 35 ICLQ 925.

Korah, V., 'EEC Competition Policy: Legal Form or Economic Efficiency', (1986) 39 *Current Legal Problems* 85.

—— 'From Legal Form Toward Economic Efficiency—Article 85(1) of the EEC Treaty in Contrast to U.S. Antitrust', (1990) 35 *Antitrust Bulletin* 1009.

Krugman, P. R. (ed.), *Strategic Trade policy and the New International Economics* (Cambridge, 1986).

—— 'Economic Integration in Europe: Some Conceptual Issues', in Padoa Schioppa, T., *et al* (eds.), *Efficiency, Stability and Equity: A Strategy for the Evolution of the Economic System of the European Community* (Oxford, 1987).

—— 'Competitiveness: A Dangerous Obsession', (1994) 73 *Foreign Affairs* 28.

Krugman, P. R., and Obstfeld, M., *International Economics: Theory and Policy* (2nd ed., New York, 1991).

Ladeur, K.-H., 'Die Neuordnung der Telekommunikation. Zur Funktion eines öffentlichen Unternehmens in hochkomplexer Umwelt', (1991) 74 *Kritische Vierteljahresschrift für Gesetzgebung und Rechtswissenschaft* 176.

Lande, R. H., 'The Rise and (Coming) Fall of Efficiency as the Ruler of Antitrust', (1988) 33 *Antitrust Bulletin* 429.

—— 'Chicago's False Foundations: Wealth Transfers (Not Just Efficiency) Should Guide Antitrust', (1989) 58 *Antitrust Law Journal* 631.

Lauber, V., 'The Political Economy of Industrial Policy in Western Europe', in Shull, S. A., and Cohen, J. E. (eds.), *Economics and Politics of Industrial Policy: The United States and Western Europe* (Boulder, 1986).

Layton, V., *European Advanced Technology: A Programme for Integration* (London, 1969).

Lenaerts, K., 'Constitutionalism and the many Faces of Federalism', (1990) 38 *American Journal of Comparative Law* 205.

—— 'Some Reflections on the Separation of Powers in the European Community', (1991) 28 CMLR 11.

—— 'Regulating the Regulatory Process: "Delegation of Powers" in the European Community', (1993) 18 ELR 23.

Lenaerts, K., and Van Ypersele, P., 'Le principe de subsidarité et son contexte: étude de l'article 3B du Traité CE', (1994) 30 CDE 3.

Lowe, Ph., 'Telecommunications Services and Competition Law in Europe', (1994) 5 EBLR 139.

MacCormick, N., 'Beyond the Sovereign State', (1993) 56 MLR 1.

—— 'The *Maastricht Urteil*: Sovereignty Now', (1995) 1 *European Law Journal* 255.

Magaziner, I. C., and Reich, R. B., *Minding America's Business: the Decline and Rise of the American Economy* (New York, 1983).

Majone, G., 'Cross-National Sources of Regulatory Policy-Making in Europe and the United States', (1991) 11 *Journal of Public Policy* 79.

—— 'Independence vs. Accountability? Non-Majoritarian Institutions and Democratic Government in Europe', in Hesse, J. J. (ed.), *European Yearbook of Public Administration* (Oxford, 1994).

Mancini, G. F., 'The Making of a Constitution for Europe', (1989) 26 CMLR 595.

Mancini, G. F., and Keeling, D. T., 'Democracy and the European Court of Justice', (1994) 57 MLR 175.

Mansell, R., *The New Telecommunications: A Political Economy of Network Evolution* (London, 1993).

Marchipont, J.-F., Ramadier, P., and Vigier, P., 'Politique industrielle: Intérêt communautaire', (1992) 17 *L'Événement Européen* 19.

Marenco, G., 'Competition between National Economies and Competition between Businesses—A Response to Judge Pescatore', (1987) 10 *Fordham International Law Journal* 420.

Mayes, D. G., 'European Industrial Policy', in Macmillen, M., Mayes, D. G., and Van Veen, P. (eds.), *European Integration and Industry* (Tilburg, 1987).

McGowan, F., 'EC Industrial Policy', in El-Agraa, A. M. (ed.), *The Economics of the European Community* (4th ed., London, 1994).

McKnight, L., 'The international standardization of telecommunications services and equipment', in Mestmäcker, E.-J. (ed.), *The Law and Economics of Transborder Telecommunications* (Baden-Baden, 1987).

Mény, Y., Wright, V., and Rhodes, M. (eds.), *The Politics of Steel: Western Europe and the Steel Industry in the Crisis Years (1974–1984)* (Berlin, 1987).

Mertens de Wilmars, J., 'The Case-Law of the Court of Justice in Relation to the Review of the Legality of Economic Policy in Mixed Economy Systems', (1982) 9 LIEI 1.

—— 'Réflections sur l'ordre juridico-économique de la Communauté européenne' in Dutheil de la Rochère, J., and Vandamme, J. (eds.), *Interventions Publiques et Droit Communautaire* (Brussels, 1988).

Mestmäcker, E.-J., 'Competing Goals of National Telecommunications Policy', in Mestmäcker, E.-J. (ed.), *The Law and Economics of Transborder Telecommunications* (Baden-Baden, 1987).

—— 'Auf dem Wege zu einer Ordnungspolitik für Europa', in Mestmäcker, E.-J., Möller, H., and Schwartz, P. (eds.), *Eine Ordnungspolitik für Europa: Festschrift für Hans von der Groeben zu seinem 80. Geburtstag* (Baden-Baden, 1987).

—— 'Fusionskontrolle im Gemeinsamen Markt zwischen Wettbewerbspolitik und Industriepolitik' (1988) 23 EuR 349.

—— 'Merger control in the Common Market: Between Competition Policy and Industrial Policy', in Hawk, B. (ed.), *Annual Proceedings of the Fordham Corporate Law Institute: 1988* (New York, 1989).

—— 'Zur Anwendung der Wettbewerbsregeln auf die Mitgliedstaaten und auf die Europäischen Gemeinschaften', in Baur, J., Müller-Graf, P.-Ch., and Zuleeg, M. (eds.), *Europarecht, Energierecht, Wirtschaftsrecht: Festschrift für Bodo Börner zum 70. Geburtstag* (Cologne, 1992).

—— 'Widersprüchlich, verwirrend und gefährlich', 10 October 1992 FAZ 10.

—— 'On the Legitimacy of European Law', (1994) 58 *Rabelszeitschrift* 615.

Metraux, A., *European Telecommunications Policy and the Regional Bell Operating Companies* (Geneva, 1991).

Milward, A. S., *The European Rescue of the Nation-State* (2nd ed., London, 1994).

—— *The European Community: The Salvation of the Nation State* (London, 1994).

Molle, W., *The Economics of European Integration: Theory, Practice, Policy* (Aldershot, 1990).

Moravcsik, A., 'Negotiating the Single Act: National Interests and Conventional Statecraft in the European Community', (1991) 45 *International Organisation* 19.

—— 'Preferences and Power in the European Community: A Liberal Intergovernmentalist Approach', (1993) 31 JCMS 473.

Möschel, W., 'EG-Industriepolitik nach Maastricht', (1992) 43 *ORDO* 415.

—— 'Hoheitliche Maßnahmen und die Wettbewerbsvorschriften des Gemeinschaftsrechts', in *Weiterentwicklung der Europäischen Gemeinschaften und der Marktwirtschaft. Referate des XXV. FIW-Symposions* (Cologne, 1992).

Moussis, N., 'Small and Medium Enterprises in the Internal Market', (1992) 17 ELR 482.

Müller-Armack, A., *Wirtschaftsordnung und Wirtschaftspolitik* (Freiburg, 1964).

Musgrave, R. A., and Musgrave, P., *Public Finance in Theory and Practice* (Auckland, 1985).

Mytelka, L. K., and Delapierre, M., 'The Alliance Strategies of European Firms in the Information Technology Industry and the Role of ESPRIT', (1987) 26 JCMS 231.

Naftel, J. M., 'The Natural Death of a Natural Monopoly: Competition in EC Telecommunications after the Telecommunications Terminals Judgment', (1993) 14 ECLR 105.

Narjes, K.-H., 'Europe's Technological Challenge: A View From the European Commission', (1988) 15 *Science and Public Policy* 395.

Neumann, M., 'Industrial Policy and Competition Policy', (1990) 34 *European Economic Review* 562.

Neuwahl, N. A., 'Principles of Justice: Human Rights and Constitutional Principles Within the European Union—A Framework for Analysis', COST A7 Project, *The Evolution of Rules for a Single European Market* (1995).

Neven, D., Nuttall, S., and P. Seabright, P., *Merger in Daylight: The Politics and Economics of European Merger Control* (London, 1993).

Nicolaides, Ph., 'Industrial policy in the European Community: An assessment of the Bangemann Report', in CEPS, *The Annual Review of European Community Affairs* (Oxford, 1992).

—— 'EC industrial policy', (1992) 28 *European Trends* (Economist Intelligence Unit) 53.

—— 'Industrial Policy: The Problem of Reconciling Definitions, Intentions and Effects', in Nicolaides, Ph. (ed.), *Industrial Policy in the European Community: A Necessary Response to Economic Integration?* (Maastricht, 1993).

Noam, E., *Telecommunications in Europe* (New York, 1992).

Nora, S., and Minc, A., *l'Informatisation de la Société* (Paris, 1978).

O'Keeffe, D., 'The Agreement on the European Economic Area', (1992) 8 LIEI 1.

O'Keeffe, D., and Twomey, M. (eds.), *Legal Issues of the Maastricht Treaty* (London, 1994).

Olson, M., *The Rise and Decline of Nations* (New Haven, 1982).

Ordover, J. A., 'Conflicts of Jurisdiction: Antitrust and Industrial Policy', (1987) 50 *Law and Contemporary Problems* 165.

—— 'The Economic Foundations of Competition Policy', in Comanor, W. S., *et al*, *Competition Policy in Europe and North America: Economic Issues and Institutions* (London, 1990).

Ostry, S., *Governments and Corporations in a Shrinking World: Trade and Innovation Policies in the United States, Europe, and Japan* (New York, 1990).

Overbury, H. C., 'Politics or Policy? The Demystification of EC Merger Control', in Hawk, B. (ed.), *Annual Proceedings of the Fordham Corporate Law Institute 1992: International Antitrust Law and Policy* (New York, 1993).

Page, W. H., 'Ideological Conflict and the Origins of Antitrust Policy', (1991) 66 *Tulane Law Review* 1.

Pappalardo, A., 'State Measures and Public Undertakings: Article 90 of the Treaty Revisited', (1991) 12 ECLR 29.

Pathak, A. S., 'EEC Merger Regulation Enforcement During 1992', (1992) 17 ELR *Competition Checklist* 132.

Pelkmans, J., 'The new approach to technical harmonization and standardization', (1987) 25 JCMS 249.

Peña Castellot, M., 'The Application of Competition Rules in the Telecommunications Sector: Strategic Alliances', (1995) 1:4 *DG IV Competition Policy Newsletter* 1.

Pescatore, P., 'Les objectifs de la Communauté européenne comme principes d'interpretation dans la jurisprudence de la Cour de Justice' *Miscellanea Ganshof van der Meersch*, Vol. 2 (Brussels, 1972).

Pescatore, P., 'Public and Private Aspects of European Community Competition Law', (1987) 10 *Fordham International Law Journal* 373.

Petersmann, E. U., 'Constitutionalism, Constitutional Law and European Integration', (1991) 46 *Aussenwirtschaft* 15.

—— 'Grundprobleme der Wirtschaftsverfassung der EG', (1993) 48 *Aussenwirtschaft* 389.

—— 'Constitutional Principles Governing the EEC's Commercial Policy', in Maresceau, M. (ed.), *The European Community's Commercial Policy after 1992: The Legal Dimension* (Dordrecht, 1993).

Peterson, J., 'Technology Policy in Europe: Explaining the Framework Programme and Eureka in Theory and Practice', (1991) 29 JCMS 269.

—— 'Towards a Common European Industrial Policy? The Case of High Definition Television', (1992) 28 *Government and Opposition* 496.

Phelan, D. R., 'Revolt or Revolution: The Constitutional Boundaries of the European Community', Ph.D. thesis (Florence, 1995).

Pinder, J., 'Problems of European Integration', in Denton, G. R. (ed.), *Economic Integration in Europe* (London, 1969).

Piore, M. J., and Sabel, C. F., *The Second Industrial Divide: Possibilities for Prosperity* (New York, 1984).

Pipkorn, J., 'Legal Arrangements in the Treaty of Maastricht for the Effectiveness of the Economic and Monetary Union', (1994) 31 CMLR 263.

Poiares Maduro, M., '*Keck*: The End? The Beginning of the End? Or just the End of the Beginning?', (1994) 3 *Irish Journal of European Law* 30.

Pollack, M. A., 'Creeping Competence: The Expanding Agenda of the European Community', (1994) 14 *Journal of Public Policy* 95.

Porter, M. E., *The Competitive Advantage of Nations* (London, 1990).

Posner, R., *Antitrust Law: An Economic Perspective* (Chicago, 1976).

Prestowitz, C. V., Thurow, L. C., Scharping, R., Cohen, S. C., and Steil, B., 'The Fight over Competitiveness: A Zero-Sum Debate?', (1994) 73 *Foreign Affairs* 186.

Rahmsdorf, D., 'Eine zweite Euro-Ordo-Debatte', (1980) 3 *Integration* 156.

—— *Ordnungspolitischer Dissens und europäische Integration* (Kehl am Rhein, 1982).

Ravaioli, P., and Sandler, P., 'The European Union and Telecommunications: Recent Developments in the Field of Competition', (1994) 2 *The International Computer Lawyer* 2 (Part I); 20 (Part II).

Raz, J., 'The Rule of Law and Its Virtue', (1977) 93 *The Law Quarterly Review* 195.

Reich, N., 'Competition Among Legal Orders: A New Paradigm of EC Law?', (1992) 29 CMLR 861.

—— 'The "November Revolution" of the European Court of Justice: *Keck, Meng* and *Audi* Revisited', (1994) 31 CMLR 459.

Reich, R., *The Work of Nations: Capitalism in the 21st Century* (New York, 1991).

Richonnier, M., 'Europe's Decline is not Irreversible', (1984) 22 JCMS 227.

Riley, A. J., 'More Radicalism, Please: The Notice on Co-operation between National Courts and the Commission in Applying Articles 85 and 86 of the EEC Treaty', (1993) 14 ECLR 91.

Rosamond, B., 'Mapping the European Condition: The Theory of Integration and the Integration of Theory', (1995) 1 *European Journal of International Relations* 391.

Ross, G., 'Sidling into Industrial Policy: Inside the European Commission', (1993) 11 *French Politics and Society* 20.

—— 'Inside the Delors Cabinet', (1994) 32 JCMS 499.

—— *Jacques Delors and European Integration* (Cambridge, 1995).

Sandalow, T., and Stein, E., *Courts and Free Markets: Perspectives from the United States and Europe* (Oxford, 1982).

Sandholtz, W., 'ESPRIT and the politics of international collective action', (1992) 30 JCMS 1.

—— 'Choosing Union: Monetary Politics and Maastricht', (1993) 47 *International Organization* 1.

—— 'Institutions and Collective Action: The New Telecommunications in Western Europe', (1993) 45 *World Politics* 242.

Sandholtz, W., and Zysman, J., '1992: Recasting the European Bargain', (1990) 42 *World Politics* 95.

Sauter, W., 'The ONP Framework: Towards a European Telecommunications Agency', (1994) 5 ULR 140.

—— 'The Rejection of the ONP Voice Telephony Directive by the European Parliament: The Entry of a New Player in European Telecommunications and its Effects on the Future of ONP', (1994) 5 ULR 176.

—— 'The Telecommunications Law of the European Union', (1995) 1 *European Law Journal* 92.

Sawyer, M. C., 'Reflections on the Nature and the Role of Industrial Policy', (1992) 43 *Metroeconomica* 51.

Scharpf, F. W., 'The Joint-Decision Trap: Lessons From German Federalism and European Integration', (1988) 66 *Public Administration* 239.

—— 'Community and Autonomy: Multi-Level Policy-Making in the European Union', (1994) 1 *Journal of European Public Policy* 219.

Scherer, F. M., and Ross, D., *Industrial Market Structure and Economic Performance* (3rd ed., Boston, 1990).

Schermers, H. G., and Waelbroeck, D., *Judicial Protection in the European Communities* (5th ed., Deventer, 1992).

Schneider, V., 'Organized Interests in the European Telecommunications Market', in Greenwood, J., Grote, J., and Ronit, K. (eds.), *Organized Interests and the European Community* (London, 1992).

—— 'The Structure of Policy Networks: A Comparison of "Chemicals Control" and "Telecommunications Policy" in Germany', (1992) 21 *European Journal of Political Research* 109.

Schneider, V., Dang-Nguyen, G., and Werle, R., 'Corporate Actor Networks in European Policy-Making: Harmonizing Telecommunications Policy', (1994) 32 JCMS 473.

Schneider, V., and Werle, R., 'Vom Regime zum korporativen Akteur: Zur institutionellen Dynamik der Europäischen Gemeinschaft', in Kohler-Koch, B. (ed.), *Regime in den internationalen Beziehungen* (Baden-Baden, 1989).

Schout, A., *The Institutional Framework for Industrial Development: New Directions for a European Industrial Policy* (Maastricht, 1990).

Schröter, H., 'Die Wettbewerbsregeln der Gemeinschaft', in Von der Groeben, H., Thiesing, J., and Ehlermann, C.-D. (eds.), *Kommentar zum EWG Vertrag* Vol. 3 (4th ed., Baden-Baden, 1991).

Seabright, P., 'Regulatory Capture, Subsidiarity and European Community Merger Control', (1994) 57 *European Economy* 109.

Seidel, M., 'Die Weisheit einer höheren Instanz', 14 March 1992 FAZ.

Serran-Schreiber, C., *Le Defi Americain* (Paris, 1967).

Sharp, M., 'The Single Market and European Technology Policies', in Freeman, C., Sharp, M., and Walker, W. (eds.), *Technology and the Future of Europe: Global Competition and the Environment in the 1990s* (London, 1991).

—— 'Changing Industrial Structures in Western Europe', in Dyker, D. (ed.), *The European Economy* (London, 1992).

Sharp, M., and Pavitt, K., 'Technology Policy in the 1990s: Old Trends and New Realities', (1993) 31 JCMS 129.

Siebert, H., 'Standortwettbewerb—nicht Industriepolitik', (1992) *Die Weltwirtschaft* 409.

Siebert, H., and Koop, M. J., 'Institutional Competition Versus Centralization: *Quo Vadis Europe?*', (1993) 9 *Oxford Review of Economic Policy* 15.

Siragusa, M., 'The Lowering of the Thresholds: An Opportunity to Harmonise Merger Control', (1993) 14 ECLR 139.

Siragusa, M., and Subiotto, R., 'The EEC Merger Control Regulation: The Commission's Evolving Case Law', (1991) 28 CMLR 877.

Slot, P. J., 'The Institutional Dimension of the EMU', in Curtin, D., and Heukels, T. (eds.), *Institutional Dynamics of European Integration: Essays in Honour of Henry G. Schermers* (Dordrecht, 1994).

Snyder, F., 'EMU—Metaphor for European Union? Institutions, Rules and Types of Regulation', in Dehousse, R. (ed.), *Europe After Maastricht: An Ever Closer Union* (München, 1994).

—— 'Soft Law and Institutional Practice in the European Community', in Martin, S. (ed.), *The Construction of Europe: Essays in Honour of Emile Nöel* (Deventer, 1994).

Stegemann, K., 'Wirtschaftspolitische Rivalität zwischen Industriestaaten: Neue Erkenntnisse durch Modelle strategischer Handelspolitik?', in Streit, M. E. (ed.), *Wirtschaftspolitik zwischen ökonomischer und politischer Rationalität. Festschrift für Herbert Giersch* (Wiesbaden, 1988).

Steindorff, E., 'Quo vadis Europa? Freiheiten, Regulierung und soziale Grundrechte nach den erweiterten Zielen der EG-Verfassung', in *Weiterentwicklung der Europäischen Gemeinschaften und der Marktwirtschaft. Referate des XXV. FIW-Symposions* (Cologne, 1992).

Streeck, W., and Schmitter, Ph. C., 'From National Corporatism to Transnational Pluralism: Organised Interests in the Single European Market', (1991) 19 *Politics and Society* 209.

Streit, M. E., 'Economic Order, Private Law and Public Policy: The Freiburg School of Law and Economics in Perspective', (1992) 148 JITE 675.

Streit, M. E., and Mussler, W., 'The Economic Constitution of the European Community: From "Rome" to "Maastricht"' (1995) 1 *European Law Journal* 5.

Sun, J.-M., and Pelkmans, J., 'Regulatory Competition in the Single Market', (1995) 33 JCMS 67.

Temple Lang, J., 'Article 5 of the EEC Treaty: The Emergence of Constitutional Principles in the Case Law of the Court of Justice', (1987) 10 *Fordham International Law Journal* 503.

—— 'Community Constitutional Law: Article 5 EEC Treaty', (1990) 27 CMLR 645.

—— 'European Community Constitutional Law and the Enforcement of Community Antitrust Law', in Hawk, B. (ed.), *Annual Proceedings of the Fordham Corporate Law Institute 1993: Antitrust in a Global Economy* (New York, 1994).

Tinbergen, J., *International Economic Integration* (Amsterdam, 1954).

Toth, A., 'The Principle of Subsidiarity in the Maastricht Treaty', (1992) 29 CMLR 1079.

Trachtman, J. P., 'International Regulatory Competition, Externalization and Jurisdiction', (1993) 34 *Harvard International Law Journal* 47.

Tsoukalis, L., *The New European Economy: The Politics and Economics of Integration* (Oxford, 1991).

Ungerer, H., and Costello, N., *Telecommunications in Europe: Free Choice for the User in Europe's 1992 Market. The Challenge for the European Community* European Perspectives Series (Brussels, 1988).

Van Bael, I., 'The Antitrust Settlement Practice of the EEC Commission', (1986) 23 CMLR 61.

Van der Esch, B., 'E.E.C. Competition Rules: Basic Principles and Policy Aims', (1980) 7 LIEI 75.

—— 'Dérégulation, autorégulation et le régime de concurrence nonfaussée dans la CEE', (1990) 26 CDE 499.

—— 'Die Artikel 5, 3f, 85/86 und 90 EWGV als Grundlage der wettbewerbsrechtlichen Verpflichtungen der Mitgliedstaaten', (1991) 155 ZHR 274.

Van Liederkerke, A., 'Developments in EC Competition Law in 1994—An Overview', (1995) 32 CMLR 921.

Van Tulder, R. and Junne, G., *European Multinationals in Core Technologies* (Chichester, 1988).

Vaughan, D. (ed.), *Law of the European Communities*, Vol. 1 (4th ed., London, 1986).

Venit, J. S., 'Review of the 1993 Decisions under the Merger Regulation', (1993) 18 ELR *Competition Checklist* 133.

Venit, J. S. 'The "Merger" Control Regulation: Europe comes of Age . . . or Caliban's Dinner', (1990) 27 CMLR 7.

VerLoren van Themaat, P., 'Die Aufgabenverteilung zwischem dem Gesetzgeber und dem Europäischem Gerichtshof bei der Gestaltung der Wirtschaftsverfassung der Europäischen Gemeinschaften', in Mestmäcker, E.-J., Möller, H., and Schwartz, P. (eds.), *Eine Ordnungspolitik für Europa: Festschrift für Hans von der Groeben zu seinem 80. Geburtstag* (Baden-Baden, 1987).

—— 'Some Preliminary Observations on the Intergovernmental Conferences: The Relations between the Concepts of a Common Market, a Monetary Union, an Economic Union, a Political Union and Sovereignty', (1991) 28 CMLR 291.

—— 'Einige Bemerkungen zu dem Verhältnis zwischen den Begriffen Gemeinsamer Markt, Wirtschaftsunion, Währungsunion, Politische Union und Souveränität', in Baur, J., Müller-Graf, P.-Ch., and Zuleeg, M. (eds.), *Europarecht, Energierecht, Wirtschaftsrecht: Festschrift für Bodo Börner zum 70. Geburtstag* (Cologne, 1992).

Verstrynge, J.-F., 'Current Antitrust Policy Issues in the EEC: Some Reflections on the Second Generation of Competition Policy', in Hawk, B. (ed.), *Annual Proceedings of the Fordham Corporate Law Institute 1984: Antitrust and Trade Policies in International Trade* (New York, 1985).

Verstrynge, J.-F., 'The System of EEC Competition Rules', in Slot, P. J., and Van der Woude, M. H. (eds.), *Exploiting the Internal Market: Co-operation and Competition Toward 1992* (Deventer, 1988).

Vickers, J., and Wright, V. (eds.), *The Politics of Privatisation in Europe* (London, 1989).

Viner, J., *The Customs Union Issue* (New York, 1950).

Von der Groeben, H., 'Die Wettbewerbspolitik als Teil der Wirtschaftspolitik im Gemeinsamen Markt', in Von der Groeben, H. (ed.), *Europa: Plan und Wirklichkeit. Reden-Berichte-Aufsätze zur europäischen Politik* (Baden-Baden, 1967).

—— *The European Community: The Formative Years. The Struggle to Establish the Common Market and the Political Union (1958–66)* European Perspectives Series (Brussels-Luxembourg 1985).

—— *Legitimationsprobleme der Europäischen Gemeinschaft* (Baden-Baden, 1987).

—— *Die Europäische Gemeinschaft und die Herausforderungen unserer Zeit: Aufsätze und Reden 1967–1987* (Baden-Baden, 1987), Weilemann, P. R. (ed.).

—— 'Probleme einer Europäischen Wirtschaftsordnung', in Baur, J., Müller-Graf, P.-Ch. and Zuleeg, M. (eds.), *Europarecht, Energierecht, Wirtschaftsrecht: Festschrift für Bodo Börner zum 70. Geburtstag* (Cologne, 1992).

Von der Groeben, H., Thiesing, J., and Ehlermann, C.-D. (eds.), *Kommentar zum EWG-Vertrag*, Vol. 4 (4th ed., Baden-Baden, 1991).

Von der Groeben, H., and Mestmäcker, E.-J. (eds.), *Ziele und Methoden der Europäischen Integration* (Frankfurt, 1972).

Wachsmann, A., and Berrod, F., 'Les critères de justification des monopoles: un premier bilan après l'affaire *Corbeau*', (1994) 30 RTDE 39.

Ward, A., 'Effective Sanctions in EC Law: A Moving Boundary in the Division of Competence', (1995) 1 *European Law Journal* 205.

Ward, H., and Edwards, G., 'Chicken and Technology: The Politics of the European Community's Budget for Research and Development', (1990) 16 *Review of International Studies* 111.

Wassenberg, A. F. P., 'Games within Games: On the Politics of Association and Dissociation in European Industrial Policy-Making', in Marin, B. (ed.), *Governance and Generalized Exchange: Self-Organizing Policy Networks in Action* (Boulder, 1990).

Weatherill, S., and Beaumont, P., *EC Law* (London, 1994).

Weiler, J. J. H., 'The Community System: The Dual Character of Supranationalism', (1982) 1 YEL 267.

—— 'Community, Member States and European Integration: Is the Law Relevant?', (1983) 21 JCMS 42.

—— 'The Transformation of Europe', (1991) 100 *The Yale Law Journal* 2403.

—— 'Problems of Legitimacy in Post 1992 Europe', (1991) 46 *Aussenwirtschaft* 411.

—— 'Journey to an Unknown Destination: A Retrospective and Prospective of the European Court of Justice in the Arena of Political Integration', (1993) 31 JCMS 417.

Wilke, M., and Wallace, H., 'Subsidiarity: Approaches to power-sharing in the European Community' RIIA Discussion Paper No. 27 (London, 1990).

Wilks, S., 'Government-Industry Relations: A Review Article', (1986) 14 *Policy and Politics* 491.

—— 'Government-Industry Relations: Progress and Findings of the ESCR Research Initiative', (1989) 67 *Public Administration* 329.

—— 'The Metamorphosis of European Competition Law', in Snyder, F. (ed.), *European Community Law* Vol. I (Aldershot, 1993).

Wilks, S., and McGowan, L., 'Disarming the Commission: The Debate over a European Cartel Office', (1995) 32 JCMS 259.

—— 'Discretion in European Merger Control: The German Regime in Context', (1995) 2 *Journal of European Public Policy* 41.

Wilks, S., and Wright, M. (eds.), *Comparative Government-Industry Relations: Western Europe, the United States and Japan* (Oxford, 1987).

—— *The Promotion and regulation of Industry in Japan* (London, 1991).

Wils, G., 'Recente ontwikkelingen in het Amerikaanse antitrustrecht', (1991) 39 SEW 214.

Winter, G., 'Drei Arten Gemeinschaftlicher Rechtssetzung und ihre Legitimation', in Brüggemeier, G. (ed.), *Verfassungen für ein ziviles Europa* (Baden-Baden, 1994).

Wishlade, F. G., 'Competition Policy, Cohesion and the Co-ordination of Regional Aids in the European Community', (1993) 14 ECLR 143.

Wright, V. (ed.), *Privatization in Western Europe: Pressures, Problems, Paradoxes* (London, 1994).

Wright, M., 'Policy community, policy network and comparative industrial policies', (1988) 36 *Political Studies* 593.

Index

Article 90 EC, *see* competition policy; telecommunications policy
Article 130 EC, *see* industrial policy; competitiveness
Article 222 EC 40, 148, 167, 180–1, 219; *see also* mixed economy

citizens, citizenship 15, 24, 49–50, 182, 221
common agricultural policy (CAP) 4, 33, 46–7, 49, 178
competition among rules 35
competition policy 109–61
  and administrative discretion 130–2, 191–3
  and industrial policy 1–8, 59–62, 97–8, 107–8, 109–16
  and European Court of Justice, Court of First Instance 128
  applied to Member States 141–6
  and public policy 117–20, 122, 130
  Article 85 EC 32, 42, 123, 133, 138, 144, 157, 180, 192
  Article 86 EC 32, 124, 126, 133, 144, 149–52, 180, 187–8, 190, 86
  Article 87 EC 124, 153, 209
  Article 90 EC 40, 125, 144, 148–55, 180–1, 220; *see also* telecommunications policy
  behavioural competition policy 126
  block exemptions 38, 125–6, 130
  convergence of national policies 155–9
  effet utile 40–2, 145–6, 151, 154–5, 160, 187
  European cartel office 132, 141, 156–9, 230, 233
  legal framework of 122–9
  merger policy 75, 98, 132–41, 160–1
  principles and objectives 111–16
  private undertakings 129–32, 141–2
  Regulation 17/62 124, 126–7
  Regulation 19/65 126–7
  role of competition policy 28, 30, 208
  state aids 32, 127, 142, 144–5
comitology 52–4, 129, 197–9, 209–11, 232–3
constitution 9–55
  constitutional charter 13–14, 18, 33
  constitutional moment 17
  constitutionalization of European law 12–16, 17–18, 23, 40, 233
  economic constitution 6–7, 11, 26–42, 49–55, 112, 180, 182, 222, 232

formal constitution 12–13, 15, 23
  limits to Community action 43–9
  material constitution 12–13, 15, 22, 55
  political constitution 11, 49–55
  structure and objectives 18–21, 55
constitutional principles 21–6, 43–9
  classification of 24
  direct effect 13–14, 22, 24, 40, 152, 225
  four freedoms 3, 32–3, 49, 148, 220
  free competition 10, 20–6, 33, 36, 46–8, 51, 56, 67, 119, 121–2, 228
  general principles of law 21–3, 33, 47
  implied powers 13, 40
  institutional balance 24, 53, 164
  limited powers, enumerated powers 13, 25, 37, 43
  non-discrimination 22, 26, 31–2, 40, 42, 45–9, 123, 147
  political principles 21
  proportionality 5, 25, 34, 45–9, 123, 147
  property rights 44–5
  solidarity 19, 23, 25–6, 37, 40, 49; *see also* competition policy, *effet utile*
  subsidiarity 5, 25, 38, 53–4, 69, 95–6, 123, 147, 203, 212, 226, 230
  supremacy 13, 17, 22, 225
  unity of European law 18
corporatism 142–7, 155

democracy, democratic deficit 14–17, 28–9, 40–1, 57, 70, 91, 96, 106, 121, 209, 212, 221, 225–7, 233

economic and monetary union 10, 17, 20–1, 37, 53–4, 58, 106–7, 112, 226, 233
economic (and monetary) policy coordination 3–4, 9–10, 15, 18–20, 32, 34, 36, 51, 53–4, 58, 68, 107, 109, 112–14, 116, 228
economic and social cohesion 20, 35, 37–8, 94
economic sovereignty 2–3, 116, 133, 142, 147–8, 156, 159–60, 229–30
employment 99–105, 115–16; *see also* industrial policy, *White Paper*
European integration (positive and negative integration) 3, 5, 19, 34, 51, 58, 61, 68–70, 75, 106
European Parliament 14–15, 39, 52, 91, 96, 98–9, 128, 140, 180, 198–9, 209–10, 225–6, 233